SCRIPTURE AND SCHOLARSHIP IN EARLY MODERN ENGLAND

To my grand parents,
Sarah & Leonard Hessayon
and in memory of
Manfred & Karla Selby

Scripture and Scholarship in Early Modern England

Edited by

ARIEL HESSAYON
Goldsmiths College, University of London, UK

NICHOLAS KEENE
Royal Holloway, University of London, UK

ASHGATE

Published by
Ashgate Publishing Limited
Gower House
Croft Road
Aldershot
Hampshire GU11 3HR
England

Ashgate Publishing Company
Suite 420
101 Cherry Street
Burlington, VT 05401-4405
USA

Ashgate website: http://www.ashgate.com

British Library Cataloguing in Publication Data
Scripture and scholarship in early modern england
1. Bible – Criticism, interpretation, etc. – England – History – 17th century 2. Biblical scholars – England – History – 17th century 3. England – Intellectual life – 17th century 4. England – Religion – 17th century
I. Hessayon, Ariel II. Keene, Nicholas
220.6'7'0942'09032

Library of Congress Cataloging-in-Publication Data
Scripture and scholarship in early modern England / edited by Ariel Hessayon and Nicholas Keene.
p. cm.
ISBN 0-7546-3893-6 (alk. paper)
1. Bible—Criticism, interpretation, etc.—History. 2. England—Church history. I. Hessayon, Ariel. II. Keene, Nicholas.

BS500.S37 2006
220'.0942—dc22

2005021015

ISBN-13: 978-0-7546-3893-3
ISBN-10: 0-7546-3893-6

Printed and bound in Great Britain by MPG Books Ltd, Bodmin, Cornwall.

Contents

Notes on Contributors

Ariel Hessayon is Lecturer in Early Modern History at Goldsmiths College, University of London. He is the author of several articles on seventeenth-century prophets and mystics, as well as *'Gold Tried in the Fire': The Prophet TheaurauJohn Tany and the English Revolution* (Ashgate, 2007). His next book will be called *'Beastly fury and extreme violence': A cultural history of football* (Hambledon & London).

William Poole is Fellow and Tutor in English at New College, Oxford. His research interests are in Milton Studies, seventeenth-century scientific writing, heterodoxy and heresy, and manuscript culture. He has written a monograph, *Milton and the Idea of the Fall* (Cambridge University Press, 2005), edited Francis Lodwick's *A Country Not Named* (Tempe, 2005), and published many articles on early modern literature and intellectual history. He also co-directs the AHRB-funded project 'Language-planning and free-thinking in late seventeenth-century England', hosted by CRASSH in the University of Cambridge (2004–07).

Nicholas Cranfield studied Art History at the University of Florence and Modern History and Theology in Britain, and was a Fellow of Selwyn College in Cambridge. His doctoral research centred on the variety of theological opinions of episcopacy current in early seventeenth-century England (1603–45). He continues to write on seventeenth-century culture, the spread of Anglicanism, into both America and the Pacific (in the nineteenth century) and is an arts correspondent for the *Church Times*. He is currently working on a project to understand the effect of twentieth-century Christian art on liturgical space. He is a member of the Diocesan Advisory Committee for the Care of Churches (Southwark) and a Director of The South London Church Fund & Diocesan Board of Finance.

Scott Mandelbrote is an Official Fellow of Peterhouse, Cambridge and a Fellow of All Souls College, Oxford. He is also an Isaac Newton Trust Lecturer in the History Faculty, Cambridge University. His publications include *The Garden, the Ark, the Tower, the Temple* (Oxford, 1998), written with Jim Bennett, and *Footprints of the Lion: Isaac Newton at Work* (Cambridge, 2001). He is one of the editorial directors of the Newton Project.

Nicholas Keene is a Leverhulme Early Career Fellow at Royal Holloway, University of London, having completed his doctoral thesis there on scriptural erudition and print culture in late seventeenth- and early eighteenth-century England. He is currently preparing an edition of the correspondence of the French biblical critic Richard Simon.

Stephen D. Snobelen is an Assistant Professor at King's College, Halifax, Nova Scotia and Adjunct Professor at Dalhousie University, Halifax. He has published on Newton's theology and prophecy, Newton's General Scholium to the Principia, the Newtonians William Whiston and Samuel Clarke, the popularization of science, John Locke's religious views, nineteenth-century prophetic interpretation and nineteenth-century pre-Adamism. He is on the editorial board of the Newton Project.

Rob Iliffe has published a number of articles on early modern history and the history of science, and is completing a book on the significance of Isaac Newton's religious views for his scientific work (forthcoming, Yale University Press). He is the editor of the journal *History of Science* and an editorial director of the Newton Project.

Warren Johnston is a sessional lecturer at the University of Saskatchewan and at St Peter's College in Muenster, Saskatchewan. His research centres on political and religious thought in later seventeenth-century England. His articles on Anglican and on nonconformist apocalyptic interpretation have recently appeared in the *Journal of Ecclesiastical History* and the *Canadian Journal of History*. His article 'Revelation and the Revolution of 1688–89' appeared in 2005 in *The Historical Journal*. He is currently preparing a book on apocalyptic thought in Restoration England.

Nicholas McDowell is Lecturer in Renaissance Literature and Culture at the University of Exeter. He is the author of *The English Radical Imagination: Culture, Religion and Revolution, 1630–60* (Oxford University Press, 2003), and the editor, with Nigel Smith, of *Seventeenth-Century Radicals* (Broadview Press, forthcoming). Currently he is completing a monograph on literary patronage and political allegiance in the English Civil War and editing *The Tenure of Kings and Magistrates* and *Eikonoklastes* for the Oxford Complete Works of John Milton.

Sarah Hutton's research interests include early modern intellectual history, Neoplatonism, and women in the sixteenth and seventeenth centuries. She has edited and co-edited volumes on Platonism and the English imagination, mysticism and mechanism, women in medicine and science, two treatises of Ralph Cudworth, the correspondence of Anne Conway and friends, and the life of Henry More.

Justin Champion has published widely on early modern political and religious ideas, attacks on the Church of England in the late seventeenth and early eighteenth centuries, and the life and thought of John Toland – including a critical edition of Toland's *Nazarenus* (1718). His ongoing project is the history of the cultural crisis in the early eighteenth century. His next book will be a history of biblical criticism between 1580 and 1750 called *Prophecying the Word.*

Alex Barber is currently a research student at Royal Holloway, University of London. His thesis is on the religious and political context of print culture in late seventeenth and early-eighteenth century England. His other interests centre on Pierre Bayle and the English republic of letters.

John Morrill is Professor of British and Irish History at the University of Cambridge and Deputy Director of its Centre for Research in the Arts, Social Sciences and Humanities. He has written extensively about early modern political, social and religious history, including six essays on Oliver Cromwell (as well as a 30,000 word life in the *New Dictionary of National Biography*).

Acknowledgements

The idea for this collection grew out of some conversations Nick and I had a few years ago. Since then we have run up a number of debts. First and foremost, we would like to thank our contributors for delivering their articles – most of them fairly promptly! We would also like to thank the staff of the various libraries and institutions that provided assistance to all those who have contributed to this volume, notably the British Library, Cambridge University Library and the Bodleian Library.

This publication has been made possible by a grant from the Scouloudi Foundation in association with the Institute of Historical Research. Both editors, myself formerly and Nick currently, have enjoyed the generous support of the Leverhulme Trust. Our special thanks also go to Mr Farhad Hakimzadeh, Chair of the Academic Committee of the Iran Heritage Foundation, for his generous permission to reproduce images from a Polyglot Bible in his possession. In addition, a big thank you goes to Heidi May at Ashgate for having faith (and patience) in the project, and to Frances Smith for the invaluable help she has given to the project. For my part, that leaves Lorenza, who has been very understanding.

Dr Ariel Hessayon
Dr Nicholas Keene
February 2005

Acknowledgements

Introduction

Ariel Hessayon and Nicholas Keene

The story of the English Bible has often been told, but the story of the Bible in England is still incomplete.[1] It has been estimated that 465 editions and 101 variant editions of the Bible in English were published between 1525 and 1700, and that during the same period 217 editions and 26 variant editions of the New Testament in English were issued. By 1700 perhaps as many as 1,290,000 copies of the Bible in English and 545,000 copies of the New Testament in English had been printed. Even allowing for wear and tear, these figures suggest that many households possessed either an English Bible or New Testament. The Geneva version of the English Bible, produced by English exiles in the heartland of Calvinism, with its helpful if sometimes provocative marginalia, was eventually supplanted by the King James Bible or so-called Authorized Version of 1611, derived largely from the translation of William Tyndale (d.1536).[2] The continued value of the Bible as a commodity is evident in the number of testators who were at pains to specify it among the possessions bequeathed to their heirs.[3]

I

It is a commonplace that the Bible was the most read and commented upon book in this era (in which period of English history has it not been?), and that its influence suffused all aspects of life from individual salvation to familial relationships to political government. The vernacular Bible became the symbol of English Protestant identity and independence in the second half of the sixteenth century, as well as the ultimate battleground for the contestation of competing ideologies to prescribe

---

[1] D. Daniell, *The Bible in English* (New Haven, 2003) is thorough. For a classic account, see F. F. Bruce, *History of the Bible in English* (New York, 1978).

[2] C.J. Sommerville, 'On the distribution of religious and occult literature in seventeenth-century England' *The Library*, 5th series, 29 (1974), 222–3; B.J. McMullin, 'The Bible trade', in J. Barnard and D. F. Mckenzie (eds), *The Cambridge History of the Book in England Volume IV 1557–1695* (Cambridge, 2002), 455–73.

[3] PRO Prob 11/191 fol. 73v; PRO Prob 11/198 fol. 34r; PRO Prob 11/205 fol. 407v; PRO Prob 11/217 fol. 251r; PRO Prob 11/223 fol. 270r; PRO Prob 11/234 fol. 124r; PRO Prob 11/297 fol. 208r; see also, PRO Prob 11/205 fol. 407v.

and regulate the operation of the sacred in the lives of the nation.[4] The work of Christopher Hill has been particularly illuminating in highlighting the centrality of the (vernacular) Bible to the religious, social, political, economic and cultural lives of English men and women.[5] The story of the Bible in England, however, remains incomplete. There is a dearth of studies concerning the scholarly criticism of the Bible between the late sixteenth and early eighteenth centuries. There are a number of works demonstrating the developing critical attention to the Bible through to the late Middle Ages in Europe,[6] complemented by a substantial body of literature focused on John Wycliffe and the Lollards.[7] The significance of new strategies of treating the Bible has been explored in the Renaissance,[8] many centred on Erasmus,[9]

---

[4] R.H. Worth Jr, *Church, Monarch and Bible in Sixteenth Century England* (North Carolina, 2000); I. Green, *Print and Protestantism in Early Modern England* (Oxford, 2000). The best study of the King James Bible is D. Daiches, *The King James Version of the Bible: An Account of the Development and Sources of the English Bible of 1611 with special reference to the Hebrew Tradition* (Chicago, 1941). Modern studies include A. McGrath, *In the Beginning: The Story of the King James Bible and how it changed a Nation, a Language and a Culture* (London, 2001), and A. Nicolson, *Power and Glory: Jacobean England and the Making of the King James Bible* (London, 2003).

[5] C. Hill, *The English Bible and the Seventeenth Century Revolution* (London, 1993).

[6] The principal work is B. Smalley, *The Study of the Bible in the Middle Ages* (rev. 3rd ed., Oxford, 1983). Also invaluable is Henri de Lubac, *Exégèse médiévale: Les quatre sens de l'écriture* (4 vols, Paris 1959–64). See also R. Gameson (ed.), *The Early Medieval Bible* (Cambridge, 1994); K. Walsh and D. Wood (eds), *The Bible in the Medieval World: Essays in Memory of Beryl Smalley* (Oxford, 1985); D.W. Lourdaux and D. Verhelst (eds), *The Bible and Medieval Culture* (Louvain, 1979).

[7] Particularly useful is K. Ghosh, *The Wycliffite Heresy: Authority and the Interpretation of Texts* (Cambridge, 2002). Other key works include A. Kenny (ed.), *Wyclif in his times* (Oxford, 1986); D.C. Wood *The evangelical doctor, John Wycliffe and the Lollards* (Welwyn, 1984); C.V. Bostick, *The Antichrist and the Lollards, apocalypticism in late medieval and Reformation England* (Leiden, 1998); A. Hudson, *Lollards and their Books* (London, 1985) and idem, *The Premature Reformation: Wycliffite Texts and Lollard History* (Oxford, 1988); M. Aston, *Lollards and reformers, images and literacy in late medieval religion* (London, 1984); M. Deanesly, *The Lollard Bible and other medieval biblical versions* (Cambridge, 1920).

[8] The best account of Renaissance Protestant biblical erudition is François LaPlanche, *L'écriture, le sacré et l'histoire: Erudits et politiques protestants devant la Bible en France au XVIIe siècle* (Amsterdam, 1986). See also Don Cameron Allen, *The Legend of Noah: Renaissance Rationalism in Art, Science, and Letters* (Illinois, 1949); idem, *Mysteriously Meant: The Rediscovery of Pagan Symbolism and Allegorical Interpretation in the Renaissance* (Baltimore, 1970). Other useful works include G.R. Evans, *The Language and Logic of the Bible: The Road to Reformation* (Cambridge, 1985), J.H. Bentley, *Humanists and Holy Writ: New Testament Scholarship in the Renaissance* (Princeton, 1983). See also D.K. Shuger, *The Renaissance Bible: Scholarship, Sacrifice, and Subjectivity* (Berkeley, 1994).

[9] Of particular value in the historiography on Erasmus is E. Rummel, *Erasmus' Annotations on the New Testament: From Philologist to Theologian*, Erasmus Studies 8 (Toronto, 1986); J.C. Olin, *Six Essays on Erasmus* (New York, 1979) and idem, *Erasmus, Utopia and the*

and biblical interpretation during the Reformation has received fulsome discussion.[10] There have been a number of useful intellectual biographies on leading late sixteenth and early seventeenth century European figures prominent in developing critical approaches to scripture, most notably Anthony Grafton's study of Joseph Scaliger,[11] but corresponding studies of English biblical scholars like Archbishop Ussher and the polymath John Selden are missing.[12] Thereafter historians seem unsure of the broader significance of scholarly treatments of the Bible and have apparently left many unwieldy tomes to gather dust on the shelves.

II

Contributors to this volume, whose interests lie in the fields of early modern history, theology, and literature, have approached the subject of biblical scholarship from a wide variety of different perspectives, but they share certain assumptions. They believe that English scriptural erudition can only be understood in a European context. English biblical scholars in this era belonged to a self-conscious European intellectual community exchanging ideas and developing strategies for excavating the sacred text. Anglophone historiography has traditionally failed to sufficiently appreciate this cosmopolitan intellectual culture and much remains to be done on the cross-fertilisation of ideas relating to the Bible across geographical, cultural and linguistic boundaries. The contributors also believe that, contrary to the impression sometimes conveyed in studies of radical thought, be it in the mid-seventeenth century or the turn of the eighteenth, biblical criticism was not the exclusive preserve of 'free-thinkers' operating outside the parameters of the ecclesiastical establishment. It was a shared dialogue, and the various interlocutors drew upon the same resources of biblical, patristic and historical material to construct their

---

Jesuits: Essays on the Outreach of Humanism (New York, 1994). See also B. Hall, *Humanists and Protestants* (Edinburgh, 1990) and T.J. Wengert, *Human freedom, Christian righteousness, Philip Melanchthon's exegetical dispute with Erasmus of Rotterdam* (Oxford, 1998).

[10] See particularly O. O'Sullivan (ed.), *The Bible as Book: The Reformation* (London, 2000); W.P. Stephens (ed.), *The Bible, the Reformation and the Church: Essays in honour of James Atkinson* (Sheffield, 1995); D.C. Steinmetz, *The Bible in the Sixteenth Century* (Durham, NC, 1990). A useful collection of essays can be found in R.A. Muller and J.L. Thompson (eds), *Biblical Interpretation in the Era of the Reformation* (Michigan, 1996). See also Muller, *Post-Reformation Reformed Dogmatics. Volume 1:Prolegomena to Theology* (Grand Rapids, 1985) and *Post-Reformation Dogmatics. Volume 2: Holy Scripture: The Cognitive Foundation of Theology* (Grand Rapids, 1993).

[11] A. Grafton, *Joseph Scaliger: A Study in the History of Classical Scholarship* (2 vols, Oxford 1983–93). See also C.S.M. Rademaker, *The Life and Work of Gerardus Joannes Vossius (1577–1649)* (Netherlands, 1981), and N. Wickenden, *G J. Vossius and the Humanist Concept of History* (Netherlands, 1993).

[12] R. Buick Knox, *James Ussher Archbishop of Armagh* (Cardiff, 1967) contains little information on Ussher's biblical scholarship. The wait with regards to Selden may soon be over with a forthcoming monograph by G.J. Toomer.

arguments, however differently they interpreted and deployed that intellectual resource to contest the status, authority and role of the Bible. An over-reliance on the binary categorisation of 'orthodoxy' and 'heterodoxy', always historically contingent and shifting categories, has perhaps obscured some of the subtleties and nuances of this shared conversation.[13] Nor was discussion of aspects of biblical scholarship the preserve of university-educated intellectuals locked away in ivory towers far from the uncomprehending masses. Over the course of the early modern period, as various essays here demonstrate, the arguments and the information upon which they were based were communicated to a far broader audience than ever before, to the delight of some observers and the consternation of others. By the end of the seventeenth century, the convention that abstruse matters relating to scripture should be locked away in Latinate discourse was observed as much in its breach as its observance. As it became increasingly difficult for the religious establishment to control the dissemination and interpretation of aspects of biblical learning, the contestation for the authority to interpret scripture became a battleground critical to the status of the Bible in England. By the mid-eighteenth century no aspect of the history, construction or transmission of scripture had gone unchallenged, but the Bible remained the most read and commented upon book.

[13] See J.G.A. Pocock, 'Within the margins: the definitions of orthodoxy', in R.D. Lund (ed.), *The Margins of Orthodoxy: Heterodox Writing and Cultural Response, 1660–1750* (Cambridge, 1995), 33–53.

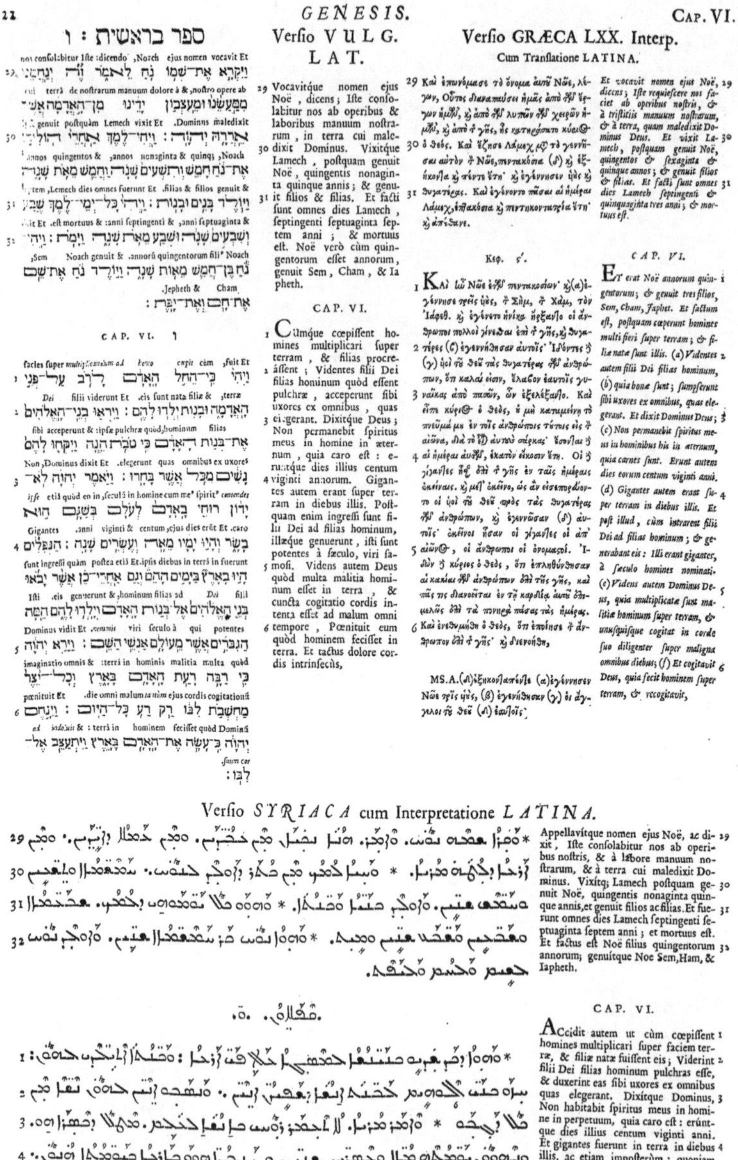
22 GENESIS. CAP. VI.

ספר בראשית : ו

Versio VULG. LAT.

29 Vocavitque nomen ejus Noë, dicens; Iste consolabitur nos ab operibus & laboribus manuum nostrarum, in terra cui maledixit Dominus.
30 Vixitque Lamech, postquam genuit Noë, quingentis nonaginta quinque annis; & genuit filios & filias.
31 Et facti sunt omnes dies Lamech, septingenti septuaginta septem anni; & mortuus est. Noë verò cùm quingentorum esset annorum, genuit Sem, Cham, & Iapheth.

CAP. VI.

1 Cumque cœpissent homines multiplicari super terram, & filias procreassent;
2 Videntes filii Dei filias hominum quòd essent pulchræ, acceperunt sibi uxores ex omnibus, quas elegerant.
3 Dixitque Deus; Non permanebit spiritus meus in homine in æternum, quia caro est: eruntque dies illius centum viginti annorum.
4 Gigantes autem erant super terram in diebus illis. Postquam enim ingressi sunt filii Dei ad filias hominum, illæque genuerunt, isti sunt potentes à sæculo, viri famosi.
5 Videns autem Deus quòd multa malitia hominum esset in terra, & cuncta cogitatio cordis intenta esset ad malum omni tempore,
6 Pœnituit eum quòd hominem fecisset in terra. Et tactus dolore cordis intrinsecùs,

Versio GRÆCA LXX. Interp. Cum Translatione LATINA.

29 Καὶ ἐπωνόμασε τὸ ὄνομα αὐτοῦ Νῶε, λέγων, Οὗτος διαναπαύσει ἡμᾶς ἀπὸ τῶν ἔργων ἡμῶν, καὶ ἀπὸ τῶν λυπῶν τῶν χειρῶν ἡμῶν, καὶ ἀπὸ τῆς γῆς, ἧς κατηράσατο κύριος ὁ Θεός.
30 Καὶ ἔζησε Λάμεχ μετὰ τὸ γεννῆσαι αὐτὸν τὸν Νῶε, πεντακόσια (δ) ἑξήκοντα καὶ πέντε ἔτη· καὶ ἐγέννησεν υἱοὺς καὶ θυγατέρας.
31 Καὶ ἐγένοντο πᾶσαι αἱ ἡμέραι Λάμεχ, ἑπτακόσια καὶ πεντηκοντατρία ἔτη· καὶ ἀπέθανε.

Κεφ. ς΄.

1 Καὶ ἦν Νῶε ἐτῶν πεντακοσίων· καὶ (α) ἐγέννησε τρεῖς υἱοὺς, τὸν Σὴμ, τὸν Χὰμ, τὸν Ἰάφεθ. καὶ ἐγένετο ἡνίκα ἤρξαντο οἱ ἄνθρωποι πολλοὶ γίνεσθαι ἐπὶ τῆς γῆς, καὶ θυγατέρες (β) ἐγεννήθησαν αὐτοῖς.
2 Ἰδόντες δὲ (γ) οἱ υἱοὶ τοῦ Θεοῦ τὰς θυγατέρας τῶν ἀνθρώπων, ὅτι καλαί εἰσιν, ἔλαβον ἑαυτοῖς γυναῖκας ἀπὸ πασῶν, ὧν ἐξελέξαντο.
3 Καὶ εἶπε κύριος ὁ Θεὸς, οὐ μὴ καταμείνῃ τὸ πνεῦμά μου ἐν τοῖς ἀνθρώποις τούτοις εἰς τὸν αἰῶνα, διὰ τὸ εἶναι αὐτοὺς σάρκας· ἔσονται δὲ αἱ ἡμέραι αὐτῶν, ἑκατὸν εἴκοσιν ἔτη.
4 Οἱ δὲ γίγαντες ἦσαν ἐπὶ τῆς γῆς ἐν ταῖς ἡμέραις ἐκείναις. καὶ μετ᾽ ἐκεῖνο, ὡς ἂν εἰσεπορεύοντο οἱ υἱοὶ τοῦ Θεοῦ πρὸς τὰς θυγατέρας τῶν ἀνθρώπων, καὶ ἐγεννῶσαν (δ) αὐτοῖς· ἐκεῖνοι ἦσαν οἱ γίγαντες οἱ ἀπ᾽ αἰῶνος, οἱ ἄνθρωποι οἱ ὀνομαστοί.
5 Ἰδὼν δὲ κύριος ὁ Θεὸς, ὅτι ἐπληθύνθησαν αἱ κακίαι τῶν ἀνθρώπων ἐπὶ τῆς γῆς, καὶ πᾶς τις διανοεῖται ἐν τῇ καρδίᾳ αὐτοῦ ἐπιμελῶς ἐπὶ τὰ πονηρὰ πάσας τὰς ἡμέρας.
6 Καὶ ἐνεθυμήθη ὁ Θεὸς, ὅτι ἐποίησε τὸν ἄνθρωπον ἐπὶ τῆς γῆς· καὶ διενοήθη,

MS.A. (δ) ἑξηκονταπέντε (α) ἐγέννησεν Νῶε τρεῖς υἱοὺς, (β) ἐγεννήθησαν (γ) οἱ ἄγγελοι τοῦ Θεοῦ (δ) ἑαυτοῖς.

29 Et vocavit nomen ejus Noë, dicens; Iste requiescere nos faciet ab operibus nostris, & à tristitiis manuum nostrarum, & à terra, quam maledixit Dominus Deus.
30 Et vixit Lamech, postquam genuit Noë, quingentos & sexaginta & quinque annos; & genuit filios & filias.
31 Et facti sunt omnes dies Lamech septingenti & quinquaginta tres anni; & mortuus est.

CAP. VI.

1 Et erat Noë annorum quingentorum; & genuit tres filios, Sem, Cham, Japhet. Et factum est, postquam cœperunt homines multi fieri super terram; & filiæ natæ sunt illis.
2 (a) Videntes autem filii Dei filias hominum, (b) quia bonæ sunt; sumpserunt sibi uxores ex omnibus, quas elegerant.
3 Et dixit Dominus Deus; (c) Non permanebit spiritus meus in hominibus his in æternum, quia carnes sunt. Erunt autem dies eorum centum viginti anni.
4 (d) Gigantes autem erant super terram in diebus illis. Et post illud, cùm intrarent filii Dei ad filias hominum; & generabant eis: Illi erant gigantes, à sæculo homines nominati.
5 (e) Videns autem Dominus Deus, quia multiplicatæ sunt malitiæ hominum super terram, & unusquisque cogitat in corde suo diligenter super maligna omnibus diebus;
6 (f) Et cogitavit Deus, quia fecit hominem super terram, & recogitavit,

Versio SYRIACA cum Interpretatione LATINA.

29 Appellavítque nomen ejus Noë, ac dixit, Iste consolabitur nos ab operibus nostris, & à labore manuum nostrarum, & à terra cui maledixit Dominus.
30 Vixitq; Lamech postquam genuit Noë, quingentis nonaginta quinque annis, et genuit filios ac filias.
31 Et fuerunt omnes dies Lamech septingenti septuaginta septem anni; et mortuus est.
32 Et factus est Noë filius quingentorum annorum; genuítque Noe Sem, Ham, & Iapheth.

CAP. VI.

1 Accidit autem ut cùm cœpissent homines multiplicari super faciem terræ, & filiæ natæ fuissent eis;
2 Viderint filii Dei filias hominum pulchras esse, & duxerint eas sibi uxores ex omnibus quas elegerant.
3 Dixitque Dominus, Non habitabit spiritus meus in homine in perpetuum, quia caro est: eruntque dies illius centum viginti anni.
4 Et gigantes fuerunt in terra in diebus illis, ac etiam imposterùm: quoniam ingressi sunt filii Dei ad filias hominum, et genuerunt eis gigantes æternos, gigantes nominatissimos.
5 Et vidit Dominus crevisse malitiam hominis super terram, & omnem affectum cogitationis cordis ejus deteriorem esse indiès.
6 Et displicuit Domino quòd fecisset hominem in terra, et doluit in corde suo.

Genesis 6 from the Polyglot Bible.

PARAPH. CHALD. cum VERSIONE LATINA.

תרגום אונקלוס TARGUM ONKELOS.

29 וּקְרָא יָת שְׁמֵיהּ נֹחַ לְמֵימַר דֵּין יְנַחֲמִנַּנָא מֵעוֹבָדָנָא וּמִלֵּאוּת יְדָנָא מִן אַרְעָא דִּי לַטְיַהּ יְיָ׃
30 וַחֲיָא לֶמֶךְ בָּתַר דְּאוֹלֵיד יָת נֹחַ חֲמֵשׁ מְאָה וְתִשְׁעִין וַחֲמֵשׁ שְׁנִין וְאוֹלֵיד בְּנִין וּבְנָן׃
31 וַהֲווֹ כָּל יוֹמֵי לֶמֶךְ שְׁבַע מְאָה וְשַׁבְעִין וּשְׁבַע שְׁנִין וּמִית׃
32 וַהֲוָה נֹחַ בַּר חֲמֵשׁ מְאָה שְׁנִין וְאוֹלֵיד נֹחַ יָת שֵׁם יָת חָם וְיָת יָפֶת׃

ו

וַהֲוָה כַּד שָׁרִיאוּ בְּנֵי אֱנָשָׁא לְמִסְגֵּי עַל אַפֵּי אַרְעָא וּבְנָתָא אִתְיְלִידָא לְהוֹן׃
2 וַחֲזוֹ בְּנֵי רַבְרְבַיָּא יָת בְּנָת אֱנָשָׁא אֲרֵי שַׁפִּירָן אִנּוּן וּנְסִיבוּ לְהוֹן נְשִׁין מִכֹּל דִּי אִתְרְעִיאוּ׃
3 וַאֲמַר יְיָ לָא יִתְקַיַּם דָּרָא בִישָׁא הָדֵין קֳדָמַי לְעָלַם בְּדִיל דְּאִנּוּן בִּשְׂרָא וְעוֹבָדֵיהוֹן בִּישַׁיָּא אַרְכָּא יְהִיב לְהוֹן מְאָה וְעֶשְׂרִין שְׁנִין אִם יְתוּבוּן׃
4 גִּבָּרַיָּא הֲווֹ בְּאַרְעָא בְּיוֹמַיָּא הָאִנּוּן וְאַף בָּתַר כֵּן דִּי יְעָלוּן בְּנֵי רַבְרְבַיָּא לִבְנָת אֱנָשָׁא וִילִידָן מִנְּהוֹן אִנּוּן גִּבָּרַיָּא דְּמֵעָלְמָא אֱנָשִׁין דִּשְׁמָא׃
5 וַחֲזָא יְיָ אֲרֵי סְגִיאַת בִּישַׁת אֱנָשָׁא בְּאַרְעָא וְכָל יִצְרָא מַחְשְׁבָת לִבֵּיהּ לְחוֹד בִּישׁ כָּל יוֹמַיָּא׃
6 וְתָב יְיָ בְּמֵימְרֵיהּ אֲרֵי עֲבַד יָת אָדָם בְּאַרְעָא וַאֲמַר בְּמֵימְרֵיהּ לְמִתְבַּר תּוּקְפֵיהוֹן כִּרְעוּתֵיהּ׃

29 Et vocavit nomen ejus Noe, dicens: Iste consolabitur nos ab operibus nostris, & à labore manuum nostrarum, de terrâ cui maledixit Dominus.
30 Et vixit Lamech postquàm genuit Noe, quingentis & nonaginta & quinque annis: & genuit
31 filios & filias. Et fuerunt omnes dies Lamech septingenti & septuaginta & septem anni: & mor-
32 tuus est. Et fuit Noe filius quingentorum annorum: & genuit Noe; Sem, Cham & Japhet.

CAP. VI.

1 ET factum est cum cœpissent filii hominum, multiplicari super faciem terræ: & filiæ natæ essent
2 eis. Et vidissent filii principum filias hominum, quòd essent pulchræ: acceperunt sibi uxores, ex omnibus quas voluerunt.
3 Et dixit Dominus; Non permanebit generatio pessima hæc coram me in æternum; eò quòd caro sunt, & opera eorum pessima; terminus dabitur eis centum & viginti annorum, si fortè convertan-
4 tur. Gigantes erant in terrâ in diebus illis: & etiam postquam ingressi sunt filii principum ad filias hominum, & genuerunt ex eis: Ipsi sunt potentes à seculo, viri nominis.
5 *Et vidit Dominus*, quòd multa esset malitia hominis in terrâ: & omnis sensus *cogitationum* cordis sui esset malus omni tem-
6 pore. Et pœnituit Dominum in verbo suo, quòd fecisset hominem in terrâ: Et dixit in verbo suo, ut contereret fortitudinem eorum juxta beneplacitum suum,

TEXTUS HEBRÆO-SAMARITANUS.

29 [illegible]
30 [illegible]
31 [illegible]
32 [illegible]

ו

1 [illegible]
2 [illegible]
3 [illegible]
4 [illegible]
5 [illegible]
6 [illegible]

VERSIO SAMARITANA.

29 [illegible]
30 [illegible]
31 [illegible]
32 [illegible]

ו

1 [illegible]
2 [illegible]
3 [illegible]
4 [illegible]
5 [illegible]
6 [illegible]

TEXT. ET VER. SAM. Translatio Latina.

Vocavitque nomen ejus Noë; dicens, Hic consolabitur nos ab operibus nostris, & à labore manuum nostrarum de terra cui maledixit Dominus. 29
Vixit autem Lamech postquam genuit Noë sexcentis annis; genuitque filios & filias. 30
Et fuerunt omnes dies Lamech, sexcenti & quinquaginta tres anni; & mortuus est. 31
Erat autem Noë filius quingentorum annorum, cùm genuit Sem, Cham, & Japhet. 32

CAP. VI.

FActum est autem cùm cœpit homo multiplicari super faciem terræ, ut filiæ nascerentur eis. 1
Et viderunt filii (a) Dei filias hominis, quòd bonæ essent: Et acceperunt sibi uxores ex omnibus quas elegerunt. 2
Dixitque Dominus, (b) Non disceptabit spiritus meus adversùs hominem in perpetuum, quia ipse caro est. Erunt enim dies ejus centum & viginti anni. 3
Gigantes autem erant in terra in diebus illis: atque etiam post hæc, cùm ingressi sunt filii Dei ad filias hominum, genueruntque illis; hi potentes sunt à seculo, viri (c) nominis. 4
Et vidit Dominus, quia multiplicata erat malitia hominis in terra: & (d) omnis imaginatio cogitationum cordis ejus tantùm malum omni die. 5
(e) Pœnituitque Dominum, quòd fecisset (f) hominem in terra: & (g) doluit in corde suo. 6

VER. SAM. (a) Dominatorum (b) Non projiciet opus meum adversùs (c) Excellentiæ. (d) omne secretum negotium (e) Inflatusq; est Dominus, (f) mundum (g) arctavit se apud cor suum.

Versio ARABICA cum Interpretatione LATINA.

29 * وسماه نوحا قايلا هذا يعزينا من اعمالنا ومن مشقة ايدينا في الارض التي لعنها الله *
30 وعاش بعد ذلك خمس ماية سنة وخمسا وتسعين سنة واولد فيها بنين وبنات * فصار
31 جميع عمره سبعماية سنة وسبعا وسبعين سنة ثم مات * ولما صار نوح ابن خمس ماية
32 سنة اولد ساما وحاما ويافث *

* الفصل السادس *

1 * ولما ابتداء الناس ان يكثروا على وجه الارض وولد لهم بنات * راي بنو الاشراف
2 بنات العامة حسانا فاتخذوا لهم نساء من جميع من اختاروه * فقال الله عند ذلك لا
3 تحل روحي على هولاء الناس ابدا لانهم بشريون * ويكون المهل مني لهم ماية وعشرين
4 سنة * وكان على الارض جبابرة في تلك الايام ومن بعدها * لان بني الوهيم دخلوا
5 على بنات قاين فولدن لهم جبابرة دهريين جبابرة مذكورين * فراي الرب ان شر الناس
6 قد كثر على الارض * وان هوية فكرهم وحقدهم ردي في جميع الايام * وكره الله خلقة
ولد ادم على الارض وكره ما جاء من معصيتهم

Et vocavit eum Nuha, dicens, Iste consolabitur nos de operibus nostris, et de labore manuum nostrarum, in terra cui maledixit Deus. 29
Et vixit posteà quingentos annos, et quinque ac nonaginta annos; in quibus genuit filios et filias. 30
Factaque est tota ætas ejus, septingenti anni, et septem ac septuaginta anni; deinde mortuus est. 31
Cùmque factus fuisset Nuha filius quingentorum annorum, genuit Sam, & Ham, et Jafeth. 32

CAP. VI.

CUmque cœpissent homines multiplicari super facie terræ, natæq; illis essent filiæ: 1
Viderunt filii illustrium filias plebis pulchras, assumpseruntque sibi mulieres ex quibuscunque elegerunt. 2
Dixitque Deus tunc, Non habitabit spiritus meus in his hominibus semper, quoniam carnales sunt. Eritque mora quam protraham ipsis, centum ac viginti annorum. 3
Eraatque super terram gigantes in illis diebus, & post illos; quia filii Elohim ingressi sunt ad filias Cain, & genuerunt eis gigantes æternos, gigantes memorabiles. 4
Viditque Dominus, quòd malitia hominum jam multiplicata esset super terram; & quòd voluntas cogitationis eorum, & pervicacia eorum mala esset in omnibus diebus. 5
Et abominatus est Deus creationem filiorum Adæ super terram, & abominatus est quod provenit ex inobedientia eorum. 6

Chapter 1

'Og King of Bashan, Enoch and the Books of Enoch: Extra-Canonical Texts and Interpretations of Genesis 6:1–4'*

Ariel Hessayon

> It is not the Writer, but the authority of the Church, that maketh a Book Canonical
> [Thomas Hobbes, *Leviathan* (1651), part III, chap. 33, 204]

> For only Og king of Bashan remained of the remnant of the giants
> (Deuteronomy 3:11)

Renaissance Humanist, Franciscan friar, Benedictine monk, Doctor of Medicine and 'Great Jester of France', François Rabelais (*c*.1490–1553?) was the author of *La vie, faits & dits Heroiques de Gargantua, & de son filz Pantagruel* (Lyon, 1564). A satirical masterpiece with liberal dollops of scatological humour, it tells the irreverent story of Gargantua, his son Pantagruel and their companion Panurge. Gargantua and Pantagruel are giants and in an allusion to the Matthean genealogy of Christ the first book begins with a promised account of how 'the Giants were born in this world, and how from them by a direct line issued *Gargantua*'. Similarly, the second book introduces a parody of the Old Testament genealogies:

> And the first was *Chalbroth*
> who begat *Sarabroth*
> who begat *Faribroth*
> who begat *Hurtali*, that was a brave eater of pottage, and reigned in the time of the flood.

Acknowledging readers would doubt the veracity of this lineage, 'seeing at the time of the flood all the world was destroyed, except *Noah*, and seven persons more with him in the Ark', Rabelais described how the giant Hurtali survived the deluge. Citing the authority of a rabbinic school known as the Massoretes, 'good honest fellows, true *ballokeering* blades, and exact *Hebraical* bagpipers', Rabelais explained that Hurtali did not get in the ark (he was too big), but rather sat astride upon it, with 'one leg on the one side, and another on the other, as little children use to do upon their wooden horses'. In this manner Hurtali steered the ark away from danger. Appreciative of his good deed those inside sent him up an abundance of food through a chimney.[1]

Rabelais's Hurtali was none other than Og the king of Bashan, whom Moses and the children of Israel slew in the battle of Edrei (Numbers 21:33). It was said of Og that he alone remained of the remnant of giants and that his iron bedstead in Rabbath was nine cubits long and four cubits broad (Deuteronomy 3:11). In *The Guide for the Perplexed* Moses ben Maimonides (1135–1204) elucidated the meaning of Og's enormous bedstead. The verse was not an example of hyperbole, for Scripture 'tells us that Og was double as long as an ordinary person, or a little less'. Undoubtedly this was an exceptional height among men, 'but not quite impossible'.[2] Maimonides's literal reading of the text was intended to negate the authority of the Talmud's commentary. According to a legend in the Babylonian Talmud (final redaction undertaken from late fifth century CE) Og uprooted a mountain to throw at the camp of Israel. God, however, sent ants which burrowed through the mountain above Og's head, so that it sank around his neck. As Og struggled to free himself his teeth projected on each side. Moses then took an axe and leaping into the air struck at Og's ankle, killing him.[3] Other interpretations accounted for Og's presence after the flood. Thus the Babylonian Talmud and the Midrash Rabbah (assembled and edited about fifth century CE) connected him with the 'one that had escaped' (Genesis 14:13).[4] Likewise, the *Pirkê de Rabbi Eliezer* (final redaction probably undertaken in the ninth century) told of how Og sat down on a piece of wood 'under the gutter' of the ark. After swearing an oath to Noah that he and his descendants would serve him as slaves in perpetuity, Noah made an aperture in the ark through which he passed victuals daily to Og.[5] A tractate of the Babylonian Talmud also gave Og's parentage. He was the son of Ahijah the son of Shemhazai. Rashi (1040–1105) noted in a gloss

---

* A condensed draft this essay was read at seminars for Early Modern History at Cambridge University and the Institute of Historical Research. I would like to thank the participants for their helpful comments and suggestions. In addition, I have profited from the advice of Mario Caricchio, Lorenza Gianfrancesco, Nicholas Keene, John Morrill, George Nickelsburg, Éamonn Ó Ciardha, William Poole, Nigel Smith, Stefano Villani and John Wilson. For reasons of space most references have been omitted. These can be found in 'Og, re di Basan, Enoc e i Libri di Enoc: testi non canonici e intrepretazioni sulla *Genesi* 6, 1–4' *Rivista di Storia e Letteratura Religiosa* (2005). I alone am responsible for any mistakes or shortcomings.

[1] François Rabelais, *The first Book* (trans. Sir Thomas Urquhart, 1653), 9; Rabelais, *Second Book* (trans. Urquhart, 1653), 5–6,8–9.

[2] Maimonides, *Guide for the Perplexed* (trans. M. Friedländer, 2nd edn, New York, 1956), part ii, cap. xlvii, 248.

[3] Isidore Epstein and Maurice Simon (eds and trans.), *Babylonian Talmud*, 34 vols (1935–48), Seder Zera'im, 331 (Berakoth 54b).

[4] *Babylonian Talmud*, Seder Tohoroth, 433 (Niddah 61a); H. Freedman and Maurice Simon (ed. and trans.) *Midrash Rabbah,* 10 vols, (1939), I 350 (Bereshith xlii.8).

[5] *Pirkê de Rabbi Eliezer* (trans. Gerald Friedlander, 1916), 167; Louis Ginzburg (ed.), *Legends of the Jews*, trans. Henrietta Szold and Paul Radin, 7 vols, (1913–38; reprinted, Baltimore, 1998), I 160.

on Numbers 13:33 that Shemhazai and Azael fell from heaven in the days of the generation of Enos.[6]

I

These stories of Og king of Bashan illustrate several important intellectual themes: Jewish exegesis of the Torah, the transmission of Jewish legends and their reinterpretation within a hostile Christian environment, and Christian awareness of Jewish sources in the Renaissance. Moreover, as a giant, as the progeny of a fallen angel, Og provides a link with texts under the name of Enoch. These influential extra-canonical writings have been discussed extensively by scholars, especially after the discovery of books attributed to Enoch among the Dead Sea Scrolls. While our understanding of the formation, reception and adaptation of the Enochic corpus within various contexts – the Hellenistic and early Roman period, sectarian Judaism, rabbinic Judaism, early Judaean, Syrian, Egyptian, North African and European Christianity, Gnosticism, Manichaeism and Medieval Jewish mysticism – has been significantly enhanced, comparable developments in Western Europe between the Renaissance and the Enlightenment have been relatively neglected. This essay attempts to fill that gap by tracing the dissemination of the Enochic corpus. In the process it explores Protestant and Catholic attitudes towards the canon; the Christian discovery of Kabbalistic literature and its appropriation and fusion with magical texts; encounters between Europeans and Ethiopians; the influence of Oriental studies; the concerns of early modern scholarship and contemporary knowledge of Hebrew, Greek, Latin, Coptic, Arabic and Ethiopic sources; Protestant opposition to doctrines based on oral traditions; and sectarian interest in extra-canonical texts.

II

> And Enoch lived sixty and five years, and begat Methuselah: And Enoch walked with God after he begat Methuselah three hundred years, and begat sons and daughters: And all the days of Enoch were three hundred sixty and five years: And Enoch walked with God: and he was not; for God took him (Genesis 5:21–4).

Etymologically, Enoch may come from the Hebrew root meaning 'to dedicate' or 'to teach'. The name may be translated as dedicated or teacher. Enoch was the seventh antediluvian patriarch. Alone of the antediluvian patriarchs he did not suffer the pains of death, though his pious life was much the shortest. His 365 years has long been recognized as a reference to the solar calendar. Moreover, the priestly editor of Genesis may have modelled the figure of Enoch on Mesopotamian traditions and a version of the so-called Sumerian King List, for the position of seventh antediluvian

[6] *Babylonian Talmud*, Seder Tohoroth, 433 (Niddah 61a); M. Rosenbaum and A.M. Silbermann (eds), *Pentateuch with Targum Onkelos, Haphtaroth and Rashi's Commentary. Numbers* (New York, 1949; reprinted, 5 vols, Jerusalem, 1973), 65.

king was usually occupied by Enmeduranki, originator of divination, recipient of divine mysteries and ruler of Sippar (city of the sun-god, Shamash). Yet it is also noteworthy that while the seventh antediluvian sage Utuabzu ascended to heaven, Enoch was taken. Even so, belief in Enoch's 'translation' to heaven, if not universal among Jews, nonetheless helped develop the legend of a beloved and wise seer of priestly character, the 'scribe of righteousness', the first man born on earth 'who learned writing and knowledge and wisdom'.[7]

A number of writings are pseudonymously attributed to Enoch. Some of these pseudepigrapha are conventionally designated 1 Enoch, 2 Enoch and 3 Enoch. The so-called Hebrew Book of Enoch (3 Enoch) is a composite work extant in several recensions of different length. What has arguably been identified as an original core (3 Enoch 3–15) has been dated to about 450–850, though this has been contested. Several strands are also present, notably traditions of the angel Metatron. This character appears to embody three originally independent figures – the angel Yahoel, the lesser YHWH, and Metatron, who himself resembles the archangel Michael. 3 Enoch has been characterized as a relatively late example of Hekhaloth literature and also as a Merkabah text. The Hekhaloth books describe the heavenly halls or palaces through which the visionary passes, while Merkabah mysticism is a rabbinic term for the assemblage of 'speculations, homilies, and visions connected with the Throne of Glory and the chariot which bears it'. Though 3 Enoch seems to have emanated from Babylonian rabbinic circles it has been observed that no mention is made of Enoch in either the Palestinian or Babylonian Talmud, nor in the Tannaitic Midrashim (exegetical Midrashim of a mainly legal nature on the books of Exodus, Leviticus, Numbers and Deuteronomy). This silence has been interpreted as rabbinic criticism of some of 3 Enoch's teachings.[8]

2 Enoch or 'The Book of the Secrets of Enoch' as it called in some documents, is extant only in Slavonic. It survives in a number of fragmentary texts and more than 10 complete manuscripts, the oldest of fourteenth-century provenance. These texts are generally taken to represent two recensions of unequal length, with the greater part of the shorter recension usually assumed to be the more original. 2 Enoch appears to be the work of one author, with few interpolations. It contains an account of Enoch's ascent into the celestial realm, his journey through the seven heavens and his metamorphosis near the Throne of Glory, as well as material about the creation of the world and the story of Melchizedek's miraculous birth to a barren old woman on the day of her death. Though 2 Enoch probably circulated among a Jewish rather than early Christian community, it is considered to be almost heterodox in character. Some scholars believe it was written in Hebrew and translated into Greek, others that is was composed in Greek but based partly on a Hebrew version. Attempts to date it have also proved inconclusive. 2 Enoch has been assigned to an Alexandrian

[7] 1 Enoch 12:4; Jubilees 4:17.

[8] Ginzburg (ed.), *Legends of the Jews*, V, 156; Gershom Scholem *Kabbalah* (New York, 1978), 373.

Jew of the first century CE. At the other extreme it is supposedly the product of a Greek monk of the ninth or tenth century.

Of all the Enochic pseudepigrapha 1 Enoch has received most attention. Undoubtedly a composite work, the longest version of the text is extant in more than 60 manuscripts. The oldest of these is clearly divided into five parts, while some later copies are divided into chapters. Modern scholarship has fixed the number of chapters and introduced verses. In this arrangement there are 108 chapters consisting of five books, with an appended chapter. Some books have been further subdivided into sections:

1–36, *The Book of the Watchers*
1–5, The Oracular Introduction
6–11, The Shemihazah narrative
12–16, Enoch's Ascent to Heaven
17–19, Enoch's first journey
20–36, Enoch's second journey
37–71, *The Similitudes of Enoch* (*The Book of Parables*)
72–82, *The Astronomical Book* (*The Book of the Heavenly Luminaries*)
83–90, *The Book of Dreams*
85–90, The Animal Apocalypse
91–107, *The Epistle of Enoch*
93:1–10; 91:11-17, The Apocalypse of Weeks
106–7, The Book of Noah
108, Concluding discourse

These five books are thought to span maybe two or three centuries, ranging from possibly before 200 BCE to the end of the first-century BCE, or perhaps later still. Four Aramaic manuscripts identified as sizeable portions of the Astronomical Book have been discovered at Qumran Cave 4. On palaeographic grounds the oldest has been dated by its editor to the late third or early second-century BCE. In its earliest form this material is considered to be probably the oldest stratum of the Enochic corpus. Aramaic fragments recognized as belonging to the Book of the Watchers have also been uncovered at Qumran Cave 4. The same editor has assigned the oldest to about 200–150 BCE. The Book of the Watchers is thus likely to date from the third-century BCE and elements are commonly deemed some of the earliest known forms of Jewish apocalyptic literature. The Epistle of Enoch conceivably originated in circles ancestral to the Essenes and was perhaps written about 170 BCE. Two fragments of this work have been found at Qumran Cave 4, the older dated to the middle of the first century BCE. The Apocalypse of Weeks, which forms part of the Epistle, was most likely an independent composition that was reused by the author of the Epistle. The Book of Dreams, it has been suggested, arose out of the conflict between pietistic Judaism and Hellenism in the late 160s BCE. An Aramaic fragment unearthed at Qumran Cave 4 has been dated to 150–125 BCE. The Animal Apocalypse within the Book of Dreams appears to have been written during the Maccabean revolt against the Seleucid empire (166–160 BCE) and contains a generally agreed reference to Judas Maccabeus as the 'great horn' (90:9). Though not found at Qumran either among the Aramaic fragments identified from Cave 4, or the Greek fragments identified from Cave 7, the Similitudes of Enoch are usually regarded as a unit of Jewish composition. They may be assigned to the late first-century BCE, with two verses (56:5–6) plausibly understood as an allusion to the Parthian invasion of Judaea in 40 BCE. Alternatively, it has been carefully argued that the work belongs to the first century CE. Notions of a later date seem far-fetched.

III

> And it came to pass, when men began to multiply on the face of the earth, and daughters were born unto them, That the sons of God saw the daughters of men that they were fair; and they took them wives of all which they chose. And the Lord said, My spirit shall not always strive with man, for that he also is flesh: yet his days shall be an hundred and twenty years. There were giants in the earth in those days; and also after that, when the sons of God came in unto the daughters of men, and they bare children to them, the same became mighty men which were of old, men of renown (Genesis 6:1–4).

The Book of the Watchers, a fusion of diverse sources and traditions, is partly eschatological (1–6, 10:14–11:2). It opens with a prophetic oracle announcing divine judgment upon everything, upon all the righteous and ungodly. What follows has been viewed as an early type of expository narrative. The core appears to be a cycle of legends that coalesced in the story of Shemihazah, leader of a rebellious band of angels. This was subsequently conflated with material concerning the angelic chieftain Asael. Full of interpolations, inconsistencies and word plays, it begins with what is commonly regarded as a paraphrase of Genesis 6:1 – though the opposite has sometimes been argued, namely that the passage predates the definitive version of Genesis.

'And it came to pass' that the 'children of heaven' saw and lusted after the 'beautiful and comely' daughters of men (6:1–2). In 'the days of Jared' they descended upon the summit of Mount Hermon, where they bound themselves with 'imprecations' (6:6). The leaders and all the rest of the Watchers 'took for themselves wives from all whom they chose'. They began to cohabit with them and to defile themselves with them. They taught them sorcery and spells and showed them 'the cutting of roots and herbs' (7:1).

> And they became pregnant by them and bore great giants of three thousand cubits; and there were [not] born upon earth off-spring [which grew to their strength]. These devoured the entire fruits of men's labour, and men were unable to sustain them. Then the giants treated them violently and began to slay mankind. They began to do violence to and to attack all the birds and the beasts of the earth and reptiles [that crawl upon the earth], and

> the fish of the sea; and they began to devour their flesh, and they were drinking the blood. Thereupon the earth made accusation against the lawless ones (1 Enoch 7:2–6).[9]

The major function of the Shemihazah narrative was to explain the origin of evil in the world. This was attributed to an act of rebellion against God. It has been suggested that the story recalls a time of conflict and parallels have been drawn with Greek myths, notably Hesiod's *Catalogues of Women and Eoiae* (*c.*750–650 BCE). Likewise, similarities with several Hurrian myths preserved in Hittite have been emphasized. A concern with the maintenance of family purity, particularly the protection of the purity of the priesthood, has also been discerned. In addition, resemblances have been observed between several rebel angels' names and astral deities, while it has been noted that Mount Hermon was a holy site where the worship of Pan was established in the Hellenistic period. In the same way, the Asael legend attributes the genesis of certain sinful acts to the teaching of forbidden knowledge. Thus Asael divulged the secrets of weapon making and metallurgy to promote advances in warfare, and the mysteries of wearing jewellery and applying make-up to enhance women's sexual charms (8:1). Moreover, the Asael material has been linked both with the ritual of sending a scapegoat [Azazel] into the wilderness on the Day of Atonement (Leviticus 16), and the Prometheus myth recounted in the writings of Hesiod and Aeschylus. Other significant aspects of the Book of the Watchers include Enoch's ascent to heaven where he beholds God seated on his throne (14:8–25). Modelled on Ezekiel's vision of the chariot throne (Ezekiel 1) and a precursor of Merkabah mysticism, it is regarded as the earliest Jewish ascent apocalypse.

IV

The author of the Book of Jubilees (*c.*160–140 BCE), a midrashic commentary on Genesis and more briefly on Exodus down to the revelation on Mount Sinai, knew the Book of the Watchers. Though dependent on parts of the Enochic corpus, Jubilees differs in several important respects. In Jubilees 'the angels of the Lord', 'those who are named the Watchers', do not descend because of their lust for the daughters of men. Rather, God sends them to instruct the children of men to 'do judgment and uprightness on the earth' (Jubilees 4:15–16). Only then do they sin by defiling themselves with the daughters of men (Jubilees 4:22). Thus heaven remains untainted since evil originated on earth.

Significantly, the myth of the Watchers was known at Qumran. *The Damascus Rule* (*c.*100 BCE), one of the earlier layers of the preserved literature, contains a catalogue of the many who were led astray by thoughts of 'guilty inclination' and 'eyes of lust'. It begins with the 'Heavenly Watchers' that fell for having 'walked in

[9] Matthew Black (ed.), *The Book of Enoch or 1 Enoch, Studia in Veteris Testamenti Pseudepigrapha*, 7 (Leiden, 1985), 27–8.

the stubbornness of their heart'.[10] Similarly, *The Genesis Apocryphon* (first-century BCE) seems to have been influenced by a form of the Enochic corpus and the Book of Jubilees. An elaboration on Genesis recast in the first person singular, it may once have contained a version of the story of the Watchers.[11] Also identified among the Aramaic fragments at Qumran are copies of the so-called Book of Giants (possibly second-century BCE). Based on the story of wicked angels begetting gigantic progeny, it has been plausibly connected with a partially extant Manichean Book of Giants (third century) and, contentiously, with a text concerning Shemhazai and Azael excerpted from *Midrash Bereshit Rabbati* (*c*.1050), commonly attributed to Rabbi Moses ha-Darshan of Narbonne.

In contrast to traditions circulating at Qumran, Philo Judaeus of Alexandria (*c*.20 BCE–*c*.50 CE) seems not to have been familiar with the Book of the Watchers. His treatise 'On the Giants' is an allegorical commentary on Genesis 6:1–4. Drawing on Greek philosophy, Philo discussed the origins and destiny of the human soul, contrasting it with the flesh. Suggestively, his rendering of 'sons of God' as 'angels of God' is found in versions of the Septuagint preserved in the Codex Alexandrinus (fifth century) and some later manuscripts.[12] Philo, however, is not without difficulty for though the majority of his works are preserved in their original Greek, it was the early Christians who saved and transmitted them. Similar issues of textual contamination cast a shadow over the corpus of the Jewish aristocrat, Flavius Josephus (*c*.37–100). Extant in corrupt manuscripts, the earliest of which date from the ninth century, Josephus' writings are bedevilled with inconsistencies. Nevertheless, Josephus remains a valuable historian. Among the traditions he recorded for his Greek-educated largely gentile audience at Rome was one concerning the descendants of Adam's son, Seth:

> They discovered the science with regard to the heavenly bodies and their orderly arrangement. And in order that humanity might not lose their discoveries or perish before they came to be known, Adamos having predicted that there would be an extermination of the universe, at one time by a violent fire and at another time by a force with an abundance of water, they made two pillars, one of brick and the other of stones and inscribed their findings on both, in order that if the one of brick should be lost owing to the flood the one of stone should remain and offer an opportunity to teach men what had been written on it and to reveal that also one of brick had been set up by them. And it remains until today in the land of Seiris.

It has been observed that some features of Josephus' story about two stelae are more appropriate in an Enochic context. Nor is it inconceivable that Josephus reworked or repeated a source containing vestiges of the Watchers myth for he continued

[10] CD, in G.Vermes (ed.), *The Dead Sea Scrolls in English* (3rd edn, Harmondsworth, 1990), 84.

[11] 1QapGen, in Vermes (ed.), *Dead Sea Scrolls*, 252–59.

[12] Philo Judaeus, 'De Gigantibus', 6, in *The Works of Philo*, trans. C.D. Yonge (1997), 152.

by relating that many 'angels of God' fathered children with women. The angels' offspring proved 'insolent' and 'despisers of every good thing'. According to tradition their outrageous conduct resembled the heinous acts 'said by the Greeks to have been done by giants'.[13]

V

The influence of 1 Enoch on the New Testament has long been debated. The Similitudes of Enoch have been compared with the eschatological figure called 'Son of man' and the parable of the last judgment (Matthew 25:31–46). Furthermore, a verse from the Book of the Watchers (1:9) is explicitly quoted in the Epistle of Jude (*c*.50–150):

> And Enoch also, the seventh from Adam, prophesied of these, saying, Behold, the Lord cometh with ten thousands of his saints, To execute judgment upon all, and to convince all that are ungodly among them of all their ungodly deeds which they have ungodly committed, and all of their hard speeches which ungodly sinners have spoken against him (Jude 14–15).

Though it has not been established if Jude's letter is an authentic or pseudonymous composition, it is evident that the author had a scribal background and was Greek-educated. His apparent borrowing from a Jewish 'farewell discourse' known as the Assumption of Moses (early first century CE) together with other allusions, suggest that he knew more than a single passage of the Enochic corpus. Indeed, his representation of the fallen angels as great sinners (Jude 6) resembles traditions about the Watchers.[14] While the Epistle of Jude may imply that its author regarded the Book of the Watchers as a genuine Enochic writing, the pseudonymous Epistle of Barnabas (*c*.70–135) is more explicit. It considers Enoch a prophet, citing as Scripture an extract supposed to be a summary of an Enochic text, as well as quoting a saying of Enoch's unknown in the extant corpus.[15] Likewise, the Apocalypse of Peter (*c*.100–150) probably uses imagery derived from a version of the Noachic book preserved in the Enochic corpus.[16]

Drawing on a combination of Jewish traditions of fallen angels and Roman adaptations of Greek myths Justin Martyr (*c*.100–165) imagined that the angels' unholy union with women produced demons. These creatures subdued the human race partly by magical writings, partly by the fear they occasioned, and partly by teaching the offering of sacrifices, incense and libations. The demons sowed

[13] Steve Mason (ed.), *Flavius Josephus. Translation and Commentary. Vol.3. Judean Antiquities 1-4*, trans. Louis Feldman (Leiden, 2000), 24–7.

[14] Cf. 1 Enoch 15:3; 2 Peter 2:4–10.

[15] Barnabas 4:3; 1 Enoch 106:19–107; Barnabas 4:4; Barnabas 16:5; cf. 1 Enoch 89:56, 66; 1 Enoch 90:26–9.

[16] Apocalypse of Peter 8; cf. 1 Enoch 106:10.

murders, wars, adulteries and wickedness among men.[17] Similarly, Justin's renegade pupil Tatian (*c*.110 x 120–*c*.173) believed that roaming demons introduced the doctrine of Fate after their expulsion from heaven.[18] In the same way a *Plea on Behalf of Christians* (*c*.176–80), traditionally attributed to Athenagoras, declared that the angels were created free agents. Some of those who were placed about the first firmament 'fell into impure love of virgins', engendering giants whose souls were wandering demons.[19]

Against Heresies (*c*.175–85) by Irenaeus of Lyons (*c*.130 x 140–*c*.202?) locates the scene of the angels' transgression in heaven and maintains that the uncircumcised Enoch discharged the office of God's legate to the fallen angels.[20] Other references confirm Irenaeus' familiarity with a Greek version of the Book of the Watchers, notably a section in *Demonstration of the Apostolic Teaching* (after *c*.175), which recounts how the fallen angels taught their wives forbidden knowledge including the 'virtues of roots and herbs', dyeing in colours, cosmetics, philtres, passion, hatred, 'spells of bewitchment', sorcery and idolatry.[21] In *Stromateis* Clement of Alexandria (*c*.150–*c*.210 x 215) attributed the angels' fall to their lack of self-control. Overcome by sexual desire they descended to earth where, in an apparent borrowing from the Book of the Watchers, they revealed secrets to women.[22] Elsewhere, he noted that Jude affirmed the truth of Enoch's prophecy and quoted an Enochic saying unknown in the extant corpus - though this may have been a gloss.[23]

Tertullian of Carthage (*c*.155 x 160 - after 220?) believed that the Holy Spirit sang through 'the most ancient prophet Enoch', who had predicted that 'the demons, and the spirits of the angelic apostates' would turn all things contained in heaven, the sea and on earth into idolatry. Tertullian quoted the Epistle of Enoch's condemnation of idol worshippers and idol makers; 'I swear to you, sinners, that against the day of perdition of blood repentance is being prepared'. He added that those angels who deserted God discovered the curious art of astrology.[24] In another work, a rhetorical defence of Christianity from charges of sacrilege and disloyalty to the Emperor, Tertullian remarked that 'we are instructed' by 'our sacred books how from certain angels, who fell of their own free-will, there sprang a more wicked demon-brood, condemned of God along with the authors of their race'.[25] It was, however, in his bitter denunciations of women's sexuality and the dangers of pagan vices that Tertullian expounded at greatest length on the fallen angels and the origin of female

[17] Justin Martyr, *Second Apology*, 5; cf. 1 Enoch 9:8–9; 1 Enoch 15:8–9; Justin Martyr, *First Apology*, 5.

[18] Tatian, *Address to Greeks*, 9.

[19] [Athenagoras?], *Plea on Behalf of Christians*, 24, 25; cf. 1 Enoch 15:3.

[20] Irenaeus, *Against Heresies*, 4.16.2; cf. 1 Enoch 14:7.

[21] Irenaeus, *Demonstration*, 18; cf. 1 Enoch 6:1–2, 7:1, 8:1.

[22] Clement, *Stromateis*, 3.7.59, 5.1.10; cf. 1 Enoch 16:3.

[23] Clement, *Commentary on the Epistle of Jude*; Clement, *Selections from the Prophets*, 2.1; cf. 1 Enoch 19:3.

[24] Tertullian, *On Idolatry*, 15,4,9; cf. 1 Enoch 19:1; 1 Enoch 99:6–7; 1 Enoch 6:1–2.

[25] Tertullian, *Apology*, 22; cf. 1 Enoch 15:8–9.

ornamentation. While moralizing *On the Apparel of Women* Tertullian acknowledged that 'the Scripture of Enoch' was not received by some, 'because it is not admitted into the Jewish canon'. Yet if it was rejected for having been 'published before the deluge' he could justify how it 'safely survived that world-wide calamity'. Recalling that Noah was Enoch's great-grandson, he reasoned that Methuselah passed on his father's teaching to him. Equally, Noah could have renewed this 'Scripture' under the Spirit's inspiration. Indeed, it seemed that the Jews had discarded Enoch's testimony since it foretold of Christ.[26]

In his controversial work *On First Principles* Origen (*c*.185–*c*.254) refers to 'the book of Enoch' in a context that suggests he distinguished it from 'holy Scripture'. He continues with two quotations from a Greek translation of the Book of the Watchers, the second a saying previously cited by Clement of Alexandria – an author whom Origen read attentively.[27] In his *Commentary on the Gospel of John* written at Alexandria Origen explained that the Hebrew name 'Jared' also yielded the meaning 'going down'. If it was legitimate to accept the Book of Enoch as sacred then it was in Jared's days that 'the sons of God came down to the daughters of men'. Moreover, in an apparent allusion to Philo:

> Under this descent some have supposed that there is an enigmatical reference to the descent of souls into bodies, taking the phrase 'daughters of men' as a tropical expression for this earthly tabernacle.[28]

In his *Homilies on Numbers* Origen spoke of Enoch's books in the plural, though it is uncertain to which parts of the corpus he referred. His vindication of Christianity against the Platonist Celsus is even more revealing. Origen's adversary allegedly claimed that other angels visited the human race before Jesus. This Origen refuted, charging his adversary with misunderstanding the Book of Enoch. Nor was Celsus apparently aware that 'the books which bear the name Enoch do not at all circulate in the Churches as divine'.[29]

When Jerome (*c*.331 x 347–420) finished his memoir *On Illustrious Men* (393?) not only was the Book of Enoch considered apocryphal, but many rejected the Epistle of Jude as well. Nevertheless, 'by age and use' Jude's Epistle had gained authority and was 'reckoned among the Holy Scriptures'.[30] Jerome also mentioned in his *Homilies on the Psalms* that he had read in 'a certain apocryphal book' that when the sons of God came down to the daughters of men they descended upon Mount Hermon. Though he did not regard this text as authoritative it is noteworthy that in his earlier *Hebrew Questions on Genesis* (*completed c.* 391–93) Jerome had

[26] Tertullian, *Apparel of Women*, 1.3; see also, Tertullian, *Apparel of Women,* 1.2, 2.10; cf. 1 Enoch 8:1–3; Tertullian, *On the Veiling of Virgins*, 7.

[27] Origen, *On First Principles*, 1.3.3, 4.35; cf. 1 Enoch 21:1; 1 Enoch 19:3.

[28] Origen, *Commentary on the Gospel of John*, 6.25.

[29] Origen, *Homilies on Numbers*, 28.2; Origen, *Against Celsus*, 5.52,54–5.

[30] Jerome, *On Illustrious Men*, 4; see also, Jerome, *Commentary on the Epistle to Titus*, 1.12.

supposed that the *Nephilim* or 'falling ones' of Genesis 6:4 was a fitting name 'both for angels and for the offspring of holy ones'.[31]

That Enoch 'the seventh from Adam' left some 'divine writings' could not be denied by Augustine of Hippo (354–430), for this was testified by 'the Apostle Jude in his canonical epistle'. Yet in *The City of God* (*c*.413–*c*.422 x 429) he dismissed as fables those 'scriptures which are called apocryphal', because their obscure origin was 'unknown to the fathers' from whom the authority of 'the true Scriptures' had been transmitted by a well-established succession. Nor was it without reason that these writings had no place in the 'canon of Scripture' preserved by the Temple priests, 'for their antiquity brought them under suspicion'. Thus the writings produced under Enoch's name with their fables about giants were not genuine since they had been judged so by 'prudent men'. Augustine did not doubt that 'according to the Hebrew and Christian canonical Scriptures' there were many giants before the flood, but these were not the offspring of angels. Without denying that some copies of the Septuagint translated 'sons of God' as 'angels of God', Augustine maintained that the 'sons of God' were 'according to the flesh the sons of Seth', sunk into community with women 'when they forsook righteousness'.[32] This was not a new Christian interpretation, for it had been tentatively advanced by Julius Africanus (*c*.160–*c*.240) – according to extracts from his chronicle made by a Byzantine chronographer.[33]

VI

In the *Apostolic Constitutions* (*c*.380), a redacted collection eventually rejected by the Church on account of the interpolations of Arian heretics, the Book of Enoch along with other writings was condemned as apocryphal, 'pernicious and repugnant to the truth'.[34] It was also denounced as apocryphal in the *Synopsis of Sacred Scripture* (early sixth century?), traditionally if erroneously ascribed to Athanasius (d.373), and the *Catalogue of the Sixty Canonical Books* (seventh century?), appended in some manuscripts to the *Quaestiones* of Anastasius of Sinai. Significantly, the Books of Enoch were not even mentioned among the apocryphal writings enumerated in the so-called *Gelasian Decree* (early sixth century?), a spurious decretal attributed in some copies to Pope Gelasius I (492–6), but more likely of South Gallic origin. One title that was rejected by the *Gelasian Decree*, however, was a 'book of the giant named Ogia who is said by the heretics to have fought with a dragon after the flood'. This work has been identified with the Manichean Book of Giants.[35]

---

[31] Jerome, *Commentary on Psalm CXXXII*, 3; Jerome, *Hebrew Questions on Genesis*, trans. C.T.R. Hayward (Oxford, 1995), 37.

[32] Augustine, *The City of God*, 15.23, 18.38.

[33] William Adler and Paul Tuffin (eds), *The chronography of George Synkellos* (Oxford, 2002), 19.25–6.

[34] *Apostolic Constitutions*, 6.16.

[35] *Synopsis Scripturæ Sacræ*, in Jacques Paul Migne (ed.), *Patrologia Graeca* (162 vols, Paris, 1857–66), XXVIII, col. 431.

VII

About 386 Priscillian, contested bishop of Avila, was executed at Trier on criminal charges. Priscillian was probably the author of a *Book on Faith and on Apocrypha* (late fourth century), a defence of his doctrine and conduct, which argued that it had been apostolic practice to 'read from outside the canon'. Though he appears not to have known the Book of Enoch, the writer used the authority of Jude, 'the twin of the Lord', to question why the prophecy of Enoch was condemned.[36] While some of Priscillian's followers were eventually reconciled with the Spanish Church others were denounced as dangerous heretics. It has been suggested that during the seventh century a collection of texts with Priscillianist affiliations, some based partly on apocryphal sources, were transmitted from Spain to Ireland. No fragments of the Enochic corpus, however, have been discovered in the rich Irish literature of the period. Even so, several scholars have detected Enochic motifs such as the constituent elements of man, the naming of Adam, the seven heavens and the seven principal archangels behind ideas expressed in disparate texts. Yet there are more likely direct and intermediate sources. Thus some of the eight angels invoked in a sacrilegious prayer of Aldebert, a Frankish bishop condemned at the Lateran Synod of 745, were probably derived from the books of Daniel, Esdras and Tobit rather than Enoch.[37] Similarly, two early ninth century Breton manuscripts contain an account of the creation of the world. Products of Early Celtic religious culture they supposedly depend on the Book of Enoch. Another manuscript, however, also identified as ninth-century Breton contains a story of the birth of Noah. This is widely regarded as an abridged Latin version of the beginning of the Noachic book preserved in the Enochic corpus (1 Enoch 106:1–18). It has been argued that this fragment represents part of a larger if not complete Latin translation of the Book of Enoch. This seems unduly optimistic. The tale is introduced with an inept scribal addition, concludes with a warning of the flood and is followed by several miscellaneous texts grouped around the theme of punishment awaiting unrepentant sinners.[38] Indeed, there are only two known references in Western literature derived from a Latin version of the Book of Enoch. These citations by pseudo-Cyprian and pseudo-Vigilius are from the same passage quoted in the Epistle of Jude.

By the tenth century the Latin fragment of the Noachic book was in England, perhaps at Worcester. Hitherto, the Book of Enoch seems to have been unknown in the British Isles. In his commentary on *The seven Catholic Epistles* Bede (*c.*673–735) had declared that the book was reckoned among the Apocrypha by the Church. Though he alluded to its extraordinary account of giants fathered by angels this

[36] A.S. Jacobs, 'The Disorder of Books: Priscillian's Canonical Defense of Apocrypha',*Harvard Theological Review*, 93 (2000), 146–7.

[37] The names of angels are Uriel (2 Esdras 4:1, 1 Enoch 19:1), Raguel (Tobit 3:7, 1 Enoch 20:4), Tubuel, Michael (Daniel 10:13, 1 Enoch 9:1), Adinus (1 Esdras 9:48), Tubuas, Sabaoc and Sirniel.

[38] BL, MS Royal 5 E. XIII, fols 79v–80r, printed in Robert Charles (ed.), *The Book of Enoch* (Oxford, 1893), 373–5.

was not a summary of the original work, but rather a paraphrase of Augustine's censorious account. Likewise, Bede's reading of *Nephilim* derived from Jerome.[39] More contentious are the various correspondence and partial correspondences noticed by some critics between the Book of Enoch and *Beowulf* (before 1025). Thus the poet's portrayal of Grendel as a gigantic creature and eater of human flesh has been compared with Enochic traditions about the giants. Yet even proponents of this misguided view have conceded that Grendel's descent is not from rebel angels, nor even Seth but Cain. While legends that Cain was the son of Satan, and that his offspring begat a mixed multitude are undoubtedly of Jewish origin, they are not Enochic. Nor is the interpretation that the daughters of Cain mated with the sons of Seth.

VIII

In his *Flowers of History* Roger of Wendover (d.1236), Benedictine monk and chronicler of St Albans Abbey related that Enoch pleased God, was translated to paradise where he lived with Elijah, discovered certain letters and wrote a book, as was contained in the Epistle of Jude. Adapted from Peter Comestor's University textbook the *Historia Scholastica* (*c*.1169 x 1175), this formula was repeated in the *Great Chronicle* of Matthew Paris (*c*.1200-1259), Roger's successor at St. Albans.[40] Variations are found in several English chronicles such as the popular *Universal Chronicle* of the Chester monk Ranulph Higden (d.1363) and the *Eulogium historiarum* (*c*.1366), compiled by a Malmesbury monk from Higden and other sources. The *Eulogium* also reiterated the explanation that the giants were the progeny of the sons of Seth and the daughters of Cain.[41] This exposition recurs in the *Chronicle of England to AD 1417* by John Capgrave (1393–1464), an Austin friar of King's Lynn. In an echo of Tertullian's belief that Enoch and Elijah were the two witnesses who would suffer bloody death at the hands of Antichrist (Revelation 11:3–12), Capgrave maintained that Enoch and Elijah would return from paradise to preach against the errors of Antichrist, when they would be martyred. Furthermore, in a passage reminiscent of Vincent of Beauvais's *Speculum Naturale* (*c*.1245), Capgrave observed that:

---

[39] Bede, *Super Catholicas Exposito* (709 x 716?), Bede, *Quæstiones super Genesim* (725 x 731), in Jacques-Paul Migne (ed.), *Patrologia Latina* (221 vols, Paris, 1844–64), XCIII, cols 128–9, 293.

[40] Roger de Wendover, *Flowers of History*, Rolls Series 84, ed. Henry Hewlett, 3 vols.(1886–89), I 4; Matthew Paris, *Chronica Majora*, RS 57, ed. Henry Luard, 7 vols.(1872–83), I 4; cf. Peter Comestor, *Historia Scholastica* (*c*.1170), in Migne (ed.), PL CXCVIII, cap. xxx, cols 1080–81.

[41] Churchill Babington et al. (eds), *Polychronicon Ranulphi Higden*, RS 41, 9 vols (1865–86), II, 222–3; Frank Haydon (ed.), *Eulogium (Historiarum sive Temporis)*, RS 9 (3 vols, 1858–63), I 22, 24.

> This Ennok mad a book of prophecie, whech the lawe acoundith among bokis that be clepid Apocripha; of whech I have mech wondir, for in the Epistil of Judas, whech is incorporate to the Bible, the same Apostil makith mynde of this book.[42]

IX

Martin Luther (1483–46) denied that Enoch would return before the last judgment, unless this was to be in spirit. Luther also noted that Enoch's prophecy was to be read nowhere in the Scriptures and that for this reason some ancient Church Fathers would not receive Jude's epistle as canonical. Dismissing this as insufficient cause to reject a book, Luther maintained that Enoch had preached and published the 'Word of the Lord', which he had learned through his father Adam, 'by influence from the holy Ghost'.[43] Similarly, Jean Calvin (1509–64) doubted that Enoch's prophecy was an apocryphal text, supposing that Jude had received it from the Jews by oral tradition.[44] Reused by reformers like Lancelot Ridley (d.1576) and Augustin Marlorat (1506–62) these arguments became part of the Protestant arsenal in the larger battle against Catholic doctrine.[45] Thus William Perkins (1558–1602) renounced all unwritten traditions that were made articles of faith and rules of God's worship, for all such doctrines were written 'in the books of the Prophets and Apostles'. Even if some book penned by a Jew under Enoch's name was extant in Jude's days and afterwards lost, knowing if Enoch had written the prophecy was unnecessary to salvation. Had the work existed it was apocryphal because Moses was 'the first penman of Scripture'. Nor was it true that some canonical books were missing, for not one sentence or tittle of the canon had perished. To doubt this was to question the fidelity of the Church, the keeper of the canon.[46]

Reiterating Protestant objections to 'traditions' and unwritten 'verities' urged by the Church of Rome, Andrew Willet set out his thoughts on Enoch's prophecy in *Hexapla in Genesin* (Cambridge, 1605). Disagreeing with Tertullian, Willet insisted that there was no genuine 'propheticall booke of Henoch'. Nor did he consider it possible that part of it might be true. Dismissing the Franciscan Miguel de Medina's opinion that a book under Enoch's name had never existed, he also supposed it unlikely that 'the true booke of Henoch' was extant in Jude's days and afterwards

[42] Francis Hingeston (ed.), *The Chronicle of England by John Capgrave*, RS 1 (1858), 12, 15; cf. Tertullian, *Treatise on the Soul*, 50; Vincent of Beauvais, *Bibliotheca Mundi* (4 vols, Douai, 1624), I, col. 7.

[43] Martin Luther, *A commentarie or exposition vppon the twoo Epistles generall of Sainct Peter, and that of Sainct Jude*, trans. Thomas Newton (1581), 168v.

[44] Jean Calvin, *The Comentaries of M. Jhon Caluin vpon the first Epistle of Sainct Iohn, and vpon the Epistle of Jude* (1580), sig. C.

[45] Lancelot Ridley, *An Exposition vpon the epistle of Jude yᵉ apostle of Christ* (1549), sig. Hii[r-v]; Augustin Marlorat, *A Catholike and ecclesiastical exposition uppon the epistle of S. Iude the Apostle*, trans. I.D. (1584), sig. Diiii.

[46] William Perkins, *A godlie and learned exposition vpon the whole Epistle of Jude* (1606), 110–11.

corrupted with fables. Rather, Willet cited Augustine's testimony, arguing that the Book of Enoch was produced by heretics and 'altogether forged'.[47] In the same vein, Samuel Otes (*c.*1578–1658) claimed that 'the Scriptures' were perfect, though why some writings were lost was best known to God. Declaring unwritten traditions superfluous he fulminated against the Council of Trent:

> Traditions are gathered of an evill egge: digge the Papists never so deep, they shall not find the myne nor spring of them in the Primitive Church.[48]

X

According to the Acts of the Apostles Philip baptized a eunuch of 'great authority' under the Candace, Queen of the Ethiopians (Acts 8:26–39). Not until the fourth century, however, with the supposed missionary activities of Frumentius of Tyre (died *c.*380), was Christianity introduced into Ethiopia. By the early sixth century Ethiopia was a predominantly Christian country, largely due to the evangelizing of most likely Syrian monks who may have arrived from South Arabia. Beginning probably with the Gospels it appears that before the end of the fifth century Greek texts of the Bible were translated into Ethiopic. Syrian monks may also have used Syriac versions in conjunction with the Greek in their Bible translations. Among the texts rendered into Ethiopic, possibly before the end of the sixth century, were the Book of Jubilees and the Book of Enoch. It seems likely that the translators of Enoch used a Greek text, though it has been argued that they relied on an Aramaic version either directly or with recourse to the Greek. The oldest known manuscript of Ethiopic Enoch was discovered in the Church of Holy Gabriel on the island of Kebran, and dates from the late fourteenth or early fifteenth century. Though it contains some textual corruptions introduced by scribal error or emendation this manuscript is superior to later copies, which indicate a process of progressive degeneration during transmission. In a number of manuscripts the Book of Enoch is usually combined with the Ethiopic Bible, frequently appearing next to the Book of Job, Daniel or books attributed to Solomon. Accorded canonical status in the Ethiopian Church the work was often quoted in Ethiopic literature and is one of many sources for the *Kebra Nagast* (final redaction about 1320). Based on the Queen of Sheba's legendary visit to Solomon (1 Kings 10:1–13), the epic *Kebra Nagast* or 'Glory of the Kings' tells of their affair, the birth of their son Menelik and his theft of the Ark of the Covenant, which he brought to Aksum, the new Zion. Conflating Enochic and Koranic traditions as well as material found in the Syriac *Cave of Treasures* (final redaction about sixth century), the hundredth chapter narrated the angels' fall. Assuming the mind and body of men, the rebel angels descended amidst the children of Cain. After playing musical instruments to accompany dancing they enjoyed an orgy with the daughters of Cain. The women conceived but died in childbirth. Their

---

[47] Andrew Willet, *Hexapla in Genesin* (Cambridge, 1605), 70.

[48] Samuel Otes, *An explanation of the generall Epistle of Saint Iude* (1633), 309–11.

surviving offspring split open their mothers' bellies and came forth by their navels. They grew to be giants, whose height reached to the clouds.[49]

XI

Enoch the 'scribe of righteousness', the first man born on earth who 'learned writing', was credited with recording 'the signs of heaven according to the order of their months' that men might know 'the seasons of the years'.[50] In a supposed citation from a Samaritan Hellenistic fragment (third or second century BCE) doubtfully attributed by the Church historian Eusebius of Caesarea (*c.*260–*c.*339) or his source to the Jewish Hellenistic historian Eupolemus, Enoch was also recognized as the discoverer of astrology and equated with the Greek Atlas.[51] Moreover, according to a quotation from the lost *Book of Imouth* by Zosimus of Panopolis (late third–early fourth century) 'ancient and divine scriptures' said that certain angels lusted after women and afterwards instructed them in 'all the works of nature'. These teachings were inscribed in the *Book of Chemes*, 'whence the art is called alchemy'. Though 'Chemes' is suggestive of Noah's son Ham (Cham), Zosimus' marriage of Enochic traditions with a mythic account of the origins of alchemy is significant in a Hellenistic Egyptian context.[52] For it may anticipate the commingling of Enoch and the Egyptian god of knowledge, wisdom and writing, 'the three times great' Thoth – considered by the Greeks as the divine equivalent of their own 'thrice-great' Hermes.[53] Thus the learned Franciscan monk Roger Bacon (*c.*1214–*c.*1294) remarked that some identified Enoch with 'the great Hermogenes, whom the Greeks much commend and laud', attributing to him 'all secret and celestial science'.[54] Similarly, the Syrian chronographer Gregory Abû'l Faraj, commonly known as Bar Hebraeus (1226–86), observed that the ancient Greeks said that Enoch was Hermes Trismegistus. It was he who 'made manifest before every man the knowledge of books and the art of writing', who invented 'the science of the constellations and the courses of the stars'.[55] Like these Greeks, the inhabitants of Harran in north-western Mesopotamia, who took the name Sabi'an when they fell under Muslim domination, were said to speak of Enoch as being the Koranic prophet Idris, asserting the same was Hermes. It is therefore noteworthy that a Hermetic treatise of probably Arab origin linking the fifteen fixed stars with fifteen plants, stones and talismen is

---

[49] Ernest W. Budge (ed.), *The Queen of Sheba and her only son Menyelek* (2nd edn, Oxford, 1932), 184–8.

[50] 1 Enoch 12:4; Jubilees 4:17; Black (ed.), *Book of Enoch*, 124; cf. Eusebius, *The Church History of Eusebius*, 7.32.19.

[51] Eusebius, *Praeparatio Evangelica*, 9.17.8–9.

[52] Adler and Tuffin (eds), *Chronography of George Synkellos*, 14.4–14.

[53] Cf. Plato, *Phaedrus*, 274D; Plato, *Philebus*, 18B–D.

[54] Roger Bacon, *Secretum secretorum*, in Robert Steele (ed.), *Rogeri Baconi, Opera*, 16 fascicule 5 (Oxford, 1909–40), 99.

[55] Ernest W. Budge (ed.), *The Chronography of Gregory Abû'l Faraj*, 2 vols (1932), I 5.

ascribed in some fourteenth-century Latin manuscripts to Enoch and in other copies to Hermes.[56] Indeed, the Arab geographer Ibn Battūta (1304?–77?) reported that Hermes was also called by the name of Khanūkh [Enoch], that is Idris. This Idris was said to have speculated on the movement of celestial bodies, to have warned men of the coming of the deluge and to have built the pyramids, 'in which he depicted all the practical arts and their tools, and made diagrams of the sciences' that they might remain immortalized.[57]

XII

A collection of several books, the greater part purporting to be the sayings of Rabbi Simeon ben Yohai (second century) and his companions but more likely written mainly by Moses de Leon (d.1305), *Sefer Ha-Zohar (The Book of Splendour)* is the most important work of Kabbalistic literature. According to the *Zohar* the Book of Enoch related that after God caused Enoch to ascend 'He showed him all supernal mysteries, and the Tree of Life in the midst of the Garden and its leaves and branches'.[58] While it has been suggested that this account derives from the Book of the Watchers (1 Enoch 32:3–6), or the Hebrew Book of Enoch (3 Enoch), more discerning commentators have observed that although the Zohar's author drew on sources ranging from the Babylonian Talmud to Joseph Gikatilla's *Ginnat Egoz (A Garden of Nuts)* (1274), he also fabricated quotations from several non-existent texts. Thus the Zohar's Enochic references may be largely unconnected with the known writings pseudonymously attributed to Enoch. Even so, with the endowment by the Medicis in the 1460s of a Platonic Academy in Florence there developed Christian circles engaged in earnest study of the Kabbalah and with it magic and texts circulating under the names of antediluvian patriarchs and Kings of Israel. Foremost among these speculators was the brilliant Giovanni Pico della Mirandola (1463–94), who spent vast sums collecting books, had Kabbalistic literature translated into Latin and consulted Hebrew manuscripts. Seventeenth-century sources citing supposedly contemporary testimony maintained that Pico had purchased a copy of the Book of Enoch.[59] This title, however, is not recorded in the catalogue of Pico's Kabbalistic manuscripts compiled by Jacques Gaffarel (1601–81). Yet Pico did possess an early fourteenth-century commentary 'according to the path of truth' on the Pentateuch by the Italian Menahem ben Benjamin Recanati. Later printed as *Perush al Ha-Torah*

---

[56] *BL*, MS Harleian 1612, fols 15r–18v; *BL*, MS Harleian 80, fols 81–4; *BL*, MS Royal 12, C. XVIII, 8; *BL*, MS Sloane 3847, no.4.

[57] H.A.R. Gibb (ed.), *'Travels of Ibn Battūta, AD 1325–54'*, *Hakluyt Society*, 2nd series, 110 trans. C. Defrémery and B.R. Sanguinetti (Cambridge, 1958), 50–51.

[58] *The Zohar*, trans. Harry Sperling and Maurice Simon, 5 vols (1931–34), I, 139 (37b); cf. *Zohar*, I, 177 (55b), I, 181 (56b), I, 189 (58b).

[59] Thomas Bang, *Cœlum Orientis* (Copenhagen, 1657), 18–19; August Pfeiffer, *Henoch* (Wittenberg, 1683), cap. 4 § 3; Gottfried Vockerodt, *Historia Societatum et rei literariæ ante diluvium* (Jena, 1687), 31.

(Venice, 1523), this contained expositions upon Enoch's translation, his prophetical books, the sons of God and the daughters of men, the fallen angels, the brevity of man's life and the giants.[60] It is therefore noteworthy that Pico observed that 'the secret theology of the Hebrews' transforms the 'holy Enoch' into an 'angel of divinity', whom they call the angel of the *Shekhinah* (the Divine Presence).[61] Indeed, in his *Apologia* (Naples, 1487), Pico condemned necromancers for the 'incantations and bestialities' they mendaciously said originated with Solomon, Adam and Enoch.[62] Like Pico, a character in Johannes Reuchlin's dialogue *De verbo mirifico* (Basel, 1494), inveighs against 'triflers in the magical art', complaining that he found only ignorance hidden behind such splendid titles as the Book of Solomon and the Book of Enoch.[63] Significantly, a character in Reuchlin's *De arte Cabalistica* (Hagenau, 1517), having spoken of books on Kabbalistic contemplation in everyday use, adduces numerous writings regarded as lost, including some cited on good authority such as the Books of Enoch.[64]

XIII

In 1513 a Psalter was issued at Rome entitled *Alphabetum seu potius syllabarium literarum Chaldaearum* (Rome, 1513). Probably based on a manuscript in the Vatican library this was the first book printed in Ethiopic. Its editors were an Ethiopian friar from Jerusalem named Thomas Walda Samuel and his pupil, the German Orientalist and correspondent of Reuchlin, Johannes Potken (1470–1524). In 1548 an Ethiopic New Testament was published in Rome, the work of another Ethiopian monk arrived via Jerusalem, Abba Täsfa Seyon (known locally as 'Pietro Indiano') and his assistants. Rome's large Ethiopian community had been granted a church, renamed Santo Stefano degli Abissini by Pope Sixtus IV in 1479, and an adjoining hospice, and it was a monk from this community who in 1546 encountered a French Orientalist recently expelled from the Society of Jesus. The Frenchman was Guillaume Postel (1510–81), who was to translate a sizeable portion of the *Zohar* and another Kabbalistic text *Sefer Yezirah (Book of Formation)* from Hebrew into Latin. In *De Etruriae regionis* (Florence, 1551), Postel declared that Enoch's prophecies made before the flood were preserved in the ecclesiastical records of the Queen of Sheba, and that to this day they were believed to be canonical scripture in Ethiopia.[65] Moreover, in another volume entitled *De Originibus* (Basel, 1553),

---

[60] Jacques Gaffarel, *Codicum Cabalisticorum manuscriptorum* (Paris, 1651), 22.

[61] Pico, *On the Dignity of Man*, trans. C.G. Wallis (Indianapolis, 1965), 5–6.

[62] Pico, *Opera Omnia*, 2 vols (Basel, 1572–73), I, 181.

[63] Johannes Reuchlin, *Sämtliche Werke* (Stuttgart, 1996), Band I, 1, 122.

[64] Johannes Reuchlin, *On the Art of the Kabbalah*, eds Martin and Sarah Goodman, (Nebraska, 1993), 90–91.

[65] Guillaume Postel, *De Etruriae regionis* (Florence, 1551), 108–9, 242–3.

Postel claimed that the Ethiopian priest had explained to him the meaning of the Book of Enoch.[66]

Postel's discovery was digested by the English Protestant exile John Bale (1495–1563), who reaffirmed that the prophet Enoch's work was held in the Queen of Sheba's ecclesiastical archives and that it remained canonical scripture in Ethiopia.[67] Postel's writings were also an important source for the mathematician and magician John Dee (1527–1608), whose copy of *De Originibus* is heavily annotated throughout.[68] Other works consulted by Dee included Johannes Pantheus' *Voarchadvmia contra alchimiam* (Venice, 1530), which displayed 26 characters purporting to be the Enochic alphabet, and Petrus Bonus's *Introdvctio in Divinam Chemiae artem* (Basel, 1572), which cited Roger Bacon's remark that some identified Enoch with 'the great Hermogenes'.[69] In May 1581 Dee gazed into a crystal ball and imagined he saw something, but a few occasions excepted, he needed the services of a scryer to communicate with spirits directly. The following March Edward Kelley (1555–95) became his scryer. Dee recorded in several volumes Kelley's supposed visions and angelic conversations, conceding that he could find no other way to attain 'true wisdome'. In 1583 these revelations took the form of a paradisical angelic language, characters represented as letters and numbers dictated to fill grids of forty-nine rows by forty-nine columns. These tables were referred to as the 'Liber mysteriorum sextus et sanctus' or the Book of Enoch. While this work has not been deciphered, its existence is testimony to Dee's conviction that Enoch had received divine mysteries through angelic intermediaries.[70]

XIV

In 1520 a Portuguese embassy under Dom Rodrigo de Lima arrived in Ethiopia, known as the land of Prester John. During their stay the embassy's chaplain Francisco Álvares composed a narrative later printed in Portuguese (Lisbon, 1540) and Italian. At Aksum they found a lengthy chronicle, which told of the Queen of Sheba's visit to Solomon and the birth of their son at Jerusalem. Though the Andalucian adventurer Leo Africanus (*c.*1494–after 1550?) omitted Ethiopia from his *Della descrittione dell'Africa* (Venice, 1550), the English version *A geographical historie of Africa* (1600) included an account of Ethiopian customs and beliefs derived from Álvares

---

[66] Guillaume Postel, *De Originibus* (Basel, 1553), title page, 10–11, 59, 72, 100.

[67] John Bale, *Scriptorvm Illustrium maioris Brytanniae posterior pars* (Basel, 1559), 3.

[68] Postel *De Originibus*, 54, 59 [*Royal College of Physicians* (London) D 144/14, 21b].

[69] Johannes Augustinus Pantheus, *Voarchadvmia contra alchimiam* (Venice, 1530), 15v–16r [*BL*, C. 120.b.4(2)]; Petrus Bonus, *Introdvctio in Divinam Chemiae artem* (Basel, 1572), 110 [*R.Coll.Phys.* D 107/3, 7c].

[70] James Halliwell (ed.), *Private Diary of John Dee*, *Camden Society*, 19 (1842), 11, 15, 89; *BL*, MS Sloane 3188, fol. 7r–v; *BL*, MS Sloane 3189; Meric Casaubon (ed.), *A True & Faithful Relation* (1659), 174, 418.

and Zagazabo, the Ethiopian ambassador who accompanied Álvares on his departure in 1526.[71] Zagazabo's confession of faith, together with letters sent by the Ethiopian Emperor to the King of Portugal and the Pope, was published by Damião de Góis (Louvain, 1540) and afterwards translated into English. Alluding to the *Kebra Nagast* it recounted how Menelik cunningly stole 'the true tables of the couenant' from the Ark.[72]

In 1613 what became the first of four ever-expanding editions of Samuel Purchas's monumental work on Ecclesiastical, Theological and Geographical History was issued at London. For his survey of Ethiopia Purchas drew principally on Álvares, a narrative ascribed to João Bermudez (Lisbon, 1565), and a relation by the Spanish 'Frier and lyer', Luis de Urreta (Valencia, 1610). According to Urreta, Pope Gregory XIII (1572–85) had despatched two priests to catalogue the matchless library of the Ethiopian Emperor housed in the monastery of the Holy Cross upon Mount Amara. This fantastical collection, supposedly begun by the Queen of Sheba, was said in Purchas's words to contain 'innumerable' books of 'inestimable' value, including texts attributed to Noah, Abraham, Solomon, Job and Esdras, as well as the Gospels of Bartholomew, Thomas and Andrew. In addition, it held:

> the writings of *Enoch* copied out of the stones wherein they were engrauen, which intreate of Philosophie, of the Heauens and Elements.[73]

Urreta's report reappeared in the Jesuit Nicolao Godigno's *De Abassinorum rebus* (Leiden, 1615).[74] It was also used by George Sandys in *A Relation of a Journey* (1615), Sandys cautiously repeating Urreta's claim that with other 'mysteries that escaped the Flood' the Ethiopians possessed written in their 'vulgar' tongue the 'oracles of *Enoch*' engraved by him upon pillars.[75] A similar paraphrase is found in Peter Heylyn's *Microcosmus* (Oxford, 1625), who seems to have relied upon Purchas and Sandys.[76]

XV

The French Humanist Nicolas Claude Fabri de Peiresc (1580–1637) owned an edition of Purchas. Though he could not read English himself Peiresc thought the voyages rather good and initially considered having the volumes translated into Latin. In July 1633 one of Peiresc's contacts, the Capuchin Gilles de Loches, visited him at Aix-

[71] Leo Africanus, *A geographical historie of Africa*, trans. John Pory (1600), 395–405.

[72] Joannes Boemus, *The manners, lawes, and customes of all nations*, trans. E. Aston (1611), 558.

[73] Luis de Urreta, *Historia Ecclesiástica, Política, Natural, y moral des los grandes y remotos Reynos de la Etiopia* (Valencia, 1610), 103–7; Samuel Purchas, *Purchas his Pilgrimage* (1613), 567.

[74] Nicolao Godigno, *De Abassinorum rebus* (Leiden, 1615), 108.

[75] George Sandys, *A Relation of a Journey begun in An. Dom. 1610.* (1615), 171.

[76] Peter Heylyn, *Microcosmus* (Oxford, 1625), 735–36.

en-Provence. Loches had returned from a seven-year stay in the Levant where he had studied Oriental languages and attempted to procure Coptic, Ethiopic, Armenian, Arabic and Turkish manuscripts for Peiresc. In October Loches supplied Peiresc with a list of rare books he had seen in divers convents and monasteries including, it seems, '*Mazhapha Einock*, or the Prophecie of *Enoch*, foretelling such things as should happen at the end of the World'. Peiresc responded by asking him to translate a passage to confirm if it was genuine or forged.[77] Loches, however, did not have it. Nonetheless, Peiresc informed his correspondents that a version of the Book of Enoch had been discovered in one of the Oriental languages and that it was written in the form of prophecies just before Enoch's ascent to heaven.[78] Hoping to locate it in the Vatican, Peiresc was promised a catalogue of the library's Coptic collection by Cardinal Barberini.[79] In July 1634 another Capuchin, Agathange de Vendôme, replied to Peiresc from Cairo about the Ethiopic books he had requested. Vendôme had found a volume of prophecies and occult things that spoke of Enoch and angels. Yet more than two years passed before gifts to the Capuchins ensured that it was removed from the Levant and shipped to Marseilles.[80]

On 25 October/4 November 1636 the small Ethiopic book written on thick parchment was finally in Peiresc's hands at Aix-en-Provence. Referring to it as the 'Revelations of Enoch' he supposed it the same volume that Postel had seen and expected the text to be, if not a faithful version, at least consistent with things mentioned by Jude, Origen and others. That same day Peiresc wrote to Loches, now guardian of the Capuchin convent at Bourges, reminding him of his undertaking to translate it.[81] While awaiting a response Peiresc spread word of the manuscript in his possession. Declining the help of learned men like Claude Saumaise (1588–1653) he kept faith with Loches, who had apparently recently completed his study of Ethiopic grammar.[82] But Loches procrastinated, pleading that he was overburdened and unable to work on a full translation before Easter. Undeterred, Peiresc settled for a sample, sending him a facsimile of the first page. Again Loches delayed, claiming that the Ethiopic script had been copied inaccurately.[83] Peiresc died on 14/24 June

---

[77] Apollinaire de Valence (ed.), *Correspondance de Peiresc avec plusieurs missionaires et religieux de l'ordre des Capucins, 1631–37* (Paris, 1891), 12–13; Pierre Gassendi, *Viri Illustris Nicolai Claudi Fabricii de Peiresc* (Paris, 1641), Book V, 269; Pierre Gassendi, *The Mirrour of true Nobility & Gentility*, trans. W. Rand (1657) Book V, 89–90.

[78] Jacques Philippe Tamizey de Larroque (ed.), *Lettres de Peiresc aux freres Dupuy* (7 vols, Paris, 1888–98), IV, 396; Agnès Bresson (ed.), *Nicolas-Claude Fabri de Peiresc. Lettres à Claude Saumaise et à son entourage, 1620–37* (Florence, 1992), 348, n.2.

[79] de Valence (ed.), *Correspondance*, 22.

[80] de Valence (ed.), *Correspondance*, 69; Gassendi, *Mirrour,* V, 90, 123.

[81] Bresson (ed.), *Peiresc*, 348, n.2; de Larroque (ed.), *Lettres*, III, 600; de Valence (ed.), *Correspondance*, 276–7.

[82] de Larroque (ed.), *Lettres*, III, 609; Bresson (ed.), *Peiresc*, 351 n. 17; Bresson (ed.), *Peiresc*, 348–49.

[83] Bresson (ed.), *Peiresc*, 360; de Larroque (ed.), *Lettres*, III, 618; de Valence (ed.), *Correspondance*, 279, 303, 308, 310.

1637. The book he had acquired after much trouble and at great expense remained untranslated.[84]

Peiresc's scholarship was commemorated by his friend the astronomer Pierre Gassendi (1592–1655) in *Viri Illustris Nicolai Claudii Fabricii de Peiresc Senatoris Aquisextiensis Vita* (Paris, 1641). Peiresc's library was bequeathed to his brother Palamède and on his demise to Palamède's son, Claude, who in 1647 sold the collection at Paris. Together with the bulk of the manuscripts the so-called '*Mazhapha Einock*' was purchased for Cardinal Jules Mazarin. In 1655 a third edition of Gassendi's biography was issued at The Hague with an appendix by the French physician and chemist Pierre Borel (1620?–71). From Paris Borel communicated the fate of Peiresc's collection to a Prussian émigré resident in London, Samuel Hartlib (*c.*1660–62). In March 1656 Hartlib wrote to John Worthington, Master of Jesus College, Cambridge with news that 'Liber Enoch est in Bibliothecâ Mazarinâ'.[85] On 16/26 July 1659 another of Hartlib's correspondents, the German émigré Henry Oldenburg (*c.*1618–77), reported from Paris his conversation with the mathematician and Orientalist Claude Hardy (*c.*1598–1678). Acting on Hardy's directions Oldenburg had found the 'Revelationes Enochi' in Mazarin's library. He described it as having '83. leaves in a good faire caracter, bound in wood, cased in calfs leather, in smal 4to'. Oldenburg had also heard a story that Peiresc got the book from Loches for having 'freed him from ye Turkish Gallyes'. Furthermore, it was said that Loches had translated the prophecy before his death at the convent.[86] Hartlib was doubtless intrigued for on 6 August 1659 the natural philosopher John Beale (*c.*1603–*c.*1682) sent him tidings from Hereford of the prophecies of Seth and Enoch. In Beale's opinion Enoch's prophecies had long ago been controverted; Origen, Jerome, Athanasius and others regarded them as 'no better than Apocryphall fables', Tertullian spoke highly of them, while Augustine was quite fair, but excluded them from 'the chastity of the Canon'.[87] Beale, moreover, was in touch with Hartlib's acquaintance John Evelyn (1620–1706), to whom the English version of Gassendi's memoir of Peiresc was dedicated. In his treatise on engraving in copper Evelyn discussed the relics of antediluvian patriarchs mentioned by Josephus and the twelfth century Byzantine chronographer George Cedrenus. Evelyn observed that:

> The *Æthiopians* are said at this day to glory much in possessing the Books of *Seth* and *Enoch*, as those who have lately written of the *Abyssines* relate. *Origen*, St. *Augustine*, and *Hierom* have likewise made honourable mention of them; and *Tertullian* plainly reproves those who (in his time) thought they could not be preserved.[88]

---

[84] de Larroque (ed.), *Lettres de Peiresc*, VI, 660.

[85] James Crossley (ed.), *Diary and Correspondence of John Worthington, Chetham Society*, 13 (1847), I, 59, 82–3.

[86] A.R. Hall and M.B. Hall (eds), *The Correspondence of Henry Oldenburg,* 13 vols (Madison, Wisc., and London & Philadelphia, 1965–86), I, 282.

[87] *SUL*, HP 65/7/1A–B, 2A.

[88] John Evelyn, *Sculptura* (1662), 13.

Like Evelyn, Sir Thomas Browne (1605–82) of Norwich mused upon '*Enochs* Pillars', considering them somewhat fabulous, though his reference to Josephus was a misattribution.[89] Browne also composed a catalogue of rarities entitled 'Musæum Clausum' or 'Bibliotheca Abscondita'. Among the remarkable books in this collection was one obtained by Peiresc – '*Mazhapha Einok*, or, the Prophecy of *Enoch*'.[90]

XVI

In his misconceived discourse on oriental tongues the German Christianus Ravius (1613–77) remarked that printed books in Ethiopic were so scarce that he believed there were none 'in all *England*'.[91] Ravius's work was dedicated to James Ussher (1581–1656), Archbishop of Armagh, who had attempted to procure an Ethiopic New Testament through an English merchant at Aleppo. Ussher was also one of the eminent scholars who supported the publication of *Biblia Sacra Polyglotta* (1653–57). Its principal editor was Brian Walton (1600–61), who had formerly supported Archbishop Laud's policies and taken refuge with the royalist garrison at Oxford. Walton credited Edmund Castell (1606–85) with correcting the Ethiopic text of the Polyglot Bible and rendering the Ethiopic version of the Song of Solomon into Latin. Castell afterwards greeted the restoration of Charles II with *Sol Angliæ Oriens* (1660), a set of laudatory verses in all seven languages employed in the Polyglot. Appended was an entreaty for aiding Castell's great enterprise, a lexicon to accompany the Polyglot. Castell was assisted with the Ethiopic part of the *Lexicon Heptaglotton* (1669) by the German Johann Michael Wansleben (1635–79). While in London, Wansleben had overseen the printing in 1661 of an Ethiopic grammar and lexicon by Hiob Ludolf (1624–1704). A counsellor of Duke Ernst of Saxe-Gotha and correspondent of Oldenburg, Ludolf later bemoaned Wansleben's inept supervision, characterizing him as a man of 'little Judgment, less Faith, and no Honesty'. Perhaps this was because Wansleben converted to Catholicism and became a Dominican.[92] Even so, in 1670 Wansleben made a complete copy of the so-called '*Mazhapha Einock*' and probably about the same time transcribed the preface, middle and end of the text for Ludolf. On examining these extracts, however, Ludolf declared that Peiresc had been deceived, for 'the knavery of those he employ'd' had foisted upon him 'another Book with a false Title'. Ludolf found nothing of either Enoch or his prophecies but only some 'very clear discourses of the Mysteries of Heaven and Earth, and the Holy Trinity' by Abba Bakhayla Mîkâ'êl-Zosimus.[93]

In late 1683 or early 1684 Ludolf examined the famous 'Revelationes Enochi', which had since been transferred from Mazarin's library to the Bibliothèque Royale,

[89] L.C.Martin (ed.), *Sir Thomas Browne. Religio Medici and other works* (Oxford, 1967), 24–5.

[90] Sir Thomas Browne, *Certain Miscellany Tracts* (1684), 200.

[91] Christianus Ravius, *A discovrse of the orientall tongves* (1649), 23, 133–4.

[92] Hiob Ludolf, *A New History of Ethiopia* (1684 edn), sig. F^{v-2}.

[93] Ludolf, *New History of Ethiopia*, 269.

Paris. Finding that the last of the volume's four tracts consisted of a discourse concerning the birth of Enoch, Ludolf concluded that this was the probable source for the manuscript's misleading title. He wrote a contemptuous note at the head of the original document, later printed in essence, charging its author with plundering refuse from old fragments. Ludolf was certain of this because he had compared the Ethiopic text with extracts from a Greek version of the Book of the Watchers copied by a Byzantine chronographer.[94]

XVII

In the early ninth century George (fl. 810), the Syncellus or adviser to the Patriarch of Constantinople Tarasius (784–806), wrote a universal history. Syncellus envisaged his *Chronography* stretching from the Creation to his own time, though he reached only the beginning of the Roman Emperor Diocletian's reign (285 AD) before his death. For the antediluvian section Syncellus drew on the work of two early fifth century Alexandrian monks, Panodorus and Annianus. Though it has been suggested that much of this part of the chronicle is a clumsy polemic against these very authorities, Syncellus's reworking of their material and his extensive excerpts from their sources has resulted in the preservation of material earlier than Panodorus and Annianus. Thus Syncellus quoted apparently by way of Panodorus and Annianus from several lost texts such as Julius Africanus's *Chronography*, the original Greek version of Eusebius of Caesarea's *Chronicle* and Zosimus of Panopolis's *Book of Imouth*. Through these and other intermediary sources Syncellus also preserved earlier works still, like an epitome of Manetho's list of Egyptian dynasties derived from recensions of Africanus and Eusebius, and an abridgement of Berossus' *Babyloniaca* extracted from recensions of the Greek antiquaries Alexander Polyhistor and Abydenus. Moreover, it was through his Alexandrian authorities that Syncellus cited or paraphrased revised Greek versions of Jewish pseudepigrapha – the Testament of Adam, the Book of Jubilees and the Book of Enoch.

Though he considered the Book of Enoch 'apocryphal, questionable in places' and 'contaminated by Jews and heretics', Syncellus preferred it to the 'lies' of Berossus and Manetho, if only because it was 'more akin to our Scriptures'. Syncellus gave excerpts from 'the first book of Enoch concerning the Watchers' (1 Enoch 6:1–9:4, 8:4–10:14, 15:8–16:1), as well as abbreviated summaries from the Book of the Watchers (1 Enoch 10:4–12) and the Astronomical Book (1 Enoch 72–82). In addition, he quoted a passage about the burning of Mount Hermon on 'the day of the great judgment' and the limiting of man's age to 120 years unknown in the extant

[94] Hiob Ludolf, *Iobi Ludolfi ... ad suam Historiam Aethiopicam* (Frankfurt upon Main, 1691), 347–8; Ernest W. Budge (ed.), *The Book of the Mysteries of the Heavens and Earth* (Oxford, 1935), 141–4.

Enochic corpus. It seems that these extracts were carefully selected by Panodorus and emended either by Syncellus or his Alexandrian predecessor(s).[95]

Syncellus's chronicle was the most important witness to the Greek version of the Book of Enoch until the late nineteenth century when a fifth- or sixth-century mutilated manuscript was discovered in a Christian grave at Akhmîm (Codex Panopolitanus) containing two corrupt copies of the Book of the Watchers. Another witness is a fourth-century papyrus codex that came to light in the first half of the twentieth century having the subscription 'The Epistle of Enoch' (in its present condition it contains an almost continuous Greek text of 1 Enoch 97:6–107:3). There is also an extract from the Book of Dreams (1 Enoch 89:42–9) in Greek found in a late tenth- or eleventh-century tachygraphical manuscript in the Vatican library and deciphered in 1855. Furthermore, a sixth- or seventh-century manuscript containing a Coptic fragment of the Apocalypse of Weeks (1 Enoch 93:3–8) was discovered in the northern cemetery of Antinoë in 1937. Then there are allusions. Thus a stichometry of canonical and apocryphal books (sixth century?) appended to a *Chronography* under the name of the Patriarch of Constantinople Nicephorus (806–15) gave the length of 'Enoch' as 4800 stichoi or lines. Moreover, the twelfth century Byzantine chronographer George Cedrenus, who slavishly followed Syncellus for much of antediluvian history, appears to have provided a laconic paraphrase of Syncellus's first excerpt from the Book of the Watchers. In addition, Michael the Syrian, Jacobite Patriarch of Antioch (1166–99) quoted in his *Chronicle* from the Book of the Watchers (1 Enoch 6:1–7). This Syriac citation relates that 200 of the sons of God under the leadership of Semiazos abandoned their angelic way of life to join their brethren, the sons of Seth and Enos. They took wives from the daughters of Cain who afterwards gave birth to 'great giants, that is plunderers, mighty and renowned assassins, and audacious bandits'. It has been argued that Michael's account by way of a Syrian chronicler, possibly Jacob of Edessa (*c*.640–708) or his younger contemporary John of Litarba, drew on Annianus's *Chronography* – the same source used by Syncellus.[96] Similarly, the Syrian chronographer Bar Hebraeus preserved a legend mediated to him from Annianus through Michael's *Chronicle*. In this version the Watchers are the sons of Seth and are called 'Sons of God' because of the chaste and holy life they led on Mount Hermon. Their leader was a man named Samyâzôs, the first king, while their offspring were 'mighty men of names' notorious for 'murders and robberies'.[97]

---

[95] William Adler, *Time Immemorial* (Washington, DC, 1989), 83, 86, 88, 151–4, 176, 179.

[96] S.P. Brock, 'A Fragment of Enoch in Syriac', *Journal of Theological Studies*, n.s. 19 (1968), 626–31.

[97] Budge (ed.), *Chronography of Gregory Abû'l Faraj*, I, 3–4.

XVIII

In 1583 the French-born Protestant convert Joseph Juste Scaliger (1540–1609) published a major work on chronology entitled *Opus novum de emendatione temporum* (Paris, 1583), which he regarded as a test for the minds of his age. But it was while collecting material for an edition of Jerome's Latin version of the second book of Eusebius's *Chronicle* that Scaliger, alerted by a reference in Cedrenus, encountered the *Chronography* of George the Syncellus. In 1601 an eleventh-century manuscript of Syncellus's chronicle was located in the library of Catherine de Medici. Extracts were made by Scaliger's friend, the Protestant scholar Isaac Casaubon (1559–1614), and by mid-June 1602 the codex sent from Paris to Leiden, where Scaliger examined it carefully. Scaliger found the text of Syncellus incoherent and mutilated, dismissing its author as silly and verbose. Yet he could not ignore the monk's 'treasury', concluding that Eusebius's *Chronicle* would have to be reconstructed.[98] This awesome if flawed endeavour duly appeared in *Thesaurus temporum* (Leiden, 1606), together with extensive notes that included some of Syncellus's excerpts from the Book of Enoch – and Scaliger's disdainful comments:

> So much for the forged first book of Enoch. I cannot decide whether it took the Jews more spare time to write all of this, or me more patience to copy it out. It contains so many loathsome and shameful things that I would not think it worth reading if I did not know that Jews make a habit of lying, and that even now they cannot stop producing such rubbish. But because it is translated from the Hebrew ... and the book is very old, and Tertullian cites from it ... I preferred to swallow the tedium of copying it out rather than bear the blame for continuing to deprive my kind readers of it.[99]

Scaliger's publication was used by Samuel Purchas in a chapter on 'the cause, and comming of the Flood'. Purchas introduced his theme with a discussion of '*Henoch the seuenth from Adam who walked with God whom God tooke away that he should not see death*'. Like Tertullian and Calvin, Purchas believed that Enoch and Elijah were 'witnesses of the resurrection', though he rejected the notion that they would come and 'preach against Antichrist' and be slain by him as a 'Popish' dream.[100] Adhering to accepted Protestant exegesis Purchas also supposed that either Jude received Enoch's 'testimony' by oral tradition or that the prophecy, perhaps forged by a Jew, was written and subsequently lost. Indeed, he thought it apparent that 'the booke bearing *Enochs* name' was 'very fabulous'. Nonetheless, Purchas considered it appropriate to translate most of Scaliger's Greek text, printing an abbreviated English version that conflated Syncellus's three longer citations from the Book of the Watchers into a single extract:

---

[98] Anthony Grafton, *Joseph Scaliger*, 2 vols (Oxford, 1983–94), II, 536–48.

[99] Joseph Scaliger, *Thesaurus temporum*, 5 parts (Leiden, 1606), Notæ 244–5; Grafton, *Joseph Scaliger*, II, 685–6.

[100] Purchas, *Purchas his Pilgrimage*, 30.

> And it came to passe when the sonnes of men were multiplied, there were borne to them faire daughters, and the Watch-men ... lusted and went astray after them: and they said One to another, *Let vs chuse vs wiues of the daughters of men of the earth*. And *Semixas* their Prince said vnto them, *I feare me you will not do this thing, and I alone shall be debter of a great sinne*. And they all answered him and said: *We will sweare with an oath, and will Anathematise or Curse our selues not to alter this our mind till we haue fulfilled it*: and they all sware together. These came downe in the dayes of *Iared* to the top of the hill, *Hermon*. And they called the hill, *Hermon*, because they sware and Anathematised on it. These were the names of their Rulers, *Semixas*, *Atarcuph*, *Arachiel*, *Chababiel*, *Orammame*, *Ramiel*, *Sapsich*, *Zakiel*, *Balkiel*, *Azalzel*, *Pharmaros*, *Samiel* & c.
>
> *These tooke them wiues, and three generations were borne vnto them: the first were great Giants; the Giants begate the Naphelim, to whom were borne Eliud; and they taught them and their wiues sorceries and inchantments. Ezael taught first to make swords and weapons for warre, and how to worke in mettals. He taught to make womens ornaments, and how to looke faire, and Iewelling. And they beguiled the Saints: and much sinne was committed on the earth. Other of them taught the vertues of Roots, Astrologie, Diuinations, & c. After these things the Giants began to eate the flesh of men, and men were diminished: and the remnant cried to heauen, because of their wickednesse, that they might come in remembrance before him ...* .[101]

Syncellus had been brought to the scholarly world's attention. The fragments from the Book of Enoch published by Scaliger were discussed in *De patriarcha Henoch* (Franeker, 1615) by Johannes Drusius (1550–1616), professor of Hebrew at Franeker University in Friesland. From Armagh Ussher wrote to John Selden pointing out a discrepancy between the Samaritan chronology and the 'corrupt' copy of Syncellus concerning Enoch's age at the birth of Methuselah (Genesis 5:21).[102] In the Vatican library another manuscript of Syncellus's chronicle was found and a transcript procured by Peiresc to assist the work of Johannes Baptista Altinus. Peiresc also had the Vatican manuscript copied, compared with the codex in the Bibliothèque Royale and then corrected by Saumaise to help Jean-Jacques Bouchard (1606?–41) with his translation of Syncellus.[103] Naturally Peiresc's interest in Syncellus became entwined with his obsession with the Book of Enoch. On 25 February/7 March 1637 the German-born Catholic convert and librarian to Cardinal Barberini, Lucas Holstenius (1596–1661) wrote to his patron from Rome. Holstenius informed Peiresc that he once heard the renowned Dutch jurist Hugo Grotius (1583–1645) say that he had done some work on the Greek version of the Book of Enoch. Peiresc told Saumaise he was willing to pay handsomely for a transcript of the Greek text and on 7/17 April he wrote to Grotius, at that time the resident Swedish ambassador in Paris,

---

[101] Purchas, *Purchas his Pilgrimage*, 31.

[102] Richard Parr, *The Life Of the Most Reverend Father in God, James Usher* (1686), 383.

[103] Gassendi, *Mirrour*, III, 208, V, 136; de Larroque (ed.), *Lettres*, I, 49, 55–6, 73 94, 108, 119; V, 287; Jean François Boissonade (ed.), *L. Holstenii Epistolæ ad diversos* (Paris, 1817), 99, 104, 110, 168.

imploring him to share his research.[104] Peiresc, however, first received a response to an earlier communication concerning his untranslated Ethiopic volume: Grotius referred him to Scaliger's *Thesaurus temporum*.[105] On 10/20 April Peiresc wrote to Grotius again, asking for his opinion on Syncellus's excerpts from the Book of Enoch and information as to the whereabouts of the manuscript used by Scaliger.[106] In May 1637, less than a month before his death, deluded, Peiresc despatched a last letter to Loches suggesting that he compare the Syncellus excerpts published by Scaliger with the facsimile of the first page of the so-called '*Mazhapha Einock*'.[107]

About 1637 the German Jesuit Athanasius Kircher (1601–80), whose study of hieroglyphic writing had been encouraged by Peiresc, made a discovery in the monastic library of San Salvatore in Messina, Sicily. According to his account in *Œdipus Ægyptiacus* (Rome, 1652–54), Kircher had found a Greek fragment of the Book of Enoch - doubtless derived from or preserved in a copy of Syncellus's chronicle.[108] Kircher printed the text together with a Latin translation and detailed notes, citing Augustine, Tertullian, Origen, Clement of Alexandria, Zosimus of Panopolis and Syncellus, as well as authors in Arabic who had reported the syncretic tradition identifying Enoch with Hermes and Idris.[109] While Kircher was engaged in his labours the Dominican Jacques Goar (1601–53) was busy editing Byzantine texts, issuing editions of Cedrenus (Paris, 1647) and Syncellus (Paris, 1652). Based on the codex in the Bibliothèque Royale and accompanied with a Latin translation, Goar's preface rebutted Scaliger's charge that Syncellus's *Chronography* was derived solely from Eusebius, arguing that the monk had relied on diverse sources.

Though Syncellus's excerpts from the Book of Enoch were translated from Greek into English by Purchas, and from Greek into Latin by Kircher and Goar, the text's provenance and authority continued to be debated by mainly learned men. On the continent Thomas Bang's *Cœlum Orientis et prisci mundi triade* (Copenhagen, 1657) provided the most exhaustive discussion yet. Bang referred to every pertinent patristic source available in Greek and Latin, cited Jewish writings such as the *Pirkê de Rabbi Eliezer* and the *Zohar*, alluded to Jewish authors like Rashi and Recanati, and mentioned relevant work by Pantheus, Postel, Scaliger and Kircher. Afterwards, the subject was treated by among others; Balthasar Bebelius in *Ecclesiæ antediluvianæ vera et falsa* (Strasbourg, 1665), Joachim Johannes Mader in *De Bibliothecis atque Archivis virorum clarissimorum* (Helmstadt, 1666), the Swiss theologian Johann Heinrich Heidegger in *De historia sacra Patriarcharum exercitationes selectae*

[104] Boissonade (ed.), *Holstenii Epistolæ*, 286–7; de Larroque (ed.), *Lettres*, V, 468; Bresson (ed.), *Peiresc*, 373; B.L. Meulenbroek (ed.), *Briefwisseling van Hugo Grotius. 1637* (The Hague, 1971), VIII, 225–6.

[105] B.L. Meulenbroek (ed.), *Briefwisseling van Hugo Grotius. 1 March–31 December 1636* (The Hague, 1969), VII, 561; Meulenbroek (ed.), *Briefwisseling van Hugo Grotius*, VIII, 200-201.

[106] Meulenbroek (ed.), *Briefwisseling van Hugo Grotius,* VIII, 233–4, 313.

[107] de Valence (ed.), *Correspondance*, 319–20.

[108] Athanasius Kircher, *Œdipus Ægyptiacus*, 4 vols (Rome, 1652–54), II 68.

[109] Kircher, *Œdipus Ægyptiacus*, I, 66–,7; II 68–78.

(Amsterdam, 1667–71), August Pfeiffer in *Henoch, descriptus exercitatione philologica ad Gen. 5 v.22.23.24.* (Wittenberg, 1683), and Gottfried Vockerodt in *Historia Societatum et rei literariæ ante diluvium* (Jena, 1687).

In England Protestant antipathy to doctrines based upon unwritten traditions continued to inform the majority of responses to Enoch's prophecy. Thus John Donne (1572–1631) scorned a Catholic theologian for suggesting that the Book of Enoch was '*Canonicall Scripture* in the time of the Jews'.[110] Similarly, in *A Practical Commentary, or an exposition with notes On the Epistle of Jude* (1657) Thomas Manton maintained that whether the prophecy was written or unwritten the same 'spirit' that spoke in Enoch inspired the Apostle. That Jude had quoted '*Enochs Prophesie*' rather than authentic Scripture was 'done by the providence of God' to preserve this ancient 'memorial to the Church'. Yet Manton also noted that the Jews have 'some Relicks of this Prophesie in their Writings' and that some spoke of a volume extant in 'primitive times' consisting of 4,082 lines called 'the *Prophesie of Enoch*'. Though that work was condemned as apocryphal it was possible for good books to be lost – but not Scripture.[111] John Edwards (1637–1716) advocated the same doctrine in a discourse on the authority and style of the Bible: it was impossible to prove that any book belonging to the canon was missing. As Jude's Epistle did not mention any '*Book* or *Writing* of *Enoch*' none could infer that such a work was lost.[112] There were, however, some dissenting voices.

The self-proclaimed '*High-Priest*' and 'Recorder to the thirteen Tribes of the Jewes' TheaurauJohn Tany (1608–59) asked:

> *Enock* the seventh from *Adam*, what wrote he? for he was higher then any; where is the hieroglyphicks he wrote in? where is that? there was such a man your riddle saith, and that man wrote more, then all the Old and New-Testaments, and we have none of them, where are they?[113]

Tany paraphrased Genesis 6:2 as 'The Sons of God came in to the daughters of men, and saw them beautiful', understanding the verse as a reference to the 'fallen' angels. He seems, moreover, to have been familiar with vestiges of the myth of the Watchers preserved in the Testaments of the Twelve Patriarchs.[114] Modelled on the 'Testament of Jacob' (Genesis 49), incorporating Jewish material - though arguably of late second-century Christian origin, alluded to by Origen and Jerome, extant in Greek, Armenian and Slavonic, this extra-canonical text was translated from a late tenth-century Greek manuscript into Latin by Robert Grosseteste (*c*.1170–1253), bishop of Lincoln, in 1242. Grosseteste's version was rendered into English in a translation attributed to Anthony Gilby (*c*.1510–85) that was frequently reprinted – 16 editions were issued between 1574 and 1647. Before the flood, according to the

---

[110] John Donne, *Fifty sermons. The second volume* (1649), 347.

[111] Thomas Manton, *A Practical Commentary* (1657), 432–33.

[112] John Edwards, *A discourse concerning the authority, stile, and perfection of the books of the Old and New-Testament* (1693), 348, 466–7.

[113] TheaurauJohn Tany, *Theous Ori Apokolipikal* (1651), 54; cf. Jude 14.

[114] Tany, *Theous Ori Apokolipikal*, 32.

'Testament of Reuben', the Watchers were deceived by women who wore make-up and jewellery and braided their hair:

> as soon as they saw them, they fell in love with one another, and conceived a working in their minds, and turned themselves into the shape of men, and appeared to them in their companying with their husband: and the woman by conceiving the desire of them in the imagination of their minde, brought forth Giants. For the Watches appeared to them of height unto heaven.[115]

Tany's interpretation of Genesis 6:2 appears to have combined this reworked Enochic tradition with a reading resembling Philo's figurative explanation enunciated in 'On the Giants'. For Tany believed that the fallen angels signified the soul, a substance derived from the 'essence of God', while the daughters of men denoted the 'spiritual body in Man' – an invisible, celestial flesh of a divine nature. His paraphrase thus represented the process whereby the soul became 'essenced' in the spiritual body.[116]

Like Tany, several Quakers showed an interest in pseudepigrapha. On 11 March 1658 Thomas Lawson wrote from Bordley Hall, Yorkshire to Margaret Fell at Swarthmore Hall, Lancashire:

> Thomas Killam was telling mee, his wife, hath gott one of the books I mentioned to thee, called the testament of the patriarchs, hee saith, it speaks very much of Enocks prophecy, which hints much ag[t] the lying priests, it rose in mee, to speak to thee, that if any freind were moved to go to Holland, and had any conference with the Jews, that they made enquiry of them, if Enocks writeings bee extant among them.[117]

While Quakers seldom cited from the Apocrypha – Jewish texts omitted from the Hebrew Bible but found in certain copies of the Septuagint and together with 2 Esdras included in the Vulgate, a few were concerned with the fate of 'those Scriptures mentioned, but not inserted in the Bible'. About 1659 a catalogue of these writings appeared in *Something concerning Agbarus, Prince of the Edesseans* (no date). Reminiscent of extra-canonical compositions identified by Priscillian, Reuchlin and others, this list included 'the Prophecy of *Enoch*, mentioned *Jude* 14' and 'the Books of *Henoch*, mentioned in the Epistle of *Thadeus Origen* and *Tertullian*'.[118] Occurring verbatim in Edward Billing's *A word of reproof and advice* (1659) and afterwards placed in some Bibles owned by Quakers, it may have been compiled by the controversialist Samuel Fisher (1604–65).[119] In *Rusticus ad Academicos* (1660) Fisher defended the Quakers from the calumny that they censured the Scriptures. Examining the bounds of the canon he enumerated '*inspired*' writings cited in

115 *The Testaments of the Twelve Patriarchs*, trans. A[nthony] G[ilby?] (1647), no sig. [Reuben 5:5–7]; cf. 1 Corinthians 11:10; 1 Timothy 2:9; 1 Peter 3:3–5.

116 Tany, *Theous Ori Apokolipikal*, 3, 32, 37, 62.

117 *FHL*, MS Swarthmore, I, 243.

118 [Anon.] *Something concerning Agbarus* (no date = 1659), 1, 8.

119 Edward Billing, *A Word of Reproof* (1659), 44; Thomas Comber, *Christianity No Enthusiasm* (1678), 58.

Scripture but missing from the Bible, observing that in addition 'the Testament of the *Twelve Patriarchs*' was extant. Furthermore, he demanded:

> Where's the *Prophecy of Enoch*, spoken of *Jude* 14. out of whose Prophesie the *Jewes* can tell you more then ye wot of from that of *Jude*?[120]

In *The Answer to William Penn Quaker* (1673), the heresiarch Lodowick Muggleton (1609–98) declared that God revealed his secrets to Enoch, showing him that 'God was in a glorious form like man from Eternity'. God gave Enoch the 'spirit of prophecy'. Indeed, the 'wonderful things' recorded in the 'books of *Enoch*' were read by Noah, Abraham and 'the twelve sons of *Jacob*'. This was evident from 'the testimony of the twelve sons of *Jacob*' and the Scriptures. Apparently taking a hint from 'the Testimony of the twelve Patriarchs at their deaths', Muggleton also asserted something analogous to the ancient heresy that Melchizedek (Genesis 14:18) was God the Father:

> This *Melchizedek* King of *Salem*, that brought forth Bread and Wine to *Abraham*, it was God himself, that did appear unto *Abraham* in the form of a man and blessed him.[121]

Though Muggleton nowhere states that the Books of Enoch or the Testaments of the Twelve Patriarchs are canonical, he regarded the former as inspired. In a letter to Elizabeth Flaggerter of Cork dated London, 22 June 1682 he claimed:

> The first man God chose, after the fall of Adam, was Enoch; and God did furnish him with the revelation to write books ... He left this revelation to Noah, and Noah left it to Shem, and Shem left it to his sons, until it came to Abraham, Isaac, and Jacob. So that Enoch's revelation and declaration to the fathers of old, and all that did believe the books of Enoch, they were as a parliament, to enact it as a statute-law to their children, from generation to generation, for ever.[122]

Similarly, Thomas Tomkinson wrote from London to Muggletonians in Ireland, referring to 'the 12 Patriarchs mention'd in Genesis & in there Testament to their Children'. In his commentary on the Epistle of Jude Tomkinson maintained that though 'wee have not Enocks prophesies on Recorde yet it is certaine there where such prophesies'. Whether they were written in 'bokes of parchment' or transmitted by oral tradition 'from father to son' was uncertain, but it was evident that 'Enocks prophesies where spoken of by the 12 patriarkes and sons of Jacob in there blesing to there children' – 'most espeshely in their gods becoming flesh'.[123] Long after Muggleton's death his followers issued their own edition of *The Testament of the*

---

[120] Samuel Fisher, *Rusticus ad Academicos* (1660), part ii, 81–2.

[121] Lodowick Muggleton, *Answer to William Penn* (1673), 29, 32.

[122] John Reeve and Lodowick Muggleton, *Volume of Spiritual Epistles* (ed. Tobiah Terry, 1820), 516.

[123] *BL*, Add. MS 60,180 fol.15r; *BL*, Add. MS 60,198, 32.

Twelve Patriarchs (1837) from a copy printed at London in 1693 for the Stationers' Company.

XIX

In 1659 Isaac Casuabon's son Florence Étienne Méric Casaubon (1599–1671) published a transcript of Dee's 'Liber sexti mysteriorum, & sancti parallelus, novalisque' (1583) as *A True & Faithful Relation of What passed for many Yeers Between Dr. John Dee ... and Some Spirits* (1659). In his preface Casaubon dwelled on the 'BOOK OF ENOCH' because 'so much of it' was 'in this Relation'. Confessing he did not know how much was extant besides 'what we have in *Scaliger*', Casaubon deemed it 'a very superstitious, foolish, fabulous writing' – in one word, 'Cabalistical'. Even so, Casaubon's edition publicized the purported heading of Enoch's books, rendered into English as:

> But behold, the people waxed wicked, and became unrighteous, and the spirit of the Lord was far off, and gone away from them. So that those that were unworthy began to read.[124]

In 1663 there appeared a condensed account of the 'Sons of God', narrating the Sethites holy life, their descent from Mount Hermon, desire for women, marriage with the daughters of Cain – who first played musical instruments and sang to them, and birth of the giants. This was Bar Hebraeus's Arabic version of his chronography entitled *Ta'rikh al-Mukhtasar al-Duwal* (late thirteenth century), translated into Latin by Edward Pococke as *Historia Compendiosa Dynastiarvm* (Oxford, 1663).[125]

XX

In John Milton's *Paradise Lost* (1667) Adam beholds a vision of the future. On a 'spacious' plain he sees 'Tents of various hue' and nearby some cattle grazing. The sound of harp and organ are heard. From the 'high neighbouring Hills' descend men that by their 'guise' seem just:

> they on the Plain
> Long had not walkt, when from the Tents behold
> A Beavie of fair Women, richly gay
> In Gems and wanton dress; to the Harp they sung
> Soft amorous Ditties, and in dance came on.

[124] Casaubon (ed.), *True & Faithful Relation* (1659), sig. E2^{r-3}, 174.

[125] Gregory Abû'l Faraj, *Historia Compendiosa Dynastiarvm* (ed. Edward Pococke, Oxford, 1663), 5, 6.

Caught in an 'amorous Net' each man chooses a woman to his liking. They treat of love till the 'Evening Star', when the 'Nuptial Torch' is lit and the 'marriage Rites' invoked. But that 'sober Race of Men, whose lives Religious titl'd them the Sons of God' have been seduced by the race of Cain; a 'fair femal Troop' empty 'of all good':

> Bred onely and completed to the taste
> Of lustful appetence, to sing, to dance,
> To dress, and troule the Tongue, and roule the Eye.

In another vision Adam sees the product of those 'ill-mated Marriages':

> Giants of mightie Bone, and bould emprise;
> Part wield thir Arms, part courb the foaming Steed,
> Single or in Array of Battel rang'd.

But the 'seventh' from Adam:

> The onely righteous in a World perverse,
> And therefore hated, therefore so beset
> With Foes for daring single to be just,
> And utter odious Truth, that God would come
> To judge them with his Saints: Him the most High
> Rapt in a balmie Cloud with winged Steeds
> Did ... walk with God
> High in Salvation and the Climes of bliss,
> Exempt from Death; to shew thee what reward
> Awaits the good, the rest what punishment.[126]

Milton's poetic elaboration upon Genesis is intriguing, for it supplements the account in the Authorized Version with other possible sources. The reference to tents and cattle amplifies the depiction of Jabal (Genesis 4:20), while the sound of music accords with the description of his brother Jubal – 'father of all such as handle the harp and organ' (Genesis 4:21). Moreover, the upright sons of God descending from the high hills are clearly the descendants of Seth (Julius Africanus, *Chronography*; Ephrem the Syrian, *Hymns on Paradise* 1.10–11; Augustine, *City of God* 15:23), versed in God's works that have not been lost (Josephus, *Antiquities* 1.2.3). Their temptresses are the daughters of Cain (Ephrem, *Hymns on Paradise* 1.10–11; Chrysostom, *Homily XXII on Genesis*; Theodoret, *Questions on Genesis* 47; *Pirkê de Rabbi Eliezer* 22). The fruit of this unholy union are the giants (Genesis 6:4), expert in war (Baruch 3:26). Enoch is the seventh from Adam, who prophesies that God will come with his saints to judge the wicked (Jude 14). He walked with God (Genesis 5:24) and did not taste death (Hebrews 11:5). There is no suggestion here that Milton

[126] John Milton, *Paradise Lost* (1668), sigs. Qq2^{r-2}–Rr^{v}, reprinted in Alastair Fowler (ed.) *John Milton. Paradise Lost* (1987), XI, ll. 556–712, 592–600.

used Syncellus's excerpts from the Book of Enoch. His sons of God are men, not angels. Their leaders are not named, nor is their number given. No reference is made to Mount Hermon or to the secrets the Watchers taught their wives. His giants are not eaters of flesh and drinkers of blood. Yet the detail that the daughters of Cain enticed the sons of Seth with music, song and dance is suggestive. In his *Commentary on Genesis* Procopius of Gaza (*c*.465–*c*.529) noted with reference to the phrase 'sons of God' that the progeny of Cain invented music, notably the lyre. More elaborate is the Syriac *Cave of Treasures* which describes how the Sethites were attracted to the Cainite camp by 'the devilish playing of the reeds which emitted musical sounds, and by the harps which the men played through the operation of the power of the devils, and by the sounds of the tambourines and of the sistra which were beaten and rattled through the agency of evil spirits'. This theme of entrapment through music and song recurs in Bar Hebraeus's Arabic version of his chronography and is also a feature of the Ethiopic *Kebra Nagast*, which relates that the dancing Cainite women accompanied their singing with tambourine, flutes, pipes and loud cries of joy.[127] Moreover, according to a highly glossed Greek translation of *Hymns of Paradise* by Ephrem the Syrian (*c*.306–73), the sons of God were lured down from the higher land by the daughters of Cain, who came to them with 'wind and string instruments'. Ephrem's account is quoted in Syncellus's *Chronography* – a work that may have been partly read to the blind Milton.[128] Indeed, Milton knew the tradition identifying the fallen angels with the sons of God from Justin Martyr. Thus Satan addresses Belial in *Paradise Regain'd* (1671):

> Before the Flood thou with thy lusty Crew,
> False titl'd Sons of God, roaming the Earth
> Cast wanton eyes on the daughters of men,
> And coupl'd with them, and begot a race.[129]

XXI

In 1698 the German-born patristic scholar and advocate of Lutheran Syncretism Johann Ernest Grabe (1666–1711) issued the first volume of *Spicilegium SS. Patrum, ut et Hæreticorum* (2 vols, Oxford, 1698–99). Included was an edition of the Testaments of the Twelve Patriarchs, together with notes that gave the Greek text of Syncellus's excerpts from the Book of Enoch with a parallel Latin translation. The Enoch fragments printed by Grabe were rendered into English as *The History*

---

[127] Procopius, *Commentary on Genesis*, in Migne (ed.), PG, LXXXVII, cols 267–8; Ernest W. Budge (ed.), *The Book of the Cave of Treasures* (1927), 87; Abû'l Faraj, *Historia Compendiosa Dynastiarvm* (ed. Pococke), 6; Budge (ed.), *Queen of Sheba and her only son Menyelek*, 184–8.

[128] Adler and Tuffin (eds), *Chronography of George Synkellos* 15.13–31; cf. Ephrem the Syrian, *Hymns on Paradise* 1:10–11.

[129] John Milton, *Of Reformation Touching Chvrch-Discipline* (1641), 24–5; John Milton, *Paradise Regain'd* (1671), II, ll. 178–81, 37.

of the Angels, and their Gallantry with the Daughters of Men (1715).[130] Syncellus's extracts from Enoch were also published in Greek accompanied with a Latin version in the German Johann Albert Fabricius's *Codex Pseudepigraphus Veteris Testamenti* (2 vols, Hamburg and Leipzig, 1713–23). Fabricius's compilation marked the culmination of research at that date on the Books of Enoch, containing selections from the writings of Postel, Dee, Scaliger, Drusius, Grotius, Bang, Mader, Pfeiffer, Vockerodt, Ludolf, Grabe and others.[131] Fabricius was followed by the most extensive treatment yet of the subject in English, William Whiston's *A Collection of Authentick Records Belonging to the Old and New Testament* (2 parts, 1727–28). This included 'Extracts out of the First Book of Enoch, concerning The Egregori', as well as:

> A Dissertation to prove that this Book of Enoch, whose Fragments we have here produc'd was really genuine, and was one of the Sacred Apocryphal or Concealed Books of the Old Testament.[132]

Far from being neglected, Enoch and the books under his name had preoccupied monks, chroniclers, rabbis, Kabbalists, Academicians, magicians, Catholic theologians, Protestant divines, Orientalists, sectarians and poets alike. So much so, that by the mid-eighteenth century the available evidence in Greek and Latin had been exhausted. Fresh impetus was needed in the form of a complete text. In March 1773 the Scottish adventurer James Bruce (1730–94), having spent two eventful years in Abyssinia, arrived at Marseilles. Before returning to the British Isles Bruce presented a specially prepared copy of the Ethiopic version of the Book of Enoch to Louis XV in Paris, subsequently deposited in the Bibliothèque Royale. Another was given to the Bodleian Library, Oxford and a third retained by Bruce. The Paris manuscript was transcribed by Carl Gottfried Woide, librarian of the British Museum. The text in the Bodleian was translated into English by Richard Laurence (1760–1838), regius professor of Hebrew at Oxford, and published as *The Book of Enoch the Prophet* (Oxford, 1821), setting off a new chain of speculation.[133]

---

[130] Johann Ernest Grabe (ed.), *Spicilegium SS. Patrum, ut et Hæreticorum*, 2 vols (Oxford, 1698–99), I, 347–54; 'The History of the Angels, and their Gallantry with the Daughters of Men', in Johann Ernest Grabe, *The History of the Seventy-two Interpreters*, trans. Mr Lewis (1715), 177–96.

[131] Johann Albert Fabricius (ed.), *Codex Pseudepigraphus Veteris Testamenti*, 2 vols (Hamburg and Leipzig, 1713–23), I, 160–223, II, 55–61.

[132] William Whiston, *A Collection of Authentick Records Belonging to the Old and New Testament*, 2 parts (1727–28), I, 260–93.

[133] James Bruce, *Travels to Discover the Source of the Nile,* eds Alexander Murray and Henry Salt, 5 vols (Edinburgh, 1790), I, 488–9, 497–500.

Chapter 2

The Genesis Narrative in the Circle of Robert Hooke and Francis Lodwick

William Poole

I

The gregarious natural philosopher Robert Hooke (1635–1703) kept a private journal for two extended periods (1672–83, 1688–93), the earlier years preserved in a folio MS now at the Guildhall, the later in a tiny pocket-book in the Sloane collection. Heavily abbreviated, these terse jottings record not only Hooke's activities as a central figure in the early Royal Society but also his career as City Surveyor, his private intrigues, his keen interest in the London book trade, and his daily meetings in the coffee shops with his circle of friends, themselves typically fellows of the Royal Society.[1] In particular, the laconic accounts of conversations held in the coffee shop reveal the breadth of Hooke's interests, and this essay addresses one such interest in particular: the Hooke circle and the book of Genesis, more precisely the Genesis accounts of the creation of the world and of man, of man's fall, and of the flood.

By 'the Hooke circle' is meant the nucleus of names, some predominant in the earlier set of journals, some in the later, gathered around Hooke in coffee shop or private house – men like the Royal Society administrator Abraham Hill (1633–1721), the astronomer Edmond Halley (1656–1742), the antiquary John Aubrey (1626–97), the bookseller John Martyn (*c.*1619–80), the merchant and agriculturalist John Houghton (1645–1705), the translators and brothers-in-law Alexander Pitfield (1659–1728) and Richard Waller (*c.*1660–1715), and the merchant and linguist

[1] H.W. Robinson and W. Adams (eds), *The Diary of Robert Hooke M.A., M.D., F.R.S. 1672–80* (London, 1935) (edited from Guildhall MS 1758, but lacking initial entries and January 1681–May 1683); R.T. Gunther (ed.), *Early Science in Oxford* (Oxford, 15 vols, 1923–67), vol. 10, 69–265 (edited from BL, MS Sloane 4024). Sloane 1039 contains further scraps. Hooke's diaries are cited by date alone. See M. 'Espinasse, *Robert Hooke* (London, 1956), 106–55; S. Shapin, 'Who was Robert Hooke?' in M. Hunter and S. Schaffer (eds), *Robert Hooke: New Studies* (Aldershot, 1989), 253–86; L. Mulligan, 'Self-Scrutiny and the Study of Nature: Robert Hooke's Diary as Natural History', *Journal of British Studies*, 35 (1996) 311–42, *cum grano salis*.

Francis Lodwick (1619–94).[2] Interests relevant to the book of Genesis include not simply comments directly relating to the interpretation and textual status of the earlier parts of the Mosaic narrative, but also topics directly or indirectly bearing on the biblical account of creation, namely chronology, textual criticism, and the sciences today gathered under earth sciences, especially geology and palaeontology. Such an enquiry must heed not only printed material produced from within the Hooke circle, including translations, editorial work, or library catalogues, but also manuscripts of various types: commonplace books (Hill, Halley), manuscripts designed for the press (Aubrey), and manuscripts seemingly never intended for print (Lodwick). I shall discuss chiefly the reading of Hooke, Hill, and Lodwick, the hypotheses concerning creation of Hooke, Halley and Aubrey, and the impact on the group of Orientalism. Finally, I show how Lodwick in particular, a hitherto neglected free-thinker, combined heretical beliefs in the extreme age of the world and the existence of men before Adam with extreme doctrinal minimalism, denying the traditional consequences of the fall of man, and effectively demolishing most of the familiar theological scaffolds erected on Genesis 1–3.[3] Lodwick's speculations, and indeed the sum of such speculation in the Hooke circle, though often not conducted under the aegis of the society itself, complicate the early Royal Society's avowed decision not to treat of religious controversy.

It is important to remember, however, the physical locations and social contexts of many of the documents examined. It is no accident, for instance, that the most heretical of Hooke's circle, Lodwick, restricted his bolder speculations to manuscript, and though we can be sure many of Lodwick's interests were inspired by those of his friends, we cannot prove he fully reciprocated, despite some minor circulation of his papers.

II

First, what kind of books did this circle buy, read or hand about? Thankfully we possess not only Hooke's posthumous library sale-catalogue, but also two manuscript catalogues of Lodwick's extensive library, and 11 of Hill's indexed commonplace books. The three men carefully organized their own collections: Lodwick's mature catalogue is preceded by a table for converting his old shelf-marks into his new system; Hill's commonplace books employ notation referring to the physical layout of his library; and Hooke records in his journal some days spent cataloguing his

[2] Details concerning fellows of the Royal Society are taken, where possible, from M. Hunter, *The Royal Society and its Fellows 1660–1700: The Morphology of an Early Scientific Institution* (2nd edn) (Chalfont St.Giles, 1994). See also Margaret J.M. Ezell, 'Richard Waller, SRS: "In the Pursuit of Nature"' *Notes and Records of the Royal Society of London* 38 (1984), 215–33. Martyn, printer to the Royal Society, but roguish in his commercial behaviour, was not a fellow.

[3] W. Poole, 'A Baboon in the Garden of Eden: the private heresies of Francis Lodwick', *TLS* 5204 (27 December 2002), 10–11.

own books.[4] And it is immediately obvious that these men paid close attention to contemporary debates concerning the textual state of the bible. Not only did Hooke own various standard and less standard commentaries on Genesis, including those of Benedictus Pererius (Cologne, 1622), David Pareus (Frankfurt, 1615), Hieronymus Zanchius (Neustadt, 1602), Johann Heinrich Hottinger (Heidelburg, 1659) and Pico della Mirandola (edition unspecified), but he also owned Buxtorf the Younger's *De Punctorum Origine, Antiquitate et Authoritate* (Basel, 1648), a contribution to the controversy over the antiquity of the vowel-points of biblical Hebrew.[5] More esoteric English productions in Hooke's library directly or indirectly affecting the interpretation of Genesis include Henry More's *Conjectura Cabbalistica* (London and Cambridge, 1653), and Van Helmont's *Two Hundred Queries* (London, 1684) – a book Francis Lodwick owned too. Both works, arguing for the pre-existence of the soul, had damaging implications for orthodoxy, and Van Helmont in another work even denied creation *ex nihilo*, a denial which went hand-in-hand, as it often did, with the rejection of creation as occurring at a dateable time in the past. In passing, Lodwick, in a lending-and-borrowing list at the end of his library catalogue, noted down in 1688 that he had lent the *Two Hundred Queries* to another member of their circle, the veteran FRS Thomas Henshaw (1618–1700).[6]

Hooke also owned the infamous triumvirate of texts denying complete Mosaic authorship of the Pentateuch – Hobbes's *Leviathan* (1651), Isaac La Peyrère's *Prae-Adamitae* (1655, English translation 1656), and Spinoza's *Tractatus Theologico-Politicus* (1670, English translation 1689).[7] He possessed, too, the first textual critique of the Old Testament to incorporate such attacks, Richard Simon's *Histoire Critique du Vieux Testament* (1678).[8] Again, Lodwick owned all of these texts, including, notably, the *Prae-Adamitae* and the *Critique*, and both La Peyrère's theory that there were men before Adam and Simon's supposal that 'the Books of the Bible that are come into our hands, are but abridgments of the ancient Records, which were more full and copious, before the last abridgment was made for the publick use of the people' were principles Lodwick took to heart.[9] Hill's engagement with these issues is likewise evident: he excerpts from Spinoza frequently, noting for instance that a 'very smal part of the Pentateuch writ by Moses. Tract. Theolopol 8o p. 151.'

---

[4] MSS Sloane 855, 859; MSS Sloane 2891–901; Hooke 5–6 August 1674. Sloane 1039, fols 143vf. may be part of Hooke's lists.

[5] E. Millington, *Bibliotheca Hookiana* (London, 1703), 1, 2, 8, 14; R.A. Muller, 'The Debate over the Vowel Points and the Crisis in Orthodox Hermeneutics' *JMedRenStud*, 10 (1980) 53–72. Hooke notes he was reading Pererius on 6 January 1689.

[6] Millington, *Bibliotheca* 45, 49; F.M. Van Helmont *A Cabbalistical Dialogue* (London, 1682) (See also [A. Conway] *The Principles of the Most Ancient and Modern Philosophy* (London, 1692), 8); MS Sloane 859, fols 49^{r}, 77^{r}.

[7] Millington, *Bibliotheca* 8, 9, 54. On the relationship between these texts, see most recently N. Malcolm, *Aspects of Hobbes* (Oxford, 2002), 383–431.

[8] Millington, *Bibliotheca*, 41, 54.

[9] MS Sloane 859, fols 12^{r}, 23^{r}, 52^{r}; R. Simon, *The Critical History of the Old Testament* (London, 1682), 5.

Hill also recorded various remarks on lost biblical books, the incompleteness of the canon, and the relative novelty of the Hebrew vowel-points. In some papers seemingly listing books he owns, he includes Spinoza's *Tractatus*.[10] Lodwick, rather remarkably, owned the *Prae-Adamitae* and the *Critique* in both their original languages and their English translations.[11]

Of course, excerpting from or owning books notorious for their implications concerning the textual state of the bible or their otherwise heretical nature is not quite the same thing as assenting to such books, but it reveals currency and discussion, something likewise confirmed by Hooke's journals. In late 1675, for instance, coffee-shop conversation revolved around universal language schemes – Hooke, Aubrey and Lodwick were all members of the group which tried to revise John Wilkins's great *Essay* (1668) after Wilkins's death[12] – and theological, particularly Old Testament, matters: 'At Spanish Coffe house with Mr Hill and Mr Lodowick, discoursd of Universall Language, of the temporall promises in the old testament' (14 December). A few days later, conversation clearly turned to Genesis itself, and La Peyrère's preadamite hypothesis: 'To Martins and Garaways club: Ludowick, Hill, Aubery, Wild. Discoursd about Universal Character, about preadamits and of Creation' (18 December). Hooke's journal is then silent on such matters until late 1677, when discussion on Genesis resumed: 'Talkd with Lodowick of Creation' (24 December 1677); 'discoursd 1st of Genesis with Lodowick, Spencer and Crawley' (15 January 1678). These are all matters dealt with extensively in Lodwick's manuscripts, and the collocation in December 1675 of universal language, preadamism, and creation provides the most persuasive piece of extant evidence for dating Lodwick's manuscript utopia 'A Country Not Named', to which we shall return.

Whether such discussions were conducted as carefully hypothetical or *sub rosa* is difficult to say. Three pieces of evidence are suggestive, though I propose them rather tentatively. First, in 1691, Halley complained in a letter to Hill that he, Halley, was under the suspicion of 'asserting the eternity of the world'.[13] Secondly, the universal linguist George Dalgarno wrote, in a long section on Adam's creation in his manuscript treatise on language, that he did not 'undertake to convince preadamites and sadducees'.[14] This, I think, is clearly a blast against La Peyrère and Hobbes respectively, but given that both Dalgarno and Lodwick were central figures in the attempt to construct a universal language, and that Dalgarno's undated but late tract is aimed, if implicitly, against the other major language-planner, Wilkins, a dig at

[10] MSS Sloane 2891, fol. 12^{v} (incompletion); 2893, fol. 3^{v} (Mosaic authorship); 2901, fol. 135^{r} (vowel points); 2893, fol. 183^{v} (Spinoza).

[11] MS Sloane 859, fols 12^{r}, 23^{r} (La Peyrère); 12^{r}, 52^{r} (Simon).

[12] R. Lewis, 'The efforts of the Aubrey correspondence group to revise John Wilkins's *Essay* (1668) and their context', *Historiographia Linguistica*, 28 (2001), 331–64.

[13] E.F. MacPike (ed.), *Correspondence and Papers of Edmond Halley* (Oxford, 1932), 88 (letter of 22 June 1691); Simon Schaffer, 'Halley's Atheism and the End of the World', *NRRSL*, 32 (1977), 17–40; Allan Chapman, 'Halley's Use of Historical Evidence in the Advancement of Science', *NRRSL*, 48 (1994), 167–91, 175–81.

[14] Christ Church (Oxford), MS 162, fol. 117^{r}.

Lodwick himself is also possible. Finally, Dalgarno's friend John Wallis, writing from Oxford against Hooke's thesis that the earth's magnetic poles might have wandered over time, said that he could think of no time when this could have taken place, 'unless it were before ye Creation of Adam', he sneered, perhaps knowingly.[15]

III

These, then, were some of the issues connected with Genesis such men discussed. What of their more public work? We have mentioned Halley, who partially conformed his various theories – that the earth, hollow, enclosed a smaller sphere, the motions of which caused variations in the magnetic poles; that extrapolation back from the current salinity of lakes could act as a dating mechanism for creation; that the flood might have been due to the impact of a comet – to biblical respectability, but not very hard, nor very convincingly, as Schaffer has demonstrated. In his commonplace book, Halley collocated incompatibilities between natural philosophical and theological types of enquiry: 'Naturall Philosophy teacheth that out of nothinge nothinge can bee made ... Divinity takes her up for these & upon Supernaturall principles teaches her a Creac[i]on a[nd] Resurrection.'[16] But his early eighteenth-century paper on salinity, despite its closing rebuttal of the eternity of the world, nevertheless opens with a rather brutal splicing of the Genesis narrative – in passing noting the chronological discrepancy between the Septuagint and the Vulgate text[17] – with the extreme age of the earth:

> There have been many Attempts made and Proposals offered, to ascertain from the Appearances of Nature, what may have been the Antiquity of this Globe of *Earth*; on which, by the Evidence of Sacred Writ, *Mankind* has dwelt about 6000 Years; or according to the *Septuagint* above 7000. But whereas we are there told that the formation of *Man* was the last Act of the *Creator*, 'tis no where revealed in Scripture how long the *Earth* had existed before this last Creation, nor how long those five Days that preceded it may be accounted; since we are elsewhere told, that in respect of the Almighty a thousand Years is as one Day, being equally no part of *Eternity*; Nor can it well be conceived how those Days should be to be understood of natural Days, since they are mentioned as Measures of Time before the Creation of the Sun, which was not till the Fourth Day. And 'tis certain

---

[15] Quoted by D.R. Oldroyd, 'Geological Controversy in the Seventeenth Century: "Hooke *Vs* Wallis" and its Aftermath' in M. Hunter and S. Schaffer (eds), *Robert Hooke: New Studies* (London, 1989), 207–30, 212. For the Wallis–Dalgarno connection see Christ Church MS 162, fol. 12^{r}, and PRO PROB 11/473, fol. 105^{r-v} (Wallis's will).

[16] E.H. Cohen and J.H. Ross, 'The Commonplace Book of Edmond Halley', *NRRSL*, 40 (1985) 1–40, 30. See *PT*, 16 (1693) 563–78 for Halley's hypothesis of the terrella within the earth.

[17] See D.S. Katz, 'Isaac Vossius and the English biblical critics 1650–89' in R.H. Popkin and A. Vanderjagt (eds), *Scepticism and Irreligion in the Seventeenth and Eighteenth Centuries* (Leiden, 1993), 142–84, 150–54.

> *Adam* found the *Eerth* [sic], at his first Production, fully replenished with other sorts of *Animals*.[18]

As Schaffer notes, despite Halley's avowed proof of non-eternity, 'it was far more dangerous to prove, as Halley had done, that the "world may be found much older than many have hitherto imagin'd", than it was helpful ... [to the] orthodox to show that at least it was not eternal'.[19] In October 1693, only two years after the troubles over eternalism, Halley was unrepentant, asserting at the end of a paper before the society: 'there still [is] wanting a valid argument to evince from what has been observed in nature that this Globe of the Earth ever did begin or ever shall have an end'.[20]

Halley did not publish this paper, and his similar papers on the flood only appeared in the *Philosophical Transactions* for 1724–25, though dated 12 and 19 December 1694. In these, he stated that the biblical account of the deluge was 'much too imperfect', clearly 'the Remains of a much fuller Account'. Moreover, the flood itself was not a substantial enough inundation to submerge the earth: given a maximum of 40 inches rainfall per day, 40 days and 40 nights would produce 22 fathoms, only enough to cover low-lying land bordering the sea. Furthermore, 'the Earth seems as if it were new made out of the Ruins of an old World', an indication that huge upheavals must have taken place before Noah's time, more evidence of the incompleteness of the Genesis narrative. Halley then proposed the impact of a comet with the earth to account for geographical and axial shift, an utterly unbiblical hypothesis, whereas other writers, such as Thomas Burnet, whom we shall next encounter, blamed such changes solely on the flood, and hence on man's sin. Halley's second paper opens with the report that 'a Person whose Judgment I have great Reason to respect' had interpreted Halley's proposed upheavals as pre-dating creation itself, being the processes by which Chaos was made. If not a mere literary device, was this person Hooke? William Whiston would later suggest something similar, and Hooke summarized his book for the Society.[21] At any rate, Halley's postscript to this second paper explicitly states that he had kept these two papers from the press in 1694, lest he 'incur the Censure of the Sacred Order'.[22]

Halley's writings, though, were comparatively late, and his attitude to the bible was influenced by other, earlier projects in the group. In 1676, Hooke's splinter 'club', a destabilising subfaction of the Royal Society who promised to speak only '*sub*

[18] E. Halley, 'A Short Account of the Cause of the Saltness of the Ocean', *Philosophical Transactions*, 29 (1714–16), 296–300, 296.

[19] Schaffer, 'Halley's Atheism', 26.

[20] RS, RBC 7.364, reproduced in Schaffer, 32–3.

[21] William Whiston, *A New Theory of the Earth* (London, 1696); RS, Classified Papers XX, no. 85.

[22] E. Halley, 'Some Considerations about the Cause of the Universal Deluge' and 'Some Farther Thoughts upon the same Subject', *Philosophical Transactions*, 33 (1724–25), 118–23, 123–4. Halley concludes by observing his priority to William Whiston's *New Theory of the Earth*, which likewise advanced the cometary hypothesis.

sigillo', had discussed at their first meeting whether the earth had once been totally submerged, and later in the year, Hooke and Wren debated the concave shell of the earth.[23] This was probably not the hypothesis of a hollow earth, but further reflection on one of Hooke's major ongoing projects, his theory of fossils, and the earthquakes he posited to account for their puzzling forms, substances and positions.[24] This work, which has been substantially discussed, originated in the 1660s and continued throughout Hooke's life, published only posthumously in 1705.

Hooke's first printed lectures date from 1668, in which he discussed the nature of 'figured stones', forwarding his prescient hypothesis that such figured stones, particularly those of seemingly marine creatures, were not *lapides sui generis* but indeed the petrified remains of once-living organisms, some of which were now extinct, and that their current resting-places, often on high mountains, indicated that the contemporary geography of the earth was very different from what it once had been.[25]

Hooke's first lecture is perhaps his boldest. He not only advances his organic interpretation of fossils, an interpretation only prominently held by Nicholas Steno at the time, but he dismisses the flood as an inadequate motor for the current position of fossils, and attempts to explain various biblical events naturalistically: the catastrophe of Sodom and Gomorrah was an earthquake; the long lives of the patriarchs can be explained by supposing that the earth once span faster and hence the days and years were shorter; the giants of the pagans' *gigantomachiae* are none other than primal earthquakes – indeed, the real giants of the old testament demonstrate the possibility of the extinction of an entire species.[26] These examples are telling: the first recalls La Peyrère's attempts to reduce similar 'miracles', such as the deluge or the sun standing still, to natural causes operating over limited areas; [27] the second is similar to Isaac Newton's suggestion to Thomas Burnet that the earth might have spun slower in the original days;[28] and the third shows that Hooke was from the beginning keen on euhemerist techniques of synthesising pagan and sacred sources.

---

[23] See Hooke for 1 January, 13 May; on the club, see Hunter, *Royal Society*, 40–41.

[24] For background, see F.D. Adams, *The Birth and Development of the Geological Sciences* (New York [1938] 1954), 250–76, 399–425; C. Schneer, 'The Rise of Historical Geology in the Seventeenth Century', *Isis*, 45 (1954) 256–68; C. Albritton, *The Abyss of Time: Changing Conceptions of the Earth's Antiquity after the 16th Century* (San Francisco, 1980), 1–67; M. Rudwick, *The Meaning of Fossils* (Chicago, 2nd edn, 1985), 1–100; Y. Ito, 'Hooke's Cyclic Theory of the Earth in the Context of Seventeenth Century England', *BJHS*, 21 (1988) 295–314; E.T. Drake, *Restless Genius: Robert Hooke and his Earthly Thoughts* (New York, 1996), 69–76, 104–11.

[25] R. Hooke, *Posthumous Works* (London, 1705), 279–328.

[26] Hooke, *Posthumous Works*, 307 (Sodom and Gomorrah), 319–20 (flood too brief to shift shells; Atlantis), 322 (axial rotation), 323, 327 (giants).

[27] [I. La Peyrère] *Men Before Adam* (London, 1656), 'A Systeme', Book 4, chs 3–9.

[28] H.W. Turnbull (ed.), *The Correspondence of Isaac Newton Volume II 1676–87* (Cambridge, 1960), 321–34. See S. Mandelbrote, 'Isaac Newton and Thomas Burnet: Biblical Criticism and the Crisis of Late Seventeenth-Century England', in J.E. Force and R. H. Popkin

Rappaport has divided Hooke's ongoing series of lectures into four stages: this first stage, in which Hooke details his hypothetical model; a second stage in which he advances his theory of polar wandering to account for the upheavals assumed by the first lecture; a third stage in which, as pagan historical sources had proved unyielding, Hooke turned to the poets and to euhemerism to convince his audience of the plausibility of his claims; and a final set of retrenchments.[29] This division, emphasising as it does the tactics of Hooke's lectures, responding to first one and then another dissenting audience as occasion demanded, is partially inchoate even in the first lecture, as Hooke's comments on the giants show. Indeed, he also suggests in the first lecture that Atlantis was an ancient civilisation destroyed by an earthquake, and that there may have been many former cultures with highly advanced philosophies of nature, which have been erased by natural change, and of whom only garbled mythological accounts remain.[30] Hooke also wondered about the Egyptian and Chinese chronologies, considerably longer than the standard biblical figures. In this, he was influenced by the Jesuit Martino Martini's *Sinicae Historiae Decas Prima* (1658), the first full account of Chinese chronology, the first to point out the questions this raised about biblical chronology, and the first to draw explicit and non-biblical conclusions from this: 'I hold it as certain that the extremity of Asia was populated before the flood,' Martini declared.[31] Hooke is cagey on the chronological debate, but it is one he returned to often, for instance in his discussion of the Chinese language. Although he rejects the Chinese age of the world (88,640,102 years old in 1686) – a figure he generated not from Martini, who dated the reign of the first king Fu Hsi from the more modest but still problematic 2952 BC, but from the tables of the Persian astronomer and grandson of Tamburlane, Ulugh Beg – he does state that Chinese writing predates any European system, and that all writing systems are devised by men.[32] Hence, although Hooke does not spell this out, Chinese is older than Hebrew, and both are humanly-devised languages, a further blow to biblical universality and the divine status of Hebrew. Isaac Vossius, who appears now and then in Hooke's journals, in his defence

---

(eds), *The Books of Nature and Scripture* (Dordrecht, 1994), 149–78. Newton's slow spin applies to the hexameron, so that the vast processes of those 'days' have sufficient time to take place; Hooke is talking of the relative life-spans of the patriarchs. The similarity thus lies in both men's attempts to accommodate early biblical 'days' to a naturalistic understanding.

[29] R. Rappaport, 'Hooke on Earthquakes: Lectures, Strategy and Audience', *BJHS*, 19 (1986) 129–46.

[30] Hooke, *Posthumous Works*, 328. See also Hooke on longitude as reported by Waller (*Posthumous Works*, v): 'it having been hid some Thousands of Years already'.

[31] *Posthumous Works*, 320; M. Martini, *Sinicae Historiae Decas Prima* (Munich, 1658), esp. 11–21, quotation from 21 ('extremam Asiam ante diluvium habitatam fuisse pro certo habeo'); E.J. Van Kley, 'Europe's 'Discovery' of China and the Writing of World History', *American Historical Review*, 76 (1971) 358–85, 363; D.E. Mungello, *Curious Land: Jesuit Accommodation and the Origins of Sinology* (Stuttgart, 1985), 124–8.

[32] Hooke, 'Some Observations, and Conjectures Concerning the Chinese Characters', *PT*, 180 (1686) 63–78, 64–5. Hooke used the Merton Orientalist and itinerant manuscript collector John Greaves' Latin–Arabic edition of Ulugh Beg, *Epochae Celebriores* (London, 1650).

of the Septuagint chronology used Martini to attack the Hebraic chronology, and stated explicitly that the Chinese had writers more ancient than Moses, and that their records extended to prediluvial times. Martini and Vossius were the chief authorities for the architect John Webb's notorious attempt in 1678 to establish Chinese as the original language of mankind.[33]

Indeed, Orientalism was popular in Hooke's circle, accessible to them through the major, typically Jesuit, works of Mendoza, Ricci, Semedo, Martini, and Kircher. Hooke and Lodwick also translated 'Backhoffs' (6 December 1689) (i.e. Fedor Isakovitch Baikov, the Czar's ambassador to China in 1656),[34] and earlier in 1689 Hooke, Lodwick and John Godfrey, Clerk of the Mercers' Company discussed the 'Siam religion' (12 January).[35] That week, in Jonathan's, they also resumed discussion on the 'flood, Atlantis etc' (17 January), a reference in all probability to Hooke's ongoing lectures. Hooke bought Tachard's *Voyage of Siam* from Boudet the bookseller (28 December 1688), and Tachard's book contains a long section on Siamese religion, supposing a succession of gods in an 'uncreated and eternal' world.[36] Later references in Hooke's journal – 'I recd from Horn 12 *Siams* and sent them by M. to Mr Pitfield' (11 January 1693, and see surrounding entries) – demonstrate that the translator of Simon de la Loubère's *Du Royaume de Siam* (Paris, 1691) was Pitfield himself, the 'A.P. Gen[tleman]. R[egalis]. S[ocietatis]. S[ocius].' of its title-page.[37] The large Jesuit edition of Confucius had appeared in 1687; Hooke was reading it in 1689 (17 December). An English abridgement, from the French, was published in 1691, opening with an account, again, of the long Chinese chronology, and an attempt to harmonize it with the Septuagint – not the Vulgate text.[38] Its preface also claims that Chinese writing is the oldest in the

---

[33] I. Vossius, *Dissertatio de Vera Aetate Mundi* (The Hague, 1659), 44–8 (Vossius next attacks the preadamite thesis (49–52)); Van Kley 'China', 363–5; John Webb, *The Antiquity of China* (London, 1678); R. Ramsey, 'China and the Ideal of Order in John Webb's *An Historical Essay*', *JHI*, 62 (2001) 483–503.

[34] Probably the 'Voyage d'un Ambassadeur que la Tzaar de Muscovie envoya par terre a la Chine L'Annee 1653 [sic]' footnoted to 'Saedor Iacovuits Boicoof' and included as the third part of M. Thévenot, *Recueil des Voyages* (Paris, 1681).

[35] See also 13 November 1688, 17, 20 March 1689 for discussion of H. Lord, *A Display of Two Forraigne Sects in the East Indies* (London, 1630); also 10 December 1689 'translated Voyage of Cathay 1620.'

[36] G. Tachard, *The Voyage of Siam* (London, 1688), 275–307, 284.

[37] S. de la Loubère, *A New Historical Relation of the Kingdom of Siam* (London, 1693). For Cassini's observations on the deficiencies of Chinese chronology see 253–4. (This has not hitherto been noted as Waller's work. To this can be tentatively added Vincenzo Coronelli, trans. R.W. Gent, *An Historical and Geographical Account of the Morea, Negropont, and the Maritime Places as far as Thessalonica* (London, 1687).) See also Waller to Hooke, undated, Sloane 4067, fols 197–8, on translation.

[38] This constant preference for the Septuagint chronology stems from 1637, when the Chinese missionary Adam Schall sent a memo to Rome, requesting guidance on the matter. Schall's adoption of 2357 BC as the inception of the reign of 'Yao' was endorsed by Rome, which thus effectively served as an official endorsement of the Septuagint over the Vulgate,

world.[39] Hooke himself presented to the Royal Society the already mentioned paper on Chinese characters and Chinese printing. Earlier, Wilkins's *Essay* had contained an engraving of the Lord's Prayer in Chinese, from a manuscript of Lodwick's, though destroyed in the Great Fire.[40] Lodwick and Hooke even got the chance, in the last months of Lodwick's life, to meet some visiting Chinese in London, with whom they took tea and attempted to talk.[41]

IV

Hooke's interest in chronology, earthquakes and fossils was spurred on, as Ito has commented, by the publications of Thomas Burnet, Master of the Charterhouse, and his *Telluris Theoria Sacra*, published in Latin 1681, and in English in 1684.[42] Two more books of it appeared in Latin in 1689, and the whole set in English in 1691. The next year followed the *Archaeologiae Philosophicae*; both works attracted wide discussion and imitation.[43] Burnet's first work was an attempted harmonisation of the earth sciences with Genesis, proposing that the initial earth had been in the form of a smooth egg, which was cracked at the time of the flood, releasing huge torrents. Although Burnet sought to further his thesis by biblical reference, he was increasingly reliant on the distinction between esoteric and exoteric layers of meaning in scripture, and relegated much of 'Moses' to the realm of exoterism, or fables for the unlearned Jews. In the *Archaeologiae*, he even allegorized the fall out of meaningful existence, and it was as a result of this later work in particular, and its adoption by Blount and his friends in *The Oracles of Reason* (1693), that Burnet had to retreat from the attentions of the court.[44]

Hooke's own geological theories, and by extension their relation to the Genesis narrative, were partially shaped by Burnet's writings, and from the beginning of the second journal, references to borrowing, reading, and criticizing Burnet abound. The

---

though the reply, as an eighteenth-century witness wrote, was careful to state that the Chinese should be told that this was neither 'un point décidé par l'Eglise, ou un point évidemment démontré.' Antoine Gaubil, *Traité de la Chronologie Chinoise*, ed. Silvestre de Sacy (Paris, 1814) 283–5. Gaubil's original MS is dated Peking, 27 September 1749; Martini, *Sinicae Historiae*, 13

[39] P. Couplet et al., *Confucius Sinarum Philosophus sive Scientia Sinensis Latine Exposita* (Paris, 1687); *The Morals of Confucius* (London, 1691), 2–18. See the review of the Jesuit edition in *PT*, 16 (1686) 376–8, focusing on Chinese chronology and ending on the observation of its incompatibility with sacred chronology. The Jesuits had, though, placed the Chinese patriarch 'Fohi' (Fu Hsi) immediately after the flood (*Morals*, 5). See Mungello, *Curious Land*, 247–99.

[40] J. Wilkins, *Essay* (London, 1668), 450–51.

[41] See Hooke for 2, 6 June; 10, 12, 31 July 1693.

[42] Ito, 'Cyclic Theory' 301–4.

[43] M.H. Nicholson, *Mountain Gloom and Mountain Glory* (Ithaca, 1959), 184–270.

[44] D.P. Walker, *The Decline of Hell: Seventeenth-Century Discussions of Eternal Torment* (London, 1964), 156–66; Mandelbrote, 'Biblical Criticism'; C. Blount et al., *The Oracles of Reason* (London, 1693), 1–19.

group was also interested to learn who else was writing about Burnet, and so they asked around, and found out about Erasmus Warren's work. John Beaumont wrote a book against Burnet, and presented it to Hooke, who only noticed after Beaumont had slipped away that he was the dedicatee. Beaumont's preface speaks infectiously of how '*the mind of Man, urg'd on by strong and Luxuriant Instincts, falls naturally a considering how far they* [matters concerning creation] *may be resolvable by humane Reason*'. Hooke also obtained the *Archaeologiae*, which he epitomized and read to the society, on Burnet's own permission, via his publisher Kettelby. The physiologist Marcello Malpighi also asked Hooke for a copy of the notorious work.[45]

Hooke's own geological thought, then, was reanimated by Burnet's ongoing theorizing. Both, it might seem, were simply striving to find the best possible fit of biblical and geological models. But there is a distinction. Burnet was trying to graft natural philosophy onto a theological understanding of history – the flood changes a perfect into an imperfect world as the result of sin (Burnet, as we saw, seriously neglected the fall 'proper' of Genesis 3). But Hooke, as Halley, was effectively separating *sacred history* from *biblical chronology*, projects which seemed identical for not only Burnet, but also for most of his detractors. On the other side, Newton was deeply uneasy with Burnet's 'accommodation' because to Newton, accommodation was to do with *layers* of meaning, not the positing of discontinuous meanings, one for the dull and another for the initiate.

A final case is provided by John Aubrey, who included as the eighth chapter of his *Natural History of Wiltshire* 'An Hypothesis of the Terraqueous globe'. This chapter, immediately following his discussion of 'figured stones', presents a few Hookeian remarks on earth history, affirming that water once covered all the earth, that fish were the oldest species, and '[t]hat this World is much older, than is commonly supposed'. He recalls himself and another Waller, the poet Edmund, walking over the Alps, Waller 'fanc[ying] that at the Creation, those Mountains were the Sweepings or Rubbish of the World heapd-up together'. He also conjectures axial shift, and quotes liberally from Ovid to support his case. Returning to the manuscript in 1691, he noted Halley's thesis of the secondary, interior earth, and related the story of the children who appeared from a cave somewhere in England, claiming to have come from a land where there was no sun. (Aubrey misattributes the story, which actually derives from William of Newburgh, the Yorkshire chronicler, who told of two green children who appeared out of a pit 'sub Rege Stephano', uttering an unknown language. The story had been used to good effect by Francis Godwin in his popular *The Man in the Moone*.)[46]

---

[45] Journals, 22 November 1688–97, May 1693 *passim*, esp. 12, 19 December 1688, 9 January 1689, 16, 20, 22 April 1689, 9, 21 December 1692, 18, 24 February 1693, 8 March 1693, 10, 13 April 1693. Hooke's digest of the *Archaeologiae* appeared in *PT*, 17 (1693) 796–812; copies in Bod., MS Eng. Misc. *c*.144; BL, MS Sloane 3828. J. Beaumont, *Considerations on a Book Entituled the Theory of the Earth* (London, 1693), A2^v. Beaumont is reviewed in *PT*, 17 (1693) 888–92; Woodward in *PT*, 19 (1695–97) 115–23.

[46] Bod. MS Aubrey 1, fols 86^v–101^r; G. Neubrigensis, *Rerum Anglicarum Libri Quinque* (Antwerp, 1567), 71–3; [Francis Godwin], *The Man in the Moone* (London, 1638) 105–6. Aubrey attributes the anecdote to the Jesuit Eusebius Nieuwebrigensis, and notes a parallel

Aubrey claimed no originality. He notes that the hypothesis is Hooke's, unprinted and liable to be forgotten without Aubrey's aid, and first delivered, at least so Aubrey claims, in '1663, or 1664'. This is unlikely, the back-dating of Hooke's first lecture thereby a little too comfortably anticipating Steno's *Prodromus* (1669, translated by Hooke's great enemy Oldenburg into English in 1671), which likewise argued for the organic origin of fossils.

Aubrey sent *The Natural History* to John Ray, another man much interested in the explanation of the deluge. Ray wrote back an encouraging letter, urging Aubrey to go ahead and publish, but with one major excision: 'I find but one thing that may give any just offence & that is ye Hypothesis of ye Terraqueous Globe, wherewith I must confesse my self not to be satisfied.' Ray was clearly troubled about the chronological implications of Hooke's work, and wrote again to Aubrey on fossils detailing his present opinion: 'my present opinion I say [–] for in such things I am not fixt, but ready to alter upon better information, saving always ye truth of ye Letter of ye Scripture'. But against the instruction to excise the digression, Aubrey has gruffly annotated the complaint: 'This hypothesis is Mr Hookes: I say so: and 'tis the best thing in the Book it (indeed) does interfere wth ye 1 chap. of Genesis.'[47] Here, stung into action by what he clearly perceived were misgivings fuelled by conservative exegisis, Aubrey, with slight exasperation, disclaims any interest in harmonizing his Hookeian 'hypothesis' with conventional chronology.

This points up the inherent danger of accommodation, because most of the natural philosophers accommodated their theories *to* the bible as well as using 'accommodation to the vulgar' as a fail-safe for when the fit was not exactly snug. Earlier writers, such as Wilkins in 1638, had simply disconnected the bible from natural philosophy, arguing that it had little concern with natural philosophy.[48] But the reconnections of Burnet, Newton and Hooke alike were dangerous, indeed more dangerous for traditional hermeneutics than the total accommodation Wilkins had at least in theory advocated, because reconnection teased out hermeneutic disagreements over the status of scripture, particularly the accounts of creation, fall and flood. As one reaction to Burnet ran, 'indeed my feare arose from the beauty of this Theory which the more it Captivats, the more are the Words of Moses in danger to be deprest.'[49] As we saw, Burnet was more sensitive to the received literal interpretation of the bible than Hooke or Halley or Aubrey – but Newton was more so than Burnet. Aubrey's own copy of Burnet's 1684 *Sacred Theory* contains light pencilling throughout, and one of the later sentences pointed up for particular attention is, tellingly: 'How necessary it is to understand Nature, if we would rightly understand those things in holy Writ that

from Kircher. See M. Hunter, *John Aubrey and the Realm of Learning* (London, 1975), 56–60.

[47] MSS Aubrey 1, fol. 13; Aubrey 13, fol. 174.

[48] J. Wilkins, *Discovery of a World in the Moone* (London, 1638), 40.

[49] MS Add. 10039, fols 65^{r}–73^{v} 'C & S discourse of Mr Burnetts, Theory of the Earth' [1684], fol. 65^{r}.

relate to the Natural World.'[50] 'Right understanding', though, was not simply a matter of better natural philosophy, but one of hermeneutics, and it was on that level too that the conflict operated.

V

All these issues receive their most heretical inflections in the manuscript writings of Francis Lodwick, writings at once outspoken in their rhetorical casting, and secretive in their apparent non-circulation. On the one hand, Lodwick organized many of his manuscripts into neat fair-copy compendia, complete with contents pages, and he also interconnected various of his short discourses: 'as I haue else where shewed'; 'I haue: 22: 8: of the first booke shewed the derivation of the word Reason.'[51] He included as an appendix of his own mature library catalogue a list 'of my Writings', 25 folios and a quarto, promoted to membership of his printed library.[52] But despite such private assertions of his writing's polished coherency and his evident pride in making private books – often so obviously redrafted from earlier fair copies that exact dating is impossible – Lodwick appears not to have circulated his writing much. We have noted that discussion of preadamism, creation, and 'temporal promises' in the Old Testament were discussed in Hooke's company, and some of Lodwick's more striking papers reside in Abraham Hill's collection of his friends' manuscripts, including pieces by William Petty, Christopher Wren and others, now Sloane 2903. Lodwick was also recognized in his time as a major linguist – his *A Common Writing* of 1647, sponsored by Samuel Hartlib, was the first printed attempt at a universal character, and he went on to publish a more sophisticated, though virtually ignored version, *The Ground-work*, in 1652. George Dalgarno knew of Lodwick, and referred to him a few times, and Lodwick helped Wilkins with parts of the *Essay*, in which Wilkins mentions Lodwick by name, twice, something he denied to Dalgarno, with whom Wilkins had fallen out by that point. After many years friendship with Hooke, Lodwick was eventually proposed and elected to the Royal Society in 1681, by John Houghton, who had himself been proposed by Hooke. The coffee-house circle looked after its own, and was obviously Lodwick's portal to the Royal Society, to whom he was an administrative asset, though only publishing one paper in the *Philosophical Transactions* (1686), his seminal phonetic alphabet.[53]

This is Lodwick the linguist, though, and that was not the whole man. As we have noted, Lodwick also assembled a library of remarkable eclecticism, far more eclectic than that of Hooke. He owned the books of Hobbes, La Peyrère and Simon, but his interests do not stop there. Apart from quite a bit of Miltonic and Leveller material,

---

[50] Bod. Ashm. G 26: Thomas Burnet, *The Theory of the Earth* (London, 1684), 221–2.

[51] MSS Sloane 897 fol. 40r; Sloane 913, fol. 61^{v}.

[52] Sloane 859, fol. 74^{r}.

[53] See principally V. Salmon, *The Works of Francis Lodwick* (London, 1972); D. Cram and J. Maat, *George Dalgarno on Universal Language* (Oxford, 2001), 109, 116, 118–19, 240–41; J. Wilkins, *Essay* (London, 1668), 357, 450; Hunter, *Morphology*, 202–3, 206–7.

he also owned some texts associated with the Ranters, including Joseph Salmon's *Heights in Depths* (1651) and Isaac Penington the Younger's *Eccho from the Great Deep* (1650), various Socinian writings, Menasseh Ben Israel's *Spes Israelis* (1650) – and Menasseh had read La Peyrère – and, finally, William Rabisha's extremely rare and radical critique of the story of the fall, *Adam Unvailed* (1649).[54] This last book is so scarce it now survives in only three copies, and references in contemporary sale catalogues are rare too (examples include Thomas Britton the 'Small-coal man', and Samuel Jeake the provincial radical).[55] Rabisha, an elusive figure who seems to have been at different times royalist cook and parliamentary captain, presented this, his only strictly theological work, 'In opposition to what ever hath been formerly declared by most men', as his title-page vaunts. He develops his own theory of the narrative of creation and fall, effectively turning it upside down by insisting that man was created 'meerly blinde, foolish, ignorant', and that the 'fall' was actually a promotion: 'as a coal is like a whole world set on fire, so was *Adam* like God in the knowledge of good and evil', for is it not God himself after the fall who declares 'Behold, the man is become as one of us to know good and evil'?[56]

No-one reads, or reads in the same way, all the books in their library, but Lodwick's own exegetical attitudes to Genesis owed much to the attitudes of these texts, on the one hand the radicalism of Rabisha and others, and on the other the biblical criticism of La Peyrère and Simon. Additionally, Lodwick was also aware of more socially conservative forms of doctrinal scepticism, specifically Jeremy Taylor's notorious attacks on original sin throughout the 1650s; Lodwick listed 'Taylor Of Original Sin', presumably either Taylor's *Unum Necessarium* (1655) or *Deus Justificatus* (1656).[57]

Lodwick's readings of Genesis exist in various generic forms. The most striking is his rather skeletal utopia, 'A Country Not Named', which features a disembodied narrator listing in brief chapters the beliefs and habits of an unknown and unlocated country. The country and its history offers a reinterpretation of the Genesis narrative, as it would have been revised by La Peyrère, Simon, and various others. First,

> Their Account of Time is of a far elder date then ours The beginning whereof is Elleue*n* Thousand seuen hundred and od yeares before we reckon the beginning of Time, beyond which they haue a tradition of far elder date by thousands of yeares ...

---

[54] MS Sloane 859, fols 38ʳ (Levellers), 47ʳ (Salmon), 36ʳ, 62ʳ (Penington), 17ʳ (Menasseh), 47ʳ (Rabisha).

[55] J. Bullord, *The Library of Mr. Tho. Britton, Smallcoal-man* (London, 1694), 7; M. Hunter, G. Mandelbrote, N. Ovenden, N. Smith (eds), *A Radical's Books: the Library Catalogue of Samuel Jeake of Rye (1623–90)* (London, 1999), 198–9.

[56] William Rabisha, *Adam Unvailed and Seen with Open Face* (London, 1649), t.p., 2, 7; Gen. 3: 22.

[57] Sloane 859, fol. 47ʳ. See P. Elmen, 'Jeremy Taylor and the Fall of Man', *MLQ*, 14 (1953) 139–48.

This 'beginning' point is, for the utopians, the date of the flood – merely for them a local flood – which pushes the original creation back uncounted millennia. In this mysterious interim men existed, long before the creation of Adam and Eve, for, as La Peyrère had said, how could Cain cry 'every one that findeth me shall slay me' if only his parents existed?[58] The utopians protest that the bible properly understood is only a record of Jewish history, and they also harbour doubts about original sin, predestination and the nature of the Atonement. Furthermore, they themselves keep records exactly in the manner Simon supposed the early Jews did: by a system of public record offices.[59] They are monotheists, following a theophany on a plain, but in possession of only the most minimal of commandments: consecrate the holy ground, celebrate the theophany annually, make no images of God, and meet every three days to sort out disputes. They later became Christians by sending 'Emissaryes' – a touch developed from Bacon's *New Atlantis* – to Jerusalem, who vouchsafe Christ's genuineness. But Christ to them is only a prophet who teaches what Reason can already instruct, and accordingly they are sceptical about the value of scripture-reading. Thus, in one of the most bizarre moments in an early-modern utopia, they entirely banish scripture-reading from their church services. Their society also shows the influence of Lodwick's language schemes and his earlier contact with the Hartlib circle: they possess a universal language imposed by the magistrate, and they have a particular interest in educational reform.[60]

It might be said that Lodwick was allowing himself to fantasize under the thin guise of fiction. But Lodwick corroborated each of his 'fictional' positions in non-fictional manuscripts, indeed even in the same manuscript in which the utopia is found. Sloane 913 is a reversed quarto: Lodwick wrote his utopia from the front in, and then when he had finished, reversed the quarto and wrote out a serious of theological disquisitions, many mirroring the concerns of his utopians. He also prepared a companion set of disquisitions in another manuscript of similar format. Thus, while the utopia starts with an adoption of a long chronology, preadamism, and a rejection of the universality of the bible, so the first disquisition starting at the opposite end of the manuscript concerns itself with 'the Originall of Mankind', offering a series of biblical and 'naturall' arguments for such beliefs. Again, when the utopians promise that in 'fitting time and place' they will explain their thoughts on original sin, the promise is not kept within the utopia, but Lodwick apportions one of the disquisitions in the companion manuscript to a comprehensive rejection of precisely that doctrine.[61]

Perhaps Lodwick's most thorough-going revisions of the Genesis narrative, though, are preserved in Abraham Hill's collection. In Sloane 2903 there is a sheaf of papers, mostly in Lodwick's hand, which comprehensively rewrites the orthodox understanding of both the status and the interpretation of Genesis. After a few

---

[58] Sloane 913, fols 2^{r}-3^{r}; La Peyrère, *Men Before Adam*, 'A Systeme', 149–50; Gen. 4:14.

[59] Sloane 913, fols 2^{v}, 21^{r}, 3^{v}–4^{v}.

[60] Sloane 913, fols 5^{r}–21^{r}, 21^{r}–5^{r}, 27^{v}–9^{r}.

[61] Sloane 913, fols 91^{v}-8^{v}; Sloane 899, fols 34^{v}–8^{r}.

pages arguing that Mosaic Law was not repealed by Christ, Lodwick settles into a discussion of the origin of the early books of the bible, noting that they were clearly compiled out of earlier records and that many books have been lost. He then lists 'Certain Queries', 32 questions comprising a radical critique of Genesis 1–4. In this list we see the conjunction of preadamism with a rejection of almost every doctrine erected on the fall narrative: men were created multiple, rational and mortal, but soon fell to sin, necessitating the creation of Adam and Eve. Adam and Eve did not really 'fall', as the fruit of the forbidden tree was as potent as God had named it, and in any case God was not that bothered by their disobedience. The curse he laid on them affected only them and not their posterity, and after they were expelled from Eden they went off to live with their neighbours.[62]

Lodwick next supplies a narrative extrapolation of his revisionary understanding of Genesis in two further documents, first, 'A Supposal of the manner of Creation', a long accommodation of Cartesian ideas of vortices to the account of the hexameron, an approach reminiscent of Newton's objections to Burnet. Secondly, he skips over the many thousands of years separating Genesis 1 from Genesis 2 and continues 'After a long succession of Time from the first Creation', a retelling of Genesis 2–3 adapted to Lodwick's various ideas on the potency of the two trees in Eden and the real benefit accrued by the fall. This position is exactly congruent with that of William Rabisha. The charge of these documents lies in their odd combination of extremely unfamiliar, heretical material with a kind of defiant commonsense. Lodwick, for instance, decides that it was not a serpent that tempted Eve but a baboon, 'Very Sportiue'.[63]

VI

The broad conclusion of this essay is unsurprising – natural philosophical speculation was informed and directed by its theological underlay, and in particular, geological and palaeontological hypotheses were reciprocally linked to heremeneutic decisions about the Genesis narrative. Now and then the connection had to be forced out into the open – Aubrey's exasperated annotation to Ray's letter, for instance, admitting incompatibility with Genesis, or Newton's unease at the liberties of Burnet's 'accommodation'. This also serves to remind us of the inherent instabilities of accommodation as a principle: at one extreme we may have a supposed literalism and at the other a complete rejection of the surface text as mere decoy, but between the extremes there are all sorts of shades of accommodation. 'Accommodation' in its original sense of Moses adapting his language to the vulgar capacity becomes entangled with 'accommodation' in the more colloquial sense of finding ways of *re*uniting the Mosaic description with contemporary natural philosophy. Lodwick is an excellent example of this entanglement. He rejected conventional chronology, attacked the textual integrity and Mosaic authorship of Genesis, abolished the fall and

---

[62] Sloane 2903, fols 145^{r}–57^{v}.

[63] Sloane 2903, fols. 158^{r}–64^{v}.

original sin, declared the flood to be a local phenomenon, and elsewhere extended his kind attentions to the trinity, to atonement, to usury, to divorce and a multitude of other topics. But his exegetical approach, like that of La Peyrère, worked with what was written. He always tries to provide some scriptural citation for heresy, and when he came to model his Cartesian-style creation, he carefully pegged each of his stages to one of the Mosaic Six Days. Like many others, Lodwick demoted the bible, but continued to take orders from it. The corollary to this within Lodwick's utopia is provided by his utopian church: anxious to be described as Christians, his utopians nonetheless forbid public readings from the bible in their services.[64]

Finally, what complicates the picture is the issue of secrecy. The geologically-driven operated in a more public fashion than the theologically-driven: Hooke and Halley delivered their ideas first as speech, not quite print, but not quite private jottings. Lodwick, I suggest, with his strong theological orientation, would have been immediately more open to question, and so he restricted his writings. What cannot be denied, though, is that Lodwick represents a hitherto unsuspected fount of heresy at the core of Royal Society administration in the 1680s. He himself was elected to the Council in 1686, and acted as an auditor of the accounts more times than anyone else in those years.[65] And he spent part of virtually every day in the company of other central society figures: particularly Hooke, Hill, and Halley. What they talked about in the coffee shops we have glimpsed; the tantalising question is *how*? 'To Martins and Garaways club: Ludowick, Hill, Aubery, Wild. Discoursd about Universal Character, about preadamits and of Creation' – if only Hooke had elaborated.

---

[64] Sloane 913, fols 16^{r}–18^{v}.

[65] Lodwick audited 1682–89, 1691. He was elected to the Council in 1686, 1689, 1691, 1693. See Hunter, *Morphology*, 206–7; T. Birch, *History of the Royal Society* (London, 1756–57), 4.167, 224, 332, 428, 502, 554; RS Library, Bray's Card Index to the Journal Books post 1687.

Chapter 3

Moral Tales at the Hearth: Jephthah's Daughter in the Seventeenth Century

Nicholas Cranfield

> Recorded stands my vow in Heav'n. Her doom is fix'd as fate. I'll hear no more. (Handel)

The narrative structure of Jephthah's vow and the sacrifice of his daughter in Judges 11 concentrates on six scenes: the embassy of the Gileadites; Jephthah's vow taken at Mizpah; his victory over the Ammonites; his triumphant return to his daughter's unaffected greeting; her lament and temporary exile in the mountains; and her final sacrifice.[1] These tableaux constituted the heart of the story as understood in the early modern period. This can be seen in the Tournai tapestries commissioned for Philip le Bon, Duke of Burgundy in 1470 and were probably represented in the tapestries once housed in the 'Greate Chamber' at Lacock Abbey.[2]

This essay explores a hitherto neglected area of biblical criticism and of commentary. It begins with a summary of the pre-Reformation literature concerning The Book of Judges, with specific reference to the passage concerning Jephthah's daughter (Judges 11:29–40) – a story better known now from Handel's late oratorio (1758). It then examines that passage from two different seventeenth-century perspectives, one literary, the other artistic, to argue that the biblical account was used to underpin the form and shape of government that further subjugated women in the age.

The first biblical commentary to appear in English on Judges is that of the leading London puritan, Richard Rogers. This essay will show that Rogers uses the biblical narrative to serve as much as an example for ordained ministers as for husbands and wives, as well as for magistrates. The daughter's willingness to die is a laudable example of feminine submission: 'her prosperitie should bee our desire and ioy'.[3] Rogers constructs a social pattern of a male-dominated hierarchy in which the

[1] L. Reau, *Iconographie de l'Art Chrétien* (Paris, 1955–58), II, 234–6.

[2] T.E. Vernon, 'Inventory of Sir Henry Sharington', *Wiltshire Archaeological Society Magazine*, 63 (1968), 75.

[3] R. Rogers, *A commentary on the Whole Book of Judges Preached First and Delivered in Sundrie Lectures* (London, 1615), 582.

'Jephthah's Daughter', artist unknown. The Royal Collection © 2003, Her Majesty Queen Elizabeth II

woman is punished for daring to come out of the house without the due permission of her father.

The second source is to be found in a painting that may have been from the inside lid of a marriage chest or other domestic coffer. The so-called 'Windsor panel' appears to be unique in its chosen subject matter. It illustrates scenes from the life of the intrepid warrior Jephthah. It conspicuously fails to include the nameless daughter's two months' sojourn in the hills and so emphasizes her submissive stance as she stands before her executioner in the seemingly incongruous surrounds of a walled garden at Windsor. By its use in a domestic context the fiery hearth at which Jephthah's daughter came to be sacrificed was a scene made all too familiar to women in a later age.

I

Jephthah's vow finds a parallel in the promise Saul made before his battle with the Philistines (1 Samuel 14:24–46). The parallel is striking as it roots the dilemma within the context of the God-given struggle for Israel's domination. Since the overriding concern for the people of Israel, then as now, was to establish a sacral homeland, the unintended consequence of a vow could not stand in the way: Jephthah's own lineage may have come to an abrupt halt (his daughter was an only child who died childless) but the nation's security had been saved.

Saul's oath is not the only parallel to be found in the pages of Holy Scripture. Many commentators are reminded of the sacrifice of Abraham and Isaac (Genesis 22) but this is less satisfactory. Dr Phyllis Trible has roundly pointed out that Jephthah is no Abraham since 'distrust, not faith, has singled out his one and only child'.[4] Also Jephthah is not called by YWHW in the same way in which Abraham experienced his call, even though both of them are celebrated saviours of their people.

Two non-biblical parallels are found in classical mythology, of which the story of Iphigenia, the daughter of Agamemnon, is the more pertinent. Agamemnon promises to sacrifice his daughter in order to gain a fair wind to set sail for Troy. He lures her to his presence pretending that she is to marry Achilles. But whereas the Mizpah vow is open-ended, the priest Calchas had already singled Iphigenia out as the sacrificial victim. Iphigenia's fate is the tragedy of a death foretold in which the parent's role has already been scripted.

This myth, and the shame of it, was commemorated yearly (cf. Judges 11:40) with a festival that was apparently first held at Brauron and then later transferred to Athens. According to Pausanias (Description of Greece III, 16, 8) this was the cult of Artemis Tauropolis, but some have said that Pausanias, for once, may have been wrong as 'she was neither Artemis nor Athena, but the native Syrian goddess Astarte'.[5]

---

[4] P. Trible, *Texts of Terror: Literary and Feminist Readings of Biblical Narratives* (Philadelphia, 1984), 102.

[5] J.G. Frazer, *Pausanias's Description of Greece* (London, 1898), III, 340–41.

The second classical tale is that of Idomeneus, King of Crete, one of the leading chiefs to fight at Troy (Iliad, xiii, 210f). At his return he was caught up in a storm that threatened to capsize his fleet. The circumstances of his own immediate personal safety, and not the outcome of a war or the ultimate survival of a whole tribe, occasions his vow and he pledges to sacrifice to Poseidon whom (or what) ever he first met. At his landfall it is his son who comes to greet him and Idomeneus is reluctantly obliged to affect his oath. On the other hand, we might remember that Odysseus made no such rash oath at *his* homecoming for all that it might have made it the more expeditious. His dog survived.

Whereas the slaughter of Iphigenia did not adversely affect the fortunes of Agamemnon, at least not directly as there is no sense that Agamemnon is under a curse for it when he sets sail, the killing of the son of Idomeneus is revenged; Idomeneus is driven out by his own people and forced into exile, going to live in Calabria where he founded a community at Salentini.

Trible has found, in authors as diverse as Origen (c.185-c.254), Chrysostom (*c*.347–407), Gregory Nazianzenus (*c*.329–90), Theodoret of Cyr (*c*.393–*c*.458), Procopius of Gaza (*c*.499–565), Ambrose (*c*.339–97), Augustine (354–430), Jerome (*c*.331 x 347–420), and Epiphanius (*c*.315–403), as well as in Ephraim the Syrian (*c*.306–78), the Venerable Bede (*c*.673–735), Hugh of St Victor (*c*.1096–141), and Thomas Aquinas (1225–74) – not all of whom would have been available to Richard Rogers – that the story concentrates on the ambiguity of false oaths without comment on the luckless daughter. The biblical hermeneutic, which she sees as being male-focussed throughout, commemorates Jephthah but not his daughter.[6] By the intertestamental period the Judge has become one of the heroes (Ecclesiasticus 46:11–12), later incorporated in the catalogue of saints (Hebrews 11:32–4). This predisposition to exalt Jephthah but to ignore his part in his daughter's death is repeated in the Early Fathers. Where there is discussion of the moral dilemma it is always argued that Jephthah performed the vow that he had made according to the promise that he had given and for that was rewarded by God.

The Levitical Code explicitly condemns human sacrifice (Leviticus 18:21, 20:2–5, Deuteronomy 13:31, 18:10). Although such outrages took place occasionally (2 Kings 16:3) they clearly breached the covenant. This obliged some Jewish writers either to suggest that God punished Jephthah or to accommodate the sacrifice in some other way. One early Jewish legend suggested that Jephthah was dismembered for breaking the Levitical Code,[7] while the Rabbinical author David Kimchi later attempted to redress the balance by reading the text of Judges 11:39 somewhat ungrammatically to argue that the sentence meted out on the daughter was one of lifelong celibacy under house arrest. Most Christian authors, on the other hand, have seen fit to follow Luther's view that while some commentators affirmed that he did not sacrifice her, the text was clear enough.

---

[6] Trible, *Texts of Terror*, 115.

[7] L. Ginzburg, *The Legends of the Jews* (Philadelphia, 1909–38), IV, 43–4.

Most writers recognised Jephthah's mistaken zeal but nevertheless commended his strong piety. In Hugh of St Victor and Joannes Arboreus, Jephthah even becomes a type of Christ with his daughter prefiguring the Church (although this reading inverts the sacrifice since Christ died for the Church).

For Thomas Aquinas the central question was how vows were to be undertaken and their obligations met – a reading that lies behind the later mid- sixteenth-century debate about vows (expressly monastic and priestly):

> Other actions are good in themselves, and for this reason can be a matter of a vow, yet they may have an evil result, in which case the vow may not be observed. This happened in the case of *Jephte*, whom as related in *Judges*, made a vow to the Lord ... This vow could have had an evil result, were he to meet some animal that should not be sacrificed, such as an ass or a human being, as indeed happened. Hence Jerome says, 'In vowing he was foolish to because he did not use his discretion, and in keeping the vow he was impious'. Yet the Scripture says that the Spirit of the Lord came upon him, because his faith and devotion which moved him to make the vow were from the Holy Spirit. For this reason, because of the victory he won, and because he probably repented of his evil deed (which, however, prefigured something good) he is placed in the catalogue of the saints.
> (T Aquinas, *Summa Theologiae* 2a, 2ae, 88.2 ad. 2)

The conscience-saving clause that Jephthah *probably* repented is breathtaking. Ambrose similarly had wrestled with the problems raised by another 'shameful promise': that given by Herod when the daughter of Herodias was sent into entertain her king's guests (Mark 6:14–29 and parallels):

> A good disposition ought to be open and straightforward, so that one may utter words without deceit, and possess one's soul with singleness of intent, and not delude another with false words, and not promise anything dishonourable. If he has made such a promise it is far better for him not to fulfill it, than to fulfill what is shameful. Sometimes people bind themselves by a solemn oath and, though they came to know that they ought not to have made the promise, fulfill it in consideration of their oath.
> (Ambrose, Duties of the Clergy 3.12, 76–7)

These readings in The Fathers were appealed to in the early modern period when Reformers debated the status of ordination, whether undertaken by secular or religious clergy. Erasmus had written first on the debate over oaths. In his *Colluquy of Rash Vows; or Pilgrimages to Sacred Places* (*c*.1509) he averred that were he Pope, 'I should not be obdurate in releasing those that are engaged by them'.[8]

Around 1544 Martin Bucer debated the issue with Bartholomew Latomus (1490–1570). Latomus argued from the Old Testament that all vows have to be fulfilled, while Bucer held that it would depend on whether the vow was or was not acceptable in the first place. Writing in 1551 Godfrey Tilmann made the link between celibacy,

[8] D. Erasmus, *Pilgrimages to Saint Mary of Walsingham and Saint Thomas of Canterbury*, ed. J.G. Nichols (London, 1849), xxii.

monasticism and oath-keeping virtually inescapable; for him Jephthah's daughter and John the Baptist are types of a nun and a monk.[9]

The Scot, George Buchanan (1506–82) wrote a Latin play, *Jepthes, sive Votum*, in France when this debate raged between Paris and Strasbourg. Buchanan, who taught in Paris, Bordeaux and Coimbra before his eventual return to Edinburgh in 1556, had wanted to translate the Euripidean tragedy of Iphigenia but Erasmus had already done so.[10] To Buchanan – who, in an earlier play, *Baptistes, sive Calumnia*, had already courted disapproval for portraying Henry VIII as Herod and Sir Thomas More as John the Baptist[11] – Jephthah was a liberator like Christ. In the voice of the angelic prologue, Buchanan concedes only that 'lest Jephthah grow proud and insolent with success he will at once be overwhelmed with domestic loss, and his arrogant airs will be shattered'.[12] Without irony Buchanan dedicated his play to Charles Cossa, Comte de Brissac, who was Marshal of France and commander of Turin.[13]

II

Though no English language considerations on The Book of Judges seem to have been produced in the sixteenth century, two such works appeared within a decade of each other in the reign of James VI and I. An anonymous ballad, *JEFFA Judge of Israel*, was one of 128 ballads entered in the register of the Stationers' Company (14 December 1624) and had probably circulated for a few years previously.[14] As with so many ballads, few copies exist. The commentary of Richard Rogers, on the other hand, was nothing if not substantial, and intended by its author to be a benchmark for the scholastic community. Its 970 folio pages contain one hundred and three sermons that treat, verse by verse, of the whole biblical book.[15] Dr Glyn Redworth has questioned whether both works may have been found to be topical when contemporaries saw James VI and I sacrifice his own daughter, Elizabeth of Bohemia, to the interests of the Emperor.

Richard Rogers (1551–1618) was a graduate of Christ's College, Cambridge (1570). Richard Bancroft cited him as a member of the Braintree classis.[16] From

---

[9] R. Lebeque, *La tragedie religieuse en France* (Paris, 1929).

[10] D. Erasmus, *Euripidis Hecuba et Iphigenia latine facte* (Paris, 1506), ed. J.H. Waszink (Amsterdam, 1969).

[11] J.M. Aitken, *The Trial of George Buchanan before the Lisbon Inquisition* (London, 1939), xviii-xx.

[12] 'porro ne Iepthes quoque/se metiatur exitu huius proelii/et intumescat insolens rebus bonis, /damno obruetur protinus domestico,/cedentque fracti contumaces spiritus' (lines 51–5).

[13] G. Buchanan, *Tragedies*, ed. P. Sharratt and P.G. Walsh (Edinburgh, 1983).

[14] E. Arber (ed.), *Transcript of the registers of the Company of Stationers of London, 1554–1640 AD*, 5 vols (London and Birmingham, 1875– 94), IV, 93, STC 14498.5.

[15] STC 21204.

[16] R. Bancroft, *Daungerous Positions and Proceedings* (London, 1593), 84.

1576 or 1577 until his death he was 'Preacher of the Word of God', in other words a Puritan lecturer, in the parish of Wethersfield in Essex. His immediate successor was Stephen Marshall, later of Smectymnuus fame. Wethersfield itself was a Trinity Hall living; from 1570 until he died in 1613 John Ludham was the vicar, succeeded by Robert Pasfield.

Throughout his life the noted puritan Rogers attracted adverse attention from the authorities of the established Church. He was suspended for eight months in 1583 for opposing Whitgift's Three Articles, was excommunicated on 30 November 1589, and later suspended by Archbishop Whitgift for refusing to subscribe to the *ex officio* oath – the order rescinding the suspension came through on the day Whitgift died.[17] In James's reign Rogers seems to have had a less provocative career, although he narrowly avoided prosecution during the primary Visitation of Bishop Thomas Ravis when Lord Knollys of Greys intervened on his behalf with Archbishop Bancroft. Rogers even dedicated the second edition of his *Seaven Treatises containing such directions as is gathered out of the Holie Scriptures* to the King in 1605.

Rogers' commentary was rooted in sermons that he had preached over the years and was far more than a compendium of past homilies. As he explained in his letter of 20 January 1615/16 to Lord Chief Justice Sir Edward Coke, to whom he dedicated the volume, it was more difficult to write a commentary than compose sermons[18] but he hoped he might benefit future students and preachers by choosing a book of Scripture for which there were no extant sermons or lectures.[19] He intended to read the book in the context of the Pentateuch and sought also the broader Christological perspective in the Old Testament, since although Christ may not be readily apparent, he is seen 'darkly and by types and figures, as God saw it meete for those ages'.[20] Above all, he offered the book 'as a poore pledge and memoriall to Gods church of my fidelitie, power and love'.[21]

The book's copyright was entered at the Stationers' Company on 29 October 1613,[22] two years before eventual publication. The well-established publisher, Felix Kingston, excused the delay, 'the coppie being very badly written and the Author farre off, and unable to tend the presse'.[23] Apparently Rogers did not attend to the actual printing; Ludham's death in Wethersfield might have increased the author's local pastoral outreach, while his increasing age may also have told against him: in 1613 he was 63 and no longer the vigorous young man who steps out of the pages of his extant diary of the Armada years.[24]

---

17 *ODNB s.v.* 'Rogers, Richard'.

18 Rogers, *A commentary*, B3.

19 Rogers, *A commentary*, B3^{v}.

20 Rogers, *A commentary*, B3*^{r}.

21 Rogers, *A commentary*, A3*^{r}.

22 Arber, *Registers*, III, 244^{v}.

23 Rogers, *A commentary*, Corrigenda.

24 M.M. Knappen, *Two Elizabethan Puritan Diaries* (Chicago, 1933).

Rogers first set out a classical exposition of his exegetical method. It defines the writing of commentaries in the early modern period and provides a textbook case history by which to judge his own work:

> The order which I purpose to observe in the Lectures upon this booke, is first to give the short summe of the chapters: then to devide every chapter into parts, for the better distinguishing the points thereof, that they may be better understood, and more clearly seene into: thirdly I give the sense of the verses more fully, and lay forth the doctrine with the reasons, and use therof, though for the most part, they be not alwaies expressly set downe, which manner of handling the diverse histories of this booke (as also I thinke the same of our preaching out of all Scriptures) namely, that after the meaning and sense, apt and fit instructions should be drawne out, with the application, the present state, need, and use of the hearers, plainely and pithily as may be for their best edifying I hold meetest to be used.[25]

To do this he discoursed on his text as a preacher might in the pulpit; two sermons, numbered 67 and 68, are given over to the account of Jephthah and the Ammonites. The first, as a prelude to the issues raised by the oath, takes up the story of the Ammonite challenge to Jephthah (Judges 11:25–8 and Rogers 564–6), while the second concentrates on the verses 29–33 (567–74) and 34–40 (575–88). The bulk of his consideration centres upon the outcome of 'the rashe oath', as the 1568 Bishop's Bible had it, and not with its undertaking or with the battle against the Ammonites themselves.

The exposition of Judges 11:29 is followed by Paul's claim that 'when the Lord appointeth any man to any speciall calling, hee gives him gifts for the discharge of it' (568). This is offered to all humanity but there is a higher duty expected of those called to be ordained Ministers: 'so the Ministers much more, as the calling is farre more excellent, when hee sendeth them to any people to convert them and make them of his militant Church, hee stores them up by love, zeale and labour, to set their gifts of knowledge a worke and maketh great change among the people by their ministerie' (568). Self-appointed ministers who set themselves up are not to be trusted: 'They who are unfit to doe the Lords message to them to whom they are sent, are not sent by him, but seeke themselves and their own profit, and not the peoples' (568).

There then follows a classic exposition of the oath undertaken at Mizpah: 'This vow, though he had meant well, was ill made and in great ignorance, in that he did not make it more distinctly and advisedly' (569). Like Luther before him, Rogers dismisses any suggestion that the vow might have been commuted to sentence the girl to lifelong virginity. Thereafter, like many other male commentators before and since, he is more concerned about likely aspects of ritual uncleanliness that might have arisen from the oath; what would have been the outcome had a dog first run out to greet its master?

---

25 Rogers, *A commentary*, B3**r.

Rogers also asks whether Jephthah was right to take an oath at all, since although he is included among the ranks of the faithful, he had nonetheless sinned greatly: 'What was a lesser sin for him became the occasion of a greater sin', that of homicide, as it would for Herod (Bede, Homilies on the Gospels 2.23). Lest God be thought to have blessed Jephthah's actions directly, Rogers argues that the spirit which descended upon him at his oath taking (Judges 11:30, 31) was the spirit of courage and not the third Person of the Trinity. The vow was to be seen as an example of how we must make a 'firme covenant, to prayer and reading,' as vows that are agreeable to God's word are lawful (571). God clearly gives his spirit and the victory to those he chooses (Judges 11:32, 33) and so 'setteth us forward in our duties doing' (572), an example not only to ordained ministers, but to husbands and wives and magistrates as Rogers concludes with a list of dutiful exemplars from Pharaoh (Exodus 14:28) to Samson (Judges 16:20).

Rogers held that Jephthah had acted wrongly: 'all may see what effect comes of rashnes, and how unbeseeming a companion it is to a wise man, who should ponder his doings, and weigh his words with reason, yea religion, even in the balances of the sanctuarie, that is, by the word of God, before they be uttered. The best fruite of it is sorrow and repentance' (575). Rather than quote Robert Cawdrey's influential *Store House of Similes* (London 1600), and its example of the city faced with its vigilant enemy, Rogers ends with the adage 'Rashnesse doth nothing well'. The Bible for its part was not short of examples of rash behaviour, whether in Herod, or 'the like had *David* done, if he had not bin staied by *Abigail* against the house of *Nabal*', or in the Prodigal Son who 'might in no wise be staied from his purpose, as though he had gone about some great and weightie worke' (575).

From Judges 11:35 Rogers teases out five distinct lessons as being the core teaching from the story of Jephthah. First, the principal theme that God humbles the proud and that those 'who have surfeited of God's own delighting, then will be brought low' (577), which Rogers then illustrates and which finds its highest recognition in the salutation of the Virgin Mary (Luke 1:38). God's ways differ from those of the society in which we live and as such can overturn human order.

Second, and even more uncomfortably perhaps for a modern readership, is the admonition that 'the best delights and greatest pleasures of this life, in which wee have had exceeding comfort, as hee had in his daughter, may possibly and doe often time to our great sorrow and discontentment', so that there is a sin in setting our hearts on riches (578). Beyond material happiness Rogers clearly knows the social joys and appetites found inside families. He himself married only because he could not cope with single life. Rogers takes the high moral ground of the seventeenth-century father and so adduces from the text the third 'instruction for children, that they had not need to be crosses to their parents, by loosenes and disobedience' (578). Without her father first giving her an exeat, Jephthah's daughter should have stayed at home. Similarly, the first row Pepys records with his wife is her refusal to accept his authority when she had gone out of doors without his consent.[26]

Rogers's fourth observation is one that all subsequent commentators have overlooked: Jephthah had ignored the provisions of Leviticus 27:2–8 that allow for the redemption of a son or of a daughter. Consequently his daughter was sacrificed through fear and ignorance of the Law. Even in the two-month interim period Jephthah had not consulted with the high priest, showing his folly. We can overlook the somewhat simplistic understanding of the Temple cult available to Rogers at this point and salute rather his perception that Jephthah's failing is as much in the taking of an oath rashly as it was in the ignorance of the Law 'that held him in that grievous error'. Crucially for Christians, therefore, the story shows the need to learn the Law so that they too can profit by its benefits: 'But the text giving occasion rather to urge this care upon the better sort, we may iustly bewaile it, how long it is ere even many a good Christian attaine to that measure of competent and necessarie knowledge, which might guide his course' (579).

Rogers concludes that all that can be said of Jephthah is that in his ignorance of the Law he at least sought to keep a good conscience: 'Better is he by many degrees, who in that which hee knowes is carefull to doe the same: then another who swelleth with pride, and is puffed up with great knowledge in the letter, when he seeth not the end of it, much lesse attaineth to it' (580). Behind this we can hear that Rogers, like so many Puritans, was as zealous for the upkeeping of the Law as he was fearful of those who claimed to keep it; a nice dilemma for many evangelicals, then and since.

Rogers shows real enthusiasm for the daughter's acquiescence to whatever the father had enjoined of the Lord, begging only a two months allowance that she and her companions (the first mention of any human society that she has enjoyed at Mizpah) might go to the hill country, and commends her honour in returning promptly to face death as an example of appropriate filial submission (587). She accedes to the unintended consequences of her father's foolhardiness and 'her prosperitie should be our desire and ioy' (582). 'This her readie and obedient affection (setting aside the error thereof) is a cleare glasse for youth to looke in, to shew their readinesse in obeying their parents, it being agreeable to the law of God, which is required of them, and so in obeying their governors set over them' (581).

The 'setting aside the error thereof' remains the stumbling block for most readers today, whether their approach is as single-minded as that adopted by Trible, or whether they view the story by the light, albeit dim, of human justice. Rogers endorses a hierarchy that placed the father at the head of the household and the godly magistrate above all, claiming that the teachings of the 'cleare glasse' are simple and to be learned by the young if society is not to decay:

---

[26] R Latham, W.Matthews, et al. (eds), *The diary of Samuel Pepys*, 11 vols (London, 1970-83) I, 16–17 (13 January 1660). Similarly, following the Soham Killings in August 2002, a writer was forced to resign from *The Herald* for suggesting, 'Had the parents of Holly Wells and Jessica Chapman kept the Lord's Day, their daughters would still be alive', an opinion commonly held by some members of the Free Church of Scotland.

> Which may go to teach our youth, and particularly the maidens of our age, to learne this point of obedience of her; namely not to bee their own carvers, to cut out their liberty to themselves, while they be under the governement and authoritie of their parents or other; to go where they list, and to thinke themselves too good to crave leave, especially for their lawfull going forth ... going commonly to such places, & to such ends, as they wish afterward that they had staied at home, doe with shame and sorrow, reape the iust fruit of their disobedience.
> (R. Rogers, 583–4)

The annual festival of mourning for her ensures that she is not forgotten 'and besides that, it is likely enough they did it, that all parents might be warned to make no such vowes' (588). The festival also provides one last admonition that Rogers is not slow to extrapolate from the text:

> And therefore the blind and wicked practise, of spending the twelve daies at the Nativitie in play, revell and disorder, also the leaud customes still retained in some parts of this land, to keepe their prophane customary feasts and drinkings in the Sabbath, with al other misrule of like sort, are utterly to be rooted out, and better plants set in their roomes, if it may be.
> (R. Rogers, 588)

III

Representing Jephthah's conquests and his daughter's sacrifice was seemingly no more common in artistic terms than in literary circles. Although the portrayal of the last scene is potentially as dramatic as the death of Holofernes or of Sisera, few artists turned their attention to it. Customarily pre-Reformation depictions show the fated girl greeting her victorious father at the gate of his home. Although representations of her final sacrifice and execution may have been confused for those which show the scene at Tauris – one myth being misunderstood for another – this may simply reflect the habit of sacralizing secular heroines because of the commonly shared cult of death in classical and Renaissance Christianity.[27]

A miniature from a German Bible painted at Augsburg in 1457 is typical.[28] A young blonde woman stands left in front of a crenellated wall that runs between the two towers of her father's castellated home in Mizpah while her father, advancing towards her on foot with his soldiery, raises his right hand above her in salutation, his fingers distinctively held out in blessing.[29] A similar illustration in the 1568 Bishop's Bible indicates that the story is one about human folly rather than about God's saving covenant, a distortion most commonly found in discussions of the narrative of the Prodigal Son where the rash acts of the protagonist form the central focus of the account (Luke 15:13, etc).

---

[27] I. Donaldson, *The Rapes of Lucretia* (New York, 1982), 167.

[28] Munich, Staatsbibliothek, Cgm. 206, fol.125^{v}.

[29] M Brion (ed.), *The Bible in Art The Old Testament* (London, 1956), pl. 142.

In the German mediaeval painting the girl plays on a fiddle, rejoicing as she comes out to meet her father and her country's saviour with music and with dancing. In the Biblical text the daughter's response before the reproof and ultimate sentence of her father is not one of self-pity; it is best paraphrased as 'Be it unto me according to thy word'. By contrast, Buchanan's heroine laments the harsh fate that awaits women at their birth when, though free of blame, they are consumed by the envious teeth of malevolent gossips.[30] The words *tuppîm* and *mêhōlôt* ('with timbrel and dancing') sound as a refrain that at once links the unnamed Gileadite woman to Miriam, who similarly turned out to greet Moses and the triumphant Israelites after they had deceived Pharaoh and crossed the Red Sea into safety (Exodus 15:19–21). They are later used for the greeting of David after his slaying the Philistines (1 Samuel 18:6, 7), a further indication that they are a quasi-formulaic pattern of words associated with the way in which Israel's saviour was heralded. Implicitly they recognise the path to preferment that Jephthah's biblical sanctity will take alongside those other types of the Christ, Moses and David.

However, Jephthah was not widely seen by artists in the Christian West as an obvious antitype for Christ. Few narrative paintings of the scenes exist and in many cases these are the decorative work of less widely recognised artists. In Baroque art, for instance, only some fifty depictions of the greeting between father and daughter, and a further three-dozen or so of her death, survive. None is listed for her self-imposed exile in the mountains.[31] Lucas van Leiden, Zanchi, Simon Vouet (for a 1623 Gobelin tapestry series commissioned by Louis XIII), Pierre Mignard, Boucher, and van Loo all tried their hand at the daughter's greeting. Strozzi, Maffei, Pittoni, Le Brun, and Rembrandt, along with van Leiden, Vouet and Mignard, are among the better known artists who at some point or other illustrated Judges 11:39, a scene which can first be identified in a carved capital at Vézelay.

With the exception of Strozzi and Vouet the absence of any interest in the gripping dramatic potential of the scenes by the Caravaggisti is perhaps the more remarkable argument from silence. Interest in the daughter's two months' solace in the hills only comes with the Romantics in the nineteenth century; Sir John Millais, Charles Ricketts, Alexandre Cabanel and even James Tissot (for an illustrated Hebrew Bible (1896-1904)), are among artists who depict this passage.[32]

The unique 'Windsor panel', as discussed by Dr Hearn,[33] is a remarkable document of domestic immediacy, feminine subjugation, and strict household control. It is painted on walnut, the scarcity of which at once suggests that it may well have come from a valuable piece of furniture; traces of hinges and a repair to where a

[30] 'o feminarum sorte vulgus aspera/productum in auras, quas, licet culpa vacent,/rumor malignus dente rodit invido'! Buchanan with the Euripidean tale in mind names her Iphis whereas in Pseudo-Philo she is named Seila (Pseudo-Philo, 39–40).

[31] Reau, *Iconographie*, and A. Pilger, *Barockthemen* (Budapest, 1974), II, 119–22.

[32] H.A. Roberts, *Iconographic Index to Old Testament Subjects represented ... in the ... Fine Arts Library, Harvard University* (New York and London, 1987), 71.

[33] K. Hearn, *Dynasties* (London, 1995), 115–16.

handle could have been inserted may suggest that it came from the inside lid of a coffer.[34] The panel measures 41.9 x 185.7 cms and comprises two horizontal boards, respectively 30.3cms and 11 cms wide. This format is not that different from some surviving Renaissance Italian *cassoni*; 'The Adventures of Ulysses' in The Walker Art Gallery, Liverpool, measures 42.8 x 153 cms, and the Pesellino 'Triumphs' in the Isabella Stewart Gardner Museum, Boston are both 42.5 x 157.4 cms.[35]

Such narratives also appear on Quattrocento *spalliere*,[36] and even in Finiguerra's picture chronicle. Unlike the well-known graffiti of the pavement in Siena cathedral which shows the two processions of the victorious Jephthah and his welcoming daughter, Finiguerra only illustrates the moment when 'IETTE' is about to kill his daughter. She kneels before his raised sword with her hands tied behind her back as he grasps her hair roughly; a representation closely based on his own 'The Sacrifice of Isaac'.[37] It is with such examples that the picture, although clearly northern in inspiration, invites comparison. Such a sequence of scenes would constitute a quotidian reminder to women of their place in contemporary society.

There is still no ready agreement about the 'Windsor panel's' actual date, place of composition or provenance. After it first came into the Royal Collection in 1955[38] Oliver Millar reckoned it was most probably sixteenth century.[39] In particular he drew attention to the Spanish style armour, and found that the Ammonite rout was reminiscent of a work from the 1540s depicting the Battle of the Spurs which is also now in the Royal Collection.[40] The decorative quality of the painting is similar to much ceramic painting,[41] and the unevenness of handling argues for at least two hands, one responsible for the architectural 'backdrop', the other for the theatrical figures in the foreground.

More recently Richard Williams of The Courtauld Institute, London, discovered that the three scenes (the daughter's two-month sojourn in the hills is omitted) are taken from four Flemish engravings of the story by Gerard de Jode after Hans Bol (1534–93),[42] but are adapted to an unmistakably English landscape; Windsor Castle,

---

[34] Hearn, *Dynasties*, 156.

[35] G. Hughes, *Renaissance Cassoni. Masterpieces of early Italian Art. Painted Marriage Chests 1400–1550* (Alfriston and London, 1997).

[36] A.B. Barriault, *Spalliera Paintings in Renaissance Tuscany* (Pennsylvania, 1994), passim and esp. 99–101.

[37] S. Colvin, *A Florentine Picture Chronicle by Maso Finiguerra* (London, 1898), pl. 42.

[38] It was purchased at Sotheby's by HM The Queen on the first anniversary of her coronation, 2 June 1954 (lot 60).

[39] O. Millar, *The Tudor, Stuart and Early Georgian pictures in the collection of HM The Queen* (London, 1963), I, 70 and pll. 28–30.

[40] Millar, *Tudor, Stuart and Early Georgian Pictures*, I, 54 and pl. 9.

[41] I owe this observation, and many other helpful comments on this essay, to Dr Dugald McLellan, Senior Tutor at St Paul's College in the University of Sydney.

[42] Hearn, *Dynasties*, 115. Photographs of the original de Jode engravings, missing from the Kupferstichkabinett in Berlin since the Second World War, are in the Warburg Institute, London.

viewed from the south, closes the landscape beyond the battle of the Ammonites, while the sacrifice of Jephthah's daughter takes place in the incongruous surroundings of a walled Tudor garden and parkland. Others, including the present author, have noted that the handling of paint on the fletton bricks of the walls of the park is strikingly similar to that in Robert Peake's now rediscovered Henry, Prince of Wales on Horseback, of 1611 (Parham Park). It may be significant that Robert Peake's son would himself later be responsible for importing and adapting engravings by Bolswert and de Vos for use in Laud's much detested illustrated Bible.[43]

The 'Windsor panel' comprises three scenes in the Jephthah saga painted as a continuous narrative, from left to right. In the first we see the rout of the Ammonite forces by Jephthah. In the background is Windsor Castle as it would have appeared in the sixteenth and seventeenth centuries. Although the accuracy of the view is remarkable, apart from the inexplicable addition of a turret above the Round Tower, direct comparison is difficult since all surviving contemporary images, both drawings and woodcuts – including that in Braun and Hogenberg's *Civitates Orbis Terrarum* (Cologne, 1572) – depict the castle from the northern aspect.[44] Depictions of the castle from the south east only emerge later, notably in the engravings of Wenceslaus Hollar. Drawn between 1659 and 1663, these were not published until 1672 in Elias Ashmole's *History of the Garter*. The spurious turret does not appear in the celebrated aerial view of the castle undertaken for John Norden's *Survey* in 1607 – a time of much new building in the castle and grounds[45] – so may be an architectural caprice or a short-lived superstructure.

The question that remains to be asked is why Windsor was depicted at all? Windsor itself was only used occasionally as a royal residence in the reign of Elizabeth I who preferred Greenwich and Richmond, where she died. Its use under James VI and I was usually limited to brief visits in July and September at the start and end of each summer progress. The reconstructed pattern for his reign suggests that the King was in residence at Windsor for rarely more than a week or 10 days at a stretch, and at times only for a day;[46] the King would be at Oatlands one day, spend the next day in Windsor with a very busy schedule before turning back to London.[47] During James's seemingly only winter visit, in December 1603, he drew up sanctions with regard to papists and recusants to be implemented by the archbishop and his suffragans.[48] Towards the end of his reign James varied his visits little: in July 1621 he planned

---

[43] G. Henderson, 'Bible Illustration in the Age of Laud', *Transactions of the Cambridge Bibliographical Society*, VIII (1986), 173–216.

[44] M. Aston, *The King's Bedpost* (London, 1993),172-5.

[45] BL, MS Harleian 3749, illustrated in R.R. Tighe, and J.E. Davis, *Annals of Windsor* (London, 1858), frontispiece. See also C.G.E. Bunt, *Windsor Castle through three centuries* (Leigh-on-Sea, 1949) plates 10, 11, 12 *et al.*

[46] As the Venetian ambassador Giovanni Battista Lionello noted on 14 July 1616.

[47] *Calendar of State Papers: Italy 1615–17*, 353.

[48] Public Record Office (PRO). State Papers (SP). 14/5/25, 15 December 1603.

his intended 1622 visit to Scotland there,[49] and was at Windsor again in April 1623, writing to Buckingham in Madrid.[50]

Apart from the city plagues two other reasons made Windsor an attractive if occasional lodging. First, the outlying woods were ideal for the King's relentless pursuit of the chase; 'the king has been hunting all day and killed a stag' one court correspondent noted in September 1609.[51] Ten years later the King got the French Ambassador out of bed early to go hunting at seven in the morning.[52] The Venetian Ambassador Contarini had noted at the end of the summer progress the year before that the King 'amuses himself with his usual pleasures of the chase, of which he never seems to be weary, increase in age by no means damping his ardour for them'.[53] When gout and arthritis took on he famously assuaged the pain by resting his legs inside the carcasses of the freshly caught trophies of the hunt.

The other calendar date that drew the King to Windsor was the installation of knights of the Most Sovereign Order of the Garter: in the first year of his reign the King held the St George's Day feast at Windsor [54] to admit his elder son to the Order, returning in 1606 to admit his Danish brother in law, King Christian IV. When he attended in person this saved the newly created knights the not inconsiderable expense of horses and liveries for the necessary pageant of their journey from the Court down to Windsor, a consideration that weighed with the King himself when the Duke of York was admitted to the Order at Whitsun 1611.[55] It was pointedly noticed that, although he remained in London in 1608 for the installation of his then favourite, the Earl of Dunbar, he accorded him the notable favour of turning out to watch him ride out of the city.[56]

The pattern that emerges of the King's attendance at Windsor and his use of the castle suggests an early summer visit in May, at least in the first years of his reign, with visits either side of the summer progress in July, and then in early September. It does not, however, suggest why any artist would seek to introduce a view of the castle that was as topographically accurate as the 'Windsor panel'. There seems to be very little to argue for a connection with either Arabella Stuart or with Hardwick and the Cavendishes as some have wondered,[57] and evidence to link the panel with the royal use of Windsor is still lacking.

---

[49] *HMC Report 15, Appendix Part I (Mar)* 95.

[50] BL, MS Harleian 6987 fol. 69.

[51] PRO, SP. 14/48/1, 1 September 1609.

[52] J. Nichols, *The Progresses, Processions and Magnificent Festivities of James I* (London, 1828), III, 569.

[53] *Calendar of State Papers: Italy 1617–19*, 525.

[54] PRO, SP. 14/2/33, 4 July 1603.

[55] *Calendar of State Papers: Venetian 1610–13*, 227.

[56] *Calendar of State Papers: Italy 1607–10*, 245.

[57] K. Hearn, letter to the author, 17 May 1995. Dr Redworth's helpful comments on the fate of Elizabeth of Bohemia might suggest a more profitable link but there is no apparent evidence for this.

The second scene is clearly intended as the principal subject as it takes up more than half the width of the overall design. The heroic Jephthah is at the centre of the picture. He is at the head of a troop of light cavalry, seven of them in all, and is followed on foot by a captain accompanied by three soldiers, attended by his sergeant at arms and by an equerry. Of the seven mounted cavalry the first three are singled out from the rest of the troop by their plumed helms, similar to their commander's and strongly reminiscent of that found in Peake's Henry, Prince of Wales.[58] From the porch doorway Jephthah's daughter has emerged to greet her father and to salute his victory over the enemy that has needfully guaranteed her safety and that of her people. She is playing the side drum while behind her are two companions, one of whom plays a lute, the other a triangle.

Splendidly caparisoned with a plumed helmet and a cloak drawn across his breastplate, Jephthah is every inch the conquering hero at his return from the field of his triumphs. Yet, for all his classical equestrian pose the artist has chosen to paint him a few moments later – taken aback at the sight in front of him Jephthah looks upwards into the heavens, shielding his breast with his left hand at the moment of awe struck terror. This is not the rending of his garments as in the Bible (Judges 11:35), nor yet the benediction of the Augsburg illumination, but it does set the mood of the painting powerfully if theatrically: Arrogance toppled by rash endeavour, pride laid low by foolhardiness. The road he has freshly taken from conquering the Ammonites, the rout still sounding distantly in his ears, has led him to be overwhelmed by impending domestic loss. For Buchanan, 'et intumescat insolens rebus bonis,/damno obruetur protinus domestico,/cedentque fracti contumaces spiritus'.[59]

The narrative sequence of the picture exceeds that of the Bible since it allows us to see Jephthah both in his victory and at the very moment when the taste of it is soured by self-realisation. The defeated troops are portrayed as they flee across Windsor Great Park, ironically set in juxtaposition behind the stateliness of Jephthah's triumphal procession. Seconds later the world is turned upside down in chaos that is both domestic, as Buchanan observed, and emotional, as we can see for ourselves. The Three Graces at the doorway, a conscious artistic tribute made all the more obvious by the stance of each of them, have now turned into the Fates. Jephthah's daughter will be the immediate victim of her father's rashness but he will be the final loser of all that he had cherished and fought for in his life.

The lodge in front of which she stands, and into whose garden she will be led to die, is a carefully observed domestic two-storey Tudor building with an attic floor. On the first floor there are oriel windows giving out from two sides of what is most likely to have been a gallery; to the north, still within the curtelage wall, there is a second domestic building, built in a style reminiscent of Netherlandish architecture, wrongly identified as the parish church.[60] The chimney and the large windows in the

[58] Hearn, *Dynasties*, 115.

[59] 'proud and insolent with success he will at once be overwhelmed with domestic loss, and his arrogant airs will be shattered', Buchanan *Jephthes*, ll.53–55.

[60] Millar, *Tudor, Stuart and Early Georgian Pictures*, I, 70.

south-facing wall suggest that this four storey high edifice is the Hall. It would appear to be one of Windsor Park's lodges. There was a flurry of Windsor appointments at the outset of the reign of James VI and I of officials who would need residences. Sir Robert Cary, for instance, had the reversion of the Keepership of the Little Park for life,[61] Sir Richard Cox was entrusted to keep an armoury at the outer park gate,[62] and Sir Henry Neville was made Keeper of the game during 1605.[63] The distant windmill itself may once have existed at Frogmore farm.

Unlike the engraving series of de Jode, the artist omits the sojourn in the hill country so that the third scene is the *denouement*. Jephthah's daughter is kneeling in submission in front of the fiery altar where she will be sacrificed. Two halberdiers stand hard by, scarcely on guard as one of them cannot even bring himself to witness the scene. Beside them is a group of four yeomen whose number appears not to include Jephthah as their dress suggests that they are household officials. The Master himself is absent. Three of her companions are grouped as suppliants opposite her but the headsman has already lifted his sword. They may be unable to alter the fate of their friend but their placement clearly looks forward to Judges 11:40 as they are the first of the daughters of Israel who will come each year for four days to lament the daughter of Jephthah the Gileadite.

The inclusion of site-specific views in the panel is striking and may therefore have been for a purpose. It may argue either for the likely residence of whoever commissioned the work or for the location in which the artist worked and knew well. This cannot determine the nationality of the artist or the provenance of the work.

Those who gathered at the hearth might risk getting too close if they disobeyed their fathers, and went 'commonly to such places, & to such ends, as they wish afterward that they had staied at home, doe with shame and sorrow, reape the iust fruit of their disobedience purpose'.[64] Disobedience of authority, whether that of the father, the head of a household, or of the magistrate, could have dire consequences in the society of early modern England as Scripture was relied upon to underpin social order.

[61] PRO, SP. 14/4/6* 16 October 1603 grant and PRO, SP 14/53/1*.

[62] PRO, SP. 14/6/59* 14 February 1604 grant.

[63] PRO, SP. 14/31/10*.

[64] Rogers, *A Commentary*, 584.

Chapter 4

English Scholarship and the Greek Text of the Old Testament, 1620–1720: The Impact of Codex Alexandrinus[1]

Scott Mandelbrote

Early modern Protestant critics were brought up to believe in the superiority of the Hebrew text of the Bible. Where they challenged this, for the most part they tried to substitute one authoritative text for another. Thus, for the translators of the English Authorised Version (1611), both the Greek Old Testament (the ancient translation of the Septuagint) and the Latin Vulgate attributed to St Jerome had value because they were versions in the vernacular of the times that had themselves been made from the original languages of Scripture.[2] Given these assumptions, Jean Morin's *Exercitationes biblicae de hebraei graecique textus sinceritate*, published at Paris in 1633, represented a new and potentially worrying development for Protestant critics.

Morin was born into a Huguenot family and had studied Greek and Latin at La Rochelle and Hebrew at Leiden. After his conversion to Catholicism, he came into the circle of Cardinal du Perron, formerly ambassador to the Papal court. On his patron's death in 1618, he joined the Oratory.[3] There he was well placed to benefit from the broader realisation of the religious and political benefits of closer links with the East that had been the goal of his first patron. One aspect of this was an interest in the ancient versions of Scripture preserved among the communities of the Middle East. Morin's particular concern became the editing of the text of the Samaritan

---

[1] This essay derives from part of the second of the Grinfield Lectures that I delivered in Oxford in May 2003. In a different form, it was later presented to the Hebrew, Jewish, and Early Christian Studies seminar in the Faculty of Divinity at Cambridge. I am grateful to the Grinfield electors for inviting me to prepare the lectures for 2002–4 and would like to thank Sebastian Brock in particular for his comments and encouragement. I have also benefited from the help and advice of Alastair Hamilton, Nicholas de Lange, Noel Malcolm, Peter Miller, Nicolette Mout, Tabitta van Nouhuys, and Jean-Louis Quantin.

[2] Muneharu Kitagaki, *Principles and Problems of Translation in Seventeenth-Century England* (Kyoto, 1981), 45–102.

[3] Paul Auvray, 'Jean Morin (1591–1659)', *Revue Biblique*, 66 (1959), 397–413.

Pentateuch, which embodied his conviction that the received Hebrew text of the Old Testament was not always reliable. This critical insight had already been developed in Morin's work on the Septuagint.[4]

In the late 1620s, Morin had helped to prepare an edition of this version of the Old Testament, with a parallel Latin translation. In the prefatory material he adapted patristic arguments about the instability of the text of the Bible and suggested the importance of returning to the original readings, which could only be recovered by the collation of different translations. Deploying the authority of Augustine, Morin argued that the witness and practice of the early Church indicated that the Septuagint was superior to the current Hebrew text, which had been corrupted by the Massoretes and later Jews.[5] By drawing attention to the modernity of the Hebrew text in its current form, Morin implicitly attacked those Protestants who were wedded to its authority. His criticism of the Hebrew text was not, however, a simple argument for the primacy of the Greek over the Hebrew text of the Old Testament. For example, although Morin constantly made reference to the work of Jerome, his use of the old Latin translation of the Septuagint, rather than the Vulgate, as the source for the parallel text that he published, implicitly undermined Roman insistence on the authority of that translation. His commitment to a Gallican view of the Church did not, however, lessen the challenge that Morin's ideas posed to contemporary Protestant scholarship.

Morin's works were widely taken up, particularly in England, which he had visited as part of a mission to the court of Henrietta Maria in the 1620s. His approach to the criticism of the Septuagint depended on the notion that an accurate text, if it could be constructed at all, would only be a product of the criticism and comparison of many different versions. This idea certainly animated a number of English critics during the seventeenth century, including both Brian Walton and John Ernest Grabe. Walton's work was indeed attacked by those who remained convinced of the importance of the current, pointed Hebrew text of Scripture. The Independent divine and Interregnum Dean of Christ Church, John Owen argued that Walton had 'taken from [the Bible's] fulnesse and perfection, its sufficiency and excellency' by creating a Massora of his own, an '*orall law* or *verbum [agraphon]*, their unknowne,

---

[4] Alastair Hamilton and Francis Richard, *André du Ryer and Oriental Studies in Seventeenth-Century France* (Oxford, 2004), 40–55; Peter N. Miller, 'Making the Paris Polyglot Bible: Humanism and Orientalism in the Early Seventeenth Century', in Herbert Jaumann (ed.), *Die europäische Gelehrtenrepublik im Zeitalter des Konfessionalismus* (Wiesbaden, 2001), 59–85; Miller, 'A Philologist, a Traveller and an Antiquary rediscover the Samaritans in Seventeenth-Century Paris, Rome and Aix: Jean Morin, Pietro della Valle and N.-C. Fabri de Peiresc', in Helmut Zedelmaier and Martin Mulsow (eds), *Die Praktiken der Gelehrsamkeit in der frühen Neuzeit* (Tübingen, 2001), 123–46; Miller, 'Les Origines de la Bible polyglotte de Paris: *Philologia sacra*, Contre-Réforme et raison d'état', *XVIIe siècle*, 49 (1997), 57–66.

[5] [Jean Morin, (ed.)], *Vetus testamentum, secundum LXX*, 3 vols (Paris, 1628), 1, Preface.

endlesse, bottomlesse, boundlesse treasure of traditions'.[6] For Owen and others, openness to the indeterminacy of textual traditions was with good reason a threat to the foundations of Protestantism.

One of the puzzles of seventeenth-century intellectual history is the remarkable growth of critical activity concentrated on the text of Scripture in the years after 1620, in the volume and variety of scholarly productivity and in the geographical distribution of the scholars undertaking original and profound work. Almost all the serious study of the Septuagint in the sixteenth and early seventeenth centuries depended on manuscripts to be found in northern Italian libraries and, to a lesser extent, on the linguistic skill of Greek exiles living there. Editions of the Septuagint printed in Spain, Germany, and the Low Countries derived their text from manuscripts copied in Italy or from printed editions produced there. The reasons for the alteration of this pattern in the early seventeenth century may also explain the more general growth of work in biblical criticism as a whole.

From the beginning of printed Septuagint criticism there had been an interest in the health of the Churches of the East. The development of that interest in sixteenth-century Rome had helped to promote biblical studies there.[7] In the early seventeenth century, however, there was an enormous burgeoning of concern for Eastern Christians, especially in London and Paris, and unprecedented opportunities to investigate the possessions and attitudes of the peoples of the Middle East, Muslim as well as Christian. War and trade, both furthered by diplomacy, promoted this development. War could be good for scholarship. Fleeing the depredations of marauding armies or the prospects of forced conversion during the Thirty Years War, émigré scholars took with them manuscripts and ideas on which their ability to earn a living in strange places depended. The knowledge that these refugees had of foreign lands whose political importance was magnified by war attracted patrons who were willing to support learned projects that they might otherwise have ignored. Looting troops who carried off archives and precious manuscripts enriched collections far from the trade routes that had originally established the scholarly centres of Western Europe in Northern Italy and South-Central Germany. In this way, great collections and important texts found their way to Sweden, for instance into the collection of Queen Christina, whose books and manuscripts eventually formed the background for the Septuagint scholarship of Isaac Vossius. Vossius's bills as the Queen's librarian were paid with valuables at her abdication in 1654: one of the manuscripts that he received was the great silver codex of the Gothic version of the Bible, the Gospels translated by Ulfilas in the fourth century, that had been looted from the Hradschin in Prague in 1648.[8]

---

[6] John Owen, *Of the Divine Originall, Authority, Self-Evidencing Light, and Power of the Scriptures* (Oxford, 1659), sig. *3r.

[7] See the relevant essays in Anthony Grafton (ed.), *Rome Reborn. The Vatican Library and Renaissance Culture* (Washington, DC, 1993).

[8] F.F. Blok, *Contributions to the History of Isaac Vossius's Library* (Amsterdam, 1974); Tönnes Kleberg, *Codex Argenteus. The Silver Bible at Uppsala*, trans. Neil Tomkinson, 6th edition (Uppsala, 1984).

The opening up of eastern markets for merchants of the English Levant Company and its French and Dutch rivals in the late sixteenth and early seventeenth centuries brought the prospect of extensive travel in the East. That in turn made the attainment of a high level of competence in the languages of the Levant, above all in Arabic, a realistic goal for enterprising scholars and their patrons. It also made essential the maintenance of a permanent diplomatic presence at Constantinople and other notable trading cities of the Ottoman empire, particularly Smyrna and Aleppo. These were nodes through which manuscripts and people passed and they became the centres from which expeditions could be mounted in search of objects that were more precious to European visitors than to native inhabitants.[9]

Politics played a role in these exchanges. The Thirty Years War was not just a matter of battles in Central Europe; it also witnessed a diplomatic dance whose purpose was to achieve the relief of military pressure on allies in far-away places by inducing others to fight on their side. To the French, the Dutch, and above all to the English subjects of the cash-strapped rex pacificus and would-be saviour of the Protestant cause, James VI and I, that meant placing their hopes in unlikely chains of consequences. For example, if only the Sultan could be persuaded to worry less about the threat to his dominions from the Persians to the East, then he might be encouraged to move again on Vienna, thus dividing the forces of the Emperor in Central Europe.

The man whom James I charged with the diplomatic task of seeking Ottoman aid, however indirect, for embattled European Protestants was Sir Thomas Roe.[10] Roe was sent out to Constantinople in 1621, having previously sailed in search of gold in the West Indies and travelled on missions both to the Netherlands and India. In addition to learning the steps of the political etiquette of the Porte, Roe soon had to cope with the demands of wealthy and influential collectors in England. Roe's first impression of the pickings to be had in the East was a discouraging one. In December 1624, anticipating the arrival of the Earl of Arundel's agent, William Petty, who was supposed to search equally for pagan and Christian antiquities in Greece and Turkey, Roe wrote 'he will find, that barbarisme hath worne out all the footstepps of ciuility and learning: yett manuscripts are plenty, old Greeke books, that are little worth; they have bene cerned ouer by many of good iudgment, and I think the gleanings are very poore.'[11] Roe maintained this line a month later in a dispatch that he sent to Arundel himself: 'barbarisme hath spitefully trodden out all worthy relicques of antiquitye. Some few medalls or coynes he may fynd rarely; but bookes haue been so often visited, that I thincke Duck-lane is better furnished then the Greeke church.'[12]

[9] G.J. Toomer, *Eastern Wisedome and Learning* (Oxford, 1996); Daniel Goffman, *Britons in the Ottoman Empire, 1642–60* (Seattle, 1998).

[10] Michael Strachan, *Sir Thomas Roe 1581–1644. A Life* (Salisbury, 1989).

[11] Samuel Richardson (ed.), *The Negotiations of Sir Thomas Roe* (London, 1740), 319–20; on Arundel's collecting habits, see Michael Vickers, 'Greek and Roman Antiquities in the Seventeenth Century', in Oliver Impey and Arthur MacGregor (eds), *The Origin of Museums* (Oxford, 1985), 223–31; David Howarth, *Lord Arundel and his Circle* (New Haven, 1985).

[12] Richardson, *Negotiations*, 334–5.

By January 1625, however, Roe's tone had begun to change. One factor in this was doubtless the success that Petty had in fact had in gathering manuscripts as well as antiquities. In April 1626, Roe remarked ruefully to Thomas Goad, chaplain to the Archbishop of Canterbury, that Petty 'is a good chooser', who had spirited away 22 fine manuscripts from the best library in Greece, despite the fact that he had only been able to gain access to the collection through Roe's help.[13] Yet Roe's sense that Petty and Arundel were only out for themselves revealed the diplomatic context for his change of heart. Early on in his embassy, Roe had met the Greek Patriarch of Constantinople, Cyrillos Lucaris, whom he summed up as 'a man of learning and wit, and in religion, tho' he durst not publickly own it, a direct Calvinist'.[14] Lucaris (1570–1638) was Patriarch of the Greek Church at a difficult time. The identity of his faith and the authority of his see were under threat from Roman Catholic diplomats and proselytisers, whose ability to win the ear of the Sultan or to bribe his rivals made ecclesiastical jurisdiction awkward and dangerous.[15]

Lucaris had close links with the anti-Papal West, having studied with Paolo Sarpi and Cesare Cremonini in Padua, and encountered the missionary efforts of the Uniate Christians as the rector of Academies at Ostrog and Vilna in Poland and Lithuania. From 1601, Lucaris served as Patriarch of Alexandria and soon began to establish links with Western Protestants, particularly through the offices of the Dutch ambassador in Constantinople, Cornelis van Haag. By 1611, he had met with proponents of Church reunion, notably Johannes Wtenbogaert, and he soon began a correspondence with a number of interested Protestants, including the convert and former Bishop of Spoleto, Marco Antonio de Dominis. In response to a suggestion from Archbishop Abbot, he sent Metrophanes Kritopulos to study in Oxford, and he later engaged in extensive correspondence with Swiss Protestants. Although his orthodoxy was by now in question, Lucaris succeeded to the Patriarchate of Constantinople in 1621.[16]

Lucaris was far from being a passive figure in his dealings with Roe, although Roe was eager to build up his own role in saving Lucaris from the machinations of Papal agents and Uniate clerics. Lucaris was even more interested in the question of ecclesiastical reunion than his contacts in the Church of England. This provided a doctrinal lifeline for his Church and his interpretation of its theology. Both

---

[13] Richardson, *Negotiations*, 500–501.

[14] Richardson, *Negotiations*, 35.

[15] Thomas Smith, *Collectanea de Cyrillo Lucario, Patriarcha Constantinopolitano* (London, 1707); George A. Hadjiantoniou, *Protestant Patriarch. The Life of Cyril Lucaris (1572-1638), Patriarch of Constantinople* (Richmond, VA, 1961); Steven Runciman, *The Great Church in Captivity* (Cambridge, 1968), 259–88; Gunnar Hering, *Ökumenisches Patriarchat und europäische Politik, 1620–38* (Wiesbaden, 1968); Gerhard Podskalsky, *Griechische Theologie in der Zeit der Türkenherrschaft (1453–1821). Die Orthodoxie in Spannungsfeld der nachreformatorischen Konfessionen des Westerns* (Munich, 1988), especially 26–30, 154–78; Hugh Trevor-Roper, *From Counter-Reformation to Glorious Revolution* (London, 1992), 83–111.

[16] For Kritopulos, see Podskalsky, *Griechische Theologie*, 220–26.

Archbishop Abbot, and his successor at Canterbury, William Laud, were curious about the doctrine of the Greek Church, which they saw as proof that Roman Catholic interpretations of tradition were not consonant with the heritage of the Christian community as a whole, and were interested in reunion as a means of asserting the antiquity of their own communion.[17] Lucaris, on the other hand, was eager to differentiate Orthodox doctrine and practice from that of the Uniate Churches and to resist Catholic proselytising. In his dealings with Lucaris, Roe could deploy money (or at least the promise of it) and authority. In managing Roe, Lucaris was forced to rely on an unusual weapon of the weak, the bargaining power of manuscripts. There was method to Lucaris's attempts to raise money and capital by expropriating monastic libraries and church treasuries. He bargained carefully with Roe and others, often keeping them in the dark about exactly what they were getting.

In June 1625, Roe took the bait that Lucaris was offering, perhaps desperate to report good news to his masters, whose diplomatic aims in Constantinople were not coming to very much. He had already described the Patriarch as a possible source of manuscripts and antiquities, writing 'By his meanes, I may procure some bookes; but they are indeed Greeke to mee'. At this stage, he was somewhat dismissive of Lucaris's offer of 'One book he hath giuen mee to present his majestie, butt not yett deliuered, beeing the bible entire, written by the hand of Tecla, the protomartyr of the Greekes, that liued with St Paul, which hee doth auerre to bee authenticall, and the greatest relique of the Greeke church'.[18] By mid-summer, however, he noticed that Lucaris was offering 'richly to store England' with manuscripts, and he had found a text that particularly interested him. This was an old manuscript history of the first seven Councils of the Church, alleged to have been owned by the Alexandrian Patriarchate, that Roe could see would generate immediate gains in the currency of anti-Catholic propaganda and polemic. This manuscript, which he again complained was 'not yet my owne', offered the prospect of contradicting the pro-Papal accounts of the ecclesiastical history of the early Church presented by Baronius and Binnius.[19]

Roe assured Abbott that 'I haue begun to deale playnly with the patriarch, who hath made a great collection, that his old books rott and rust by him, among ignorant Greeks, that neuer will vnderstand, nor make vse of them; that in right they belong to the church of God, that will publish them; that they are weapons fitt for champions … I find he scarse knowes the names of many, I am sure, not their contents, nor the reputation of their authors …'.[20] By 1626, Roe was negotiating a swap of books. With Goad's help, he had prepared a list of manuscript titles that he would look out for and of suitable printed books that might be sent in return. His negotiations with Lucaris ran on into the following year and were not wholly successful. They encompassed the offer of a press and type for the Patriarch to print literature in Greek

[17] Anthony Milton, *Catholic and Reformed* (Cambridge, 1995).

[18] Richardson, *Negotiations*, 334–5, 343–4.

[19] Richardson, *Negotiations*, 414, 499.

[20] Richardson, *Negotiations*, 414.

at Constantinople for his flock, as well as various other schemes.[21] Yet, despite Roe's impatience, significant manuscripts did change hands, perhaps because of Lucaris's desperation to obtain something worthwhile from his ally.[22] Roe, however, was quite unsure whether the book that he finally accepted at New Year 1627, and brought back to England in 1628, was what it seemed, and described the gift, which bore a new dedication to Charles I in the Patriarch's hand, in the following terms:

> the old Bible formerly presented to his late majestie ... What estimation it may be of is aboue my sckill; but he valewes yt, as the greatest antiquitye of the Greeke church. The letter is very fayre, a character that I haue neuer seene. It is entyre, except the beginning of St Matheiw. He doth testifye vnder his hand, that it was was written by the virgin Tecla, daughter of a famous Greeke, called Abgierienos, who founded the monastarye in Egypt vpon Pharoas tower, a deuout and learned mayd, who was persecuted in Asya, and to whom Gregorye Nazianzen hath written many epistles. At the end wherof, vnder the same hand, are the epistles of Clement. She dyed not long after the councell of Nice. The book is very great, and hath antiquitye enough at sight ... .[23]

Roe had never seen handwriting of such antiquity. As English critics quickly noted, the manuscript was written in a large, square uncial hand and showed almost no sign of the accent or breathing marks of later codices. It was, in other words, something that looked to them very like the descriptions that they had received of Codex Vaticanus, the manuscript of the Septuagint that had been discovered in Rome and formed the basis for the best sixteenth-century editions of the Greek Old Testament. Moreover, this new codex came with an impressive tradition, albeit one that we now suspect that it may only have acquired in the early seventeenth century, perhaps from Lucaris himself. This stated that it had been written by the virgin martyr, Thecla, the supposed date of whose death meant that this was, in all likelihood, an even older manuscript than any that Catholic editors had used. It implied that this was also a manuscript which had been written by someone who had corresponded with one of the most significant of the Greek Fathers, whose own witness to the readings of the Septuagint was regularly cited by critics of the text.[24]

Early seventeenth-century English collectors had already achieved several remarkable coups relating to classical and biblical manuscripts, most notably the

---

[21] R.J. Roberts, 'The Greek Press at Constantinople in 1627 and its Antecedents', *The Library*, 5th series, 22 (1967), 13–43.

[22] Colin Davey, 'Fair Exchange? Old Manuscripts for New Printed Books', in Robin Cormack and Elizabeth Jeffreys (eds), *Through the Looking Glass. Byzantium through British Eyes* (Aldershot, 2000), 127–34.

[23] Richardson, *Negotiations*, 618; Matthew Spinka, 'Acquisition of the Codex Alexandrinus by England', *Journal of Religion*, 16 (1936), 10–29.

[24] On the difficulties that English scholars had in interpreting the manuscript, see Scot McKendrick, 'The Codex Alexandrinus or the Dangers of being a Named Manuscript' in McKendrick and Orlaith A. O'Sullivan (eds), *The Bible as Book. The Transmission of the Greek Text* (London, 2003), 1–16; cf. Stephen J. Davis, *The Cult of Saint Thecla. A Tradition of Women's Piety in Late Antiquity* (Oxford, 2001).

Earl of Pembroke's purchase and donation to the new Bodleian Library in Oxford of the collection of Giacomo Barocci, consisting of more than 240 Greek manuscripts, which had recently been sold in Venice. The Barocci manuscripts, together with 26 manuscripts collected by Roe (but which did not include the manuscript of the Septuagint that Lucaris and Roe intended for the Royal Library), were installed in the Bodleian Library in May 1629 and catalogued by two of Laud's assistants, Augustine Lindsell and Peter Turner.[25] They were intended to furnish material for the Greek press that Laud had established at Oxford, to succeed the one that Sir Henry Savile had operated at Eton. In 1620, Savile himself had given to the University the manuscript from which he had printed the Eton edition of St John Chrysostom, another author whose comments on the text of the Septuagint were well known to seventeenth-century Englishmen.[26] Laud, as Oxford's Chancellor, would later give the university many of the books that had been collected for him by his agents in the East.[27]

These collections made the Bodleian Library the pre-eminent repository of Greek learning in England and one of the most important in the world. During the course of the seventeenth century, moreover, the libraries of the Oxford Colleges also came by important manuscripts for the study of the Septuagint, in particular the twelfth-century copy of the Octateuch that John Bancroft gave University College, of which he was Master, in 1632. This bequest, and much later donations like those that Sir George Wheler, who travelled in Greece in the mid-1670s, made to Lincoln College, joined the earlier acquisitions made by Corpus Christi College in the 1530s and Cardinal Pole's munificent gift of Greek manuscripts to New College in the 1550s. With the collections of the Bodleian, they ought to have made Oxford the natural location for the work of early modern English scholars of the Septuagint.[28]

By and large, however, those scholars remained in London. A few, most notably James Ussher, Archbishop of Armagh, visited the Bodleian Library and made extensive first-hand use of Oxford manuscripts.[29] Many others employed amanuenses and scribes in Oxford, just as they would to obtain manuscripts from foreign libraries. But the libraries of London also contained manuscripts of interest to editors of the Septuagint, above all the text of Genesis to be found in the library of Sir Robert

---

[25] Ian Philip, *The Bodleian Libary in the Seventeenth and Eighteenth Centuries* (Oxford, 1983), 37–41.

[26] S. van der Woude, 'Sir Henry Savile's Chrysostomus Edition in the Netherlands', in van der Woude (ed.), *Studia bibliographica in honorem Herman de la Fontaine Verwey* (Amsterdam, 1966), 437–47; Bodleian Library, Oxford, MS. Auct. E. 3. 7.

[27] [R.W. Hunt, R. Barbour and J.J.G. Alexander], *Greek Manuscripts in the Bodleian Library* (Oxford, 1966), 8–9.

[28] [Hunt, Barbour, and Alexander], *Greek Manuscripts*, 9, 28; I. Hutter, 'Cardinal Pole's Greek Manuscripts in Oxford', in A.C. de la Mare and B.C. Barker-Benfield (eds), *Manuscripts at Oxford. An Exhibition in Memory of Richard William Hunt (1908–79)* (Oxford, 1980), 108–13.

[29] See the notes preserved in Bodleian Library, Oxford, MSS. Rawlinson C 850, D 280, and D 1290.

Cotton. Ussher considered this to be the most ancient manuscript in the world.[30] As his sentiments indicate, English scholars were particularly interested in finding a text that would give them more direct access to the words of Scripture and that might thus solve the critical riddles that had been posed by post-Tridentine Catholic editors of the Vulgate and the Septuagint. They had, perhaps, now located that text in the huge manuscript that Lucaris had presented to Roe, which soon found its way into the capable hands of the Royal Librarian, Patrick Young (1584–1652).[31]

Jean Morin received news of the manuscript from a fellow Oratorian, Father Philip, who served in the entourage of Queen Henrietta Maria at Greenwich. His reaction was sceptical. From his English correspondents, Morin picked up the view that the manuscript had come with Lucaris from Egypt. He therefore, naturally enough, at first supposed that it must be a copy of a late version of the Greek Old Testament, based on the recension of Hesychius.[32] This was one of three texts of the Septuagint thought to have circulated in late antiquity and was supposed to have been the version that was used in Egypt and Africa. Another version, the Lucianic, was believed to have circulated in Syria and Anatolia, whereas Greek speakers in Palestine were at the same time thought to have used texts based on the allegedly more authentic traditions preserved by Origen in the third century. These had circulated from the library and scriptorium at Caesarea in the lost original Septuagint column of the polyglot manuscripts of the Hexapla. Morin therefore felt confident in telling Thomas Comber, Dean of Carlisle, that the manuscript now in the Royal Library at Westminster was not 'a pure and sincere text of the Septuagint', but a mixture of sentences and pericopes that had been made consonant with the readings of the Hebrew text. Origen himself had marked such departures from the original text of the Septuagint in the edition that he had prepared using a critical sign deployed by contemporary Alexandrian grammarians, the obelisk (-).[33]

Morin accepted that the fame of the association with Thecla implied that the English had acquired a manuscript of importance. He had no difficulty, however, in downgrading it in comparison with the texts prepared by Origen. Morin suggested that further comparison with the citations from the Greek text of Isaiah recorded by Procopius and with Andreas Masius's edition of the book of Joshua (which had deployed a Syriac text to help establish the readings of the Septuagint) might reveal what sort of state the newly discovered codex was in. After some delay, however, Morin received communications from Young himself, who wanted collations of

[30] Ussher's estimation of the manuscript is reported by Brian Walton, *The Considerator Considered* (London, 1659), p. 141; cf. Ussher's notes at Bodleian Library, Oxford, MS. Rawlinson, D 1290, fol. 98r.

[31] Ruth Spalding (ed.), *The Diary of Bulstrode Whitelocke 1605–75* (Oxford, 1990), 602; Edward Maunde Thompson (ed.), *Facsimile of the Codex Alexandrinus*, 4 vols (London, 1879–83); British Library, London, MSS Royal, I, D. v–viii.

[32] Jean Morin, *Antiquitates ecclesiae orientalis* (London, 1682), 235–7; for the activities of Father Philip, see Milton, *Catholic and Reformed*, 362–5.

[33] Morin, *Antiquitates*, 236 ['Textus ille non est 70 Interpretatum purus & sincerus textus ...']

manuscripts in Paris to compare with his newly acquired treasure. The denouement for Morin's vision of Codex Alexandrinus, however, had to wait until Young's own works based on the manuscript began to appear.[34]

In 1633, Young published an edition of the first epistle of Clement of Rome to the Corinthians, an apocryphal work written around 96 CE, based on Lucaris's manuscript.[35] This provenance provided evidence for the canonicity of the Clementine Epistles. Their importance to Young lay in the testimony that they provided for the appointment of bishops in the days of the Apostles. They thus underpinned the claim that the hierarchy of the Church of England replicated the structures of the primitive Church, supporting arguments that could be derived from later texts such as the Ignatian epistles. By this time, some of Young's English correspondents had decided that the manuscript now in the Royal Library must be 'the true Septuagint, or at least nearest to the true Septuagint of any now extant' and the least corrupt of manuscripts of the Old Testament.[36] In 1637, Young published his edition of the catena on Job, dedicated to William Laud, to which he attached the first Septuagint text to be printed from the codex in the Royal Library. This edition of the book of Job was set out in verses (stichs) according to the practice of the scribe of that part of the manuscript. Young argued that this provided evidence of the scribal practice of Thecla. He suggested that it was a rarity of great antiquity and that his work gave a taste of the exegetical feast that would come once the entire manuscript was printed.[37]

When Morin received a copy of Young's edition of Job from Father Philip, he began to revise his earlier opinions about the manuscript. He accepted that specimens of the letter of the manuscript that he had been sent suggested that it was indeed ancient; nevertheless he continued to stress the superiority of Codex Vaticanus and its greater similarity to the tradition of Origen. He insisted that Young should make further collations of the newly discovered manuscript to determine its true nature, proposing that it should be compared with the Septuagint portions of Codex Bezae in Cambridge or with manuscripts from Roman and Parisian libraries.[38]

The foremost British biblical critic of the period, James Ussher, whose chronologies, which were eventually published in the 1650s, supported the authority

---

[34] Morin, *Antiquitates*, 235–7, 242–3; cf. Andreas Masius (ed.), *Iosuae imperatoris historia illustrata* (Antwerp, 1574).

[35] Patrick Young (ed.), *Clementis ad Corinthios epistola prior* (Oxford, 1633).

[36] Johannes Kemke (ed.), *Patricius Junius (Patrick Young) Bibliothekar der Könige Jacob I. und Carl I. von England* (Leipzig, 1898), 79–80 (Mr Glen to Young, 23 May 1636). For the identity of Glen, see Noel Malcolm (ed.), *The Correspondence of Thomas Hobbes*, 2 vols (Oxford, 1994), 2, 837.

[37] Patrick Young (ed.), *Catena graecorum patrum in beatum Iob* (London, 1637), which included Young's edition of the text of Job drawn 'ex venerando bibliothecae regiae Ms. codice, & totius orbis antiquissimo, ac praestantissimo' ['out of the venerable manuscript codex in the Royal Library, which is the most ancient and the most excellent in the whole world'].

[38] Morin, *Antiquitates*, 277–88.

of the Hebrew Bible over the Septuagint text of the Old Testament, was also sceptical about the witness of the manuscript that was presented in Young's edition of Job. Ussher suggested that both the codex in the Royal Library and the Roman edition of the Septuagint, based on Codex Vaticanus, showed signs of Origen's critical intervention in the text. As evidence for this, he referred Young to his own forthcoming edition of the Vulgate of Job. He argued that despite the novelty of the text that Young had recovered from the recently discovered manuscript 'that, I can most certainly assure yow, is not the pure Septuagint; but that which was interlarded by Origen out of Theodotion'.[39]

While English scholars, unlike Morin, were indeed looking for the true text of the Septuagint, they remained in need of convincing that any particular manuscript really represented it. Young's correspondence at this time reveals the deep-seated nature of the division in attitudes to the manuscript that Lucaris had given to the King. The Regius Professor of Greek at Cambridge, James Duport, wrote hopefully of 'that rare and singular Cimelium of Thecla's Greek Bible' and of his desire to consult the most authentic translations, including the best copies of the Septuagint, in his own work on Job. Others shared Ussher's uncertainties, which were compounded by the changing nature of English politics.[40] Despite the interest of Parliamentarians like John Selden in the manuscripts in the Royal Library, as well as the decision of the Westminster Assembly in spring 1646 'to incourage Mr Patrick Young to print the old Testament of the Septuagint translation', Young's position as librarian at St James's was precarious because of the upheavals of the civil war.[41]

Eventually, Young secured an annual pension to make progress on the work of collating the manuscript of the Septuagint, and, by the start of 1648, he had completed the scholia on the first chapter of Genesis. With Ussher's help, he was able to compare the text with that of other manuscripts, for example the important Parisian codices to which Morin had referred him. These included the manuscript of the Octateuch owned by Claude Sarràve, and one of the Prophets that had been in the possession of Cardinal de la Rochefoucauld (Codex Marchalianus).[42] Ussher's Parisian agent, the Irish physician Arnold Boate, who had already attacked Morin's arguments against the primacy of the Hebrew text of the Bible, acted to try to secure copies of manuscripts for Young. He failed, however, to win the trust of the relevant librarians, and was unable even to obtain a copy of the collations that the Jesuit scholar, Fronto de Duc, had made from the Cottonian Genesis almost 30 years before. However, Boate believed Young could live without this information, since

---

[39] Kemke, *Patricius Junius*, 92-4; cf. James Ussher, *The Annals of the World* (London, 1658); James Barr, 'Why the World was Created in 4004 BC: Archbishop Ussher and Biblical Chronology', *Bulletin of the John Rylands University Library of Manchester*, 67 (1984–85), 575–608.

[40] Kemke, *Patricius Junius*, 103–4.

[41] Spalding, *The Diary of Bulstrode Whitelocke*, 185; cf. *Journals of the House of Commons*, 4 (1644–46), 9; Stationers' Hall, London, MS. Court Book C, fol. 226r–v.

[42] See Kemke, *Patricius Junius*, xxiii–v.

the manuscript had now returned to the Cottonian library in London.[43] In due course, Young did indeed collate it for himself.[44]

Young's work came to a halt with his death in 1652. Debate, though, still continued on the significance of the various manuscripts of the Septuagint. Meric Casaubon, for example, who provided Young with evidence of the Septuagint readings used by his father, Isaac, in his arguments against the chronology of Baronius, urged that the codex in the Royal Library should be printed unaltered, 'there being some use to be made (sometime very good) of the very errations of such ancient copies'. Others, particularly in Ussher's circle, worried about the danger that this sort of scholarship posed to the authority of the Hebrew text of the Old Testament.[45]

Young's death thus ensured the perpetuation of a state of scholarly uncertainty about the manuscript. His commitment to the edition seems to have prevented anyone from commissioning one of the circle of young divines and orientalists around the deprived priest, Brian Walton, from taking on the project. These young men assisted Walton in the early 1650s in the completion of a major project that Ussher had been mooting for over 30 years: an English polyglot Bible.[46] With the encouragement of Selden, and with money granted by the Council of State, these scholars embarked on one of the most ambitious publishing projects of early modern England. The polyglot, whose printing Walton oversaw between 1653 and 1657, contained texts in Arabic, Aramaic, Ethiopic, Greek, Hebrew, Latin, Persian, Samaritan, and Syriac, as

---

[43] Kemke, *Patricius Junius*, 111–13; for the visit of the Cottonian Genesis to France, see British Library, London, MSS Cotton Julius C.iii, fol. 290; Cotton Julius C.v, fols 220–22, 229–30, 236r–v, 283–4, 288–9; James Carley, 'Thomas Wakefield, Robert Wakefield, and the Cotton Genesis', *Transactions of the Cambridge Bibliographical Society*, 12 (2000–2003), 246–65. Boate was a long-term critic of Morin's attitude to the Septuagint, see Bodleian Library, Oxford, MS Selden supra 108, fols 80, 86; cf. Arnold Boate, *De textus hebraici veteris testamenti certitudine* (Paris, 1650). See also Elizabethanne Boran, 'An Early Friendship Network of James Ussher, Archbishop of Armagh, 1626–56', in Helga Robinson-Hammerstein (ed.), *European Universities in the Age of Reformation and Counter Reformation* (Dublin, 1998), 116–34.

[44] Young's collations of various manuscripts were eventually printed in Brian Walton (ed.), *Biblia sacra polyglotta*, 6 vols (London, 1653–57), vol. 6.

[45] Kemke, *Patricius Junius*, 115–17. The position of Ussher and his associates, particularly Boate, was complicated by the publication of Louis Cappel, *Critica sacra* (Paris, 1650), which Morin had encouraged. See Georg Schnedermann, *Die Controverse des Ludovicus Cappellus mit den Buxtorfen über das Alter der Hebraïschen Punctation* (Leipzig, 1879); J.C.H. Lebram, 'Ein Streit um die Hebraïsche Bibel und die Septuaginta', in Th.H. Lunsingh Scheurleer and G.H.M. Posthumus Meyjes (eds), *Leiden University in the Seventeenth Century* (Leiden, 1975), 20–63.

[46] For Ussher's long-term interest in such a project, see Richard Parr (ed.), *The Life of the most Reverend Father in God, James Usher, late Lord Arch-Bishop of Armagh, Primate and Metropolitan of all Ireland. With a Collection of Three Hundred Letters* (London, 1686), 2–11 (*Letters*); James Ussher and William Eyre, *De textus hebraici veteris testamenti variantibus ad Ludovicum Cappellum epistola* (London, 1652); Bodleian Library, MS Rawlinson, C 849, fols 262–3.

well as an extensive critical apparatus and a wide-ranging selection of Prolegomena. The Pentateuch had already been printed by the end of 1653.[47]

Given the existence of Young's plans, it becomes easy to understand why the editor of the London Polyglot should have chosen to print the text of the Septuagint from the edition published at Rome under the authority of Sixtus V in 1587, which was based on Codex Vaticanus. Both Walton and his critics respected this manuscript and valued it for its antiquity. It is true that the text of Codex Vaticanus was accompanied in the main body of the Polyglot by a running list of variants based in part on a collation of the manuscript in the Royal Library, whose New Testament text was also collated for the Polyglot by Alexander Huish, Prebendary of Wells. In the Prolegomena, Walton also gave the manuscript the name 'Codex Alexandrinus', by which it has since been known and which testified to his faith in the story of its having been brought to England from the library of the Egyptian patriarchate.[48] Amongst other things, that story hinted that this particular manuscript might preserve the tradition of the very first text of the Septuagint, which was widely supposed to have been translated at Alexandria.[49] Walton also expressed his confidence in the value for Christian scholarship of the witness of the Greek translation of the Old Testament, quoting St John Chrysostom's opinion of it as a gateway to Christ.[50] He discussed the advantages and disadvantages of the various published editions of the text, and described the manuscripts whose readings he had been interested in obtaining, in addition to those that had been taken from Codex Alexandrinus. These included many of the texts for which Boate had searched on Young's behalf, including Codex Marchalianus, as well as manuscripts from the library of Cardinal Barberini, to which Morin had had access, and a manuscript in the University Library at Cambridge of the Septuagint of Chronicles, which was believed to have belonged to Theodore of Tarsus, the seventh-century Greek Archbishop of Canterbury.

Walton's sense of the importance of collation as a demonstration of the variety of the Septuagint text was made apparent in the sixth volume of the Polyglot. This printed the readings obtained from the manuscripts to which he and his collaborators had had

[47] The clearest narratives of the preparation and publication of the London Polyglot remain Adam Clarke, *A Succinct Account of Polyglot Bibles* (Liverpool, 1802); Henry John Todd, *Memoirs of the Life and Writings of the Right Rev. Brian Walton, DD*, 2 vols (London, 1821), vol. 1; see also Nicolas Barker, 'The Polyglot Bible' in John Barnard, D.F. McKenzie and Maureen Bell (eds), *The Cambridge History of the Book in Britain. Volume IV: 1557–1695* (Cambridge, 2002), 648–51. Walton himself described progress on the work in a letter to Johannes Buxtorf the younger (20 January 1656), Öffentliche Bibliothek der Universität Basel, MS G.I. 62, fols 4–5.

[48] Walton, *Biblia sacra polyglotta*, 1, preface and pp. 54–[72] (ninth prolegomenon).

[49] For more recent scholarship on the question of the origins of the manuscript, see T.C. Skeat, 'The Provenance of Codex Alexandrinus', *Journal of Theological Studies*, New Series, 6 (1955), 233–5; T.S. Pattie, 'The Creation of the Great Codices', in John L. Sharpe III and Kimberley van Kampen (eds), *The Bible as Book. The Manuscript Tradition* (London, 1998), 61–72; McKendrick, 'The Codex Alexandrinus'.

[50] Walton, *Biblia sacra polyglotta*, 1, preface ['ostium ad Christum'].

access, particularly those of the Cottonian Genesis, and reprinted the variants given in the scholia of Flaminius Nobilis from the Sixtine edition of the Septuagint. Yet because of the death of Young, Walton's work remained fundamentally incomplete and uncertain with regard to the Septuagint. On the one hand, in his preface, Walton expressed confidence in the recovery of the original, integral text of the Septuagint through the critical study of manuscript witnesses. At the same time, his discussion of the state of the text in the Prolegomena often echoed the more cautious and critical sentiments of Morin. Neither Walton nor Ussher, who, in 1655, published a consideration of the variants in the text of the Septuagint whose content was at times very close to that of Walton's prolegomena, were able to go beyond this.[51] Walton was thus sceptical about some of the miraculous evidence adduced for the purity and antiquity of the Septuagint, but he was nevertheless adamant that its language preserved elements of an original Hebrew text of the Old Testament that was now lost. He was certain that Morin was wrong in his initial arguments about the value of Codex Alexandrinus but was unsure what he himself thought its worth was.[52]

One aspect of Walton's work was, however, more definite. This was the disdain with which he treated the first published edition of the Septuagint from an English printer; Roger Daniel's version of the text of the Sixtine edition prepared for the use of the scholars at Westminster school. This appeared in 1653 and was edited by the Socinian, John Biddle. Its publication may have owed something to the interest in the Septuagint generated by Codex Alexandrinus and the frustration produced by the failure of Young's attempts to edit it. Walton was scathing in the Prolegomena to the London Polyglot about the shortcomings of this edition, in particular attacking the mixture of texts and versions that it provided. He denied that it had even followed the Sixtine edition in any meaningful way.[53] This criticism was later echoed in John Pearson's introduction to the edition of the Sixtine text that was published at Cambridge in 1665, although in practice this version followed that of 1653 in many particulars. Pearson also reiterated Walton's hope that the critical reconstruction of the original text of the Septuagint might eventually be possible.[54] The combination of such expectation with anxieties about the presentation of the Sixtine edition may explain the growth of a general sense among English authors of the second half of the seventeenth century that Codex Alexandrinus could indeed provide evidence of the true Septuagint and might thus help to confute Catholic claims about the

---

[51] James Ussher, *De graeca septuaginta, interpretum versione syntagma* (London, 1655).

[52] On the critical stance adopted by Walton in the London Polyglot, see Peter N. Miller, 'The "Antiquarianization" of Biblical Scholarship and the London Polyglot Bible (1653–57)', *Journal of the History of Ideas*, 62 (2001), 463–82.

[53] Walton, *Biblia sacra polyglotta*, 1, 65–6 (ninth prolegomenon); [John Biddle, (ed.)], *Vetus testamentum graecum ex versione septuaginta interpretum* (London, 1653). On Biddle, his work, and its publication, see H.J. McLachlan, *Socinianism in Seventeenth-Century England* (Oxford, 1951), 163-217; Stephen B. Dobranski, 'Licensing Milton's Heresy', in Dobranski and John P. Rumrich (eds.), *Milton and Heresy* (Cambridge, 1998), 139–58.

[54] [John Pearson, (ed.)], *Vetus testamentum graecum ex versione septuaginta interpretum* (Cambridge, 1665), preface.

uncertainty of the witness of Scripture. Scholars, however, knew that this conclusion was yet to be proved.

One of the principal objects of the Oxford University Press, re-founded by John Fell, was to settle this issue. Fell's prospectus of 1672 stated that 'We purpose to Print, if we may be encouraged: 1. The greek Bible in a royal folio, to w[hi]ch purpose we have procured the use of the Alexandrian Ms. out of his Ma[jes]ties: library, with others of good note from diuerse Places & have of our own seueral copies of venerable Antiquity nevre yet collated'.[55] Despite the publication of the Psalter in a text derived from Codex Alexandrinus by Thomas Gale, shortage of money meant that no significant progress was made with this ambitious project.[56] Had it been accomplished, it would surely have attempted to enthrone Codex Alexandrinus as the pre-eminent manuscript witness to the Old Testament. The Oxford orientalist, Thomas Smith, who was involved with the planned edition of the Septuagint, commented at this time that existing versions of the Greek Old Testament were:

> confessedly corrupt in a thousand places; and therefore several, & B[isho]p Usher among [th]e rest, pretend that the Greeke translation wee enjoy is of a later date, and is not [th]e copy, that was put into [th]e Library of Ptolemy at Alexandria [tha]t being destroyed by [th]e fire w[hi]ch consumed [th]e great treasure of learning deposited there, or lost by time. But for all this pretence the contrary opinion is abundantly more probable, that this is the very copy, notwithstanding those seemingly great dissonancyes from [th]e original Text, w[hi]ch are owing partly to [th]e negligence of the Librarian in the frequent transcribing, and partly to the boldness of Interpolators who have added or substracted, what they thought fittest. But take it as it is, with all its faults, it is a most excellent, nay inestimable, treasure: but without w[hi]ch it would bee very difficult, not to say impossible, to understand several considerable places in [th]e Ebrew, w[hi]ch by this great helpe are now become plaine & easy ... .[57]

Although Fell and his disciples failed to complete their edition of the Septuagint, late seventeenth-century Oxford scholars, largely as a result of their efforts, began to explore the manuscript heritage to which they were heirs and did set about the serious editing of the works of the Greek Fathers that Laud had intended his benefactions to encourage.

In this context, it is worth drawing attention to an important change in the mentality of those Englishmen who worked most extensively on Greek Patristic

---

[55] All Souls College, Oxford, MS 239a, fol. 1r. On Fell's plans for the Oxford Press, see particularly John Johnson and Strickland Gibson, *Print and Privilege at Oxford to the Year 1700* (London, 1946); Harry Carter, *A History of the Oxford University Press. Volume I: To the Year 1780* (Oxford, 1975); Nicholas Keene, 'John Fell: Education, Erudition and the English Church in Late Seventeenth-Century Oxford', *History of Universities*, 18 (2003), 62–101.

[56] [Thomas Gale (ed.)], *Psalterium, juxta exemplar Alexandrinum* (Oxford, 1678).

[57] Bodleian Library, Oxford, MS. Smith 60, 130 (Smith to Matthew Delamott, 16 June 1678); cf. Smith's comments on the failure of the Oxford edition of the Septuagint, MS Smith 62, 251–2.

texts in the wake of the schism that split the Church following the imposition of oaths to the new King and Queen, William III and Mary, as part of the settlement that followed the Revolution of 1688. Although its effects were exaggerated among the non-jurors, they were not confined to them. There was, more generally, a growth of sentimental attachment to the liturgy and practices of the Greek Church as the embodiment of purity in the Christian past. This arose out of the interest in reunion that had characterised earlier involvement with the Greeks but it was in many ways quite distinct from it. Such an attachment shaped the publishing efforts of John Ernest (Johann Ernst) Grabe (1666–1711), which were carried out with the material assistance of leading Whig bishops and supporters of the Revolution, notably John Sharp, Archbishop of York, and William Lloyd, successively Bishop of St Asaph, Coventry and Lichfield, and Worcester.[58]

Grabe had been born in Königsberg and educated at the Lutheran university there, but afterwards begun to have doubts about the validity of the Lutheran Church. After toying with conversion to Catholicism, he was persuaded to enter the Anglican Church and arrived in England in 1697. He was first welcomed by the non-juror Edward Stephens, who was a strong proponent of the establishment of a Greek College in Oxford, a scheme which also interested a number of Whig Bishops, notably Edward Stillingfleet of Worcester.[59] Grabe settled initially at St Edmund Hall in Oxford, where he fell under the spell of the great New Testament critic, collator of manuscripts, and collector of variant lections, John Mill.[60] Initially, Grabe's work concentrated on the preparation of editions of the Fathers, and on the editing of the works of George Bull, the most prominent contemporary English interpreter and defender of the Council of Nice.[61] This editorial activity brought Grabe into controversy with anti-Trinitarians, some of whom later attempted to use manuscript evidence for the doctrines of the early Church that Grabe had uncovered against his own position.[62]

---

[58] George Every, 'Dr. Grabe and his Manuscripts', *Journal of Theological Studies*, New Series, 8 (1957), 280–92; Günther Thomann, 'John Ernest Grabe (1666–1711): Lutheran Syncretist and Anglican Patristic Scholar', *Journal of Ecclesiastical History*, 43 (1992), 414–27; Jean-Louis Quantin, '*Apocryphorum nimis studiosi?* Dodwell, Mill, Grabe et le problème du canon néo-testamentaire au tournant du XVIIe et du XVIIIe siècle', in Simon Claude Mimouni (ed.), *Apocryphité. Histoire d'un concept transversal aux religions du livre* (Turnhout, 2002), 285–306.

[59] E.D. Trappe, 'The Greek College at Oxford, 1699–1705', *Oxoniensia*, 19 (1954), 92-111; for evidence of Stephens's activity at this time, see Queens' College, Cambridge, MS 73, nos 11 and 13.

[60] Mill's own plans to work on the Septuagint are discussed at Bodleian Library, Oxford, MS. Smith 62, 55–8; cf. Adam Fox, *John Mill and Richard Bentley* (Oxford, 1954).

[61] John Ernest Grabe (ed.), *Spicilegium ss. patrum*, 2 vols (Oxford, 1698–99); George Bull, *Opera omnia*, ed. John Ernest Grabe (London, 1703); cf. Bodleian Library, Oxford, MSS Grabe 21–2.

[62] See, in the context of his later work on the Septuagint, John Ernest Grabe, *An Essay upon Two Arabick Manuscripts of the Bodlejan Library*, 2nd edn (London, 1712).

After working on the apparatus of the visually impressive but textually disappointing Oxford edition of the Greek New Testament that appeared in 1703, Grabe came to arrangements with the booksellers who were operating the Oxford press at the time to publish a critical edition of the Septuagint.[63] He collected and collated manuscript variants through a wide correspondence that built on the networks that Mill had established. Mill and others at Oxford had continued to show an interest in the idea of editing the Septuagint during the years after 1688.[64] Through Mill's contacts, Grabe received facsimiles of manuscripts made for him by Isaac Newton in Cambridge, and by Bernard de Montfaucon in Paris, as well as from the Vatican Library.[65] St Amand, Grabe's contact in Rome, complained bitterly about the help he received from the librarian at the Vatican: 'Zacagnia is [th]e idlest, ignorantest, uncivil Librarian, [tha]t has ever been I believe …'.[66] Nevertheless Zacagnia also proved to be one of Grabe's informants, sending tracings of manuscripts as well as discussions of their age and contents. Grabe collated the texts that he received with a copy that he had made of the Codex Alexandrinus, entering the variant readings that he hoped to publish as corrections to a copy text of the Sixtine edition of the Septuagint.[67]

Much of this work was done at a distance, since from autumn 1705 Grabe spent more and more time in London, and he was almost as reliant on Oxford informants and collators for the information that he obtained from the manuscripts in University, Lincoln, and New Colleges, as he was on foreign ones.[68] Through his network of patrons, who included Robert Harley, Grabe succeeded in obtaining royal sponsorship for his edition of the Septuagint. He planned this in the grandest of terms and rapidly started to run out of money once the business of engraving headpieces, drawing frontispieces, and setting and correcting complex Greek texts (all of which also required carriage to and from London to the press at Oxford) was underway. Subscription money did not cover the full amount of Grabe's costs and the book trade was slow to pick up the slack: the major Dutch bookseller Reinier Leers was reluctant to subscribe at all, since he was confident that, once Grabe's grandiose edition appeared, it would pirated by German printers in a smaller and cheaper format.[69]

---

[63] Bodleian Library, Oxford, MS. Grabe 23, fols 86–98.

[64] Cf. John Ernest Grabe, *Epistola ad clarissimum virum, D[omi]nu[m] Joannem Millium* (Oxford, 1705). For evidence of the continuity of interest in printing the Septuagint at Oxford, see Kongelige Bibliotek, Copenhagen, MS NKS 1675 2o, no. 76; Bodleian Library, Oxford, MS Smith 62, 55–8.

[65] Newton's work for Grabe can be found in Bodleian Library, Oxford, MS Grabe 36, 16, 38–49; correspondence with Montfaucon and with Lorenzo Alessandro Zacagnia is in MS. Grabe 23, fols 5–10.

[66] Bodleian Library, Oxford, MS Grabe 23, fols 102–3

[67] Bodleian Library, Oxford, MSS Grabe 49, 51–2.

[68] Bodleian Library, Oxford, MS Grabe 49.

[69] Bodleian Library, Oxford, MS Grabe 23, fols 104–33; MS Grabe 53. A version of Grabe's work, prepared by Johann Jacob Breitinger, did eventually appear in four volumes, printed at Zurich between 1730 and 1732.

Nevertheless, Grabe pressed ahead, believing his work promised once and for all to establish Codex Alexandrinus as the best surviving version of the text of the Greek Old Testament that Origen himself had used in compiling the Hexapla. Turning Morin's argument on its head, Grabe argued that Codex Vaticanus was itself a later Hesychian recension of the Septuagint. Grabe deployed Origen's own extensive vocabulary of critical signs to indicate divergences from the presumed original version of the Septuagint that had been supplied in the text from other sources (particularly the Hebrew Bible) or to point out readings that were peculiar to the Septuagint itself.[70] Yet, as a consequence of this re-enactment of the editorial procedure of Origen, Grabe himself began to produce a mixed text of the Septuagint, rather than demonstrating the purity of Codex Alexandrinus as he had perhaps envisaged. Nevertheless, Grabe's edition ought really to have been the culmination of seventeenth-century English interest in Codex Alexandrinus. It should have proved the importance of that manuscript as source for the true text of the Septuagint. Why did it fail?

The simple answer is that, despite the traditional role ascribed to providence in the protection and dissemination of biblical texts, Codex Alexandrinus was astonishingly unfortunate in or unforgiving of its editors. Grabe died in 1711, when he had published only the first and fourth parts of his edition.[71] Francis Lee, a former follower of the teachings of Pierre Poiret and Jane Lead, took up the edition, but he died in 1719, after only completing the second part of the work.[72] The third and final part appeared in 1720 and was seen through the press by William Wigan. The delayed and erratic nature of its publication ensured that Grabe's work suffered in the marketplace. Many subscribers had presumably died before the second and third parts of the edition that they had helped to pay for had appeared. Yet the level of subscription and the relative success of Grabe's appeals for financial support also draw attention to the prestigious nature of his project. Grabe's initial transcriptions of the text of Codex Alexandrinus were checked by prominent and active scholars – Humfrey Wanley, the librarian to the Harley family, and John Potter, an expert on Greek history and antiquities who had become Bishop of Oxford by the time that Grabe's edition was finished.[73] It is therefore worth considering why Grabe's patrons and supporters could not have found a more secure way to ensure the completion of his work.

---

[70] See the prefaces in John Ernest Grabe (ed.), *Septuaginta Interpretum*, 4 vols (Oxford, 1707–20); Grabe, *Epistola*, 45–56; Grabe, *Dissertatio de variis vitiis LXX interpretum versioni* (Oxford, 1710).

[71] An account of Grabe's death may be found at pp. 35–6 of volume 1 of the casebooks of Dr Richard Mead, in the archives of C. Hoare & Co., 37 Fleet Street, London [Papers of Richard Mead, Box A].

[72] For evidence of the distress that Lee's involvement with mystical theology caused in Oxford, see Bodleian Library, Oxford, MS Smith 62, 244–6; for examples of Lee's work, see MS Grabe 50.

[73] Bodleian Library, Oxford, MS Grabe 53, fols 310–11.

Here, it becomes important to register the place of the Septuagint and, more generally, the status of the Greek Church in Grabe's wider scheme of activities. For much of his career in England, Grabe was a friend of and apologist for the schismatic non-jurors. At Oxford, he had refused to communicate in the Church of England and was even suspected of retaining sympathies with Roman Catholicism. He had compiled private liturgies that were based on Greek models, but whose use the Church of England had not sanctioned.[74] Moreover, his scholarship had unwittingly given aid to critics of the established Church from both ends of the spectrum. Not only was it favourable to non-juring high churchmen, but it also supplied evidence that doctrinally suspect low churchmen, in particular the proponent of Arianism, William Whiston, attempted to use in their own programmes of liturgical and theological reform. The main intention of establishing that Codex Alexandrinus represented a more perfect text of the Septuagint had always had a polemical aspect, with implications for the identity of the true Church. By the time that Grabe's edition was completed, his own commitment to ecclesiastical purity had apparently led him away from the notion that most of his English contemporaries had of orthodoxy. In his hands, commitment to the primitive witness of the Greek Church seemed more like a badge of party than a demonstration of conformity. Moreover, the conviction that a single, pure text of Scripture might still exist had begun to seem the preserve of enthusiasts, rather than of serious and broad-minded scholars.[75]

There is, however, a final reason for Grabe's failure. Despite his commitment to Codex Alexandrinus, his edition was always conceived in critical terms. The idea that a single manuscript might confute Catholic critics of the clarity and authority of Scripture almost seemed unworthy of late seventeenth-century Protestant scholarship. When the royal librarian, Richard Bentley, strode down the burning staircase of Ashburnham House in 1731, he abandoned to the flames the Cottonian Genesis, which had once been a talisman for the hopes of early seventeenth-century English Old Testament scholarship. On the other hand, he carried with him Codex Alexandrinus.[76] Yet the scholarship for which Bentley was already famous was the work of the conjectural reconstruction of ancient texts. This depended on the evidence of many manuscripts, not the witness of a single codex. The same was true of the

[74] See Günther Thomann (ed.), *John Ernest Grabe's Liturgies – Two Unknown Anglican Liturgies of the Seventeenth Century* (Nuremberg, 1989); cf. the critical comments of Thomas Smith, Bodleian Libary, Oxford, MS Smith 62, 153–82.

[75] See, for example, the comments of the Leicester divine, John Jackson, who was sympathetic to Arianism and whose interest in the Septuagint derived from a conviction (which had once been even commoner among English theologians) that 'the *Hebrew*, tho' not so often transcrib'd as the *Septua[gint]* hath suffer'd by the perfidiousness of the Jews.' Cambridge University Library, MS Add. 7113, no. 20.

[76] Andrew Prescott, '"Their Miserable State of Cremation": The Restoration of the Cotton Library', in C.J. Wright (ed.), *Sir Robert Cotton as Collector* (London, 1997), 391–454; the collations that Bentley made from the Cottonian Genesis survive at Trinity College, Cambridge, MS B.17.20, fols 89–92. There had been plans to print the manuscript in the early 1690s, see Bodleian Library, Oxford, MS Smith 47, fol. 86r.

best of English Old Testament criticism in the second half of the seventeenth century and it implied a much more complex attitude to Codex Alexandrinus than the one displayed by many of those who first made its acquaintance. It would, no doubt, have sold books to claim that here was the earliest and truest text of Scripture. It might even have helped to construct a powerful confessional argument to demonstrate that the best surviving testimony to the content of ancient revelation lay in a vernacular translation that had circulated in the early Church. Yet neither of these claims about Codex Alexandrinus in the end would have satisfied sceptical eyes like those of Jean Morin. The demands of a particular form of critical and antiquarian scholarship, therefore, eventually overcame the blandishments of polemical advantage. Codex Alexandrinus retained its importance, but it did not become 'a pure and sincere text'.

Chapter 5

'A Two-Edged Sword': Biblical Criticism and the New Testament Canon in Early Modern England

Nicholas Keene

I

The religion of Protestants was the religion of the book, and that book was the Bible. Yet it is one of the defining paradoxes of early modern Protestantism that its elevation of the written record of divine revelation to totemic status stimulated an explosion of scholarship that would ultimately serve to forge a critical discipline that could be mimicked and manipulated to undermine the sacred text it had been designed to protect. The New Testament canon was the exclusive body of texts written by the apostles or their companions, inspired by the Holy Spirit, that provided a self-sufficient guide to Christian belief and practice and had, according to orthodox tradition, been preserved through the ages by divine providence. It provided one of the arenas of biblical discourse in which this paradox unfolded.

The battle over the status of Christian scriptural texts had been vigorously waged within the early Church, but the debate lay largely dormant through the Middle Ages.[1] It was not until the dawn of humanism, with its re-evaluation of the textual bases of religious, political and cultural authority that the controversy was re-ignited. This age of criticism and philology witnessed the dethroning of cherished forgeries like the Donation of Constantine and the *Corpus Dionysiacum* by Lorenzo Valla and the *Corpus Hermeticum* by Isaac Casaubon.[2] Within this culture of textual re-evaluation, reformers on both sides of the new religious divide argued over the merits of canonical scripture with a candour that would prove discomforting to standard-bearers of a later orthodoxy. Cardinal Cajetan, Erasmus, Luther and Calvin all cast

---

[1] B.M. Metzger, *The Canon of the New Testament: Its Origin, Development and Significance* (Oxford, 1987); F.F. Bruce, *The Canon of Scripture* (Glasgow, 1988); B.D. Ehrman, *Lost Christianities: The Battles for Scripture and the Faiths We Never Knew* (Oxford, 2003).

[2] The best discussion of Renaissance scholarship is A. Grafton, *Defenders of the Text: The Traditions of Scholarship in an Age of Science, 1450–1800* (Cambridge, Massachusetts 1991).

doubt on the Pauline authorship of the Epistle to the Hebrews. Luther notoriously described James as an 'epistle of straw', and could not accept the book of Revelation as either an apostolic or prophetic text. Calvin suggested that a disciple wrote 2 Peter at the apostle's command. Erasmus argued, on stylistic grounds, that the author of the Fourth Gospel and Revelation could not be the same person.[3] The canon emerged intact, but many of the questions raised reappeared in various guises within English debate in the late seventeenth and early eighteenth centuries. A consensus regarding the defining characteristics of canonicity – authorship, contents, or the judgement of the early Church – proved elusive. The authorship of some canonical texts was uncertain, and the canon might have to be expanded if lost texts were recovered. A judgement based on textual content was subjective, unless the infallible authority of the Church was conceded. Yet the early Church Fathers were not unanimous regarding the status of individual scriptural texts.

The Welsh biblical critic Jeremiah Jones, who, at the time of his premature death in 1726, had completed an exhaustive study on the canonicity of ancient Christian writings, addressed all these issues and provides a vantage point from which to look back over the debates regarding the construction, contents and claims to authority of the New Testament canon. Jones regarded New Testament canonicity both as a complex aspect of biblical scholarship – he knew of 'no question involved with more intricacies and perplexing difficulties' – and a neglected one.[4] Most Christians, he believed, still had little idea of why they received the scriptures as the word of God; more significantly, for all their gainsaying, most Protestants accepted the canon upon the same authority as Catholics – that of the Church.[5] Jones echoed the sentiments of Richard Baxter in *The Saints Everlasting Rest*, a work that had claimed a permanent place in the canon of Protestant devotional literature, when he asked, 'Where is the man that ever knew the Canon from the Apocrypha, before it was told him?'[6]

Jones was intimately familiar with both the writings of the early church fathers, and recent scholarship – both domestic and European. He constructed the most coherent and comprehensive defence of the traditional canon then published in England. He rejected, as the primary yardstick of canonicity, the authority of the present-day Church, as the Catholics affirmed, for, by this standard, Aesop's Fables might 'become as good a part of Scripture, as Saint Paul's Epistles'. He rejected reliance on the internal evidence of the texts as such a subjective criterion of judgement could only result in division between Christian sects. He rejected falling back on the guidance of the Holy Spirit, for whilst the Spirit might illuminate divinely inspired texts for the individual Christian, this could not provide an argument to convince agnostic minds, and, unrestrained, led to the excesses of enthusiasm. Jones rested

---

[3] Metzger, *Canon of the New Testament*, 239–47.

[4] J. Jones, *A new and full method of settling the canonical authority of the New Testament* (3 vols, London 1726–27), i. 2.

[5] Ibid., i. 13–15.

[6] R. Baxter, *The Saints Everlasting Rest: or, A Treatise Of the Blessed State of the Saints in their enjoyment of God in Glory* (London, 1650), 176; Jones, *New Testament*, i. 53–8.

the New Testament canon on the authority of the early Church, the judgement of the Christians in the first ages after Christ who read the texts in their assemblies and were best placed to detect forgeries.[7] Jones's work, held in high regard through the eighteenth century, can be seen as the closing remarks of the debate in early modern England, a debate between Protestants and Catholics, between Anglicans and enthusiasts, between Christians and sceptics, and between scholars who just could not agree.

This essay will present a dialogue between Jones and three scholars who employed their critical, philological and literary skills to query the formation, challenge the identity and undermine the authority of the New Testament canon, bringing upon their heads the vituperation of the spokesmen of orthodoxy. These three critics were the bombastic Quaker Samuel Fisher, the freethinking deist John Toland and the intrepid Arian William Whiston. The confessional identities and religious agendas of these three scholars were very different, but each obliged those who wished to defend the status and authority of scripture to re-examine the texts of their Bibles and the tradition through which they had been handed down.

It does not appear that Jones ever read the work of Samuel Fisher – in its original or posthumously republished form – although he did refer to Quaker treatments of scripture.[8] Fisher, the son of a Northampton hatter, graduated BA from Trinity College, Oxford in 1627, and was ordained deacon on 1 January 1628. On 25 March 1643, he was presented by Parliament as lecturer at Lyd, Kent, and was vicar of the parish there by 1645. Sometime before 1649 he resigned his vicarage to join the Baptists, and became pastor to a nearby congregation at Ashford. He was prominent in the organisation of Baptist churches, and established a reputation as a formidable theological disputant. In 1655, following meetings with prominent Quakers including George Fox, Fisher defected to the Society of Friends, the final step on a spiritual peregrination undertaken by many in mid-seventeenth-century England. He proved an effective propagandist for the cause at home and on the continent.[9]

In April 1659, he held a series of three disputes with Thomas Danson at Sandwich, Kent, following which he published *Rusticus ad Academicos*, aimed at 'Four Fore-men' of the 'Fraternity of Fiery Fighters' seeking to destroy the children of Christ – Danson, Baxter, John Owen, Independent minister and vice-chancellor of Oxford University, and the skilful Baptist disputant John Tombes. At a time when Quakers and other sectarians were being accused of tearing books out of their Bibles and even burning them, Fisher provided the most scholarly and scathing dismissal of the

[7] Ibid., i. 43–52 (quotation, 46); cf. J. Owen, *Of the divine originall, authority, self-evidencing light, and Power of the Scriptures* (Oxford, 1658), 34–5, 68–122.

[8] Fisher's principal work as a Baptist was *Baby-Baptism Meer Babism* (London, 1653), republished in 1655 and 1669 as *Christianismus redivivus, Christ'ndom both Unchrist'ned and New Christ'ned*; his principal publication as a Quaker was *Rusticus ad Academicos in exercitationibus expostulatoriis, apologeticis quatuor The rustick's alarm to the rabbies* (London, 1660), republished with other Quaker writings in 1679 under the title *The Testimony of Truth Exalted.*

[9] New DNB 'Fisher, Samuel (bap. 1604, d. 1665)'.

traditional Protestant conception of a providentially preserved collection of sacred scripture.[10] Fisher's rambling invective was a rustic Quaker's alarm to the clerical rabbis, an erudite rejection of learning as a means of divining God's truth, and a vehement statement of the primacy of the light within over the mere letter of God's word.[11]

John Toland was the principal target of Jones's scholarly ire throughout his work on the New Testament. Born on 30 November 1670 on the Inishowen peninsula in county Donegal, Ireland, supposedly the illegitimate son of a Roman Catholic priest, Toland traced his ancestry through Irish historians and bards. Rejecting at sixteen the 'insupportable Yoke' of Catholicism, his education at European seats of learning, including Leiden under Friedrich Spanheim the Younger, was partly funded by Presbyterian sponsors. At ease moving among the circles of Benjamin Furly and John Locke in Rotterdam and London, in more conservative Oxford he acquired a reputation as a controversial coffee-house disputant in matters of religion.[12]

Toland's notoriety was sealed in 1695 with the publication of *Christianity not Mysterious*, in which his conclusion that all apparent Christian mysteries were either puzzles that could be solved or superstitions peddled by priests plunged him into a maelstrom of criticism.[13] In 1698, in an edition of the canon of John Milton, Toland dismissed the royal authorship of *Eikon basilike* and appeared to insinuate that even the New Testament canon was not free from the contamination of forgery. Called to the bar by Offspring Blackall, chaplain to William III and later Bishop of Exeter, Toland 'clarified' his position, providing in *Amyntor* in order to 'convince all the World' of

[10] The anonymous *The Quakers Dream* (London, 1655), spoke of 'the burning of the Bible by sundry Quakers, Ranters, or Shakers' (3); John Deacon's *The Examination and exploits of James Nayler* (London, 1657) accused the Quaker's followers of saying that 'the Bible ought to be burned' (43–4). I owe these references to Dr Hessayon. Fisher, *Rusticus*, title-page.

[11] C. Hill, *The World Turned Upside Down: Radical Ideas during the English Revolution* (London, 1972), 260. Hill has suggested that Fisher deserves 'greater recognition as a precursor of the English enlightenment'; ibid., 268. R.H. Popkin has suggested that *Rusticus* was 'strikingly novel for the time; 'Spinoza and Samuel Fisher', *Philosophia* 15 (1985), 219-236 (quotation, 231–2). N. McDowell has suggested that *Rusticus* was the 'most strident and comprehensive rejection of the Bible as a framework for understanding man and the universe written in early modern England'; *The English Radical Imagination: Culture, Religion and Revolution 1630–60* (Oxford, 2003), 139. D.S. Katz has suggested that Fisher possesses 'some claim to being among the founding fathers of modern biblical criticism'; *God's Last Words: Reading the English Bible from the Reformation to Fundamentalism* (New Haven, 2004), 73. Dissenting, N. Malcolm, has suggested that Fisher 'is sometimes hailed, quite unjustifiably, as an innovatory biblical scholar'; *Aspects of Hobbes* (Oxford, 2002), 430._

[12] New DNB 'Toland, John 1670–1722'. On Toland, see J.A.I. Champion, *Republican Learning: John Toland and the crisis of Christian culture, 1696-1722* (Manchester, 2003), idem, *The Pillars of Priestcraft Shaken: The Church of England and its enemies 1660–1730*, and assorted articles; see also S. Daniel, *John Toland: his methods, manners and mind* (Kingston, 1984).

[13] P. McGuinness, A. Harrison and R. Kearney (eds), *John Toland's Christianity not Mysterious: text, associated works and critical essays* (Dublin, 1997).

his innocence, a catalogue, replete with scholarly apparatus and patristic references, of spurious, forged and heretical works 'father'd upon CHRIST, his Apostles, and other great Names'.[14] Three respondents were the biblical scholar Samuel Clarke, the Cambridge minister John Richardson, and the religious controversialist Stephen Nye. Nye noted that the work was 'much magnified by the Anti-Christian Party about Town'.[15] Toland returned to the subject of the New Testament canon in *Nazarenus*, a work published in 1718 but which had pre-existed in a more polemically heterodox scribal form for more than a decade and may have been intellectually conceived in the 1690s.[16] Toland announced that he had discovered, in 1709, in an Italian manuscript in the library of Prince Eugene of Savoy in Amsterdam, a 'Mahometan Gospel' attributed to the apostle Barnabas, a textual bond between the religions of Islam and Christianity that enabled Toland to postulate a shared divine economy in which the followers of Mahomet were a 'sort of Christians'.[17] One critic, Thomas Brett, accused Toland of attempting 'to invalidate the authority of the New Testament'. Jones characterized it as a 'trifling book', but went to great lengths to refute the legitimacy of Toland's line of argument.[18]

Jones was equally familiar with the writings of William Whiston, having crossed pens with him over the Gospel of Matthew.[19] Whiston, son of the Presbyterian minister Josiah Whiston, rector of the parish of Norton in Leicestershire, entered Clare College, Cambridge in 1686, where he developed an avid interest in mathematics, graduating BA in 1689 and MA in 1693. That year he was ordained deacon by the latitudinarian Bishop Lloyd of Coventry and Lichfield, whose study of biblical chronology and prophecy may have sparked Whiston's interest.[20] Like most of the Cambridge academic

---

[14] J. Toland, *A complete collection of the historical, political and miscellaneous works of John Milton* (Amsterdam, 1698); O. Blackall, *A Sermon preached before the Honourable House of Commons at St Margaret's Westminster January 30th 1698/99* (London, 1699), 15–17; J. Toland, *Amyntor: Or, A Defence of Milton's Life* (London, 1699), 18, 14. Toland continually updated and enlarged the catalogue, circulating it in manuscript; J.A. I. Champion, 'Cultura sovversiva: erudizione e polemica nel l'amyntor canonicus di Toland, *c*.1698–1726', in A. Santucci (ed.), *Filosofia e cultura nel settecento britannico* (Bologna, 2002), 343–70.

[15] S. Clarke, *Some Reflections on that part of a Book called Amyntor, or the Defence of Milton's Life, which relates to the Writings of the Primitive Fathers and the Canon of the New Testament* (London, 1699); J. Richardson, *The Canon of the New Testament Vindicated; In Answer to the Objections of J.T. in his Amyntor* (London, 1700); S. Nye, *An Historical Account: A Defence of the Canon of the New Testament* (London, 1700), 108.

[16] Champion, *Republican Learning*, 169–70; J. Toland, *Nazarenus*, ed. J.A.I. Champion (Oxford, 1999), 56–7.

[17] Ibid., 116.

[18] T. Brett, *Tradition Necessary to explain and interpret the Holy Scriptures ... and a Preface containing some Remarks on Mr. Toland's Nazarenus* (London, 1718), xxiii; Jones, *New Testament*, i. 160.

[19] J. Jones, *A Vindication of the Former Part of St. Matthew's Gospel, from Mr. Whiston's Charge of Dislocations* (London, 1719); W. Whiston, *A short view of the chronology of the Old Testament, and of the harmony of the four evangelists* (Cambridge, 1702).

[20] New DNB 'Whiston, William (1667–1752)'.

fraternity, Whiston was initially an uncomprehending auditor at Newton's lectures, but he worked through the *Principia Mathematica* to become a convert to the philosophy and a friend to the philosopher. His first work, *A New Theory of the Earth* in 1696, appropriated Newtonian physics and the latest geological scholarship to demonstrate that scriptural accounts of Creation and the Flood were conformable to reason and philosophy.[21]

Whiston also followed Newton down the treacherous theological path to Arianism, identifying it as the primitive doctrine of Christ, the apostles and primitive Christians. Whiston broached his Arian views with John Ernest Grabe, a Prussian scholar whose rejection of Lutheranism had led him to England, where he established a reputation as one of the foremost biblical and patristic scholars of his generation.[22] Whiston professed himself dissatisfied with Grabe's 'poor, unintelligible, ill Grounded Evasions' and resolved to have 'Recourse to the Original Primitive Texts and Testimonies themselves for Satisfaction'.[23] He found in the *Apostolic Constitutions* – a collection of ecclesiastical regulations purportedly handed down by Christ to his apostles after his resurrection, but dismissed by most Protestant and Catholic scholars as a forgery – confirmation of his beliefs, and informed the leaders of the Anglican Church that they were continuing to propagate fraudulent doctrine. His claims of authenticity on behalf of the Constitutions received short shrift.[24] Based on the Constitutions, Whiston expanded the scriptural canon to include the two epistles of St Clement, the Pastor of Hermas and the Apocalypse of St John, and continued to investigate the canonicity of other texts.[25] After his tumultuous exit from Cambridge prompted by public heresy, Whiston announced that he had recovered, in two Arabic manuscripts in the Bodleian Library, the lost Christian text *The Doctrine of the Apostles,* which he promised to publish alongside an edition of the Apostolic Constitutions.[26] A printed exchange with Grabe ensued.

[21] J.E. Force, *William Whiston: Honest Newtonian* (Cambridge, 1985), 32–62; S.D. Snobelen, 'William Whiston: Natural Philosopher, prophet, primitive Christian' (unpublished Cambridge PhD, 2000), 20–21.

[22] J.E. Grabe, *Spicilegium S.S. Patrum ut et Haereticorum, Seculi post Christum natum,* &c., (2 vols, Oxford 1698–99); idem, *Septuaginta Interpretum* (4 vols, Oxford 1707–20) Two volumes of the Septuagint were published after Grabe's death by Francis Lee and George Wigan from his transcript.

[23] W. Whiston, *An Historical Preface to Primitive Christianity reviv'd. With an Appendix containing An Account of the Author's Prosecution at, and Banishment from the University of Cambridge* (London, 1711), 7–8.

[24] Ibid., 13–47; Force, *William Whiston,* 17. Refutations included W. Beveridge, *The Opinion of the Right Reverend Father in God William Beveridge ... concerning the Apostolical Constitutions* (London, 1712); R. Smalbroke, *The Pretended Authority of the Clementine Constitutions confuted* (London, 1714); R. Turner, *A Discourse on the pretended Apostolic Constitutions* (London, 1715).

[25] W. Whiston, *Sermons and Essays upon Several Subjects* (1709), 296.

[26] Whiston, *Historical Preface*, 115–16.

The reinterpretations presented by Fisher, Toland and Whiston of early Church history and the formation of the New Testament canon, and their championing of extra-canonical texts, provided a fundamental challenge to the principles and practices of orthodox biblical criticism. In forming answers to these challenges, and engaging with the problems inherent in constructing an unimpeachable foundation for the authority of the New Testament canon in its current form, Jones rejected both traditional European Protestant conceptions of the self-evidencing and self-authenticating nature of sacred scripture and the English Church's traditional sympathy towards a variety of 'worthy' texts hovering on the margins of canonicity.

II

Was it God or was it Man that set such distinct Bands to the Scriptures?[27]

Jones acknowledged that, unlike the Old Testament, no inspired individual or body determined the contents of the New Testament canon and no one date could be indubitably advanced as a *terminus post quem* the book was closed.[28] The forging of the canon was a slow-burning process, in which the pure metal of divine writ was separated from the dross over a period of centuries as the Church struggled to develop a stable identity against external persecution and internal deviation. In these turbulent times the circulation of texts, the exchange of ideas, and the assembling of Christians were restricted.[29]

Evidence about the interaction, oral and textual, between early Christian churches was scarce. Jones recognized that the lack of an authoritative historical account to demonstrate this process by which the books of scripture became the book of the Bible opened up a window of opportunity for sceptics to challenge the validity of the New Testament canon. The principal literary source for the history of the early Church in the early modern era was the *Ecclesiastical History* of Eusebius of Caesarea, compiled during the early fourth century from an array of sources that had not survived, which was published in various English editions throughout the early modern period.[30] Alongside Eusebius, biblical scholars were obliged to glean information from other

---

[27] Fisher, *Rusticus*, 269.

[28] Jones, *New Testament*, i. 3.

[29] Ibid., i. 8; Metzger, *Canon of the New Testament*, 90–99; Bruce, *Canon of Scripture*, 134–44; J. Knox, *Marcion and the New Testament: An Essay in the Early History of the Canon* (Chicago, 1942); N. Hyldahl *The History of Early Christianity* (NY, 1997), 288–92.

[30] The most popular version was [Eusebius of Caesarea], *The auncient ecclesiasticall histories of the first six hundred yeares after Christ, wrytten in the Greeke tongue by three learned historiographers, Eusebius, Socrates and Euagrius ... translated out of the Greeke tongue by Meredith Hanmer*, &c., (London, 1577). See also R.M. Grant, *Eusebius as Church Historian* (Oxford, 1980); A.J. Carriker *The Library of Eusebius of Caesarea* (Leiden, 2003).

patristic sources regarding the New Testament scriptures. Among the western Fathers, Justin Martyr, Irenaeus and Tertullian were the most prolific; among their Eastern counterparts, valuable materials survived from the writings of Clement of Alexandria, Ignatius, Origen and Athanasius. The partial nature of these records, though, and the problems of interpreting the authority these Fathers ascribed to texts during a period when the canon was still evolving, made any attempts to construct a *consensus patrum* problematic.

The lack of evidence invited speculation. The non-juring theological and patristic scholar Henry Dodwell had advanced the notion that canonical texts had lain concealed in the possession of particular Churches or individuals until at least the early second century partly to prevent them from being overwhelmed by the host of spurious and forged texts proliferating amongst early Christians. Toland praised Dodwell as one who 'understands as much of Ecclesiastic History as the Divines of all Churches put together'. He was sufficiently impressed with this line of argument, which precluded any early development of a canon among the scattered Christian churches, to quote Dodwell's work at length.[31] Jones rejected this thesis as utterly false. He emphasized that the conception of the canon, as an authoritative body of texts, possessed an early genesis that slowly took shape as geographical, communicational and political barriers were overcome, spurious texts identified and dissenters ostracized.[32]

Church Councils provided a rare record of Christian assembly, and sometimes the results, if not the processes, of deliberations. Protestant authorities regarded the Council of Laodicea (*c*.364) as the Christian assembly that provided authoritative confirmation of the scriptural canon. The Laudian scholar and future bishop of Durham, John Cosin, had argued that Christ bequeathed to his apostles a fixed body of texts that was formulated into a canon some sixty years after the death of the last apostle John, by Melito, Bishop of Sardis, who had consulted with the Eastern Church. This canon was confirmed by individual Church Fathers before receiving a collective ecclesiastical blessing from the Laodicean assembly. Cosin believed that this Council was held 'in such Reverence and Estimation by All men in those elder Ages following', that its canons were generally received by all the churches in Christendom.[33]

Thomas Hobbes had provided, in *Leviathan*, a very different character assessment of this body. He spoke of the 'Doctors of the Church' in this era who 'thought such frauds as tended to make the people the more obedient to Christian Doctrine, to be pious', although he magnanimously acquitted them of falsifying scripture on the

[31] H. Dodwell, *Dissertationes in Irenaeum* (Oxford, 1689), 65–7; Toland, *Amyntor*, 69–78 (quotation, 69).

[32] Jones, *New Testament*, i. 41–3.

[33] J. Cosin, *A Scholastical History of the Canon of the Holy Scripture* (London, 1657), 29–55. (quotation, 55); Cosin's work, directed primarily at the Roman Church not Protestant dissenters, was republished in the 1670s and 1680s. On Melito of Sardis, see Metzger, *Canon of the New Testament* 122–3.

grounds that they would undoubtedly have made the sacred texts more supportive of clerical pretensions to temporal power.[34] Similarly cynical about the worthiness of ecclesiastical assemblies, Fisher demanded to know 'Who was it, God or Man, the Spirit in the Scripture it self, or the Scribes in their Synods, Councils, and Consistories that so Authorized or Canonized these, and expunged those?' 'Was it not', the Quaker concluded, 'meer Men in their Imaginations?'[35]

Toland ascribed to the Laodicean body a more creative, formative role, observing that it was 'the first Assembly wherein the Canon of Scripture was establisht'. He suggested that its members could only have discriminated the genuine from the spurious amongst the 'variety of Books as were then abroad in the World' by one of two means – 'a particular revelation from Heaven', or by 'crediting the Testimony of their Ancestors'. The former was nowhere attested, and if it was the latter, Toland assured his readers that 'for the Books I defend, I have the same Testimony which is usually alleg'd in the behalf of others'.[36] Toland further speculated that political considerations may have influenced the composition of the canon. He feared that, just as unworthy texts had been intruded into the canon 'in the dark Ages of Popery', worthy texts may have been excluded 'in ignorant Ages before' because they did not suit 'the Opinions of the strongest Party'.[37] Whiston described Church Councils as 'the great Contrivance of the Enemy of Mankind'.[38]

Nye refuted any ascription of a constructive role to the Council of Laodicea, but he did however allow that the Council endorsed previously doubted texts as canonical scripture. Although he maintained that they acted 'on most convincing reasons', he did not elaborate on what those convincing reasons may have been.[39] These doubted texts were 2 Peter, Jude, James, 2 and 3 John, Hebrews and Revelation. Eusebius had accounted the epistles of James, Jude, 2 Peter, and 2 and 3 John as *antilegomena*, 'disputed books, yet familiar to most people of the church'. He listed Hebrews as *homologoumena* – universally acknowledged – but recognized that some Christians rejected the text, whilst he seemed unable to decide whether Revelation was canonical or spurious, placing it in both categories. Eusebius' uncertainty over the status of certain scriptural texts meant that sceptics like Fisher and Toland could, and did, mine the rich intellectual resource of the 'Father of Church history'.[40] Toland noted that these texts 'were a long time plainly doubted by the Ancients', and Jones recognized that these works had taken longer to find universal acceptance in the early Church

[34] T. Hobbes, *Leviathan*, ed. R. Tuck (Cambridge, 1997), 266.

[35] Fisher, *Rusticus*, 270.

[36] Toland, *Amyntor*, 57–8.

[37] Ibid., 49.

[38] Whiston, *Sermons and Essays*, 246.

[39] Nye, *Historical Account*, 83.

[40] Eusebius of Caesarea, *The History of the Church*, trans. G.A. Williamson (rev. ed., London 1989), iii. 25; Metzger, *Canon of the New Testament*, 201–7; E. von Dobschutz, 'The Abandonment of the Canonical Idea', *American Journal of Theology* 19 (1915), 416–29; Ehrman, *Lost Christianities*, 243–4.

than others.[41] Richardson described it as inevitable that the scattered churches would more swiftly adopt certain texts than others.[42] Toland, however, pushed the point further, arguing that 'there is not one single Book in the New Testament which was not refus'd by som of the Ancients as unjustly father'd upon the Apostles, and really forg'd by their Adversaries'.[43] Nye was forced to wonder whether his opponent had found some of the first (lost) Historians of the Church, pack'd up in a close Chest, or Hogshead, and buried so many Ages under ground'.[44]

Jones recognized that a wide variety of texts competed for acceptance among early Christians. The churches did not unanimously and simultaneously receive proto-canonical texts. Numerous individuals and groups rejected the authority of the evolving canon. Faustus Manichaeus and his followers rejected the entire New Testament, but adopted three apocryphal early Christian texts – the Gospel of Thomas, the Teaching of Addas, and the Shepherd of Hermas.[45] The Alogians – so named by the fourth-century heresiographer Epiphanius because they rejected the Logos – dismissed the Gospel of St John as authored by Cerinthus, a Gnostic contemporary of the apostle.[46] The Ebionites, Jewish Christians, and a Gnostic splinter group called the Helkesaites, rejected the Acts of the Apostles and Epistles of Paul.[47]

Similarly, Jones recognized that many texts claiming divinely inspired authorship were in circulation. It was, he noted, 'the constant artifice of evil-minded designing men, to publish their errors under the great name of some Apostle, or inspired writer, in order the more effectually to propagate them among the unthinking multitude'.[48] Early heretics – Basilides, the second-century Alexandrian Gnostic, Apelles, the Gnostic pupil of Marcion, and the Nicolaitans, had all adopted this strategy.[49] In the succeeding centuries, the number of texts claiming apostolic authorship multiplied. Many of these texts, Jones observed, had been entirely lost, some survived in fragmentary form, whilst others could be partially reconstituted through patristic sources.[50]

---

[41] Toland, *Amyntor*, 57; Jones, *New Testament*, i. 8; Metzger, *Canon of the New Testament*, 213; B. D. Ehrman, *The New Testament: A Historical Introduction to the Early Christian Writings* (Oxford, 2000), 378–84, 420–21, 425–37; idem, *Lost Christianities*, 243–6; K. Aland, *The Problem of the New Testament Canon* (London, 1962), 10–12.

[42] Richardson, *Canon of the New Testament vindicated*, 9–19.

[43] Toland, *Amyntor*, 56.

[44] Nye, *Historical Account*, 74.

[45] Jones, *New Testament*, i. 8; R. Seddon, *Mani: his life and work*, (London, 1998); P. Mirecki and J. BeDuhn (eds), *The light and the darkness: studies in Manichaeism and its world* (Leiden, 2001); J. van Oort, O. Wermelinger and G. Wurst (eds) *Augustine and Manichaeism in the Latin West* (Leiden, 2001).

[46] Jones, *New Testament*, i. 8; Metzger, *Canon of the New Testament*, 72.

[47] Jones, *New Testament*, i. 8; Ehrman, *Lost Christianities*, 99–103; idem, *Lost Scriptures: Books that did not make it into the New Testament* (Oxford, 2003), 9–14.

[48] Jones, *New Testament*, i. 12.

[49] Ibid., i. 12.

[50] Ibid., i. 28.

Toland had suggested that spurious pieces were forged for a variety of reasons – by zealous Christians seeking to 'supply the brevity of the Apostolic Memoirs', by 'designing Men to support their privat Opinions', and by 'Heathens and Jews to impose on the Credulity of many wel-dispos'd Persons'.[51] Jones pointed out that some forgeries were the product of pious Christians. Tertullian and Jerome had observed that the spurious Acts of Paul and Thecla had been written by a presbyter in Asia who, when identified, confessed he did it out of love for the Apostle.[52] What mattered, Jones stressed, was not the number of spurious texts in circulation – he suggested Toland's catalogue was still incomplete – or the time of their composition – the *Gospel according to the Egyptians* might have predated at least some of the canonical gospels - but the manner in which they were received or rejected by most of the early Church so that by the end of the fourth century there was near-universal agreement on the canon.[53]

III

'Is all Extant? All remaining? All Preserved to this day that was written by Holy men, as moved by the holy Spirit?'[54]

Jones recognized that the issue of whether apostolic writers had penned more texts than those preserved for Christian posterity posed problems for the New Testament scholar concerning inspiration and the operation of divine providence. He was at pains to deny, as disagreeable to the conduct of divine providence and unlikely in light of the zeal of early Christians, that any texts accepted as canonical had subsequently been lost.[55] The issue had been picked up by Quaker controversialists seeking to use scripture to undermine scripture. If, Fisher wondered, divine providence had operated to preserve inspired scriptures, where were those texts mentioned or implied in canonical works, for instance Paul's first epistles to the Corinthians and Ephesians. Where, indeed, the Quaker disputant pondered, was Paul's epistle to the Laodiceans.[56] In Paul's epistle to the Colossians, the apostle wrote, 'And when this Epistle is read among you, cause that it be read also in the Church of the Laodiceans, and that ye likewise read the Epistle from Laodicea'.[57] A text purporting to be Paul's epistle to the Laodiceans did exist, as Fisher well knew. In a brief letter of just 20 verses, the author, apparently experiencing imprisonment, delights in the faith and virtue of the Laodiceans, warns them to be on their guard against heretics, and

[51] Toland, *Amyntor,* 42, 43.

[52] Ibid., i. 38–40; Ehrman, *Lost Christianities*, 29–46; S.J. Davis, *The Cult of Saint Thecla: A Tradition of Women's Piety in Late Antiquity* (New York, 2001).

[53] Jones, *New Testament*, i. 28, 197–216.

[54] Fisher, *Rusticus*, 275.

[55] Jones, *New Testament*, i. 130–35.

[56] Fisher, *Rusticus*, 275–7.

[57] KJV, Colossians 4:16.

encourages them to adhere to Christian faith and practice. Various church authorities from the fourth century onwards, notably Gregory the Great, mentioned the text. It was incorporated into many Vulgate manuscripts, and appeared in a number of early English versions. The tenth-century English monk Aelfric the Grammarian listed it among the Pauline Epistles, although the twelfth-century philosopher and historian John of Salisbury separated it from the other 14 epistles. The text appeared in the first German Bible, published in 1488, between Galatians and Ephesians, and in all subsequent editions before Luther's, and in the first Bohemian Bible, published at Prague in 1488 and reprinted in the sixteenth and seventeenth centuries. It was not until the Council of Florence (1439'43), in which the Western Church issued a definitive biblical canon, that Paul's so-called fifteenth epistle was excluded. The sixteenth-century converted Jew, biblical scholar and exegete Sixtus Senensis found two manuscripts of the epistle, one in the Sorbonne Library in Paris, and the other in the library of Joannes a Viridario in Padua, the latter of which he transcribed and published.[58]

Fisher used this epistle, a text that 'hovered about the doors of the Sacred Canon' for a millennium,[59] in his public dispute with Danson at Sandwich to lay a trap for his unwary opponent. In an extraordinary episode, Danson apparently declared that he doubted whether a copy of this text was extant, only for a member of the audience to stand up and declare that he personally possessed a copy. A triumphant Fisher declared that the epistle was found 'in the oldest Bible that was Printed at Worms' and 'in a certain Antient Manuscript of the New Testament Text, which I have seen and can produce, written in Old English three hundred and forty years since'. On the basis of these sources, Fisher jumped rather precipitously to the conclusion that the text was evidently 'owned as Canonical in the Church of England in those days'.[60]

Jones noted that the Quakers had pleaded for this epistle, and confessed that he had encountered a bewildering variety of opinion regarding this epistle from scholars, ancient and modern, Catholic and Protestant, English and European.[61] Digging amongst his patristic sources, he had found that Epiphanius had attested to the existence of an epistle under this name in the early second century, and that Marcion made use of it. Tertullian supposed that Marcion actually affixed the title to

---

[58] J.K. Elliott, *The Apocryphal New Testament: A Collection of Apocryphal Christian Literature in an English Translation* (Oxford, 1993), 543–7; M.R. James, *The Apocryphal New Testament* (Oxford, 1924), 478–9; Metzger, *Canon of the New Testament*, 182–3, 239–40. On Sixtus Senensis, see F.J. Crehan, 'The Bible in the Roman Catholic Church from Trent to the Present Day', in S.L. Greenslade (ed.), *The Cambridge History of the Bible: Volume III The West from the Reformation to the Present Day* (Cambridge, 1963), 206–7.

[59] J.B. Lightfoot, *Saint Paul's Epistles to the Colossians and to Philemon* (London, 1890), 297.

[60] Fisher, *Rusticus*, 282–3; H.J. Cadbury, 'Early Quakerism and Uncanonical Lore', in *Harvard Theological Review*, XL (1947), 185; J.A.I. Champion, 'Apocrypha, Canon and Criticism from Samuel Fisher to John Toland 1660–1718', in A.P. Coudert, S. Hutton, R.H. Popkin, and G.M. Weiner (eds), *Judaeo-Christian Intellectual Culture in the Seventeenth Century* (Leiden, 1999), 105–6.

[61] Jones, *New Testament*, ii. 32.

Paul's epistle to the Ephesians, but Jones gave greater credit to Epiphanius's account. Modern scholars, including the Laudian biblical scholar Henry Hammond and John Mill, editor of the seminal 1707 edition of the Greek New Testament, had continued the speculation regarding the relationship between the Laodicean and Ephesian texts.[62] Jones was adamant that Paul never wrote an epistle to the Laodiceans, but that the church of Laodicea wrote to the apostle. The confusion was the consequence of a linguistic hazard occasioned by translation. Jones 'excused' Catholic commentators, like Cardinal Bellarmine, who relied on the ambiguous Latin, but held Protestant commentators culpable, for they did not 'take the corrupt translation of the Vulgate for their infallible guide'.[63]

'What think ye', Fisher asked of John Owen, 'of that sweet, short, pretious Reply of Christ Jesus himself in his Letter to Agbarus, King of Edessa '?[64] The correspondence to which Fisher referred was a supposed exchange between Agbar, son of Uchomo, the seventeenth toparch of Edessa, and Christ. Agbar sent a letter to Christ in Jerusalem by the runner Ananias, professing belief in his divinity and mission, asking that he come and cure him of an incurable disease and offering him refuge in his city from his enemies. Christ replied, blessing the Mesopotamian king for believing in him when he had not seen him, and promising to send one of his disciples after the fulfilment of his mission and ascension. The apostle Thomas sent Judas Thaddeus, one of the Seventy, who healed Agbar and converted Edessa. Eusebius discovered the correspondence in the archives of Edessa, and provided a translation of the Syriac into Greek. Fisher had read 'the Ecclesiastical History of Eusebius Pamphilius'.[65] Fisher sought to engage Owen in an exercise of comparative textual analysis. He saw no reason why some of the Apocrypha may not be judged to be 'as divine an Original and Authority as some of those particular letters to private men, as that of Paul to Philemon'. If the Philemon epistle was included, why should not, he demanded of Owen, the correspondence with Agbarus warrant 'a room in your Canon'.[66] Fisher's 'sympathy' for apocryphal texts was a disputatious posture, enabling him to lament to his clerical protagonist that worthy texts were excluded from 'the Confines of your Congregationally Constituted, Synodically Composed, Ecclesiastically Authorized, Clerically conceived Canon'.[67]

Jones rejected the correspondence on the grounds of its lack of mention in the early Christian records, its general rejection by churches following its publication by Eusebius, and textual inconsistencies. He noted that most scholars, Catholics like Simon and Protestants like Le Clerc, had also deemed the correspondence spurious, but he was critical of the decidedly equivocal judgement offered by a few English

[62] Ibid., ii. 31–9. The version identified by Epiphanius was different from that later incorporated into manuscripts of the Vulgate; Ehrman, *Lost Scriptures*, 165–6.

[63] Jones, *New Testament*, ii. 39–49, (quotation, 40).

[64] Fisher, *Rusticus*, 277.

[65] James, *Apocryphal New Testament*, 476–7; Fisher, *Rusticus*, 277.

[66] Ibid., 270, 277.

[67] Fisher, *Rusticus*, 277.

divines. The patristic scholar William Cave had judged that there was nothing in the letters that 'may justly shake their credit and authority', and opined that there was 'no wise argument' against the correspondence, save for the lack of reference to it in the early historical record. He ascribed this silence to the fact that the letters had only survived in Syriac, and 'the Ancients' had been 'generally strangers to the Language, the Customs, and Antiquities, of those Eastern countries'.[68] Grabe had not ruled the arguments against the validity of the correspondence conclusive.[69] William Wake did not dissent from the majority opinion, but he chose to 'leave it to every one to judg as he pleases, than determine any thing in this Case'.[70] Jones strongly concurred with those critics, including Simon, Du Pin, Fabricius and Le Clerc, who had dismissed the correspondence, observing that no Christian writers mentioned it before the fourth century, and Christ's epistle contained inconsistencies and had been rejected following its publication by Eusebius.[71] Jones discounted the notion that Christ had written any texts and accused Toland, as previous critics had, of mischievously misattributing patristic references to suggest otherwise.[72]

Jones reserved swingeing criticism for those whose motives he distrusted and whose scholarly attainments he depreciated, but he also carefully distanced himself from what might loosely be termed a High Church school of clerical learning that was essentially Laudian in origin and whose principal proponent in the Restoration Church had been Bishop John Fell. The work that particularly concerned Jones was an edition, published in 1693 and twice reprinted, of the writings of the apostolic Fathers by William Wake, ordained deacon by Fell in 1681 and, at the time Jones wrote, the archbishop of Canterbury. In *The Genuine Epistles of the Apostolical Fathers*, a work of popular scholarship, Wake presented a cogent argument for the acceptance of other texts besides those in the New Testament canon as inspired, infallible and instructive for Christian faith and practice, although he stopped short of claiming for them a place in the canon. Their authors were contemporaries of the holy apostles, and their works should be received 'if not with equal Veneration, yet but with a little less Respect, then we do the Sacred Writings of those who were their Masters and Instructers'.[73]

Toland did not refer directly to Wake's work but seemed to have the future archbishop of Canterbury in his sights when he ridiculed the veneration proffered by some in the Church of England towards the writings of the apostolic Fathers. He described the *Pastor of Hermas*, a lengthy prophetic and instructive text, as 'the sillyest Book in the World'. If, Toland asked, their defenders believed them to be the genuine work of companions of the apostles, as the gospel authors Mark and Luke

68 W. Cave, *Apostolici: or, the History of the Lives, Acts, Death, and Martyrdoms of those who were Contemporary with, or immediately succeeded the Apostles* (London, 1677), iv.

69 Grabe, *Spicilegium Patrum*, i. 1–12.

70 Wake, *Genuine Epistles*, 134–9.

71 Jones, *New Testament*, ii. 1–26.

72 Ibid., i. 186–7, 193–4; Toland, *Amyntor*, 20, 21; Nye, *An Historical Account*, 23–4.

73 W. Wake, *The Genuine Epistles of the Apostolic Fathers* (London, 1693), 156–75 (quotation, 160).

were, why did they not incorporate them into the canon of the New Testament? It was 'mere Evasion' to exclude them on the grounds that the early Church excluded them, when some canonical texts were received by the whole Church only after Eusebius' time. Toland also asserted that were other lost texts recovered, they would doubtless prove to be 'as foolish and fabulous as the rest'. These texts had been 'fraudulently impos'd on the Credulous'.[74]

Jones had intended to address the writings of the apostolic Fathers in a separate work – one that he did not live long enough to write – but he did discuss the epistle of Barnabas, a text that seemed 'to lay a more pompous claim to Canonical authority than many others'.[75] Jones thought that Bishop Fell and other English divines had delivered their opinions on this and other texts of the apostolic Fathers ambiguously because they thought them worthy of as much respect as some canonical texts. He judged Fell's opinion to be that the Epistle of Barnabas was entirely orthodox in content, stylistically close to Paul's writings, that the early church fathers who ascribed it to Barnabas were in the best position to judge, and that its reading in churches was only discontinued because of its obscure and mystical elements.[76] Dodwell thought the epistle was the genuine work of the apostle, and pre-dated several canonical texts. This enabled Toland to demand to know on what grounds the epistle had been excluded from the canon.[77] Jones's judgement sought to deprive sceptics and dissenters of this potential ammunition. He argued that the Epistle of Barnabas, omitted from early catalogues of sacred texts and absent from the Syriac version, was 'a spurious, Apocryphal and silly piece' of Gentile authorship, written after the destruction of Jerusalem in CE 70, that contained falsehoods, inconsistencies, trifles and foolish allegories.[78]

IV

'Others perhaps are still extant.'[79]

Toland and Whiston both claimed to have discovered lost Christian texts from the times of the early Church, discoveries that necessitated a reappraisal of Christian theology and the New Testament canon. In *Nazarenus*, Toland announced that he had recovered the Gospel of Barnabas. *Nazarenus* was a carefully constructed piece of scholarship designed to operate on several levels depending on the educational attainments and acuity of the reader. The main body of the text was in English, with biblical references in the margins, but the footnotes, and occasional quotations

---

[74] Toland, *Amyntor*, 48, 38.

[75] Jones, *New Testament*, ii. 412.

[76] Ibid., ii. 426–7; [J. Fell], *Sancti Barnabae ... epistola catholica. Accessit S. Hermae ... Pastor* (Oxford, 1685).

[77] Jones, *New Testament*, ii. 427–8; Toland, *Amyntor*, 38–48.

[78] Jones, *New Testament*, ii. 412–62 (quotation, 413).

[79] Ibid., i. 28.

in the text, were in Latin and sometimes Greek. The knowledge of early Christian texts and patristic writings evident in *Amyntor* was again on display, but this time buttressed by a greater range of modern scholarship, including rabbinical scholars like Jacob Rhenferd, patristic scholars like Denis Patau, and orientalists like Johan Jacob Cramer.

Toland's gospel was 'a Mahometan Gospel, never before publicly made known among Christians', which 'very probably is in great part the same book' as the ancient Gospel of Barnabas mentioned in the *Gelasian Decree*, an early sixth-century list of canonical texts commonly attributed to Pope Gelasius I (492–96).[80] Toland noted that a fragment of the gospel was recorded in the thirty-ninth manuscript in the Baroccian collection in the Bodleian Library, and had been transcribed by Grabe in his *Spicilegium Patrum*. He observed that this fragment was to be found 'almost in terms' in his gospel, with the sense 'evidently there in more than one place'.[81] He noted, rather contentiously, that the Mahometans had been more careful in the preservation of their texts than Christians. Furthermore, they were more consistent in their position that if a text was inspired, 'every line and word of it must necessarily be so', leaving no room for the 30,000 various readings Mill had uncovered for the New Testament.[82] Jones observed that the *Gospel of Barnabas* (a text that in *Amyntor* Toland had boasted of proving spurious if it ever surfaced, but in *Nazarenus* now opined could be 'as old as the time of the apostles'),[83] did not appear to have fallen within the cognizance of any of the Christian writers of the first four centuries. He declared it 'a very late and notorious Mahometan imposture' and expressed his doubts that this spurious text even contained the saying of Barnabas identified by Grabe. Jones suggested, from a story related by Theodorus Lector, the early ninth-century Patriarch of Constantinople Nicephorus, and a late tenth-century Byzantine lexicon wrongly attributed to Suidas, that the Gospel of Barnabas was actually an interpolated and corrupted translation of the Gospel of Matthew composed or discovered in the time of Zeno, Emperor of the Eastern Roman Empire in the late fifth century.[84]

Toland found in this version of Barnabas, in which Mahomet was named as the Paraclete, the 'ancient Ebionite or Nazaren System' that depicted Jesus as a mere man, although divinely conceived, whose place on the cross was taken by another allowing him to preach afterwards to his disciples before being taken up to heaven.[85]

In *Amyntor*, Toland had called the Ebionites or Nazarenes – he did not discern a difference between them – 'the oldest Christians'.[86] Nye had accused Toland of

---

[80] Toland, *Nazarenus*, 115.

[81] Ibid., 138, 147; Grabe, *Spicilegium Patrum*, i. 302.

[82] Toland, *Nazarenus*, 140. Toland, Anthony Collins and other sceptics often referred to Mill's thirty thousand variant readings as a numerical indication of the instability of the New Testament text.

[83] Toland, *Amyntor*, 40, *Nazarenus*, 145.

[84] Jones, *New Testament*, i. 160–70.

[85] Ibid., 144.

[86] Toland, *Amyntor*, 64.

conflating the Ebionites and Nazarenes when 'they were no more the same Sect of Christians, than the Church of England and the Quakers are'.[87] Other commentators accepted that they were one group, at least originally, that may later have divided. This sect, or sects, stressed the importance of still keeping the Jewish Law, and gave preference to the Gospel of Matthew because of its greater emphasis upon Christ's Jewish identity. Early Church authorities speculated as to whether this group composed their own gospel, or used an Aramaic translation of Matthew, and opinion varied among Toland's critics.[88] Toland asserted that Irenaeus and Epiphanius, 'the most ignorant and partial of all historians', had been ignorantly mistaken in speculating that their gospel was an interpolated translation of Matthew. Two critics, Thomas Mangey and Thomas Brett, described the Nazarenes as enemies of the first Christians, and Brett accused Toland of following an opinion of Grabe that the Prussian scholar had later retracted.[89] Jerome, Origen and Eusebius, Toland claimed, had made use of the text, which had been read in the Nazarene churches for over 300 years, listing it among the ecclesiastical books, 'that is, books whose antiquity they were not able to deny, but whose authority they were not willing to acknowledge'.[90] Its disfavour in certain quarters, he suggested, was politically motivated. In the early Church, 'every side and sect pretended they were the onely true Christians', and all appealed to apostolic tradition, an appeal used then, as now, 'to introduce or countenance whatever men had a mind to advance without the authority of Scripture'.[91]

Jones recognized some biblical scholars had attributed considerable authority to *The Gospel according to the Ebionites*, otherwise termed *The Gospel according to the Nazarenes*, *the Hebrews*, and *the Twelve Apostles*, exalting it to 'a degree of authority very near equal, I had almost said superior to some, or even any, of the Canonical books of the New Testament'.[92] Sixtus Senensis had claimed that most of the ancient Fathers received the Nazarene Gospel amongst other sacred scriptures, whilst the ecclesiastical historian Cardinal Baronius had believed that the Gospel was the true original of the present Greek text of Matthew.[93] Jones judged though, that it was the Oratorian priest Richard Simon who had 'carried the authority of this Gospel to a very great height'. He had claimed that the Gospel of Matthew had been written originally in Hebrew for the Christians of Palestine called Nazarenes, who were not heretics. Simon argued that the work should not be regarded as apocryphal and were it extant it should be preferred to the present Greek text even with interpolations as

---

[87] Nye, *An Historical Account*, 76.

[88] Ehrman, *Lost Christianities*, 99–103.

[89] Toland, *Nazarenus*, 169; T. Brett, *Tradition Necessary to explain and interpret the Holy Scriptures* (London, 1718), iv (quotation xv); Grabe, *Spicilegium Patrum*, i. 21; T. Mangey, *Remarks upon Nazarenus* (London, 1718), 7; Jones, *New Testament*, i. 266–82.

[90] Toland, *Nazarenus*, 188, 189 (quotation, 189).

[91] Ibid., 190–92 (quotations 190, 192).

[92] Jones *New Testament*, i. 266. Jones believed that Paul referred to the text in one of his epistles, Gal. 1:6.

[93] Ibid., i. 283–4.

these had been added by the Nazarenes upon trustworthy testimonies.[94] Jones thought Grabe's assessment of the text was more judicious. The Prussian scholar rejected the supposition that it was an interpolated version of Matthew, suggesting instead that it was a genuine composition by Jewish converts at Jerusalem before the canonical gospels were written, to which the Nazarenes and Ebionites later affixed the title of Matthew to bolster its authority.[95]

Jones denied that any early Christian writer had cited the Gospel as an authoritative text, suggesting that earlier scholars, including Ussher, Pearson, Grabe, Fabricius, and Simon as well as Toland, who believed that the apostolic Father Papias had used the Gospel had misunderstood Eusebius.[96] Toland's notion that Origen alleged it to be a true Gospel was dismissed on the grounds that the Greek Father rejected it under the title of *The Gospel according to the Twelve Apostles*. Far from making frequent use of the text, as Toland asserted, Eusebius made no use of the Gospel at all – another 'unpardonable falsehood' on this part of this critic.[97] *The Gospel of the Nazarenes* was not to be found in any ancient catalogues of sacred books, was not read in churches, contained evident falsehoods – that Christ was a sinner and unwilling to be baptised – and idle stories, and Jones therefore ascribed its composition to Jewish converts still attached to their old faith and with some odd ideas about Christianity – the Nazarenes, out of whom emerged the Ebionites – translating and rewriting the Greek text of Matthew.[98] Toland's design, Jones asserted, was to advance his project of 'abolishing the doctrines of Christianity' by introducing the 'most ridiculous and impious scheme of Nazarene, or Jewish, or Ebionite, or Mahometan, or (which is the undoubted truth) of no Christianity at all'. To accomplish this end, he pursued the unscrupulous policy of 'ransacking and mustering together all the silly trumpery of the antient hereticks, grossly misrepresenting the books he cites, only with design to satisfy a bigotted humour against the Christian religion'.[99]

V

By the early eighteenth century, biblical criticism was not just a matter of discerning genuine texts from spurious ones; it was equally important to distinguish the genuine biblical critic from the fake. Jones was confident that he could identify the sceptics like Toland masquerading as believers, and that he could spot the heretics lurking among the orthodox Christians, like William Whiston. Whiston, unlike others, never sought to camouflage his heresy behind silence or dissimulation, but behind Jones'

[94] Ibid., i. 284–5; R. Simon, *A Critical History of the Text of the New Testament* (2 pts, London 1689), i. 59–83 (corrected pagination).

[95] Grabe, *Spicilegium Patrum*, i. 15–37; Jones, *New Testament*, i. 285–6.

[96] Ibid., i. 289–98.

[97] Ibid., i. 298–300 (quotation 300).

[98] Ibid., i. 300–311.

[99] Ibid., i. 217–21(quotations 218, 219).

invective against him and Toland perhaps lay the fear that other readers of their work would not tell the difference.

There may have been only muted surprise amongst biblical scholars at the announcement by William Whiston, the greatest advocate of extra-canonical texts of his generation, that he had recovered *The Doctrine of the Apostles*. This text, otherwise known as *The Teaching of the Twelve Apostles*, or the *Didache*, was a lost text of the early Church, surviving only in tantalising fragments scattered amongst ancient writings, including the *Apostolic Constitutions*. It purported to be a work of collective authorship by the twelve apostles. It contained a section of moral instruction, seemingly designed for those preparing for baptism and membership of the Church, a manual of church order and practice, and a brief closing section of apocalyptic hue. Eusebius accounted the text as spurious; Whiston's contemporaries concurred.[100] Whiston announced that he had, with the assistance of Simon Ockley, soon to be Sir Thomas Adams's professor of Arabic at Cambridge and a distinguished orientalist whom Toland also knew, recovered a version of this ancient Christian work amongst the manuscripts in the Bodleian Library. Whiston believed the work to have been extracted from the *Apostolic Constitutions* and therefore worthy to be esteemed canonical.[101]

Grabe, whose engagement with Whiston had the blessing of the ecclesiastical hierarchy, was aroused by what he perceived as an ill-informed trespassing into learned territory by 'a Presbyter only of the Church of England'.[102] Assisted by Jean Gagnier, a notable Arabist patronized by Archbishop Lloyd, Grabe trawled the Bodleian collection looking for anything relating to the *Doctrine of the Apostles*, as well as closely reading through the two manuscripts in question.[103] Upon discovering the text to be a translation out of the Constitutions, with a number of minor alterations attributable to the idiosyncrasies of the Arabic interpreter, Grabe declared himself to be 'perfectly amazed' at the claims made on its behalf by Whiston. Surely, he conjectured, out of 'common Prudence and Piety', Whiston would not have ventured upon printing a supposedly canon-worthy text without fully determining its nature and contents, lest he should 'prostitute that Sacred Name and Authority to the Scoffs and Derision of Infidels'. In passing, Grabe observed that the Arabic text followed Trinitarian orthodoxy.[104]

Reading manuscripts in an eighteenth-century library was not always a private affair. The activities of the former Cambridge scholar in the fortress of Oxford learning

---

[100] Eusebius, *History of the Church*, 88–9; Ehrman, *Lost Christianities*, 48, 244.

[101] New DNB 'Ockley, Simon (bap. 1679–1720)'; A. Kararah, 'Simon Ockley: His contribution to Arabic studies and influence on Western thought' (unpublished PhD, Cambridge, 1955); Champion, *The Pillars of Priestcraft Shaken*, 103–4.

[102] J.E. Grabe, *An Essay upon two Arabick Manuscripts of the Bodlejan Library, and that ancient Book, call'd The Doctrine of the Apostles, which is said to be extant in them, wherein Mr Whiston's Mistakes about both are plainly prov'd* (Oxford, 1711), dedication to the Bishop of Worcester.

[103] New DNB 'Gagnier, John (*c*.1670–1740)'.

[104] Grabe, *Essay*, 8–9, 75–8.

had not gone unobserved. Grabe had, he claimed, been informed that his protagonist had 'spent there but a little Time, and very few Hours only about the two Manuscripts'. Ockley informed Grabe that he had only translated chapter titles and occasional passages for Whiston and later accused him of undertaking 'to dictate to all Mankind in a Part of Learning' which he was 'entirely ignorant of'.[105] Whiston retaliated that Grabe, like other establishment scholars, obeyed the dictates of prudence that 'they must not own plainly in publick what they cannot but think and grant in private', and denied misusing Ockley. He accepted that the body of the Arabic text was a corrupt translation of the *Constitutions*, ascribing it on account of its misrepresentation of Christ's eternity to fourth-century Athanasians, but maintained that the preface to the Arabic text was the genuine preface of the *Doctrine of the Apostles*. He also tantalized his readers with news that an Arabic version of the Constitutions had been unearthed in Cambridge, promising a fuller account when further information came to hand.[106] Whiston, in elegant and sensationalist prose depicted his opponent as part of a learned coterie perpetrating long-standing frauds regarding scriptural texts. Grabe depicted his opponent as an amateur scholar, lacking in authority, temperament and scholarly attainment. Jones thought that Grabe possessed a 'too fond affection for Apocryphal books', but reserved scathing criticism for Whiston, whom 'one cannot without compassion behold honestly paying the greatest regard to the pretended Constitutions of the Apostles'.[107]

VI

It was a matter of 'the greatest Consequence and Importance', Jones stressed, to distinguish those texts that were genuinely inspired, for failure to do so was to impute lies and deceits upon God. To accept the *Gospel of the Nazarenes* was to accept that Jesus was unwilling to be baptised by John whilst to accept *Acts* supposedly penned by Peter, John, Andrew, Thomas, or Paul was to accept that Christ was not really human and that someone else had been crucified in his place. To receive spurious texts under specious pretences, or to reject canonical texts without justification, lead to errors in doctrine and practice.[108]

Looking back over more than 200 years of European history and biblical scholarship, Jones could identify many of those 'errors'. The emergence, and

---

[105] Ibid., 10; S. Ockley, *An Account of the Authority of the Arabick Manuscripts in the Bodleian Library, Controverted between Dr. Grabe and Mr. Whiston. In a Letter to Mr. Thirlby* (London, 1712), 30–31.

[106] W. Whiston, *Remarks on Dr. Grabe's Essay upon two Arabick Manuscripts of the Bodleian Library* (London, 1711), 20, viii. Whiston shared Newton's low regard for Athanasius; idem, *Athanasius convicted of Forgery* (London, 1712). See R. Iliffe, 'Prosecuting Athanasius: Protestant forensics and the mirrors of persecution', in J.E. Force and S. Hutton (eds), *Newton and Newtonianism: New Studies* (Dordrecht, 2004), 113–54.

[107] Jones, *New Testament*, i. 208, 13.

[108] Ibid., i. 9–12.

obstinate maintaining of these errors, had meant that the optimism of Renaissance scholars that the application of critical and philological skills to the scriptural texts would produce only further insights into the divine message had been replaced by greater caution. Jones did not employ the language of panicked outrage of one of Toland's critics, who spoke of 'Innumerable Detachments of Pamphleteers' asserting that sacred Writ was unintelligible in it original, spurious in its Translation, 'erected at first by human Invention, and upheld ever since by the concurring Politicks of Prince and Priest'.[109] Jones's exhaustive historical and philological examination and defence of the New Testament canon was, despite occasional invective, reasoned, scholarly and written in English. He provided translations of dozens of apocryphal texts previously only available in Latin.[110] This was a deliberate attempt to deny critics like Toland the opportunity of undermining the canon by sensationally producing lost scriptures and claiming, as Toland did in his response to the critics of *Nazarenus*, only to be performing the offices of a responsible biblical critic in the interests of Christians and the Church.[111] Jones sought to invalidate the charge that the religious 'establishment', or 'mungrel Divines' as Toland termed some its members, was able to perpetrate textual deceits upon 'ordinary' Christians by discussing matters of biblical criticism only in Latin.[112]

Jones's decision to publish in English was also a recognition that interest in, and discussion of, matters of biblical criticism had reached far beyond the academic confines of Latinate discourse to a much broader, if nebulous, constituency of curious public opinion. After periodical publications providing synopses of European works of scholarship included an extended dissertation on the vowel points and accents of the Hebrew Old Testament it was obviously too late to put that genie back in the bottle.[113]

Jones's work was republished in 1748, 1798 and 1827, and incorporated into William Hone's edition of *The Apocryphal New Testament*, first published in 1820 and frequently reprinted. By the early nineteenth century, New Testament apocryphal scholarship was uncontroversial, but Jones's work served as a reminder

---

[109] J. Paterson, *Anti-Nazarenus. By Way of Answer to Mr. Toland* (London, 1718), 'Dedication'.

[110] Jones published the texts from Johann Albert Fabricius, *Codex Apocryphus Novi Testamenti* (2 vols, Hamburg 1703; 3 vols, enlarged, 1719); Metzger, *Canon of the New Testament*, 14.

[111] J. Toland, 'Mangoneutes', in idem, *Tetradymus* (London, 1720), 141, 147–8.

[112] Ibid., 144.

[113] [J. Dunton], *The Young Students Library* (London, 1692), 248–88. There was a proliferation of English journals providing access to Latin and foreign language works of scholarship in the late seventeenth century. During the early 1690s John Dunton's *Athenian Mercury* and *The Young Students Library* competed with J. de la Croze's *The works of the learned* in providing popularized synopses of scholarly works; S. Parks, 'John Dunton and *The works of the learned*', *The Library*, series 5, 23 (1968), 13–24. See also idem, *John Dunton and the English Book Trade* (NY, 1976).

that its systematic formulation had been prompted by the need to respond to hostile criticism. In formulating that defence, Jones dispensed with traditional Protestant doctrines regarding the self-evidencing nature of sacred writ and the guidance of the Holy Spirit, to rest his case entirely on the testimony of the early Church. It is ironic, though, that by the time of his posthumous publication, the historical and patristic scholarship upon which Jones rested the ultimate authority of the New Testament canon was already in decline, as was the authority of the text itself.

Chapter 6

'To us there is but one God, the Father': Antitrinitarian Textual Criticism in Seventeenth- and Early Eighteenth-Century England

Stephen D. Snobelen

> This is he who came by water and blood – Jesus Christ; not by the water only but by the water and the blood. And the spirit is the one who testifies, because the Spirit is the truth. For there are three that testify: the Spirit and the water and the blood; and these three agree. (1 John 5:6–8 ESV (2001))

Antitrinitarianism and biblical criticism

Biblical criticism was central to early modern antitrinitarian theology from the very beginning. From its emergence a few short years after the commencement of the Reformation, antitrinitarianism was marked by both a fervent primitivism and a thoroughgoing biblicism. Although doctrinal primitivism and biblicism played important roles in Trinitarian Protestantism as well, the antitrinitarians pushed these dynamics much further. In early modern antitrinitarianism we see a passionate belief that Christianity had become corrupt in late antiquity combined with a powerful rejection of Church tradition, authority and the ecumenical creeds. This radical theological primitivism was a shaping force of their religious ethos, as they sought to retrieve from the original text of the Bible the pure teaching of monotheism, namely, the oneness and unipersonality of God. This doctrine, they believed, had been taught to the Israelites by Moses and reaffirmed in the New Testament by the Apostles and the Son of God himself.

But elements of this story can be traced further back than the early Reformation. Early modern antitrinitarians owed much to the philological and linguistic tools developed by Renaissance humanists such as Lorenzo Valla, who is famous for his exposure of the Medieval forgery known as the Donation of Constantine. These philological and linguistic tools had already been applied in a limited way to biblical criticism by Valla in the fifteenth century, but it was principally the sophisticated and extensive way they were used for biblical criticism in the early sixteenth century by Desiderius Erasmus of Rotterdam, the prince of the humanists, that cleared the path for antitrinitarian biblical criticism. This paper begins with a summary of the insights provided by Erasmus's biblical and textual criticism. After this, highlights of early antitrinitarian biblical criticism are traced in the thought of Michael Servetus and the Polish Brethren. This treatment of the birth of antitrinitarian biblical criticism will serve as an illustrative backdrop to the major focus of this paper, the deployment of biblical criticism by antitrinitarians in England beginning in the middle of the seventeenth century. In sum, this paper will make four claims about English antitrinitarian biblical criticism. First, the tools of biblical criticism developed by Erasmus on the eve of the Reformation were taken up by antitrinitarians in England, sometimes consciously and directly and sometimes through the mediation of antitrinitarians of earlier generations. Second, the English antitrinitarians or Unitarians were likewise cognizant of and partly dependent on the legacy of earlier antitrinitarians on the Continent. Third, the radical doctrinal primitivism of early modern antitrinitarianism helped to energise and give purpose to their biblical and textual criticism. Fourth, the powerful biblicism that was apparent from the very beginning of antitrinitarian thought in the early sixteenth century is every bit as evident in the thought of their English heirs in the latter half of the seventeenth century and beyond.

The birth of antitrinitarian biblical criticism

No single event was more important to the birth of antitrinitarian biblical criticism than the publication of Desiderius Erasmus of Rotterdam's *Novum instrumentum* in 1516. This work included along with a revised Latin translation of the New Testament the first critical edition of the Greek New Testament to be published. The *Novum instrumentum* embodied the textual critical ideals of Renaissance humanism, played a central role in bringing them into biblical studies and dramatically raised the status of the philologists in the Church at the expense of the theologians. It also helped restore the Bible as the major focus for discussions of Christian doctrine. Erasmus's Greek text, and its later editions, was the basis of the first two vernacular translations of the Reformation: Martin Luther's German New Testament of 1522 and William Tyndale's English New Testament of 1525. These texts, in turn, helped unleash the Reformation on northern Europe. This is not all. Erasmus' Greek text, its suggestive annotations and the philological tools it exemplified, also caught the notice of theologians who began to move away from the received doctrine of the Trinity. But the most striking feature of this text was what it did not include. Finding no extant Greek manuscript with 1 John 5:7, the passage about the three heavenly witnesses of the Father, The Word and the Holy Spirit, Erasmus published the first edition of his Greek New Testament without this so-called *comma Johanneum*. The English King James Version of 1611, which retained the comma, rendered the passage as follows: 'For there are three that bear record in heaven, the Father, the Word, and the Holy Ghost: and these three are one'. Erasmus's non-inclusion of the *comma* stirred up a controversy that lasted well into the eighteenth century. Although he succumbed to pressure from his critics, including the English theologian Edward Lee and the Spaniard Diego Lopez de Zúñiga (Stunica), the chief editor of the rival Complutensian Polyglot, and included the *comma* in all subsequent editions of his New Testament, no-one forgot that Erasmus had originally omitted this chief proof-text of Trinitarianism, least of all early modern critics of this doctrine.[1]

Also important for antitrinitarian biblical criticism was Erasmus' seminal exegetical observation that Christ is rarely called God in the Bible and that when the term 'God' is used without qualification it refers exclusively to the Father.[2] In the preface to his edition of Hilary, Erasmus had written that Hilary never applied the title 'God' to the Holy Spirit and that Hilary had observed that the Bible only calls the Son 'God' occasionally and the Holy Spirit 'God' not at all.[3] These observations were repeatedly cited in the sixteenth and seventeenth centuries by antitrinitarians, for whom it was but a small step to move from this exegetical observation to the theological conclusion that the Father is uniquely God. Erasmus also provided suggestive philological and exegetical commentary on such Trinitarian proof-texts as John 20:28, Acts 20:28, Romans 9:5, 1 Timothy 3:16 and 1 John 5:20. Early modern antitrinitarians also embraced Erasmus' Christian primitivism, his insinuations that the early church had become corrupt and his humanist programme of returning to the sources (*ad fontes*). Leaving aside the tricky question of Erasmus' own orthodoxy, it is clear that his opponents believed that he was undermining the traditional doctrine of the Trinity. This much was made clear when a group of his opponents formulated a series of charges against Erasmus at the Conference of Valladolid in 1527. The first three of these charges were that he had written against the Trinity, the deity of Christ and the deity of the Holy Spirit.[4] Although Erasmus answered these accusations and defended his orthodoxy the following year in his *Apologia adversus monachos quosdam hispanos* (*Apology against some Spanish monks*), many continued to perceive in Erasmus' biblical criticism attacks on the scriptural evidence for the central doctrine of orthodoxy.

Orthodox defenders of the faith were not the only ones to notice that Erasmus's scholarship could be used to undermine support for the Trinity. Present at the

[1] For more on Erasmus and the *comma*, see Joseph M. Levine, 'Philology and history: Erasmus and the Johannine comma', in idem, *The Autonomy of history: truth and method from Erasmus to Gibbon* (Chicago, 1999), 25–51; H.J. de Jonge, 'Erasmus and the *Comma Johanneum*', *Ephemerides Theologicae Lovanienses* 56 (1980): 381–9; Erika Rummel, *Erasmus' Annotations on the New Testament: from philologist to theologian* (Toronto, 1986), 40, 132–4; Bruce M. Metzger, *The Text of the New Testament: its transmission, corruption, and restoration* (Oxford, 1968), 101–2; Cornelius Augustijn, *Erasmus: his life, works and influence* (Toronto, 1991), 93–4. A general account of examples of Catholic opposition to Erasmus can be found in Erika Rummel, *Erasmus and his Catholic critics I: 1515–22* (Nieuwkoop, 1989) and eadem, *Erasmus and his Catholic critics II: 1523–36* (Nieuwkoop, 1989).

[2] See for example, Erasmus, *Paraphrase on John*, ed. Jane E. Phillips (Toronto, 1991), 344 and idem, *Annotations on Romans*, ed. Robert D. Sider (Toronto, 1994), 252.

[3] Gerard Brandt, *The History of the Reformation and other ecclesiastical transactions in and about the Low-Countries, from the beginning of the eighth century, down to the famous Synod of Dort, inclusive* (London, 1720), vol. I, 19–20 (second pagination series).

[4] Augustijn, *Erasmus*, 156.

Conference of Valladolid was a teenaged Spaniard named Miguel Servet. This young nobleman had come to Valladolid as the personal attendant of Juan de Quintilla, Erasmus' chief critic at the conference. Rather than take the side of his employer, Servet became impassioned at Valladolid with a zeal for Erasmus's biblical humanism. Having not displayed much interest in theology before, he took up the study of Scripture in earnest.[5] The most significant result of this study was the recognition that the traditional doctrine of the Trinity was not adequately supported by biblical testimony. Michael Servetus's conclusions on this matter were soon published in the form of the provocatively titled book *De erroribus Trinitatis* (*On the errors of the Trinity*), which appeared in 1531 when the author was only 20 years old.[6] In arguments that echo even as they radicalize the exegetical conclusions of Erasmus, Servetus states that the Father is referred to as God 'by common usage of Scripture', something not true of Christ:

> For that only the Father is called God by nature is plainly enough shown by Scripture, which says, God and CHRIST, CHRIST and God. It so joins them as though CHRIST were a being distinct from God. Likewise, when it says, God is the Father of Jesus CHRIST, a difference is noted between God and CHRIST, just as between father and son. And also when it says, *the* CHRIST *of God, the God of our Lord* JESUS CHRIST, *the head of* CHRIST *is God*. And CHRIST cries to God, *My God, my God*. And by common usage of Scripture the Father is called God; and CHRIST, Lord and Master. And Christ himself says, *That they should know thee, the only true God, and him whom thou didst send, even* JESUS CHRIST.[7]

Although it was not as radical as its title suggested, this book earned Servetus the status of the arch-heretic of the Reformation era. The outcry was such that Servetus was forced to go underground, emerging only when he published his equally heretical *Christianismi restitutio* (*Restitution of Christianity*) in 1553. This time, Servetus did not elude the authorities. Passing through Geneva on the run, Servetus was arrested by John Calvin and burnt alive at the stake. Servetus' arguments against the orthodox doctrine of the Trinity, along with the example of his martyrdom for the cause of the oneness of God, served to inspire several generations of antitrinitarians.[8]

The most important of these were the Polish Brethren or Socinians. The Polish Minor Church became a distinct entity after it broke off from the Trinitarian Polish Reformed Church in 1565. Already unitarian in doctrine at this juncture, the sophistication of the Polish Brethren's theology and biblical criticism grew over

[5] Augustijn, *Erasmus*, 157–8.

[6] Servetus, *The two treatises of Servetus on the Trinity*, trans. Earl Morse Wilbur (Cambridge, Massachusetts, 1932).

[7] Servetus, *Two treatises*, 21–2.

[8] On Servetus see Marian Hillar with Claire S. Allen, *Michael Servetus: intellectual giant, humanist, and martyr* (Lexington, 2002); George Huntston Williams, *Radical Reformation*, (Kirksville, Missouri, 1992, 3rd edn), 52-8 and passim; Jerome Friedmann, *Michael Servetus: a case study in total heresy* (Geneva, 1978); Roland H. Bainton, *Hunted Heretic: the life and death of Michael Servetus, 1511–53* (Boston, 1953); Earl Morse Wilbur, *A History of Unitarianism: Socinianism and its antecedents* (Boston, 1945), 49–75, 113–85.

the years – particularly after the Sienese nobleman Fausto Sozzini (Socinus) aligned himself with the Church in 1579.[9] The theology of the Polish Brethren was codified in the various editions of the *Racovian Catechism* of the seventeenth century.[10] This work is replete with humanistically-inspired antitrinitarian biblical criticism. Although the biblicist Socinians upheld the inspiration and original textual integrity of the Bible, they did come to believe that certain key texts had been deliberately corrupted by the orthodox party over the centuries – a view that serves as an important backdrop to the polemical exegesis in the *Catechism*. Through the use of biblical and textual criticism, the Socinians sought to restore the Scriptures to their original purity. Early on in its pages the *Catechism* establishes the most distinctive doctrine of Socinianism, namely that the one true God is a single person and that this person is the Father. Verses they believed sharply distinguish between the person of God and the person of Christ, such as John 17:3, 1 Corinthians 8:6 and Ephesians 4:6, are presented in support of this tenet.[11] These passages, and others like them in the New Testament, were regularly used by early modern antitrinitarians to argue for a distinction between God and Christ, not merely between the Father and Christ, as in Trinitarianism. The second of these three verses reads in the King James Version: 'But to us there is but one God, the Father, of whom are all things, and we in him; and one Lord Jesus Christ, by whom are all things, and we by him'. For the biblicist Socinians, the text is clear: the one God is the Father alone.

The *Catechism* also engages in textual criticism. With respect to the *comma Johanneum*, the *Catechism* observes, 'that since it is known that these words are wanting in most of the older Greek copies, and also in the Syriac, Arabic, Æthiopic, and the more ancient Latin versions, as the principal persons even among our adversaries have themselves shown, nothing certain can be concluded from them'.[12] To this, the *Catechism* adds: '[t]here are some persons who deem the genuineness of the passage suspicious; – that is to say, Erasmus, Beza, Franc. Lucas, and the Louvain divines'.[13] Although it is quite clear that the compilers of the *Catechism* rejected the veracity of the *comma*, they contend that even if it were a part of the original text, the Trinitarian sense of three consubstantial persons cannot be

[9] On the Polish Brethren, see Lech Szczucki, ed., *Faustus Socinus and his heritage* (Kraków, 2005); Williams, *The Radical Reformation*, 3rd edn; Lech Szczucki, ed., *Socinianism and its role in the culture of XVIth to XVIIIth centuries* (Warsaw, 1983); Robert Dán and Antal Pirnát, eds, *Antitrinitarianism in the second half of the 16th century* (Budapest/Leiden, 1982); Stanislas Kot, *Socinianism in Poland: the social and political ideas of the Polish Antitrinitarians in the sixteenth and seventeenth Centuries* (Beacon Hill, 1957); Wilbur, *A History of Unitarianism: Socinianism and its antecedents*. On the similar Transylvanian Unitarians see Mihály Balázs and Gizella Keserá, eds, *György Enyedi and Central European Unitarianism in the 16–17th centuries* (Budapest, 2000) and Earl Morse Wilbur, *A History of Unitarianism: in Transylvania, England, and America*, vol. 2 (Cambridge, Massachusetts, 1952).

[10] *The Racovian Catechism, with notes and illustrations, translated from the Latin*, trans. and ed. Thomas Rees (London, 1818; repr. by The American Theological Library Association, 1962).

[11] *Racovian Catechism*, 25–34.

[12] *Racovian Catechism*, 39–41.

[13] *Racovian Catechism*, 41.

sustained, as verse 8 amply demonstrates that the expression *unum sunt* ('they are one') cannot denote persons, but rather agreement 'IN ONE THING',[14] thus helping to validate Erasmus's observation that Arians could interpret 1 John 5:7 in a way that did not imply essence.[15] In all, Erasmus's biblical criticism is cited fifteen times in the final edition of the *Racovian Catechism*.[16] Over a century after his death, Erasmus continued to supply antitrinitarian biblical criticism with authority and practical support.

Antitrinitarian biblical criticism comes to England

While the relative toleration in Hungary and the Polish-Lithuanian Commonwealth allowed antitrinitarian communities to flourish in the late sixteenth and early seventeenth centuries, the less tolerant Catholic and Protestant regimes of western Europe helped ensure that unitarian belief there remained limited and diffuse throughout the same period. However, the reversal of fortunes brought about by the closing of the Racovian press in 1638 and the expulsion of the Socinians from Poland in 1660 drove Socinian émigrés to Germany and particularly to Holland in the mid- to late seventeenth century. The arrival of these doctrinal refugees in the Low Countries coincided with a time of increasing religious toleration, especially in the Netherlands. After arriving in Holland, Socinian scholars continued to produce publications and republications, including the monumental *Bibliotheca Fratrum Polonorum* ('Library of the Polish Brethren'). Socinian works from Raków and Holland also made their way across the Channel into England. This contributed to a flowering of antitrinitarian thought in Britain and in particular England in the second half of the seventeenth century.[17] But the two earliest notable English Unitarians did not initially become heretics through reading Socinian literature in England. The first, Paul Best, initially encountered Socinian teachings while travelling in central and eastern Europe in the early part of the century.[18] The second, John Biddle, appears to have arrived at antitrinitarian conclusions on his own and only afterward became aware of Socinian writings.[19]

Sometime after his return to England from his travels on the Continent, Cambridge-educated Paul Best began to disseminate his Socinian beliefs – thus providing one

---

[14] *Racovian Catechism*, 41–2.

[15] See Levine, 'Erasmus and the Johannine comma', 49.

[16] *Racovian Catechism*, 41, 80 n. 15, 121 n. 23, 121 n. 24, 128 n. 28, 129 n. 29, 130 n. 30, 134 n. 31, 151 n. 36, 161 n. 38, 255 n. 48, 291–2 n. 57, 329 n. 60, 329 (in an additional unnumbered note).

[17] For an overview see H. John McLachlan, *Socinianism in Seventeenth-Century England* (Oxford, 1951).

[18] McLachlan, *Socinianism in Seventeenth-Century England*, 149–62; Snobelen, *New DNB* entry on Best.

[19] McLachlan, *Socinianism in Seventeenth-Century England*, 163–217; Snobelen, *New DNB* entry on Biddle.

of the earliest links between Socinian theology and England. After showing some of his heretical papers to a minister in his native Yorkshire he was imprisoned in February 1645. By July of the same year he had been sent down to Westminster to be examined by Parliament. Exasperated by his continued incarceration, Best published first an appeal for toleration in April 1646,[20] and then a powerful *apologia* for the Socinian faith in the summer of 1647, his *Mysteries discovered*.[21] Although the English Parliament ordered it burnt by the hangman, at least 11 copies survive. These copies reveal a fiery pamphlet brimming with antitrinitarian exegesis. Careful to take into account biblical idiom and figures of speech, Best is suspicious of *novitas verborum* (a philological concern with doctrinal repercussions) and is convinced that the doctrine of the Trinity is an unbiblical corruption foisted on the early Church. Like previous antitrinitarians, along with Erasmus, Best laments the introduction of the Nicene Creed, noting that 'human Councils are but external and accidental means of truth'.[22] For Best only the Father is truly God, with Christ 'to us both God and his Word, as *Moses* was to *Aaron*, and *Aaron* to him, *Exod*. 4.16', stressing that this language is used 'in a figurative sense after a Scripture manner and meaning, according to the character of that beloved Apostle [John]'.[23] To explain the dignified language used of Christ in John's writings, Best refers to the authority of Erasmus' comments on the Epistles of John along with Jerome's introduction to the Gospel of John, which had both posited that one of the contexts of John's writings was the need to combat the teachings of Cerinthus and the Ebionites, who had taught that Christ was a mere man.[24] Best is also at pains to stress that 'God and Christ are distinguished, *Iohn 14.1. 1 Thess. 3.11*', adding that it was 'an observation of the learned Erasmus, that where God is put absolutely the Father is understood', giving John 8:54 as additional support for the synonymy between 'God' and 'Father'.[25] Best also answers a series of Trinitarian proof-texts. He cites Romans 1:25 and 2 Corinthians 11:31 to suggest that the doxology at the end of Romans 9:5 applies to the Father rather than to Christ as most Trinitarians claimed.[26] As for John 20:28, he uses Philippians 2:9 to assert that the titles given there are due to the exaltation of Christ after his resurrection and are meant in the sense of 'Lord and Master' and '*Elohim* and *Adonim*', as it was Christ's resurrection, not the deity of Christ, for which 'doubting' Thomas wanted evidence.[27] The context helps suggest the intended

---

[20] Best, *A letter of advice unto the ministers assembled at Westminster, with severall parcels of queries recommended to their saddest Considerations* [London, 1646].

[21] Best, *Mysteries discovered: or, a Mercuriall Picture pointing out the way from Babylon to the Holy City, for the good of all such as during that night of generall Errour and Apostasie, 2 Thes. 2.3. Revel. 3.10. have been so long misled with Romes hobgoblins* (London, 1647).

[22] Best, *Mysteries discovered*, 12–13.

[23] Best, *Mysteries discovered*, 3.

[24] Best, *Mysteries discovered*, 3. Socinians did not believe that Christ was a mere man, but the literal Son of God with a human mother but no human father.

[25] Best, *Mysteries discovered*, 4.

[26] Best, *Mysteries discovered*, 7.

[27] Best, *Mysteries discovered*, 7.

meaning. While he does not mention the textual difficulty when providing a non-Trinitarian reading of 1 John 5:7, he does note the *varia lectio* for Acts 20:28 that reads 'that peculiar blood' rather than 'God's own blood', the latter of which, he says, 'is absurd'.[28] Although brief and acerbic, Best's *Mysteries discovered* displays great learning and sophistication.

Sometimes called 'the Father of English Unitarianism', John Biddle published his first antitrinitarian work later the same summer that Best released his *Mysteries discovered.* Biddle's inaugural controversial tract is devoted to a dynamic to which Erasmus drew attention in the preface to his edition of Hilary, namely, that the Holy Spirit is never called God in the Bible. In this tract, as the title declares, Biddle presents twelve arguments '*drawn out of the Scripture*' against the deity of the Holy Spirit.[29] In his introductory letter Biddle states that it is wrong to 'give the worship of the supream Lord of Heaven and Earth, to him whom the Scripture no where affirmeth to be God'.[30] In the main body of this work, the Oxford-trained heretic uses syllogistic logic to dismantle the deity of the Holy Spirit, including the fact that in the Bible God and the Holy Spirit are distinguished, that the Holy Spirit is sent by God and that the Holy Spirit is called 'the gift of God'.[31] Then, at the end of the work, Biddle tackles five passages he believes are wrested by Trinitarian apologists to affirm the notion that the Holy Spirit is God. One of these is 1 John 5:7. Biddle first challenges the orthodox interpretation that has the phrase 'are one' denoting a unity of essence. This, he says, is against scriptural usage, which employs this language elsewhere to denote 'an union of agreement'. At the conclusion of his discussion on this verse he briefly mentions 'the suspectedness of this place', and how it is not found in the ancient Greek copies, the Syriac version, the oldest Latin version and that it is 'rejected by sundry Interpreters both Ancient and Mordern [sic]'.[32] Biddle also discusses Acts 5:3–4, thought by some to refer to the Holy Spirit as God since it speaks of Ananias lying both to the Holy Spirit and to God. Biddle contends that even if the standard translation of this passage were correct, through 'a metonymie of the adjunct' is it ultimately God to whom Ananias was lying. But he also argues that the Greek is better translated 'Why hath Satan filled thy heart to bely or counterfeit the Holy Spirit?' For this translation, he enlists the support of Erasmus, Calvin and Aretius.[33]

In 1648 Biddle published a second tract entitled *A confession of faith touching the Trinity*, in which he expanded the scope of his writing to discuss the scriptural roles of the Father and Christ.[34] This work consists of six articles of faith, the first

[28] Best, *Mysteries discovered*, 7.

[29] Biddle, *Twelve arguments drawn out of the Scripture, wherein the commonly received opinion touching the deity of the Holy Spirit, is clearly and fully refuted* (London, 1647).

[30] Biddle, *Twelve arguments*, 5.

[31] Biddle, *Twelve arguments*, 7–10.

[32] Biddle, *Twelve arguments*, 15.

[33] Biddle, *Twelve arguments*, 15–16.

[34] Biddle, *A confession of faith touching the Trinity, according to the Scriptures* (London, 1648).

of which is the belief that the Most High God is the Father. Like the Socinian Johann Crell, he begins this work and his first article with the testimony of John 17:3.[35] He contends that Christ can be called God in such passages as Isaiah 9:6 and Romans 9:5 'by reason of the Divine Empire over all things, both in Heaven and on earth, conferred to Him by the Father'.[36] In referring to John 20:28, he notes that Jesus is called 'God' in his human nature.[37] In Article IV, he gives a non-essential interpretation of the word God, arguing with copious scriptural illustration that the primary meaning of this term in both the Old and New Testaments denotes might and divine empire.[38] Sometime after this, Biddle released a book outlining testimonies from the early Church that support a non-Trinitarian reading of the Bible.[39] Like Erasmus, early modern antitrinitarians were extremely interested in the writings of the early Church, which they believed supported their unitarian faith, especially as one approaches the Apostolic period. He begins with the testimonies of Irenaeus, an early Father who was a favourite of Erasmus. In fact, he uses the 1545 Paris printing of Erasmus's edition of Irenaeus.[40] Biddle devotes 16 pages of testimonies from this early Christian theologian to show that he believed only the Father is the true God.[41] Later in the same work, Biddle refers to the gloss of Hilary on Matthew 28:19 and also notes that Hilary 'nowhere said that the Holy Spirit is God', just as Erasmus had asserted over a century before.[42]

A third example of English Unitarian thought from the middle of the seventeenth century is found in the Gloucester antitrinitarian John Knowles (*c.* 1625–77).[43] Evidence of his antitrinitarian biblical criticism is recorded in a 1650 literary debate between him and the Independent Samuel Eaton on the divinity of Christ. This book opens with four pages of proof-texts assembled by Eaton in favour of this conclusion; the remainder of the 60-page book consists of Knowles's scriptural responses. Among the texts offered by Eaton are Isaiah 9:6, 1 John 5:20 and 1 Timothy 3:16, with Eaton giving the reading of the last of these as 'God manifested in the flesh'.[44] He does not proffer 1 John 5:7. In replying to Isaiah 9:6, Knowles disputes the

[35] Biddle, *A confession of faith touching the Trinity*, 3–6; Johann Crell, *The Two Books of John Crellius Francus, touching One God the Father* (Kosmoburg [i.e. London], 1665), 1–27.

[36] Biddle, *A confession of faith touching the Trinity*, 11.

[37] Biddle, *A confession of faith touching the Trinity*, 11.

[38] Biddle, *A confession of faith touching the Trinity*, 12–14.

[39] Biddle, *The testimonies of Irenæus, Justin Martyr, Tertullian, Novatianus, Theophilus, Origen, (who lived in the two first centuries after Christ was born, or thereabouts;) as also, of Arnobius, Lactantius, Eusebius, Hilary, and Brightman; concerning that One God, and the Persons of the Holy Trinity. Together with observations on the same* (London, *c.*1653).

[40] Biddle, *The testimonies of Irenaeus*, 1.

[41] Biddle, *The testimonies of Irenaeus*, 1–16.

[42] Biddle, *Testimonies of Irenaeus*, 76–7.

[43] McLachlan, *Socinianism in seventeenth-century England*, 263–87.

[44] Eaton, in Knowles, *A friendly debate on a weighty subject: or, a conference by writing betwixt Mr Samuel Eaton and Mr John Knowles concerning the divinity of Christ: for beating out, and further clearing up of Truth* (London, 1650), 1, 3 (quotation 3).

interpretation that the term 'mighty God' makes Christ 'the most high God', noting that some interpreters, including Calvin, acknowledge the plausibility of a translation that applies the title 'mighty God' to the Father. Knowles also mentions the view of Hugo Grotius that the titles in this verse refer 'typically' to King Hezekiah. Finally, Knowles points out that the Hebrew word for 'God' used in Isaiah 9:6 is *'el* (אל), which means 'mighty', and which is demonstrably used of Israelite magistrates in Psalm 82:1: 'Ælohim *standeth in the assembly of* Æl' (the King James Version translating *'el* here as 'mighty').[45] In his rejoinder on 1 John 5:20, Knowles draws attention to the reading of Erasmus and Tyndale, '*and we are in him that is true through his Son Jesus Christ*', and stresses that while Christ is never called 'true God' elsewhere in Scripture, the Father is in John 17:3.[46] In tackling the Trinitarian interpretation of 1 Timothy 3:16, he first raises the textual difficulties with the text, stating that the Latin, Syriac and Arabic, along with Ambrose and Augustine, all read 'which' instead of 'God' in the relevant clause. As in the *Racovian Catechism*, he also relates that Hincmarus testifies that the Nestorians added the word 'God' to the text.[47] Even if this reading were genuine, Knowles continues, the text should be translated 'a *God* was manifest in the flesh'.[48] Thus, as with many other antitrinitarian exegetes before and after him, Knowles provides an exegetical response in case the textual solution is not accepted.

The Unitarian tracts

A much greater flurry of antitrinitarian publication in England occurred at the end of the seventeenth century. The so-called Trinitarian Controversy, which began in 1687 and lasted throughout most of the 1690s, saw the exegetes of the incipient English Unitarian movement lock horns in print with the English defenders of the Trinitarian faith.[49] One stimulus that helped bring about the first of a string of Unitarian publications in these years was the *Declaration for the liberty of conscience* issued by James II on 4 April 1687. As Stephen Trowell points out, the Catholic king had both intended the *Declaration* to make life easier for Roman Catholics in England and to allow non-conformists to meet legally outside the structure of the Anglican Church with the thought that this would divide the opposition of Protestants to his rule. As the events of the Glorious Revolution of 1688 demonstrate, it was singularly unsuccessful in this goal. Nevertheless, the *Declaration* did help foster the conditions that led later in 1687 to the printing of Stephen Nye's anonymously

[45] Knowles, *A friendly debate*, 7–9 (quotation 8).

[46] Knowles, *A friendly debate*, 11–12.

[47] The *Racovian Catechism* uses the testimony of both Liberatus, Archdeacon of Carthage, and Hincmarus (Hincmar) to support the contention (*Racovian Catechism*, 121 n. 24).

[48] Knowles, *A friendly debate*, 51.

[49] Stephen Trowell, Unitarian and/or Anglican: the relationship of Unitarianism to the Church from 1687 to 1698', *Bulletin of the John Rylands University Library of Manchester* 78 (1996): 77–101.

published *A brief history of the Unitarians* – a provocative attempt to try the waters of increased toleration.[50] This and other writings by Nye were later included in the so-called Unitarian Tracts of the 1690s. After the ouster of James, the Parliament under the Protestant regime of William and Mary brought out the Act of Toleration in 1689. Although this Act did not extend toleration to Catholics or antitrinitarians, it did serve to entrench further the principles of toleration. It was in this climate of growing toleration that antitrinitarian dissenters increasingly sought to publish their scriptural arguments and contest openly the Trinitarian orthodoxy of the established church.

Nye's *Brief history*, the opening shot in the Trinitarian controversies, both lays out many of the antitrinitarian arguments directed against orthodoxy and reveals dependence on Erasmus and the humanist tradition of philology. At the end of his first letter he supplies a list of four learned worthies who 'have certainly been either *Arians* or *Socinians*, or great Favourers of them; though they have used much Caution in so expressing themselves, as not to lye too open to Exception, Envy, or a legal Prosecution'.[51] Erasmus heads this list:[52]

> *D. Erasmus*, the restorer of Learning, hath given occasion both to his Friends and Enemies to think him an *Arian*. He saith, that *Phil.* 2.6. was the principal Argument of the Fathers against the *Arians*; but that to say true, it proves nothing against them. He notes on *Eph.* 5.5. that the word *God* being *used absolutely*, doth in the Apostolick Writings always signifie *the Father*. In his *Scholia* on the third Tome of St. *Jerom's* Epistles, he denies that the *Arians* were Hereticks; he adds, farther, that they were superior to our Men in Learning and Eloquence. 'Tis believed, *Erasmus* did not make himself a party to that which he esteemed the ignorant and dull side of the Question. In his Epistle to *Bilibaldus*, he speaks as openly as the time would permit a wise Man to speak, I (saith *Erasmus*) could be of the *Arian* Perswasion, if the Church approved it.[53]

Nye's hint that Erasmus was an Arian Nicodemite echoes the accusations of some of the humanist's early sixteenth-century opponents. It also was perhaps meant to provide succour for secret Unitarians and crypto-Socinians of the late seventeenth century (of whom Nye himself was one).

Nor is this the only reference to the authority of Erasmus. Nye goes on to cite him six additional times in his *Brief history*. Thus, he appeals to Erasmus's writings, usually along with those of other authorities, for support in arguing that the title 'the first and last' used of Christ in Revelation 1:17 applies to Christ as a man; that the word 'before' in John 1:15 means before in dignity; that the expression 'who is in heaven' in John 3:13 should be translated 'who was in heaven'; that the blood of Christ is called the blood of God in Acts 20:28 because 'it was *the Blood which God gave* for the Redemption of the World'; that the doxology in Romans 9:5 should be

---

[50] Trowell, 'Unitarian and/or Anglican', 78.

[51] [Nye], *A brief history of the Unitarians, called also Socinians. In four letters, written to a friend* ([London], 1687), 30.

[52] The others are Hugo Grotius, Denis Petau (Petavius), Simon Episcopius and Christopher Sand (Sandius) ([Nye], *Brief history*, 31–6).

[53] [Nye], *Brief history*, 31.

separated from the word Christ earlier in the verse; and that the *comma Johanneum* is spurious.[54] Antitrinitarian biblical criticism is applied in the *Brief history* to such pivotal verses as Romans 9:5, 1 Timothy 3:16 and 1 John 5:7.[55]

Nye extended his arguments in works published in the ensuing years. His *An accurate examination* of 1692, written against a book published by the Trinitarian Luke Milbourne, opens with a detailed refutation of the corrupt reading 'God' in 1 Timothy 3:16,[56] citing through Grotius the testimony of Hincmar, who had stated that the original reading 'which' had been replaced with 'God' by the 'Nestorian Trinitarians'. Nye jettisons the reading he terms a 'forgery' in favour of the reading with the relative pronoun 'which'. For this he calls to his aid Erasmus, who approved of this reading and who, in a dig against his opponent, Nye notes is 'somewhat learneder than our Author'.[57] In a two-page response to his opponent's assertion that Romans 9:5 applies the title 'God' to Christ, Nye notes that Erasmus had observed 'that the Copies of St. *Cyprian*, St *Hilary*, and St *Chrysostom*, had only *the Blessed over all*, or above all, without the word *God*'.[58] But even if the original text included 'God', one would suspect, as did Erasmus and Curcellaeus, that if the doxology did refer to Christ, it would have begun with a relative pronoun, rather than the nominative article of the established text.[59] Later in the same text Nye asserts that Erasmus, Petavius, Grotius and other modern critics had claimed that the ante-Nicene fathers were Arian in theology.[60] Although this statement is exaggerated, the cautious and sometimes equivocal observations of these learned men still provided useful and powerful testimony.

In 1695 John Smith intervened in the debate with a 63-page book favouring the Unitarian cause. It bore the ambitious short title *A designed end to the Socinian controversy*; the rest of the title bore witness to the principal claim of Socinians and Unitarians.[61] Despite its design, not only did this work fail to end the controversy, but it stirred up one of its own. Parliament ordered the book burnt the same year it was published; its author (whose name appeared on the title page) was also prosecuted.[62] With the antitrinitarian proof-text John 17:3 emblazoned on the title page, Smith made his position clear from the outset: there is a God and this God is

[54] [Nye], *Brief history*, 59, 88, 90, 113, 118, 152.

[55] [Nye], *Brief history*, 117–19, 137–9, 151–3.

[56] [Nye], *An accurate examination of the principal texts usually alledged for the divinity of our savour; and for the satisfaction by him made to the justice of God, for the sins of men: occasioned by a book of Mr. L. Milbourn, called, mysteries (in religion) vindicated* (London, 1692), 1–5.

[57] [Nye], *An accurate examination*, 3.

[58] [Nye], *An accurate examination, 34.*

[59] [Nye], *An accurate examination*, 35.

[60] [Nye], *An accurate examination*, 44.

[61] Smith, *A designed end to the Socinian controversy: or, a rational and plain discourse to prove, that no other person but the Father of Christ is God most High* (London, 1695).

[62] Wallace, *Antitrinitarian biography*, 3:389–99.

both one essence and one person.[63] And this '*one Person who is truly God, is him who is the Father of Jesus Christ*', a statement Smith backs up with a series of texts from the Old and New Testaments, including Isaiah 44:6, Isaiah 46:9, John 17:1,3, 1 Corinthians 1:3, Ephesians 1:3 and 1 Corinthians 8:6.[64] Smith also argues that the Bible indicates that Christ is subordinate to God,[65] and that Christ and God (not merely Christ and the Father) are distinguished in the New Testament.[66] In tackling John 10:30 and 1 John 5:7, two passages put forward by Trinitarians as articulating a unity of essence, without mentioning the dubious textual authority of the *comma*, Smith reasons that the context of 1 John 5:7 argues for an agreement in *witness*, just as John 17:11 and 21 show that the oneness expressed of John 10:30 speaks of a oneness that is 'Mystical and Moral' rather than 'Natural'.[67] Thus in both cases Smith explains these passages by looking to other examples of the same language from the same author.

Isaac Newton and the Newtonians

Biblical criticism was the chief apologetic tool of antitrinitarians in seventeenth-century England. The English Socinians and Unitarians were in part seeking to purify Scripture – the foundation of their faith – and with it Christianity itself. But they were also actively seeking to undermine support for the Trinity, a doctrine they believed was based on the accretions of post-Apostolic philosophizing and tradition. The assault on the Trinity was carried out partly through exegesis that supported unitarian theology, but also by robbing the Trinitarians of some of their chief proof-texts, such as 1 John 5:7 and 1 Timothy 3:16. The most sustained attempt to deny Trinitarians these two important *loci biblici* in the seventeenth century came at the hands of Isaac Newton, the most prominent British intellectual of the late seventeenth and early eighteenth centuries. With the Trinitarian Controversy already well underway, in November 1690 Newton sent his friend and fellow antitrinitarian John Locke a document entitled: 'An historical account of two notable corruptions of Scripture, in a Letter to a Friend'.[68] The 'two notable corruptions' were 1 John 5:7 and 1 Timothy 3:16. The letter that accompanied this treatise explained that he wanted it first translated into French and then published. Newton also spoke of publishing it in English at a later date.[69] Although Newton was to suppress it before it appeared in print, the treatise's title, tone and contents imply that it was intended as an intervention in the Trinitarian Controversy. Had it been published in the 1690s, there can be little question that an informed observer would have recognized the

[63] Smith, *Designed end*, 5–9.

[64] Smith, *Designed end*, 9–10 (quotation 9).

[65] Smith, *Designed end*, 12.

[66] Smith, *Designed end*, 14–15.

[67] Smith, *Designed end*, 26–7 (quotations 27).

[68] A modern edition of this treatise, along with two addenda, can be found in Newton, *The correspondence of Isaac Newton*, ed. H.W. Turnbull (Cambridge, 1961), vol. 3, 83–146.

[69] Newton to Locke, 14 November 1690, *Correspondence of Newton*, vol. 3, 82.

'Two notable corruptions' as an antitrinitarian document. Not only does the title revealingly characterize 1 John 5:7 and 1 Timothy 3:16 as 'corruptions', but the text portrays these passages as representing pious frauds introduced by ruthless supporters of the Trinitarian dogma. By speaking in the opening sentence of 'the discourses of some late writers' on 1 John 5:7, Newton commences his treatise with a direct reference to disputes about the verse and thus identifies the 'Two notable corruptions' as a controversial tract. The concluding words of the title ('in a Letter to a Friend') may echo the subtitle of Stephen Nye's 1687 *Brief history* ('*In four letters, written to a friend*').[70] Newton's 'Two notable corruptions' would have filled a lacuna in the Unitarian Tracts, for although these Tracts are replete with examples of textual corruptions, not one of them was devoted entirely to textual criticism. One can only imagine the sensation this treatise would have caused had it been published in the early 1690s as originally planned. Even rumours about his association with the text would have been dangerous for Newton, which may explain why he ordered Locke to suppress its publication in February 1692.[71] When the text finally appeared in print in 1754, Newton was dead and gone.

The contents and tone of the 'Two notable corruptions' reveal that Newton was working in the tradition of continental Socinian and English Unitarian textual criticism. As with both these antitrinitarian movements, Newton identifies the *comma* as a sham foisted on the text by the orthodox party and that the sense of the text was vastly superior without it. Unlike nominally Trinitarian textual critics (such as Erasmus) who were exercised mainly by philological integrity, Newton's conscious aim, like that of antitrinitarians before him, was both philological integrity and the reduction of the putative evidence for the Trinity in the Bible. As for 1 Timothy 3:16, he argued that the word 'God' was a devious corruption of the original reading. This, too, is consistent with the agenda of other antitrinitarians, who sought to reduce the occasions where the traditional text calls Christ 'God'. All this would have been recognized by Newton's contemporaries. Today, we need not rely only on a cautious text intended for the public. Newton's private manuscripts reveal that he was a convinced antitrinitarian as well as a mortalist and an espouser of believers' baptism (in theory, if not in practice).[72] Although an advocate of these beliefs in the late seventeenth century did not have to fear the stake, there was still a need for circumspection. And Newton was nothing if not extremely circumspect in these

---

[70] There is no surviving evidence of any contact between Newton and Nye at this time. Although the two were at Cambridge together and took their undergraduate degrees in the same year (1665), Newton did not become an antitrinitarian until after this, in the early 1670s.

[71] Newton to Locke, 16 February 1692, *Correspondence of Newton*, 3:195.

[72] On Newton's antitrinitarian non-conformity and biblical criticism, see Snobelen, 'Isaac Newton, heretic: the strategies of a Nicodemite', *The British Journal for the History of Science* 32 (1999): 381–419 (Newton's mortalism and espousal of believers' baptism is mentioned on p. 387); Scott Mandelbrote, '"A duty of the greatest moment": Isaac Newton and the writing of biblical criticism', *The British Journal for the History of Science* 26 (1993): 281–302; and James E. Force and Richard H. Popkin, *Essays on the Context, Nature, and Influence of Isaac Newton's Theology* (Dordrecht: Kluwer, 1990).

matters. In private, Newton believed that '[t]he word God <put absolutly> without particular restriction to ye Son or Holy ghost doth always signify the Father from one end of the scriptures to ye other',[73] a statement strikingly similar to the one cited above and made about Erasmus by Nye in 1687 and, clearly, a position reminiscent of the Dutch humanist's observations of almost two centuries before. But Newton also owed explicit debts to Erasmus, who is mentioned as early as the third sentence of the treatise.[74] In the section on the *comma Johanneum*, Newton refers extensively to Erasmus for support, displaying knowledge of all five editions of his New Testament, and outlining some of the details of the controversies with Lee and Zúñiga.[75] In the 'Two notable corruptions' Erasmus plays a heroic role in the epic struggle Newton sets up between the forces of truth and the conniving Catholic upholders of orthodoxy, who insisted on the inclusion of the *comma* in the New Testament even though they were not able to produce any tangible evidence from a Greek manuscript to support its authenticity. It is also clear that Newton owed debts to fellow antitrinitarians. Newton's reference to the work of the German Arian Christopher Sand (Sandius) on the *comma* would have raised eyebrows.[76] And even though in the single direct reference to Socinian antitrinitarian textual criticism he finds fault with a particular interpretation,[77] the reference nevertheless reveals that he had read their works, or was at least familiar with them.[78] In the final year of Newton's life, he met with the Socinian Samuel Crell and, it appears, supported the latter's publication of a work of antitrinitarian textual criticism.[79] Although the 'Two notable corruptions' was not to do the work for which it was intended until it appeared in 1754, Newton managed to weave some pregnant antitrinitarian biblical criticism into the theological portion of the General Scholium he added to the *Principia mathematica* in 1713. This included the argument that 'God' is a relative term denoting dominion (which allows it to be applied to Christ in a non-essential way), an argument he supports using passages such as Psalm 82:6 and John 10:35, where humans are called 'gods' (*'elohim* in the

---

[73] Newton, Jewish National and University Library (Jerusalem), Yahuda MS 14, fol. 25r (Newton's insertion placed within angle brackets). Cf. Keynes MS 8. The sheets making up Yahuda MS 14 appear to have been written in the 1670s. I am grateful to the Jewish National and University Library, Jerusalem for permission to quote from this manuscript.

[74] Newton, *Correspondence of Newton*, 3:83.

[75] Newton, *Correspondence of Newton*, 3:89, 94, 96–98, 100–109.

[76] Newton, *Correspondence of Newton*, 3:89. The reference is to Sand's 'Appendix interpretationum paradoxarum', which is appended to his *Interpretationes paradoxæ quatuor evangeliorum* (1670).

[77] Newton, *Correspondence of Newton*, 3:84.

[78] Newton possessed at least eight Socinian works, along with one by a Transylvanian Unitarian (Harrison, *Library of Newton*, items 421, 458, 459, 495, 496, 557, 985, 1385, 1534). On Newton's engagement with Socinianism, see Snobelen, 'Isaac Newton, Socinianism and "the one supreme God"', *Socinianism and cultural exchange: the European dimension of Antitrinitarianism and Arminian networks*, (ed.) Martin Mulsow and Jan Rohls (Leiden, 2005), 241–93

[79] Snobelen, 'Isaac Newton, heretic', 404.

Hebrew and *theoi* in the Greek).[80] These arguments, and the texts used to support them, had been commonplaces of antitrinitarian biblical criticism for over a century before the General Scholium appeared in print and were recognized as such by some of the more astute readers of the document.[81] Thus it is that one of the greatest works in the history of science concludes with a document embedded with antitrinitarian biblical criticism.[82]

Newton's antitrinitarian desire to emasculate and remove these verses must be placed against the backdrop of contemporary Trinitarian apologetics, as orthodox theologians continued to rely on these two verses through the late seventeenth century and beyond. In a 1696 publication, the English Calvinist John Edwards (a second generation anti-Socinian) includes these two verses in a list of seven New Testament passages he believes call Christ God. In referring to 1 Timothy 3:16, he cites the relevant phrase as '*God was manifest in the Flesh*' without mentioning the textual difficulties of this verse. When speaking about the *comma Johanneum*, he likewise makes no mention of textual uncertainties, and argues that the Greek word ἕν (one) in this verse refers to one essence, even though the same word in verse 8 cannot carry this meaning. These verses, Edwards contends, show 'that there is a necessity of believing the *Messias* to be *the very God*, of the same Essence with the Father and the Holy Ghost'. The other five verses in Edwards's list are: John 1:1, John 1:14, Acts 10:36, Romans 9:5, Titus 2:13 and 1 John 5:20.[83] Edwards's arguments represent the views of a large number of orthodox defenders of the Trinity. Finding biblical support for doctrine was deemed essential in Protestant England.

Two of Newton's closest followers, Samuel Clarke and William Whiston, also came to reject the Trinity in favour of the position that only the Father is the one true God. Further examples of antitrinitarian biblical criticism can be found in the works of these two Newtonians. In 1712 Clarke published the first of several editions of his *Scripture-doctrine of the Trinity*, a careful and sophisticated work that articulates a highly subordinationist view of Christ and a generally heterodox view of the Trinity, albeit one that is less radical (at least in public) than that of Newton or most contemporary Unitarians. Still, it was sufficiently unorthodox to receive the strong censure of most his Anglican confreres. At the conclusion of Part I of the *Scripture-doctrine*, in which he lists 1,251 scriptural passages mentioning God, Christ and the Holy Spirit, Clarke tersely observes: 'From All these Passages, it appears beyond contradiction, that the Words [*God*] and [*the Father*,] not [*God*] and [*the Three Persons*] are always used

---

[80] The most recent translation of the General Scholium can be found in Isaac Newton, *The Principia: mathematical principles of natural philosophy* (Berkeley, 1999), 939–44.

[81] Larry Stewart, 'Seeing through the Scholium: Religion and Reading Newton in the Eighteenth Century,' *History of Science* 34 (1996): 123–65.

[82] For more on this, see Snobelen, '"God of Gods, and Lord of Lords": the theology of Isaac Newton's General Scholium to the *Principia*', *Osiris*, 16 (2001): 169–208.

[83] Edwards, *Socinianism unmask'd: a discourse shewing the unreasonableness of a late writer's opinion concerning the necessity of only one article of Christian faith* (London, 1696), 10–11 (quotations from page 10).

in Scripture as Synonymous Terms'.[84] In a later publication, and in words that are strikingly similar to statements by Nye and Newton cited above, he elaborates on the scriptural testimony outlined in the *Scripture-doctrine*, declaring: 'The Truth of the Matter is plainly This: The Word, *God*, when used *absolutely*, always signifies the *Father*'.[85] He emphasizes that he brought forward over 300 texts from the Bible to support this conclusion, but had only been able to list 13 texts 'wherein the Word *God* has by some been thought to signify the *Son*'.[86] Of these passages,[87] five clearly refer to the Father, not the Son,[88] while another six 'are justly contested as ambiguous' on either textual or exegetical grounds.[89] The two remaining texts (John 1:1 and Hebrews 1:8), Clarke contends, distinguish the Son from the supreme God.[90] These were bold claims for an Anglican clergyman. They were also claims that closely conform to the conclusions of Erasmus two centuries before, and the overall effect was to reduce scriptural support for the deity of Christ.

Clarke undermines the authority of the *comma Johanneum* in his *Scripture-doctrine* as well. After briefly observing that the Greek uses ἕν (neuter singular) rather than εἷς (masculine singular) for 'one', and thus expresses that the Father, Word and Holy Spirit are 'One and the *Thing* in Effect; One and the same *Testimony*' rather than 'One and the same *Person*', Clarke goes on to say that since the text has not been found in any Greek manuscript prior to the invention of printing, nor was used in the Arian controversy, it 'ought not to have much Stress laid upon it in any Question'. Furthermore, he points out that 'the Sense of the Apostle is very complete without it', that it was not cited by any Greek Father before Jerome and that in the first English Bibles after the Reformation during the reigns of Henry VIII and Edward VI it was set in a different type 'to signify its being wanting in the Original'.[91] Clarke also discusses the questionable authority of the *comma* in other works.[92] In three of these examples, he appeals to the authority of Erasmus.[93] In every case, Clarke attempts to demonstrate the spuriousness of the

---

[84] Clarke, *The Scripture-doctrine of the Trinity*, in *idem*, *The works of Samuel Clarke, D.D.* (London, 1738; reprinted by Garland Publishing, 1978), vol. IV, 121.

[85] Clarke, *An answer to the remarks of the author of some considerations concerning the Trinity*, in *Works*, vol. IV, 348 (see also 347).

[86] Clarke, *An answer*, in *Works*, vol. IV, 348.

[87] Matthew 1:23, Luke 1:16, John 1:1, John 10:33, John 20:28, Acts 20:28, Romans 9:5, 1 Timothy 3:16, Titus 2:13, Hebrews 1:8, 2 Peter 1:1, 1 John 3:16 and 1 John 5:20.

[88] Luke 1:16, Titus 2:13, 2 Peter 1:1, 1 John 3:16 and 1 John 5:20.

[89] Matthew 1:23, John 10:33, John 20:28, Acts 20:28, Romans 9:5 and 1 Timothy 3:16 (Clarke, *An answer*, in *Works*, vol. IV, 348).

[90] Clarke, *An answer*, in *Works*, vol. IV, 348.

[91] Clarke, *Scripture-doctrine*, in *Works*, vol. IV, 121.

[92] Clarke, *A letter to the Reverend Dr. Wells*, in *Works*, vol. IV, 237–9; Clarke, in *Works*, vol. IV, 322–4; *A letter written to the late Reverend Mr. R. M.*, in *Works*, vol. IV, 369; *A letter to the author of a book, entitled, The true Scripture-doctrine of the most holy and undivided Trinity*, in *Works*, vol. IV, 446–7.

[93] Clarke, *A letter to the Reverend Dr. Wells*, in *Works*, vol. IV, 237; *A commentary on forty select texts of Scripture*, in *Works*, vol. IV, 322–3; *A letter to the author of a book, entitled, The true Scripture-doctrine of the most holy and undivided Trinity*, in *Works*, vol. IV, 447.

text because defenders of Trinitarian orthodoxy were still deploying it apologetically in the early eighteenth century. Although Clarke's work was much more learned and sophisticated than most of the previous writings by English Unitarians, clear affinities can be seen between his work and that of the seventeenth-century English Unitarians and the continental Socinians before them.[94]

Much less cautious than Clarke, Whiston openly proclaimed his commitment to antitrinitarianism at the end of the first decade of the eighteenth century – something that cost him his position as Lucasian Professor of Mathematics at Cambridge in 1710.[95] Whiston committed himself unambiguously in print to what Newton believed in private and what Clarke hinted at in public, namely, that the Father alone is truly God. In 1711 he declared '[t]hat the One and Only Supreme God of the Christians is no other than God the Father'.[96] Whiston was familiar with contemporary antitrinitarian biblical criticism and used it in his own campaign to expose Athanasian Trinitarianism as a post-biblical fraud. He wrote against the authenticity of the *comma* in his *Primitive Christianity Reviv'd*, citing the authority of Erasmus, John Mill's 1707 critical edition of the New Testament and the Arian Christopher Sand's 1670 *Interpretationes paradoxæ*.[97] In a note on Romans 9:5 in the same volume, Whiston comments that a 'Learned Foreigner' proposed to him in a recent letter that the beginning of the doxology originally read 'to them [the Israelites; *cf.* the beginning of the verse] belong the one who is over [ὧν ὁ ἐπὶ] all God blessed forever' instead of 'the one who is over [ὁ ὢν ἐπὶ] all God blessed forever' as in the common reading. Whiston was inclined to conclude that the proposed emendation was the original wording of Paul.[98] That the emendation was first proposed by the Socinian Jonazs Szlichtyng,[99] and apparently favoured by the Socinian Samuel Crell,[100] suggests that Whiston's learned correspondent was a

[94] On affinities between Clarke and Socinianism, see Snobelen, 'Socinianism and Newtonianism: the case of Samuel Clarke', *Fausto Sozzini e la filosofia in Europa* (ed.) Mariangela Priarolo and Emanuela Scribano (Siena, 2006), 251–302. For evidence that Clarke possessed at least one copy of the *Bibliotheca Fratrum Polonorum*, Snobelen, 'The library of Samuel Clarke', Enlightenment and Dissent 16 (1997),185–97.

[95] Snobelen, 'Suffering for Primitive Christianity: William Whiston and toleration in eighteenth-century Britain', in Miguel Benítez, James Dybikowski and Gianni Paganini (eds), *Scepticisme, clandestinité et libres pensée/Scepticism, clandestinity and free-thinking* (Paris, 2002), 269–98.

[96] Whiston, *An historical preface to primitive Christianity reviv'd* (London, 1711), 65.

[97] Whiston, *Primitive Christianity reviv'd. Part IV* (London, 1712), 171–3.

[98] Whiston, *Primitive Christianity reviv'd. Part IV*, 210.

[99] Both the emendation and Szlichtyng's name can be found in the apparatus for Romans 9:5 in the Deutsche Bibelgesellschaft's *Novum Testamentum Graece*, 26th edn (1979), in the *Nestle-Aland Greek-English New Testament*, 2nd edn (Stuttgart: Deutsche Bibelgesellschaft, 1985), 425. The suggested emendation is also discussed in Bruce M. Metzger, *A Textual Commentary on the Greek New Testament* (London, 1975), 522-23.

[100] Samuel Crell to Richard Bentley, 7 June 1726, *The correspondence of Richard Bentley, D.D. Master of Trinity College, Cambridge*, 2 vols (London, 1842), vol. 2, 664–5. Evidence that suggests that Whiston knew Samuel Crell personally is given in Snobelen, 'Socinianism and Newtonianism: the case of William Whiston', in Szczucki (ed.), *Faustus Socinus and his heritage*, 405–10.

Socinian, if not Samuel Crell himself. A collection of arguments against Trinitarian interpretations and putative corruptions of Acts 20:28, Romans 9:5, 1 Timothy 3:16, 1 John 5:7, 1 John 5:20 is assembled in his *Athanasian forgeries* of 1736.[101] In a letter he published late in life with his *Memoirs*, Whiston asserted that the reading of 1 Timothy 3:16 with 'God' is corrupt and that the use of Romans 9:5 as an example of Christ being called God is 'against the constant language of Christians in the two first centuries'.[102] A sensitivity to linguistic anachronism and a strong Christian primitivism formed integral components of his apologetic.

Whiston also engaged with Trinitarian opponents on matters of textual and biblical criticism. In referring to the Anglican Trinitarian Daniel Waterland's apparent reluctance to use such Trinitarian proof-texts as 1 John 5:7, Acts 20:28, John 3:13 and John 8:58, Whiston contends not only that Waterland 'lays no stress upon them', but also insinuates 'that he suspects the two former Readings to be spurious'. To this, Whiston confidently adds that 'if the *Athanasians* once lose these Texts, which have been of such vast Advantage to them, in these latter Ages, that Loss can never be compensated by all the Citations they can pretend to from the Fathers, since the Days of *Montanus* and *Tertullian*'.[103] Here Whiston reveals that he was committed to the common Unitarian belief that the removal of these key Trinitarian proof-texts would sufficiently undermine the doctrine as to make it untenable – a belief that reflects the strong biblicism of the Socinians and early English Unitarians.

Whiston also appears to have been instrumental in the publication of one of the period's most powerful attacks on the *comma Johanneum*. According to Whiston's recollections, sometime in 1719 Clarke asked him to write a commentary on the First Epistle of John.[104] This was accomplished the same year, with Whiston in the end writing on all three epistles. In this volume, Whiston omits the *comma* in both the adapted King James Version text and his expanded paraphrase of the epistles – something he pointedly notes in his introductory remarks.[105] Whiston's antitrinitarian agenda included the production of a purer text of the New Testament, freed from the corruptions of the Athanasian party. If Whiston's testimony is accurate, Clarke 'also at another time recommended to [him] to write against the Genuineness' of 1 John 5:7. Whiston declined this request, he says, because they both knew that Newton had already written against the *comma* and because he was otherwise occupied.[106] Nevertheless, they both agreed to commend this task to Thomas Emlyn, a known Unitarian who had already been prosecuted for his antitrinitarian views.

[101] Whiston, *Athanasian forgeries, impositions, and interpolations* (London, 1736), 5–16.

[102] Whiston, *Memoirs of the life and writings of Mr. William Whiston* (2nd edn, 2 vols, London, 1753), 1:306.

[103] Whiston, *The true origin of the Sabellian and Athanasian doctrines of the Trinity* (London, 1720), 90.

[104] Whiston, *Historical memoirs of the life of Dr. Samuel Clarke* (London, 1730), 100.

[105] Whiston, *A commentary on the three Catholic Epistles of St. John: in agreement with the ancientest records of Christianity now extant* (London, 1719).

[106] Whiston, *Memoirs of Clarke*, 100.

Emlyn's comprehensive exposé of the *comma Johanneum* appeared in 1715.[107] This testimony opens a window on the private agenda of English opponents of the Trinity at this time. It is also possible that Clarke and Whiston desired a replacement (or temporary replacement) for Newton's unpublished 'Two notable corruptions' and that Newton himself saw less need to publish his own text once Emlyn's had appeared. At the same time, Whiston's emergence as a strident antitrinitarian with known associations with Newton at the end of the first decade of the eighteenth century may have contributed to Newton's decision not to proceed in 1709 with the publication of a Latin translation of the portion of the 'Two notable corruptions' on 1 John 5:7. One wonders what Newton might have done had Whiston not been so outspoken.

Biblicism, primitivism and the purification of scripture

Beginning in the middle of the seventeenth century, English antitrinitarian biblical critics carried on and developed further a tradition that had matured earlier in the works of the Continental Socinians. Believing that they were freeing the original meaning of the Bible from the Trinitarian hermeneutic web artificially imposed on God's Word and dictated by the extra-biblical orthodox *magisterium* of the institutional Medieval Church (sometimes with physical as well as conceptual brutality), early modern antitrinitarians on both sides of the Channel drove Christian primitivism and the doctrine of *sola scriptura* much further than Martin Luther had envisioned when he broke with the Church of Rome. Not only was the Bible important to their Trinitarian Anglican and Calvinist foes, who used the Scripture to assert their own doctrinal claims, but it was especially important to the biblicist antitrinitarians, who not only rejected all Creeds except the Apostles', but believed that the pristine divine message was to be found in the Bible alone.

In speaking out against the majority opinion within Christendom and attacking what was after all the central doctrine of orthodoxy – a doctrine protected by the long arm of the law – antitrinitarians needed effective and convincing weapons to justify their minority cause. Because of the theological culture created by the twin agendas of doctrinal primitivism and biblicism, and due to the intolerant politico-religious environment that saw them persecuted and politically marginalized, antitrinitarians both chose and were forced to rely mainly on rhetorical forms of legitimation. In this climate the interpretation of Scripture and the establishment of its original text became crucial apologetic tools for early modern antitrinitarians. Unlike their Catholic and Protestant foes, Continental and English antitrinitarians did not seek clarification in the ecumenical creeds or in the majority opinion of the *corpus christianum*, even though they were happy to use these testimonies to detail what they believed to be the decline in doctrinal purity that afflicted the early church. Instead, they sought to tear down the hermeneutic edifice that fixed the meaning of Scripture and that they

[107] Emlyn, *A full inquiry into the original authority of that text, 1 John v. 7.* (London, 1715). Emlyn drew extensively on Erasmus's work.

believed was illegitimately enforced with the iron rod of an imperial church – rather than good sense and the persuasion of the Word of God itself.

Antitrinitarians did not ask, How did the Fathers interpret the relevant texts? Instead, the question they asked was, What are the scriptural doctrines of God and the Son of God when the Bible is read within the context of it own times and without the weight of later tradition? Their questions and methods were subversive, but they were subversive of the *magisterium* upheld by the dominant church rather than of the Bible or biblical faith. In the seventeenth century the Socinians, English Unitarians and especially Isaac Newton began to suspect that ecclesiastical *realpolitik* was colouring the work of the ancient and Medieval Christian copyists. The antitrinitarians explored the historical and controversial backdrops to these corruptions, not merely the weighing of manuscript evidence. These backdrops convinced the antitrinitarians that the corruptions were often deliberate and driven by theological rivalries and apologetics. In sum, the early modern antitrinitarians tell a Machiavellian story in which it is not only history, but also in part the Bible that is written by the victors.

In all of this the work of the nominally Trinitarian Erasmus looms large. The Socinians, the mid- and late-seventeenth-century English Unitarians and Newton, Clarke, Whiston and Emlyn all used the scholarship of Erasmus to bolster their excursions into antitrinitarian biblical criticism. In a more general sense, the antitrinitarians also owed much to Erasmus for the role he played in bringing into biblical studies the Renaissance ideals of primitivism and of returning to the sources (*ad fontes*). Additionally, Erasmus's compelling application of philology to biblical studies helped erode the relative autonomy of theology and guaranteed that the theologians would have to contend with and acknowledge the work with the grammarians. At the same time, the increasing scrutiny of the biblical text brought on by humanist philology led to a greater focus on the biblical testimony in discussions of Christian doctrine. Although they radicalized Erasmus' thought in ways that would have alarmed the great humanist, there can be no question that, more than anyone else, he showed the way.

While it is certainly true that they were motivated partly by sectarian concerns, the insight of early modern antitrinitarian textual critics – maintained against vociferous opposition – that some key *loci biblici* were corrupted by the orthodox (Trinitarian) party has in general terms been redeemed by modern scholarship. A review of modern English translations of the Bible reveals that many of textual difficulties argued over by early modern Trinitarians and antitrinitarians have been settled in favour of the latter party. For example, virtually no modern translations now include the *comma Johanneum*. The word 'God' now rarely appears in modern translations of 1 Timothy 3:16. Although these textual decisions came largely at the hands of Trinitarian scholars who removed the corruptions for reasons of philological integrity, there can be no question that this is an outcome with which the early modern antitrinitarian textual critics would have been pleased.

Chapter 7

Friendly Criticism: Richard Simon, John Locke, Isaac Newton and the *Johannine Comma*

Rob Iliffe

The existence of Isaac Newton's 'Historical Account of Two Notable Corruptions of Scripture' has long been known to scholars. Sent to John Locke in November 1690, when interest in the history and authenticity of the doctrine of the Trinity was already beginning to overwhelm theological debate in England, it is an impassioned but scholarly text. The 'Historical Account' comprises two analyses of the Trinitarian proof texts 1 John 5:7 (containing the so-called 'Johannine comma') and 1 Tim. 3:16; a so-called 'Third Letter' is extant in draft, which deals with about 20 other variant readings of Scripture. According to Newton these were all corruptions that either failed or succeeded in changing the text of the Bible as it was in the Textus Receptus of the Greek New Testament and in the King James Bible. Fascinatingly, Newton sent the 'Account' to Locke on the understanding that Locke would both get the tract on the comma translated into French *and then published*. Although Newton was notoriously loath to let any of his productions appear in print, he seemed strangely intent on releasing to a European audience a heterodox discourse on two of the most disputed biblical passages on the Trinity that would hit the Republic of Letters at the very moment when guardians of orthodoxy were most primed to detect heretical productions and discover their authors. [1]

[1] In the King James Bible of 1611, 1 John 5:7–8 reads 'For there are three that bear record in heaven, the Father, the Word, and the Holy Ghost: and these three are one. And there are three that bear witness in earth, the spirit, and the water, and the blood: and these three agree in one. ' The words in dispute run from 'in heaven' to 'in earth'. The 'Historical Account', written to 'A Friend', is reprinted in H. W. Turnbull et al. (eds), *The Correspondence of Isaac Newton*, 7 vols (Cambridge, 1959–77), 3:83–122 (hereafter, Newton, *Correspondence*). The so-called 'Third Letter', or rather a draft thereof, is reprinted at ibid. 3: 129–42, with a related note at 144–6. The main text was initially published as *Two letters of Sir Isaac Newton to Mr. Leclerc, . . . in Holland. The former containing a dissertation upon . . . I John, v. 7. The latter upon . . . I Timothy, iii. 16. Published from authentick MSS . . .* (London 1754), although it was republished in 1785 in S. Horsley, ed. , *Isaaci Newtoni Opera quæ exstant omnia,*

Although historians have examined efforts to publish it in the early eighteenth century, the 'Historical Account' itself has not received serious scholarly attention since the early nineteenth century, when Newton's theological commitments were of interest and importance to both Unitarians and orthodox Anglicans. I am concerned here much more narrowly with the content of Newton's text and also with the immediate aftermath of its composition. As a means of shedding light on Newton's approach, I contrast the demonstrative approach adopted in his 'Historical Account' with that of the Oratorian priest, Father Richard Simon, in the virtually contemporaneous *Critical History of the Text of the New Testament* (1689). This provided an examination in unprecedented detail of printed editions of the New Testament, as well as of original manuscripts that were either cited in these editions or that he saw with his own eyes. Approaching the authenticity of the *comma* from opposite ends of the theological spectrum, there are dissonances and consonances between their positions. The latter is less surprising when one considers that both had in their sights the views of orthodox Anglicans. In the second half of the paper, I examine the work in the light of the intellectual relationship that had developed the previous year between Locke and Newton. [2]

Although public discussion of the Trinity exploded in the early 1690s, it was James II's Declaration of Indulgence in 1687 that facilitated publication of overtly antitrinitarian texts and doctrines. Many, like the anonymous productions of Stephen Nye and the posthumous reprinting of the writings of John Biddle, were financed by Thomas Firmin, and they triggered a spate of attacks from orthodox divines. Apart from the unhealthy stress on 'reason' and 'private judgement' that the orthodox feared in their writings, antitrinitarians invariably promoted a vision of a tolerant society in which people such as themselves could worship what they took to be the true religion without fear of persecution. These topics engaged the exile John Locke, former personal secretary to the Exclusionist Earl of Shaftesbury, who returned to England in the entourage of Princess Mary and organized the publication of three major works – *The Essay Concerning Human Understanding*, the *Two Treatises of Government*, and the *Epistola de Tolerantia*. Whatever his exact doctrinal allegiances, Locke's sympathy for many religious and political views espoused by antitrinitarians ensured that his relationship with Newton would bloom when they met towards the end of 1689. [3]

(London, 1779–85), 5: 493–550. For accounts of the fate of the document after Newton sent it off, see R. S. Westfall, *Never at Rest: A Biography of Isaac Newton*, (Cambridge, 1980), 489–91 and J. -F. Baillon, 'Newton's dissertation on 1 John 5:7' (unpublished typescript).

[2] R. Simon, *A Critical history of the Text of the New Testament; wherein is firmly established the truth of those acts on which the foundation of Christian religion is laid* (London, 1689).

[3] See in general R. Iliffe, 'Prosecuting Athanasius: Protestant forensics and the mirrors of persecution', in J. E. Force and S. Hutton (eds.), *Newton and Newtonianism* (Kluwer, 2004), 113–54; J. Champion, ''Acceptable to inquisitive men': some Simonian contexts for Newton's Biblical criticism, 1680–92', in J. E. Force and R. Popkin (eds), *Newton and Religion: Context, Nature and Influence* (Kluwer, 1999), 77–96. The general significance for Locke of Socinian doctrines and practices is well explored in John Marshall, *Resistance, Religion*

Newton's stock rose at exactly the same time as Locke's. The publication of the *Principia Mathematica* in 1687 had made good all the promise of his early work in mathematics and natural philosophy. He became a Member of Parliament for the University of Cambridge in the Convention Parliament and was allied to a cohort of radical Whigs that included John Hampden, an erstwhile disciple and onetime patron of Richard Simon. Locke shared many of Newton's views on toleration and religion, and, with his patron Lord Monmouth, strove to obtain for Newton a public position in London. Amongst other patronage-related activities Newton was approached to find a tutor for Monmouth's son at the start of 1690 but after some months without contact Locke wrote a now lost letter to Newton enquiring about the nature of the *comma*. Newton wrote to Locke at the end of October saying that he would have responded sooner to this but that he had 'staid to revise & send' him the 'papers' Locke desired. As much as he may have wished to find out Newton's view on this burning issue, Locke felt a continuing obligation to provide copy for his friend Jean Leclerc's *Bibliothèque Universelle*; as we shall see, it was thanks to promptings by Leclerc that Newton revised his tract after reading Richard Simon's *Critical History of the New Testament*. [4]

The 'consulting of Authors proving more tedious' than expected, Newton advised Locke that he would have to wait until the following week for the papers. When it arrived, the opening sentence from Newton's main discourse (sent on 14 November) reveals that Locke's 'curiosity' about the authenticity of 1 John 5:7 had apparently been provoked by 'the discourses of some late writers' but Newton told Locke that he had come across new evidence concerning 1 Tim. 3:16 'wch I thought would be as acceptable to inquisitive men, & might be set down in a little room.' The whole thing had now become extremely large, so Newton believed that it would be better if only the text relating to 1 John were 'done into French'. Clearly Locke had raised the possibility of Leclerc or somebody else translating the text; as a master of anonymous publication he would have known exactly how to manage Newton's anonymity. For the latter, this represented an ambitious and perilous exercise, but also another opportunity to strut the European stage, with the possibility of publishing it in English 'after it has gone abroad long enough in French.'[5]

---

and Responsibility (Cambridge, 1994) and Marshall, 'Locke, Socinianism, 'Socinianism' and Unitarianism', in M. A. Stewart, *English Philosophy in the Age of Locke*, (Oxford, 2000), 111–82. For the political situation of England in 1689 see J. Spurr, 'The Church of England, comprehension and the Toleration Act of 1689', *English Historical Review*, 104 (1989), 927–46; G. Schochet, 'From persecution to 'toleration'', in J. R. Jones (ed.), *Liberty Secured: Britain before and after 1688* (Stanford, 1992), 122–57. More generally, see J. Coffey, *Persecution and Toleration in Protestant England 1558-1689* (Harlow, 2000). For Socinianism in England see H. J. McLachlan, *Socinianism in Seventeenth Century England* (Oxford, 1951).

[4] Newton to Locke, 28 October 1690, Newton, *Correspondence*, 79.

[5] Newton to Locke, 28 October and 14 November 1690, Newton, *Correspondence*, 3: 79, 82, esp. 83 and 185 n. 6. For Hampden see Justin Champion, 'Acceptable to inquisitive

Newton's individualist epistemological self-presentation rested on the apparent right and duty of people like himself to interpret 'disputable places' in Scripture according both to implicit criteria of comprehensibility and to settled interpretive techniques. Nevertheless, in his theological research he was not working alone but was a member of a group that included John Mill, author of the major Greek New Testament of 1707 and John Covel, Master of Christ's College, Cambridge, and possessor of a number of Scriptural exemplars brought back from his stay in the Ottoman Empire. At the start of 1687, when printing of an earlier manifestation of his New Testament was well underway, Mill wrote to Covel about some of these manuscripts and asked him to present his services to 'Dr Montague, Mr Professor Newton, and Mr Laughton'. John Montagu was Master of Trinity College, Cambridge from 1683 to 1700, and John Laughton – who was almost certainly the most frequent visitor at Newton's rooms in the late 1680s – was University Librarian from 1686 to1712. The printing of Mill's edition had reached Galatians in June 1689, but the publication of Simon's *Critical History of the Texts of the New Testament* in that month forced him to undertake a mammoth investigation of patristic citations of Scripture and stopped the production of the work in its tracks. Nevertheless, according to Mill, Simon's work pleased him immensely and thrust him into a new world. In the same year, Richard Bentley became a student of Mill, immersing himself in a wide range of Christian and pagan sources. Bentley, who was soon to ally himself closely to Newton, secured his reputation in 1691 with his radical reassessment of the date and significance of Joannes Malalas's Chronology; it was published in the form of a Letter to Mill. [6]

A friendly letter

Evidence from Newton's private theological notebook confirms that with the help of Covel, Mill and others, Newton had used material of every doctrinal hue to address the issue of disputable trinitarian passages in Scripture. This engagement predated any exposure that he had to Simon's *Critical History*; for example, the attitudes of Grotius and Erasmus to the *comma* were readily available in the variant readings scattered in the 'Appendix' to Brian Walton's *Biblia Sacra Polyglotta*, which also contained readings from the Codex Alexandrinus. An often verbatim compilation from the most authoritative printed and patristic sources was available in Matthew Poole's *Synopsis Criticorum*, which also contained a relatively balanced account of

---

men', 77-96, and Jonathan Scott, *Algernon Sidney and the Restoration Crisis, 1677–83*, (Cambridge, 1991).

[6] See Mill to Covel, 22 January 1686/7; British Library Additional MS 22910, fol. 256; King's College Cambridge, Keynes MS 135; Wotton to Bentley, 14 May 1689 and Bentley to Mill, 31 March 1691, in C. Wordsworth (ed.), *The Correspondence of Richard Bentley* 2 vols (London, 1842), 1: 1–5; A. Fox, *John Mill and Richard Bentley: A study of the textual criticism of the New Testament, 1675–1729* (Oxford, 1954), 61–2, 64–6, and esp. 145 and 151 for the collation of Covel's MSS.

the meanings of words and phrases. However, whether he actually took information directly from the primary sources or from compendia such as John Pearson's *Critici Sacri*, Newton invariably referred to the primary sources that he also undoubtedly consulted. Detailed evidence about manuscript additions, deletions and emendations was available in a somewhat inchoate form in the Appendix to Walton's *Polyglotta*, where variant readings from Hugo Grotius were followed by a new pagination of variant readings from Robert Stephens and others, and finally by a collation of the annotations made by Lucas of Bruge from the Greek and Latin New Testaments. John Fell's *New Testament* of 1675, which added antitrinitarian-slanted readings from Stephanus Curcellæus's edition of 1658, presented this in a truncated but more assimilable way. A more selective and pointed presentation of similar information was available in Socinian texts such as the Racovian Catechism or in the analysis of the fate of the text in Sand's *Appendix*, which Newton cited in his own account. Virtually every relevant edition of the Greek New Testament, as well as all the original patristic works were available to him either in the Trinity College Library, or in the 'Public' (i. e. University) Library. Nevertheless, he owned many patristic texts and at various points in his career possessed a substantial number of Greek New Testaments. [7]

Simon's *Critical History* was an eagerly awaited production that threatened to cause even more consternation to Protestants than had his same treatment of the Old Testament. In essence, he claimed that since there were no more (and indeed never had been any) original copies of the texts of the New Testament, the only guarantee that texts were authentic rested upon the authority of proper tradition, which was to be found in the Roman Catholic Church. In his examination of the *comma*, Simon began with an account of his trawl through the manuscripts in Louis XIV's and Colbert's libraries, an enterprise that had revealed the *comma* to be missing in the vast majority of the copies, although he had also noticed trinitarian glosses to the text extant in the margins of others. Evidence suggested that in time, the marginal passage had been 'inserted' in the main text by transcribers. He had then gone on to deal with Stunica's criticisms of Erasmus for leaving it out of his first and second editions, and consequently with the rationale by which Erasmus had justified including it in his third. He also discussed the authenticity of the Preface to the Canonical Epistles that had falsely been attributed to Jerome and he analysed Cyprian's and Athanasius's alleged citations of the comma. Finally he concluded with an assault on Erasmus and the Socinians' attacks on the authority of Jerome (whose virtue he vigorously defended), and also with internal inconsistencies in the way that Lutherans had dealt with the text in their printed bibles.

---

[7] For Newton's consultation with Covel see Keynes MS 2 fol. 20^{r}. For the central orthodox sources on the comma see Walton, *Biblia Sacra Polyglotta*, 6 vols (London, 1654–57), 5: 922–3; Ussher et al. , 'Variantes lectiones', (separately paginated in the 'Appendix' that constitutes volume 6 of the Polyglot), 34; 'Annotationes Hugonis Grotii' (separately paginated in the 'Appendix' to the Polyglot), 55; M. Poole, *Synopsis Criticorum aliorumque S. Scripturae interpretum operâ Mathaei Poli* (London, 1669), 3: cols 1623–25; [Fell], *Novi Testamenti Libri Omnes. Accesserunt Parallela Scripturæ Loca, necnon variantes Lectiones ex plus 100 MSS. Codicibus et antiquis versionibus collectæ*, (Oxford, 1675), 600.

Although his view on the *comma*'s textual origin is obscure, Simon appears to have accepted that despite its absence in the earliest manuscripts (including the Vulgate) Church tradition had always held that the *comma* was authentic. [8]

In his 'Historical Account', Newton largely agreed with Simon over the mechanism by which the passage had insinuated itself into the main text, but wove a very different and impassioned argument to explain the motivations behind the process. In stark contrast to Simon's view, Newton held that the Preface to the Canonical Epistles – in which manuscripts lacking the *comma* were decried as perverted – was probably Jerome's. Jerome began the corruption, after which it quickly spread to Africa and elsewhere, finally ending up in the printed Greek editions. Newton analysed the existence of the text in the pre-Vulgate writings of Cyprian and Athanasius, finding with Simon (and against the view of John Fell) that the passage was *not* referred to in those texts, and he then moved on to convict Jerome of having concocted the verse for the nefarious aims of the Catholic Church. As in all his forensic work on Christian history, his central evidence was the lack of reference to the text in the Fathers, but he dealt with this absence in a vast range of sources, including the oldest bibles, references to contemporary texts, and extant manuscript copies. Having rehearsed this evidence he scrutinized printed editions of the Greek New Testament, convicting sixteenth century authors such as Robert Stephens and Theodore Beza for misleading readers about the nature and force of the manuscript support for the reading. Finally, he concluded that the text made much more sense without the trinitarian addition.

The 'Historical Account' assumed an easy anti-Catholic animus in both writer and recipient. With the additional text directed against the authenticity of 1 Tim. 3:16, there could be no doubt either of Newton's antitrinitarian leanings, or of Locke's sympathy with them. Nevertheless, the letter was throughout couched as an exercise in textual criticism, based on 'records' and involving 'no article of faith', and 'no point of discipline'. Newton told Locke that he had written his letter 'the more freely because to you who understand the many abuses wch they of ye Roman Church have put upon ye world, it will scarce be ungratefull to be convinced of one more y^{n} is commonly believed'. Truth had to be 'purged of things spurious'. He continued:

> But whilst we exclaim against the pious frauds of ye Roman Church, & make it a part of our religion to detect & renounce all things of that kind: we must acknowledge it a greater crime in us to favour such practices, then in the Papists we so much blame on that account. For they act according to their religion but we contrary to our's. In the eastern nations, & for a long time in the western the faith subsisted without this text & it is rather a danger to religion then an advantage to make it now lean upon a bruised reed.

Just as the content of his discourse implied a shared attitude to doctrine, so Newton invoked a cultural and epistemological community of which he and Locke were members. At the outset he referred to Locke's 'prudence & calmnesse of temper',

[8] Simon, *Critical history*, 2: 2–3, 9–11.

and told him: 'I am confident I shal not offend you by telling you my mind plainly'. The pose of agreement with Locke in various attitudes and practices continued throughout the letter. [9]

Newton's claim that Jerome was responsible for inserting the *comma* explicitly into Scripture – and thus for instigating its acceptance by Catholics – flowed from his belief that the canonical preface was genuine. Partly based on this view, Newton criticized Socinians for holding that a Cyprianic passage that ostensibly cited the *comma* was corrupt, for the same Father had asserted the unity of the Trinity elsewhere. Christoph Sand, for example, had pointed to the vast amount of additions, emendations and deletions that were present in manuscripts of Cyprian's writings, indicating how easy it was for people 'who were not afraid to corrupt the sacred writings out of fear of heretics'. Instead, Newton argued that the Cyprianic passage was genuine, but it did not refer to the *comma*. For orthodox Protestant scholars, Cyprian's trinitarian gloss on 1 John 5:8 appeared to be incontrovertible evidence that the *comma* had existed in Cyprian's time, but a closer reading of the text showed Newton that his notion of the Trinity was derived from baptism and not from the *comma*. The fact remained that no other text in the next centuries mentioned the *comma*:

> had it been in Cyprian's Bible, the Latines of the next age when all the world was engaged in disputing about the Trinity & all arguments that could be thought of were diligently sought out & daily brought upon the stage, could never have been ignorant of a text, w[ch] in our age now the dispute is over is chiefly insisted upon.

The spirit, water and blood in verse eight were routinely understood as a 'type' of the Trinity, as the works of Augustine and others showed. In general, the very need for such a gloss showed that the 'expresse words' of the testimony of the three in heaven 'was not yet crept into their books'. If Augustine and others had been able to cite the *comma* they would have done so, rather than resorting to a typological understanding of the spirit, water and blood. [10]

Just as Simon's analysis of Cyprian was followed by an account of a supposed reference to the comma in Athanasius's *Works*, so was Newton's. This is not entirely surprising, as this was one of the three passages added by Newton on the basis of Leclerc's suggestion that he should read Simon. Nevertheless, Newton again went beyond the Catholic critic in his own analysis, and indeed drew evidence from another area of Simon's treatment of the *comma* in order to do so. Simon had noted that the compilers of Athanasius's writings had composed a table of his citations of Scriptural passages *as if* he had referred to the *comma* in the seventh verse. Yet Simon pointed out that in his 'dispute against the Arians', Athanasius had only cited the words και 'οι τρεις 'εις το 'έν 'εισι, 'and these three are one', without

---

[9] Newton, *Correspondence*, 3: 83, 122. Sand referred to Luther and Bullinger – as well as Bugenhagius (whom Newton never mentions) and Erasmus – in his *Interpretationes paradoxæ quatuor Evangeliorum: quibus affixa est Dissertatio de Verbo, una cum appendice*, (Amsterdam, 1670), 386.

[10] Newton, *Correspondence*, 3: 84–6; Sand, *Interpretationes paradoxae*, 380–81.

reference to the three in heaven. This text could not therefore be used as evidence of the existence of the longer reading for the seventh verse. In his account, Newton referred pejoratively to the 'feigned disputation of Athanasius wth Arius at Nice' but concurred with Simon that although the text allegedly cited by Athanasius had come from the seventh verse, there was no reference in it to the persons of the Trinity. Although he took the disputant with Arius to be a pseudo-Athanasian, he accepted that it had been deeply influential on the subsequent attitude to the authenticity of the passage. In this his view was again at one with that of Simon, who had merely commented that the work had caused some 'Greek Scoliastes' to put a note in their copies that 'afterwards was put in the text'. The Newtonian narrative was inevitably more colourful; it seemed to him that the 'mystical application' of the spirit, water and blood had 'given occasion to some body either fraudulently to insert the testimony of the three in heaven in expresse words into ye text for proving the Trinity, or else to note it in the margin of his book by way of interpretation, whence it might afterward creep into the text in transcribing. ' The finger of guilt pointed at Jerome. [11]

At the bar

Whilst Simon had striven to uphold the integrity of Jerome at every opportunity, Newton followed Erasmus, Luther and many Socinian writers who had convicted Jerome of falsifying Scripture, noting barely in passing that the Preface to the Canonical Epistles 'which goes under his name' might not in fact be his. Assuming his authorship, however, Jerome had stated that he was 'correcting' the Ancient Vulgar Latin (Newton added: 'as learned men think') and had inserted the *comma* as one of his emendations. According to Newton, Jerome complained in his Preface that in doing this he had been accused by contemporaries of falsifying Scripture; however Jerome responded that previous translators had erred by 'omitting the testimony of the three in heaven whereby the Catholick faith is established'. For Newton, the fact both that Jerome admitted it was not in the Ancient Vulgar Latin, and that he had been accused by others of falsifying the Scriptures, confirmed that he had altered the 'public reading'. Assuming such charges actually had been levelled against him, such accusations could not have been made if the reading had been accepted as merely doubtful. In any case he had betrayed his guilt by confessing the rationale behind his action:

[11] Simon, *Critical history*, 2: 10 (MSS cited from pp. 2–3); Newton, *Correspondence*, 3: 87–8. Remarking (on p87) on a gloss to the fuller passage 'Οτι τρεις ε'ισιν 'οι μαρτυρουντες 'εν τη γη το πνευμα και το 'αίδωρ και το αιμα ('For there are three that beare record [in earth] the spirit that water &the blood') in one of the texts cited by Simon, Newton noted that he suspected that ''εν τη γη' was not in the original; this is presumably because as he pointed out later in the essay (p. 91), 'in terra' was always lacking from texts lacking the 'three in heaven' passage.

> whilst upon this accusation he recommends the alteration by its usefulnesse for establishing the catholic faith, this renders it the more suspected by discovering both the designe of his making it, & ye ground of his hoping for successe. [12]

Yet the Preface by itself was inadequate to determine Jerome's guilt or innocence. 'He being called to the barr,' Newton opined, his own testimony should be ignored since 'no man is a witnesse in his own cause.' Instead, he decreed, 'laying aside all prejudice we ought according to the ordinary rules of justice to examin the businesse between him & his accusers by other witnesses.' In the first place others had charged Jerome of writing fanciful histories, while Erasmus had mentioned in his notes on the comma that he was 'frequently violent & impudent & often contrary to himself'. In addition to Jerome's own admission that the passage was lacking in the Ancient Vulgar Latin, Walton claimed in his Polyglot that the Syriac and Ethiopic bibles (which lacked the text) predated the Vulgate. There was a substantial bank of other evidence: Newton also cited the Egyptian Arabic bible from Walton's Polyglot, Sand's reference to the Armenian version (a copy of which he had seen in Amsterdam) in his *Interpretationes Paradoxae*, as well as the Slavonic bible of which Newton had personally seen an edition of 1581. From this and other evidence he concluded that the comma was lacking in the ancient Greek version 'by the unanimous consent of all the ancient & faithful Interpreters.'[13]

The passage was not in ancient bibles, nor was it referred to in any patristic text before the fifth century; 'in all that vehement universal & lasting controversy about the Trinity in Jeromes time & both before & long enough after it,' it had never even been 'thought of'. No trace of it existed 'till at length when the ignorant ages came on it began by degrees to creep into the Latine copies out of Jerome's Version', and to prove it Newton invoked its absence in a string of what were on the whole exceptionally obscure patristic sources. Again he offered a more substantial analysis than could be found in Sand or Simon, and located sources that were not generally available in the critical literature. [14]

What of the suggestion, common amongst Protestant and Catholic interpreters but dismissed by Simon, that the Arians had excised the passage from the copies that formed the basis of the versions cited by Augustine and others? Simon had invoked the attack on textual falsities in Jerome's spurious preface to explain why this ludicrous story had gained currency, and precisely because the Preface was spurious had dismissed the idea that any corruption hatched by Arians could have spread so quickly. Newton emphasized that heretics had invariably been falsely accused of corrupting Scripture, and like Simon mocked the idea that Arians could have erased the passage from every bible in the world at the same time, but the question remained of how the comma came to be inserted in the text. Simon had barely passed

---

[12] Ibid. , 3: 88–9. For comments on Jerome's parentage of the comma in Scripture see Simon, *Critical history*, 2: 4 and Sand, *Interpretationes paradoxae*, 386.

[13] Newton, *Correspondence*, 3: 89–90. For Sand's examination of the Armenian Codex, which he dated to before 400 CE, see *Interpretationes paradoxae*, 376.

[14] Newton, *Correspondence*, 3: 90–92.

comment on the orthodox critics who had accused heretics of perverting sacred texts, other than to say that in making these accusations they had usually been incorrect. On the other hand, Newton argued that the likelihood of Jerome being the author of the Preface was increased *precisely because* of the attack on Scriptural corrupters. Ignoring – of course – the fact that his own text was a sustained diatribe against perverters of God's word, Newton claimed that those who made false accusations were themselves worthy of condemnation:

> they that w^th^out proof accuse hereticks of corrupting books, & upon that pretense correct them at their pleasure without the authority of ancient manuscripts, (as some learned men in the fourth & fifth Centuries used to do,) are Falsaries by their own confession. [15]

According to Simon, the existence of different versions of the old Latin text in Jerome's time meant that the latter had been obliged 'to have recourse to the Original *Greek*, to correct the great number of faults that were in that Version.' Apart from the standard errors introduced by transcribers, 'everyone did presume to change this ancient Latin Edition according to the *Greek* taken in his own sense'. But the Greek copies were no more correct than the Latin, 'and so it seems that the Rule to be followed was very uncertain'. Simon believed that the Greek copies used by Jerome to amend the Ancient Latin Vulgar, although they were imperfect, were no longer extant. All that remained from this period were texts whose best exemplar was the diglot 'Bezæ-Claromontanus', which were ancient but which had nevertheless been produced by the Latins *on the basis of* the Ancient Vulgar. In holding that the Preface to the Canonical Epistles was genuine, and also that Jerome's Vulgate *did* contain the offending testimony of the three in heaven, Newton's analysis veered dramatically away from Simon's. For Newton, Jerome's professed use (in the Preface) of Greek copies that contained the *comma*, which were different from those publicly used by the Greeks, convicted him by his own words. This action was to 'overthrow the authority' of the Vulgate, which should have been authoritative because it was public. Moreover, Jerome's action was also inconsistent with his condemnation of the interpreters of the Ancient Vulgar Latin for deviating from the received text. According to Newton, Jerome never justified himself 'for receding from the received Greek to follow a private copy' but merely accused other interpreters for not following the received Greek. Yet the Greeks 'knew nothing' of the extra passage, and so 'the authority of his Version sinks'. Where Simon had argued that Jerome's *comma*-less edition had in time been altered to include it, Newton interpreted the absence of the 'three in heaven' text from early copies to be proof of Jerome's inability to 'perswade either the Greeks or Latines of those times to receive' the corrupted passage. [16]

---

[15] Ibid. , 3: 93; Simon, *Critical history*, 2: 125.

[16] Ibid. , 2: 129; Newton, *Correspondence*, 3: 93–4. Simon argued that the codices Bezae and Claromontanus had once comprised a single text.

Manuscripts of the scriptures are things of value

Unaware of each other's work, the Oratorian priest and the Cambridge don developed radically different accounts of the manuscript evidence relating to the *comma.* Both critiques were based on the mass of primary and critical information that was contained in the many editions of and commentaries on the Greek New Testaments that had so absorbed the European intelligentsia for nearly two centuries. Evidence in the form of ancient manuscripts was close to hand, although for Simon no originals survived. In apparently confirming that pro-trinitarian passages were absent from the oldest copies, manuscripts had an unrivalled evidential significance for Newton. Indeed, all the upgrades made to his essay after it was initially sent to Locke concerned the marshalling of new manuscript evidence. To the original missive Newton later added a reference to a gentleman 'who in his travels had consulted 12 manuscripts in several Libraries in Italy' and who had assured Newton that it was lacking in all of them. This included an inspection of 'that most ancient & most famous MS in the Popes Library written in Capital Letters' (the Codex Vaticanus). In the original letter sent to Locke it was John Covel to whom Newton was alluding when he wrote 'I am told by those who have been in Turkey that it is wanting to this day in Greek manuscripts of those parts as well as in the manuscripts wch have been brought from thence to the west'. Later in the paper Newton reworded a sentence relating the fact that Covel had brought five manuscripts from Turkey that were now being collated by Mill for his edition of the Greek New Testament in order to remove his friends' names. Leclerc's promptings also permitted him to add more first hand evidence from Simon's *Critical History* and Burnet's *Travels*. In addition, Newton was in direct contact with Mill, who gave him evidence that 1 Tim. 3:16 had been tampered with in the Alexandrinus, and he was undoubtedly on close personal terms with Covel. By the time he added new information to his letter he had probably begun to collate two of Covel's manuscripts that were in Cambridge, since he mentioned a different reading of 1 Cor. 10:9 from one of Covel's texts in the 'Third Letter' which he sent to Locke afterwards.[17]

As Simon and numerous other authors had concluded, the passage simply did not exist in the oldest manuscripts. The earliest citation Newton could find was its use in 484 CE by a bishop named Eugenius; soon afterwards the 'abused authority' of Cyprian was invoked by Fulgentius to urge the text, which was wheeled out, as it had been in the case of Eugenius, 'in the disputes with the ignorant Vandals'. Putative earlier uses of the text, such as in Athanasius's *De Unita Deitate Trinitatis*, were false, as Chiffletius had shown. As for the early transmission of the Vulgate, for Simon it was a simple matter of the false Preface convincing transcribers that the comma ought to be noted in the margins of the Vulgate, and later, included as an authentic text. For Newton the history was inevitably darker and more involved. It

[17] Ibid., 3: 94, 105, 127, n. 51 and 137; early notes from the two Covel mss in Cambridge are at Keynes MS 2, fol. 99; notes from Rom. 7:5, 1 John 3:16, 1 John 5:6, 1 John 5:7–8 and 1 Tim. 3. 16. The reference to the Italian MS evidence belongs to a section that contained an excerpt from Simon and was added later.

was 'the received opinion', he argued, that the current Vulgar Latin was 'mixed of the old Vulgar Latine & of Jerome's Version together'. The *comma* had passed from Jerome to the Vulgar Latin in such a way that the present version 'is no where to be found sincere … who that inserted ye rest of Jerome into ye text would leave out such a passage for the Trinity as this has been taken to be?'[18]

Although many features and conclusions of their approaches were similar, both scholars used the same primary evidence to reach deeply opposing views. For Simon, the fact that there were marginal additions of the *comma* to the most ancient copies of the Vulgate proved that the passage had been added in on the authority of the Preface. Accordingly, he was offering evidence from Colbert's and the King's libraries of marginal additions *to* the Vulgate. Newton referred only to 'some old Manuscripts' where there were 'footsteps of the insertion still remaining' and cited 'varieties' of alteration detailed in the works of Erasmus, Lucas of Bruges and Hesselius that demonstrated to him how the text had been insinuated *from* the Vulgate into the new hybrid Vulgar. Exactly the same material text could be used for very different ends. In order to prove that the oldest copies of the Vulgate lacked the *comma,* Simon cited a 'certain Version of the French Church' published by Jean Mabillon that was apparently over a thousand years old, which contained the passage in a marginal comment to the main text. In reading Simon to bolster his essay, Newton cited the very same evidence – while ignoring the fact that it was ostensibly an example of Jerome's Vulgate – to show that very old manuscripts of the French Church lacked the passage. [19]

Simon concluded his examination of the *comma* by pointing out how attitudes to it had caused consternation in Protestant editorial circles. Sand's citation of numerous bibles which refrained from printing the text meant nothing, since successive editions of Protestant bibles tended to blindly reproduce the text those published immediately before without the addition of new manuscript evidence. Nor in any case had it been obvious to Calvin and others how the notorious 'Preface' could be reconciled with the absence of the *comma* from the manuscript record. Newton pointed to a mirror image of this situation in which modern editors of Greek New Testaments blithely included the *comma* on the authority of existing editions. He rehearsed the standard story of how Erasmus had omitted the *comma* from his first two editions and had then included it from the authority of a doubtful manuscript. From Sand, he cobbled together a list of some early Protestant texts that had also excluded the passage although for once he was not tempted to outdo his source in extending its length. Nevertheless, a minute examination of the way early editions had cited manuscripts, from the Complutensian and Erasmus to Beza, paid massive dividends. It became clear to Newton – as if it had ever been in doubt – that no sixteenth century editor had personally set eyes on an ancient text with the full seventh verse. Rather, those that had realized the truth, and excluded the passage from their editions, had been pressured into including it, and the corrupt reading remained in printed bibles to

[18] Newton, *Correspondence*, 3: 94–6; Simon, *Critical history*, 2: 6–8.

[19] Ibid. , 2: 8; Newton, *Correspondence*, 3: 96 and 90.

Newton's day. Along the way, various editors, particularly Beza, were lambasted for sloppiness in their citation of previous authors, or were condemned for citing in favour of certain (trinitarian) readings copies that lacked the entire Epistle in which the passage was supposed to exist. [20]

No English manuscript now known contained the *comma* and from research that must have formed much of the tedious consulting of editions he complained of to Locke, Newton concluded that the only manuscript that could possibly have been cited was that 'Phœnix' which came to light in Erasmus's controversy with Lee. Naturally he doubted its authenticity: 'I cannot forbear to suspect that it was nothing but a trick put upon him by some of the Popish Clergy ... Let those who have such a manuscript at length tell us where it is.' Apart from that, the influential Complutensian edition merely offered a translation into Greek from the Vulgate. The editors did not condescend to cite a particular manuscript in support of the *comma* but instead appealed to the authority of Aquinas, who had claimed that the Arians had eradicated the seventh verse and had inserted 'and these three are one' in the *eighth*. According to Newton, since Aquinas did not understand Greek his account was only relevant to the Latin copies: 'in Spain where Thomas is of Apostolic authority [this] might passe for a very judicious & substantial defense of ye printed Greek.' However, he reminded Locke, 'to us Thomas Aquinas is no Apostle; we are seeking for the authority of Greek manuscripts'. [21]

The Complutensian Greek 1 John 5:7 and the concocted Greek passage in the 'pretended English manuscript' recorded by Erasmus differed from one another, and Newton argued that the second was merely a different translation from the Vulgate. On the other hand, examples of the shorter comma-less passage were virtually identical and therefore closer to the original. There might be Greek copies containing the longer passage, Newton concluded, but in that case the onus was on those who took it seriously to show that it had not been contaminated by the Latin. Finally, Newton followed standard antitrinitarian practice in assuming that the passage made more sense if it was interpreted as unity of testimony. If anything, this was the most radical part of the dissertation, for it was now no longer an historical investigation of the text's corruption, but rather (as he put it) an exercise of Newton's 'understanding'. As for the idea that testimony in heaven could add anything to what was given on Earth, he wrote:

> Let them make good sense of it who are able: for my part I can make none. If it be said that we are not to determin what's scripture & what not by our private judgments, I confesse it in places not controverted: but in disputable places I love to take up wth what I can best understand.

---

[20] Simon, *Critical history*, 2: 11–12; Newton, *Correspondence*, 3:97–8. The initial list is presumably from Sand, *Interpretationes paradoxae*, 377–8. For Simon's view of the Protestant Bibles and Walton's Polyglot see his *Critical enquiries into the various editions of the Bible*, (London, 1684), 215–20 and 226–48.

[21] Newton *Correspondence*, 3: 98–102, 106.

Apart from begging the question as to how one could tell whether a particular passage was disputable or not, he went on to virtually equate predilection for mystery with the ignorance of the bulk of humanity. Accordingly he told Locke:

> 'Tis the temper of the hot and superstitious part of mankind in matters of religion ever to be fond of mysteries, & for that reason to like best what they understand least. Such men may use the Apostle John as they please: but I have that honour for him as to beleive he wrote good sense. [22]

Newton backed his own intelligence in seeking to determine the true sense of a disputable text, and implicitly equated his own sense of what the meaning of a text was with that of Scripture. However, if the impression were given that his understanding operated alone in assessing the meaning of the text, the massive arsenal of patristic sources that he had marshalled gave it the lie. The appeal to these patristic sources was double-edged. They were significant because they could clear the path to the true meaning of the disputed passage, which at the end of both analyses (of the *comma* and 1 Tim. 3:16) was presented as plain and simple. However, analysis of these same texts also showed how unreliable and corrupt they were. At the end of his analysis, he appealed to the 'freedome' with which he had expressed himself and urged that Locke 'interpret it candidly', adding that he supposed this would to someone with Locke's 'integrity prove so much the more acceptable'. Again, a dispassionate critical demeanour was suggested by his comment that: 'it's ye character of an honest man to be pleased, & of a man of interest to be troubled at the detection of frauds, & of both to run most into those passions when the detection is made plainest'. However, the litigious structure of the argument placed an intolerable burden on Newton and the pose of objectivity that he was promoting, and the conclusion to his assessment of the *comma* was charged with indignation. All evidence, especially the oldest, supported his case, and there was nothing against him 'but the authority of Jerome, & the credulity & heat of his followers'. The learned world had been 'impose[d] upon', and the behaviour of the wrongdoers 'ought not to passe any longer for fair dealing'. [23]

Textual suppression

In the first few days of 1691 Newton briefly visited Oates, home of Sir Francis and Lady Damaris Cudworth Masham and refuge of Locke, where amongst other things he and Locke discussed various prophetic passages. A letter from Locke to Phillip Van Limborch of mid-June 1691, enquiring about post Locke had sent to Leclerc in late December, indicates that the 'Account' had been part of the package and had been carried by 'the hand of a very carefull friend who was travelling to Amsterdam'. At the start of April, Leclerc informed Locke that he would translate

[22] Ibid., 3: 108.
[23] Ibid., 3: 108–9.

the dissertation on 1 John 5:7 into Latin or French, since it was worthy of seeing the light of day. Nevertheless, he urged that 'it would have been better if the author had read carefully what Monsieur Simon has said on the subject'. That summer Locke was still actively seeking a possible position for Newton in London; Newton told him at the end of June that if the Historical Account was not going to see the printed light of day they could discuss what to do about it at their next meeting, but at some point Locke must have passed on the advice from Leclerc, since as we have seen, Newton acted upon it. Locke received a letter from Leclerc in July saying that the piece would have to appear with other tracts since it was too small to publish alone. His comment that a book that was too small would 'get lost' indicates that he was not contemplating publishing it in the *Bibliothèque*. [24]

By the end of the year Newton was having second thoughts about publishing such explosive material. Disillusionment with London may well have prompted the view that another all-purpose retreat to his Trinity rooms was in order. In December he told Locke that he was not interested in the Mastership of Charterhouse, remarking in a draft that 'confinement to ye London air & a formal way of life is what I am not fond of'. However, Robert Boyle died on the last day of 1691 and Newton immediately left Cambridge to attend the funeral. He stayed there for three weeks, meeting Pepys and John Evelyn on 9 January. But the trip did not go well. On the 16 January, Locke's friend Robert Pawling told him that he had by chance met one of Boyle's servants, who had promised to procure Locke some of Boyle's alchemical 'earth' that the latter had apparently requested. Pawling mentioned that he had seen Newton 'up two pairs of Stairs in a pittifull room' in Suffolk Street, and that Newton had claimed that a 'great man' (presumably Monmouth) had made some odd remark to him. Newton was 'puzzled to know whether it was a reflection on him or designed for good advice' and Locke had 'seemed to take notice of it afterwards, but how you apprehended it he knew not'. Nevertheless, Pawling continued, 'I blamed him that he was not so free with you as to know your mind more fully, in that he was well assured of your friendship to him'. Pawling very tellingly wrote that Locke could take over John Wallis's position of royal decipherer if he could work out what Newton's problem was. Newton wrote to Locke on 26 January asking him to bring the 'Historical Account' documents with him if he came, or to send them by a convenient messenger. However, a letter written by Leclerc a fortnight earlier shows that Locke had already sent him the additions Newton had culled from Simon and Burnet, and that Leclerc was about to translate the text on 1 Tim. 3:16 into Latin. [25]

---

[24] Locke to Newton 7 February 1690/91, Leclerc to Locke, 1 April 1691; Locke to Van Limborch, 18 June 1691; Newton to Locke, 30 June 1691, Leclerc to Locke 21 July 1691; E. S. de Beer, ed. , *The Correspondence of John Locke*, 8 vols (Oxford 1976–89) (hereafter Locke, *Correspondence*), 4: 197–8, 187 n1, 248, 277, 288–9 and 302. The Trinity College Exit and Redit Book indicates that Newton was away from Trinity between 2 and 16 January 1690/1. Locke was in London between the 5 and 17 January, possibly in connection with William III's return to the Netherlands on the 16 January.

[25] Newton to Locke, 13 December (and draft of letter); Newton *Correspondence*, 3: 184 and 185–6; Leclerc to Locke, 10 January 1691/92; Pawling to Locke, 16 January 1691/92;

Alarmed by Pawling's news, Locke wrote repeatedly to Newton in late January and early February. Newton replied in a terse, clipped letter of mid-February that he had assumed that the translation and publication process had been put on hold. He now 'entreated' Locke to stop both: 'I designe', he wrote, 'to suppress them'. Leclerc wrote to Locke at the start of April saying that he was disappointed that the edition had been stopped, not least because he had worked on them in such a way that it was impossible to detect that they were translations. In any case, the printer had created a fuss over the small size of the book. Locke and Newton presumably met up in Cambridge in early May, shortly after Newton expressed his pleasure at the publication being stopped, and in July Locke asked him to comment on the eighth chapter of his forthcoming *Third Letter on Toleration*, promising to send further chapters for Newton to 'read correct censure and send back'. As it happens, the eighth, ninth and tenth chapters of the *Third Letter* covered Newton's favourite bête noire concerning the use of force to persuade people into a particular religious profession. In any case, the epistolary exchange with Locke now turned almost exclusively to the subject of a recipe that Boyle had apparently left for trying his 'red earth'. [26]

A friendship in study

In trusting Newton with his views on toleration, Locke was reciprocating Newton's sharing of the 'Historical Account' with him. In the same manner in which Locke had received the 'Historical Account', so Newton understood the sensitivity of – and sympathized with – the doctrines in the *Third Letter*, and he was well aware of the need for its author to remain anonymous. This exchange can be seen as an extension of the personal discussions that Locke and Newton had over certain passages in the Bible. By the summer of 1692 the furore over the 'Historical Account' was over, and Leclerc told Locke that he would keep the text with him until Locke gave him further instructions about the intention of the author. [27]

Newton to Locke, 26 January 1691/92; Locke, *Correspondence*, 4: 353–4, 364–5 and 376. The Trinity College Exit/Redit book indicates that he returned on 21 January. See also M. Jacob, *The Newtonians and the English Revolution, 1689–1720* (Ithaca NY, 1976), 155 and R. Iliffe, 'Isaac Newton: Lucatello Professor of Mathematics', in C. Lawrence and S. Shapin, (eds), *Science Incarnate: Historical Embodiments of Natural Knowledge* (Chicago, 1998), 121–55, esp. 139–40.

[26] Newton to Locke, 16 February and 3 May 1691/2, Leclerc to Locke, 1 April 1692; Locke, *Correspondence*, 387, 434, 450 and 453.

[27] Leclerc to Locke, 5 July and 25 December 1692, Locke to Newton, 26 July 1692; Locke, *Correspondence*, 434, 473, 485 and 586. For Newton and anonymity see R. Iliffe, 'Butter for parsnips: Newton, anonymity and the authorship of the *Principia Mathematica*,' in M. Biagioli and P. Galison (eds), *Scientific Authorship* (London, 2003), 88–131. For evidence in Locke's notes and marginalia of discussions with Newton over Scriptural exegesis, see Marshall, *Resistance*, 390.

The sincere study of the Scriptures and of the foundations of morality underpinned Locke's views about the need for continuous self-education and self-scrutiny, and he argued that promoting and engaging in this sort of behaviour was constitutive of a just and tolerant society. In his short essay 'Of Study', written in May 1677, he asserted that the goal of study was knowledge and 'the end of knowledge practice or communication'. For Locke, 'ingenious' friendship with gentlemen and scholars such as Van Limborch, Newton and William Molyneux was essential to a virtuous life. Of equal importance was the study and practice of good conduct, which outside the Scriptures was exemplified in the pagan writings of Cicero. In Cicero, Locke read of the key roles played by temperance, honesty, modesty, self-control and practical wisdom, all of which aided in study. [28]

According to Locke, the great duty was to make Truth the object of study and to seek it impartially. Yet the prejudices that were implanted in people from an early age made this almost impossible. The cultures and beliefs in which men grew up were usually erroneous, and only self-sustained study could correct the epistemic fallibility of humanity. In a sense, the study of the Bible itself, just as much as the practical use of the works of 'Criticks', was subordinate to attaining the prudence and moral knowledge that would allow one to live well. False opinions imbibed from birth 'put a man quite out of the way in the whole course of his studies' while later 'the things he meets with in other men's writings or discourses [are] received or rejected as they hold proportion with those anticipations which before have taken possession of his mind'. This was the problem for Catholics and indeed for all those of 'corrupted appetites'. To make us interrogate errors that might reside in our own 'party', Locke claimed, 'we had need of all our force and all our sincerity; and here 'tis we have use of the assistance of a serious and sober friend who may help us sedately to examine these our received and beloved opinions'. It behoved men to be neither too confident nor too sceptical of their own reasoning abilities and to 'consider what proofs the matter in hand is capable of' – when all proofs of which a matter were capable were to hand, 'there we ought to acquiesce and receive it as an established and demonstrated truth. 'Only when armed with a moral wisdom could one return to historical writings and 'see the rise of opinions and find from what slight and shameful occasions some of them have taken their rise, which yet afterwards have had great authority and passed almost for sacred in the world, and borne down all before them'. There too, one might 'learn great and useful instructions of prudence, and be warned against the cheats and rogueries of the world'. [29]

---

[28] Locke, 'Of Study' in J. L. Axtell, (ed.), *The Educational Writings of John Locke*, (Cambridge 1968), 405–22, esp. 406–13. These ideas were expanded in 'Of the Conduct of Understanding', where Locke made the study of theology 'every man's duty'; see F. Garforth, (ed.), *Of the Conduct of the Understanding* (New York, 1966) and in particular Marshall, *Resistance*, 76–7, 195–6, 363–5 and 444–6. For Locke's view on the significance of friendship and of the virtues of Cicero, see ibid. , 297, n. 12, 299–310.

[29] Locke, 'Of Study', 414-22. See also the remarks in the short essay 'Error' of 1698, in Nuovo, 'Writings on Religion', 81–3.

By these terms, Newton's and Locke's interactions in the early 1690s were built around a mutual and intimate exchange of views on theology and politics that constituted part of an ideal friendship. Newton was a 'nice' man to deal with, as Locke put it later to Peter King, but he also told King that in divinity Newton was 'a valuable man' who had few equals in knowledge of the Scriptures. Newton's individualist pose was modelled on a central ideological plank of Protestantism, and his claim to be engaging in textual purification was a standard radical Protestant appropriation of a humanist commonplace. Although we do not know of Locke's reaction to the piece in any detail, Newton's letter was presumably crafted along lines that he believed Locke would find palatable. As such, although he professed little interest in patristic literature, the 'Historical Account' was highly consonant with the strictures for study promoted by Locke. Although Newton's letter was sent to a 'friend', an action that assumed an identifiable and restricted audience, the objectivist, *critical* pose within implied a more generalized ethic and community consonant with his wish to see it reach a larger audience. Alongside this, the language of the tract depicted a social group of interpreters of which he and Locke were implicitly members; seekers of truth were people who did 'tedious' work, unbiased men of 'integrity' who were 'quick-sighted', 'prudent', 'calm', 'plain', 'cautious', 'inquisitive', 'considering', 'modest' and 'candid'. They were neither duplicitous, nor 'men of interest', 'hot', 'superstitious', 'violent', 'impudent', 'cunning' or 'sly'. Nor were they 'pious' (the last usually attached to 'fraud' and a codeword for 'popish' hypocrisy) pseudo-critics who engaged in 'corrupt & forct' interpretations. Nevertheless, whatever social accomplishments Newton's implied audience shared with orthodox interpreters, the antitrinitarian content of the 'Historical Account' set Newton adrift from the large number of divines whose work more closely resembled his own local interpretive circle of Mill and Covel.[30]

In a period of intense cultural and political crisis, this language defined a restrained and trustworthy private culture and bad behaviour could still result in expulsion from it. As Justin Champion has shown, such etiquette was location-sensitive and Locke was obliged to cut off contact with John Toland after he proved overly candid in expressing his views in coffee-houses and other public arenas. Friendship with Newton was no bed of roses either. In September 1693 Newton wrote out of the blue apologising for 'uncharitableness' and 'hard thoughts' about Locke, including taking Locke for a Hobbist, for thinking that Locke had tried to 'embroile' him with women, for 'saying or thinking' that there was a plan to sell Newton an office in London, and for remarking – when told that Locke was fatally ill – that it would be better if he were dead. In reply to the letter, which Newton signed as 'your most

---

[30] For Locke on positive social attributes see Locke, *Some Thoughts Concerning Education* of 1693, passim; Marshall, *Resistance*, 292–326 and John Dunn, 'Bright enough for all our purposes: John Locke's conception of a civilized society', *Notes and Records of the Royal Society*, 43 (1989), 133–53. Locke had inquired about miracles in preparation for the *Third Letter on Toleration*, ch. 10; see http://oll. libertyfund. org/Texts/Locke0154/Works/0128-05_Bk. html#hd_lf128. 05. head. 015.

humble & most unfortunate servant', Locke told him that ever since they had met he had always been 'so intirely & sincerely your friend & thought you so much mine' that he would not have believed what Newton had said had it come from someone else. [31]

The critical mass

Despite the fact that he read Sand and other Socinian texts, there is no evidence that Newton was part of an English or European Socinian/antitrinitarian network at this time, nor is there evidence to conclude that Socinian writings were the sources of Newton's antitrinitarianism rather than significant later resources. Evidence for constructing an overwhelming critique of Protestant and Catholic orthodoxy was available in orthodox printed editions, both of the Fathers and of the New Testament. Furthermore, Newton had been immersed for many years in patristic literature and biblical study. Scrutiny of these sources allowed him to engage at a personal level with actions that had taken place in the deep historical past, but which were nevertheless freighted with theological and moral implications. Newton was also keenly aware of the generic and stylistic conventions that governed analysis in this area. For this reason, it is necessary to take seriously the discursive conventions according to which he put historical personages such as Jerome and Beza on trial. According to this way of proceeding, played out in seventeenth-century printed books and correspondence, moderns in this genre were treated no differently from the Fathers and others. In this sense, the juridical function and objectivist language of evidential analysis clashed with the litigious imperative to present Newton's audience with a plausible case. [32]

Newton's 'Historical Account' was presented as a private piece of criticism, the free exercise of a dispassionate and untrammelled understanding. Nevertheless, even if an appeal to good old-fashioned Protestant honesty and simplicity played a substantial role in this fiction, the extensive scholarship displayed therein placed a massive strain on it. Newton was thus ambivalent about the value of learning, and antitrinitarian heroes and Catholic villains were termed 'learned' at various points in his analysis. There is no doubt too, that from this perspective he was playing the role of the critical outsider. This was precisely the problem raised by the availability of works like Walton's Polyglot, for any heterodox writer with a decent grasp of Latin could find resources for their hideous views. Although to some extent Newton placed himself inside the forensic scholarly critical tradition mentioned above, his presentation of self is arguably closer to the authorial role adopted by John Knowles, Stephen Nye and some of the earlier Socinian writers. As Snobelen shows in this book, the latter could do this precisely because the Erasmian and Complutensian

[31] Newton to Locke, 16 September 1693 and Locke to Newton 5 October. For Toland see Champion, *Republican Learning: John Toland and the Crisis of Christian Culture, 1696–1722* (Manchester, 2004), 73–5.

[32] For a similar technique used to convict another (allegedly) guilty historical character, see Iliffe, 'Prosecuting Athanasius'.

editions, and discussion surrounding their readings, had laid the foundations for the cumulative sedimentation of printed resources. By the second half of the seventeenth century these resources were much more substantial, and they were more accessible. These heterodox English authors appealed to, but went some way beyond the more overtly simple renditions of antitrinitarian minimalism promoted by Biddle and others, to engage with detailed theological discussions about the sources and nature of the Trinity. Just like Newton, in showing off their critical prowess to demonstrate the simplicity of Scripture, they created a new community of believers in which the old division between the learned and the vulgar was reconstituted. This created an occasionally unresolvable tension in their writings, a situation from which Newton was hardly immune. He marshalled critical and patristic sources as well as anyone but could nevertheless play the role of the unbiased labourer, engaging in the ultra-tedious business of collating for others some variant readings in texts such as the Codex Bezæ (as he did later for Mill). [33]

Newton composed the 'Historical Account' with a view to it being translated into French, and later possibly into Latin. It would have made a major contribution to the debates that were then raging in England, and since its radical implications were obvious – despite its empiricist and critical veneer – the grapevine would have probed mercilessly for information about its authorship. Punishment for such a work would perhaps never have gone as far as prosecution, but in the early part of the decade social ostracism was not an option when a plum post in London was still a possibility. However, a printed Latin version of the text, shorn of the personal touches that marked out Locke as the recipient and addressed to a faceless audience, would have left no clues as to its authorship. In Locke, Newton was addressing a master of personal and authorial disguise who valued not merely the content of Newton's work, but also the sort of restricted environment in which people could freely exchange their views. [34]

The 'Historical Account' is animated by tensions between public and private, passion and impartiality, simplicity and learning. Given that Simon's views were designed to corrode complacent Protestant orthodoxy, it is an irony that Newton found palatable many of the same notions. However, despite their ignorance of each other's work, it was not a coincidence that they wrote at almost exactly the same time. Indeed, to arrive at his conclusions, Newton did not *need* Simon, for his tract was in any case radically and excessively determined. This was the production of a radically antitrinitarian university don, self-trained in the art of sifting through historical evidence, expert in most aspects of fourth and fifth century Church history,

---

[33] For Knowles's use of Erasmus and Grotius, see McLachlan, *Socinianism*, 270.

[34] For Locke's assumption of different names while in Holland, see Ashcraft, *Revolutionary Politics and Locke's Two Treatises of Government*, (Cambridge 1986), 338–520 and for Locke's public non-statements on the Trinity, see Marshall, 'Socinianism', passim. On his extraordinary attention to preserving anonymity see Laslett, 'Two Treatises', 4–15 and 79–80; on 'caution', see V. Nuovo, *John Locke: Writings on Religion* (Oxford, 2002), xxv. As Laslett points out (ibid. p. 6), Locke even classified the *Two Treatises* as anonymous on his own bookshelves.

with a critical mass of resources at his disposal. When Simon argued that attempts to pervert Scripture were relatively unimportant, Newton remarked in a draft letter to Locke, 'all corruptions are for imposing a new sense'. At the end of his analysis of 1 Tim. 3:16 he chastised the Catholics of the fourth and fifth centuries for attempting to corrupt every text – patristic, Scriptural or otherwise – that they got their hands on. 'Such was the liberty of that age', he pontificated splendidly, 'that learned men blushed not in translating Authors to correct them at their pleasure & confess openly y^{t} they did so as if it were a crime to translate them faithfully.' Newton retained sufficient composure to proclaim sanctimoniously that his analysis was aimed as a general warning motivated by 'the great hatred I have to pious frauds, & to shame Christians out of these practises', and in writing to Locke the great conspiracy theorist was only fulfilling his duty as a 'serious and sober friend'. [35]

[35] Newton, *Correspondence*, 3: 132 and 138–9. Even if there were a confessional view from nowhere, it would be a difficult job to decide whether Newton or Simon was more 'correct'.

Chapter 8

Thomas Beverley and the 'Late Great Revolution': English Apocalyptic Expectation in the Late Seventeenth Century*

Warren Johnston

On 28 August 1697 Narcissus Luttrell's diary recorded that the previous week 'Mr Beverley, an independant [sic] preacher, who wrote a book to prove that Christs coming to judge the world would be the 23d instant, made publick recantation in a meeting house' in London 'before diverse teachers and a full congregation; he said he was mistaken in the time'.[1] This entry refers to Thomas Beverley's frequent declarations that the fulfilment of the biblical prophecies of the fall of the beast, the resurrection of the two witnesses, and the advent of Christ's millennial kingdom on earth would all begin in 1697. Beverley was the most prolific English apocalyptic writer of the late seventeenth century, publishing over forty works expounding the prophecies of the Book of Revelation. The public renunciation of the cornerstone of his apocalyptic predictions must have been humiliating setback (though it was by no means a final admission of defeat).

Despite his prodigious authorial output in the 1680s and 1690s, surprisingly little comment on Beverley has been made by modern historians.[2] The basis for this disregard

*I am grateful to Lisa Smith for her careful reading and helpful suggestions for this chapter. All early modern works were published in London unless otherwise noted. Abbreviations used in the notes for the titles of Beverley's works are found in square brackets after the initial citation.

[1] Narcissus Luttrell, *A Brief Historical Relation of State Affairs from September 1678 to April 1714*, vol. IV (Oxford, 1857; reprint Westmead, Farnborough, 1969), 269.

[2] The most extensive treatment is found in William Lamont's consideration of Beverley's debate with Richard Baxter over proper interpretation of Revelation's prophecies during the1680s and early 1690s in his *Richard Baxter and the Millennium: Protestant Imperialism and the English Revolution* (London, 1979), 19, 23, 39–40, 54–6, 252, 257, 266–7, and *passim*. Beverley's apocalyptic ideas are summarized in LeRoy Froom's, *The Prophetic Faith of Our Fathers: the Historical Development of Prophetic Interpretation*, vol. II (Washington, 1948), 581–6, although there is little effort to place Beverley's thought in historical context, as well

stems from the mistaken assumption that the intellectual and political relevance of apocalyptic exegesis vanished at the restoration of monarchy and episcopal church in 1660. However, a considerable number of recent works have shown that apocalyptic thought after 1660 was not nearly so moribund as once imagined.[3] Beverley's prophetic interpretations were the product of the Restoration political, religious, and intellectual climate, and his eschatological explanations reflect the continued relevance of such beliefs to understanding the events and circumstances of later seventeenth-century England. And for a brief but exciting moment in the late 1680s and early 1690s it appeared to Beverley and many of his contemporaries that those events clearly presaged an impending apocalyptic climax.[4]

---

as several factual errors concerning Beverley's imprisonment and the publication dates of his works. Mention of Beverley in passing is found, for example, in: Hillel Schwartz, *The French Prophets: The History of a Millenarian Group in Eighteenth-Century England* (Berkeley, 1980), 37, 42, and 50n. 39; David Brady, *The Contribution of British Writers between 1560 and 1830 to the Interpretation of Revelation 13.16–18* (Tübingen, 1983), 134; William E. Burns, *An Age of Wonders: Prodigies, Politics and Providence in England 1657–1727* (Manchester, 2002), 113, 139.

[3] See for example Paul J. Korshin, 'Queuing and Waiting: the Apocalypse in England, 1660-1715' in C.A. Patrides and Joseph Wittreich (eds), *The Apocalypse in English Renaissance Thought and Literature: Patterns, Antecedents and Repercussions* (Manchester, 1984), 240–65; Richard H. Popkin, 'The Third Force in Seventeenth-Century Thought: Scepticism, Science and Millenarianism' in Popkin (ed.), *The Third Force in Seventeenth-Century Thought* (Leiden, 1992), 90–119; Sarah Hutton 'Henry More and the Apocalypse' *Studies in Church History* 10 (1994), 131–40; Sarah Hutton, 'More, Newton, and the Language of Biblical Prophecy' in James E. Force and Richard H. Popkin (eds.), *The Books of Nature and Scripture: Recent Essays on Natural Philosophy, Theology, and Biblical Criticism in the Netherlands of Spinoza's Time and the British Isles of Newton's Time* (London, 1994), 39–53; Rob Iliffe, '"Making a Shew": Apocalyptic Hermeneutics and the Sociology of Christian Idolatry in the Work of Isaac Newton and Henry More' in Force and Popkin (eds), *Books of Nature and Scripture*, 55–88; Philip C. Almond, 'Henry More and the Apocalypse', *JHI*, 54 (1993), 189–200; Johannes van den Berg, 'Continuity Within a Changing Context: Henry More's Millenarianism, Seen Against the Background of the Millenarian Concepts of Joseph Mede', *Pietismus und Neuzeit*, 14 (1988), 185–202; Robert G. Clouse, 'The Millennium That Survived the Fifth Monarchy Men' in Jerome Friedman (ed.), *Regnum, Religio et Ratio: Essays Presented to Robert M. Kingdon* (Kirksville, 1987), 19–29; Dennis Bustin, 'Papacy, Parish Churches, and Prophecy: The Popish Plot and the London Particular Baptists – A Case Study', *Canadian Journal of History*, 38 (2003), 493–504; Warren Johnston, 'The Patience of the Saints, the Apocalypse, and Moderate Nonconformity in Restoration England', *Canadian Journal of History*, 38 (2003), 505–20; Warren Johnston, 'The Anglican Apocalypse in Restoration England', *JEH*, 55 (2004), 467–501.

[4] Warren Johnston, 'Revelation and the Revolution of 1688–89', *HJ* (forthcoming 2005). See also for example: Margaret C. Jacob *The Newtonians and the English Revolution 1689–1720* (Hassocks, Sussex, England, 1976), chapter 3 and passim; Kenneth Newport ,'Benjamin Keach, William of Orange and the Book of Revelation: a study in English prophetical exegesis', *Baptist Quarterly,* 36 (1995), 43–51; Johannes van den Berg, 'Glorious Revolution and Millennium: the 'Apocalyptic Thoughts' of Drue Cressener' in J. van den Berg and

Very little can be said about Beverley's life before the 1680s. His birthplace and parentage is unknown. He is on the roll of King's College, Aberdeen, and graduated MA from there in 1643.[5] Of Beverley's activities during the 1640s and 1650s nothing is known. He next surfaced at the end of the 1660s, by this time in England, with the publication of *A Discourse of the Judgments of God* (1668) commenting on the mid-1660s occurrences of plague, fire, and war with the Dutch, and he published two more works during the 1670s.[6] At this point Beverley was not yet out of favour with the Restoration regime and by the early 1680s had gained preferment within the Church of England as the 'Rector of Lilley in Hertfordshire'.[7] However, this official approbation would soon disappear and Beverley's career would take a new turn in the mid-1680s.

Beverley seems to have abandoned conformity around 1683. In 1697 he recounted having served for 14 years in 'that Beautiful-Rachel-State of the Church of Christ ... in the Wilderness, weeping for her children in Sackcloth, and under Death'.[8] The anniversary date of this religious exile coincided with the publication of *The Principles of Protestant Truth and Peace*, a collection of four treatises (*The Whole Duty of Nations*, *The Woe of Scandal*, *A Catholick Catechism*, and *The True State of Liberty of Conscience*) which argued for freedom of conscience, comprehension of divergence in the national church, independence of the church from secular authority, and against compulsion of religious uniformity in non-essential aspects of public worship. Indicating his ecclesiological leanings, Beverley asserted that 'Private, particular Congregations that cannot conform to publique settlement' were the truest form of Christian worship and created 'the first Churches, when Christianity had no publique allowance', concluding that 'such may be still'.[9]

Beverley chose an inopportune time to voice his criticisms of the established church and secular jurisdiction over religious matters. Coming in the wake of the crisis over exclusion, Beverley's ideas must have attracted some notice in the clampdown on dissent occurring in the last years of Charles II's reign. Although it is not clear when or on what charge, by 1685 Beverley was in prison, and he would

---

P.G. Hoftijzer (eds), *Church, Change and Revolution: Transactions of the Fourth Anglo-Dutch Church History Colloquium* (Leiden, 1991), 130–44.

[5] Peter John Anderson (ed.), *Roll of Alumni in Arts of the University and King's College of Aberdeen 1596–1860* (Aberdeen, 1900), 14; J.F. Kellas Johnstone and A.W. Robertson, *Bibliographia Aberdonensis*, vol. II (Aberdeen, 1930), 424.

[6] Beverley, *A Discourse of the Judgments of God* (1668) – Beverley is identified as the author of this work in Donald Wing (ed.), *Short Title Catalogue of Books Printed in England, Scotland, Ireland, Wales, British America and of English Books Printed in Other Countries 1641–1700,* 3 vols (2nd edn, New York, 1972) [Wing]); Beverley *The General Inefficacy of a Late, or Death-bed Repentance* (1670; 2nd edn, 1692); Beverley *The Great Soul of Man* (1676; 2nd edn, 1677).

[7] Beverley, *The Principles of Protestant Truth and Peace, in Four Treatises* (1683) [*PPT*], title page.

[8] Beverley, *An Apology for the Hope of the Kingdom of Christ* (1697) [*Apology*], 3.

[9] Beverley, *The True State of Liberty of Conscience, in Freedom from Penal Laws and Church-Censures*, in *PPT*, 118.

remain there until the early 1690s. In 1691 Beverley acknowledged he was 'Justly a Prisoner in the Fleet', and the next year recounted having 'Labour'd these Seven Years last past, in a Confined Condition', making special mention of the benevolence of the warden of the Fleet.[10]

Beverley marked his separation from the Church of England by something other than assessments of ecclesiastical organisation and government. He also located his emergence into dissent from the time 'since I have seen into Prophecy' at which point he 'made the most Modest and Silent Recesses I could from Conformity'.[11] From the mid-1680s, exegesis of apocalyptic prophecy dominated Beverley's writings, and even his extended imprisonment did not hinder the publication of a vast body of works articulating those convictions.

Beverley's first apocalyptic exposition was *A Calendar of Prophetick Time* (1684). Although published anonymously, it is readily apparent that this work is by Beverley. Already in its extended title were several points that became characteristic of his interpretive framework, including the belief that the witnesses' prophesying (Rev. 11:3–7) would end in the year 1697, that the seven vials (Rev. 15–16) would begin pouring out in 1727, and that the beast would be finally destroyed and the millennium begun in 1772.[12] These distinctive exegetical assertions would be developed and expounded in a series of writings published between 1684 and 1701.

Beverley interpreted the Book of Revelation as a sequence of prophecies that spanned the period from the early Christian church to the end of the world and foretold the important developments throughout that time. In this historicist exegetical approach Beverley followed several of the most prominent apocalyptic exegetes of the seventeenth century, warning that it was 'a very frivolous Undertaking, to attempt to blast the Interpretation ... of Mr [Joseph] Mede, Mr. [Thomas] Brightman, and that to me above all others most Indear'd Name of the most Learned, Pious, and Honoured Dr. [Henry] More'.[13] He noted that Mede and More had 'brought forth some very Remarkable Ministerial unsealings ...of the Prophesies of Scripture, especially of the Prophecy of Daniel, and of the Revelation'.[14] This general adherence to Mede and More's exegetical method did not, however, prevent Beverley from placing his own interpretive hallmarks on his explanation of the prophecies of Revelation, and especially upon the times when those prophecies would be fulfilled.

---

[10] Beverley, *To the High Court of Parliament* (n.p., 1691) [*HC*], broadside; Beverley, *The Scripture-Line of Time, from the First Sabbath, to the Great Sabbatism of the Kingdom of Christ. Given in One View* (1692) [*SLT*,1692b].

[11] Beverley, *The Thousand Years Kingdom of Christ* (1691) [*TYK*], 4.

[12] Beverley, *A Calendar of Prophetick Time, Drawn by an Express Scripture-Line* (1684) [*Calendar*], title page. Beverley acknowledged his authorship of this work in his *An Appendix to a Discourse of Indictions* (1700) [*Appendix*], 18: 'I could not ... Conceal: That when God had ... been pleas'd to Found me on this very Scripture Line of Time, as appears by the Treatise Entituled [sic], the Scripture Calendar of Prophetick Time, Publish'd 1684'.

[13] Beverley, *An Exposition of the Divinely Prophetick Song of Songs* (1687) [*SS*], sig. A3r.

[14] Beverley, *The Prophetical History of the Reformation* (n.p., 1689) [*PHR*], 41.

Beverley described the opening of the sealed book (Revelation 5.1–8:1) as the history of the Roman Empire and the seven trumpets (Rev. 8:2–9:21, 11:15–19) as the growth of the Roman Catholic church from its origins to its eventual destruction, with the pouring of the vials detailing a series of final retributions meted out against it. Of course Beverley, like most early modern Protestant interpreters, perceived the dragon and the various beasts (Rev. 11:7; 12:3–4, 7–9, 13–17; 13:1–18; 16:13; 17:3, 8–17; 19:19–20; 20:2, 10) – as well as the false prophet (Rev. 16:13; 19:20; 20:10), the whore (Rev. 17:1–7, 16, 18), and Antichrist (1 John 2:18, 22; 4:3; 2 John 7) – as representing the supposed false religious practices of the papacy and the church of Rome. The millennium and the establishment of the New Jerusalem (Rev. 20:1–6; 21:1–22:5) depicted a 1,000-year era of true Christian practice on earth after the destruction of the Roman church, which would be followed by a short resurgence of Satan, and brought to an end by the Last Judgment (Rev. 20:7–15).[15] Additionally, Beverley regarded prophetic sections of the Book of Daniel (especially Dan. 2:31–45; 7:2–27; 12:1–13) as referring to the same historical epoch of the Christian church reaching to the founding of the millennial kingdom.[16] A last prophetic image central to his exegesis was the vision of the two witnesses (Rev. 11:3–13), representing the struggle of true Christianity against the power of the papacy, which Beverley declared an 'Apocalyptical Compass, or Sea Chart to guide us concerning Prophetical Times'.[17]

The interpretation of Revelation as a series of historical developments during the Christian era and stretching to the end of time furnished a chronological framework fundamental to Beverley's apocalyptic exegesis. From a sequence of time periods set out in Revelation and Daniel, Beverley discerned a 'Scripture-Line of Time' corresponding with prophetic accomplishment. The pinpointing of the year 1697 in initiating the fall of the beast was the keystone of Beverley's apocalyptic thought and the result of an intricate scriptural chronology.

The underlying exegetical principle behind historicist apocalyptic chronology was the belief that time periods measured in days in scriptural prophecy actually represented an equivalent number of years, based on the equating of a day with a year in Ezekiel 4: 6.[18] The beginning of the period covered by Revelation's prophecies was the start of apostolic ministry in the year AD 37, which was followed by 400 years

[15] The identification of all of these prophecies is found throughout Beverley's works and are too numerous to cite completely here. For a summary of these interpretations, see for example, *Calendar*, 36–77.

[16] *Calendar*, 33; Beverley *A Scripture-Line of Time, Drawn in Brief* (n.p., [1687]) [*SLT*, 1687]], Part I: 3; *PHR*, 3.

[17] Beverley *The Grand Apocalyptical Vision of the Witnesses Slain* (n.p., 1690) [*GAV*], 1.

[18] *Calendar*, 10; *SLT*, 1687, Part I: 1. This idea of a 'prophetic' day equalling a year (see also Numbers 14:34) was a common exegetical tenet among seventeenth-century apocalyptic expositors.

of the seven seals (Rev. 6:1–17; 8:1), ending in 437.[19] This date, in turn, anchored crucial overlapping segments of apocalyptic time of 1260, 1290, and 1345 years.

Beverley viewed the period of 1260 years from the opening of the seventh seal as incorporating a number of essential prophetic images. The 1260 days (Rev. 11:3; 12:6), 42 months (Rev. 11:2; 13:5), and the time, times, and half a time (Dan. 7:25; 12:7; Rev. 12:14) depicted the same period of 1260 'prophetic' days, 42 months of 30 days, and three and a half 'times' or years (1260 days), with each corresponding to a particular aspect of Christian history. The 1260 days specifically determined the time when true Christian belief and worship, in the figures of the witnesses and the woman in the wilderness, were suppressed following the decline of Roman political power in western Europe and the creation of the papacy.[20] This inauguration of Roman Catholic authority also coincided with the rise of what Beverley labelled 'Beastian' or Antichristian power during the 42 months.[21] The period of the three and a half years of 'times' was associated with the ascendancy of papal authority during the first 'time' (360 years from AD 437 to 797), then with the expansion of Muslim power in the Near East as a curb to papal power during the 'times'; the final half time began at the start of the Reformation in 1517 and ended at the resurrection of the witnesses (Rev. 11:11–12), with the accompanying defeat of the church of Rome, in 1697.[22] Beverley further differentiated between the witnesses' testimony for true religion and the beast's false power. The witnesses' 1260 days were measured using solar years, while the 42 months of the beast were computed in lunar years because the imperfect moon symbolized the flawed nature of Antichristian rule. Calculating the lunar year as 11 days shorter than the solar (354 days to 365 days), and adjusting this figure to compensate for the measurement of prophetic years in 12 regular months of 30 days, Beverley subtracted five days from the regular lunar year. This prophetic lunar year was 349 days and the 42 months equalled three and a half prophetic years multiplied by 349, coming to roughly 1222 years. Thus, the reign of the beast began

[19] *Calendar*, 41–51; *SLT*, 1687, Part I: 36, 46–7, 51; Part II: 16, 55; Beverley, *The First Part of the Scripture Line of Time* (n.p., 1697) [*FP*], 4. For a summary of the key dates in Beverley's apocalyptic chronology, see 'A Table of Sabbatical Time' in Beverley, *The Patriarchal Line of Time* (1688; second edition 1692), no pag..

[20] *Calendar*, 'A Further Advertisement to the Reader', no. pag.; *SLT*, 1687, Part II: 20; *SS*, 41; Beverley, *The Command of God to His People to Come Out of Babylon* (n.p., 1688) [*Command*], 34.

[21] *SLT*, 1687, Part II: 19–20; *Calendar*, 'Further Advertisement', no. pag.; Beverley, *The Late Great Revolution in This Nation* (1689) [*LGR*], 2; *PHR*, 12, 30; *SS*, 41 n. 3; Beverley *The Kingdom of Jesus Christ Entering its Succession at 1697* (n.p., 1689) [*KJC*], 31–2, 34, 38–9, 49–53.

[22] *Calendar*, 56–8; *SLT*, 1687,, Part II: 21–2, 39, 145–6, 149, 156; *PHR*, 8–9, 30; *FP*, 5; *SS*, 42; *LGR*, 2, 9–10; *KJC*, 60–61; Beverley *A Summary of Arguments for the 1,000 Y. Kingdom* (n.p., [1692]), 2; Beverley, *A Fresh Memorial of the Kingdom of Christ* (1693) [*FM*], 21–6.

in AD 475 at the final fall of the Western Empire in Romulus Augustulus's reign but still concluded with the 1,260-year interval in 1697.[23]

The last concurrent apocalyptic periods of 1290 and 1335 'days' (Dan. 12:11–12) integrated the prophecies of the book of Daniel with those of Revelation. These segments began with the 1260 years in AD 437, adding another thirty and then 45 years after its completion. These additional sections were the time of the seventh trumpet (Rev. 11:15–19) which encompassed several other prophetic episodes. Beverley explained the first 30 as the voices of the seven thunders (Rev. 10:3–4), which were preparations for the final punishments of Antichrist, concluding in 1727; this was followed by the pouring of the vials, symbolizing the reprisals culminating in the annihilation of beast and the false prophet in 1772.[24] That year would usher in the 1,000 year kingdom. This millennial reign would see Christ with the resurrected saints resident and visible in the sky, with the New Jerusalem created on earth and inhabited by the living saints.[25]

Beverley's apocalyptic chronology and explanations show that he believed in an imminent earthly millennium. While moderate in his own political and religious stance, eschewing violent and militant responses to temporal authorities, Beverley was not unaware of the reputation millenarian convictions had attained during the mid-seventeenth century as an instigation to extreme and radical action. Because of this, he was careful to make his own position clear, as well as rebutting those who might use his ideas as a motive for political radicalism. In his initial exposition of Revelation's prophecies, Beverley was careful to declare that apocalyptic exegesis did not justify rebellion or resistance in any form, avowing 'That if the Events expectable according to this Calendar shall not be conducted by the most unquestionable, lawful Authority of every Nation, I own all I have writ groundless and mistaken', and affirming that his 'whole undertaking is so far from any seditious Inclination, either in Church or State'.[26] He went on to assert that Christ would 'do all by purest and most unblemish'd Instruments, and by Princes of Great Brittain [sic] among others; beginning, as we may hope, and ought to pray, in our present Gracious Sovereign, preserv'd to the longest-course of Life'.[27] Writing this in 1684, Beverley could not have known that Charles II would be dead in less than a year, and other sovereigns would soon play their own parts in advancing his apocalyptic predictions.

---

[23] *Calendar*, 'Further Advertisement', no pag.; *SLT*, 1687, Part II: 7–8, 19–20, 39, 100; *FP*, 5; *SS*, 41; *Command*, 21–4; *LGR*, 2; *KJC*, 56–8; Beverley, *An Humble Remonstrance Concerning Some Additional Confirmation of the Kingdom of Christ* (n.p., n.d.) [*HR*], 2; Beverley, *The Catechism of the Kingdom of Our Lord Jesus Christ* (2nd edn, 1696), 18; Beverley, *The Wonderful Confirmation of the Succession of the Kingdom of Christ* (n.p., n.d.), 1–2, 4; *FM*, sig. A1v, 36–7.

[24] *Calendar*, 35, 68–72; *SLT*, 1687, Part I: 51–2, 56–7; Part II: 177; *FP*, 6–7; *SS*, 51 and n. 6; *PHR*, 54–7; *GAV*, sig a1r.

[25] *SLT*, 1687, Part II: 189; *FP*, 9; Beverley, *An Appeal Most Humble* (1691), 4; Beverley, *The Catechism of the Kingdom of Our Lord Jesus Christ* (1690) [*Catechism*1690], 2–5.

[26] *Calendar*, Preface and 'Further Advertisement', no pag..

[27] *Calendar*, 73.

During that time Beverley's convictions began to take on much more immediate significance, providing a compelling measure of apocalyptic correspondence not relegated to a distant historical past but instead playing out in rapidly unfolding political and religious circumstances.

The death of the king in February 1685 brought the Catholic James II to the English throne. With the predominant theme of Beverley's, and indeed of most English commentators', apocalyptic interpretation being the false doctrine and inevitable destruction of the papacy and Roman church, any consideration of Revelation's prophecies after James's succession required a balance between continued anti-papal convictions on the one hand, and due loyalty to the rightful monarch on the other. Beverley's first effort to achieve this came with the publication of *A Scripture-Line of Time, Drawn in Brief* in 1687, which confirmed both his anti-Catholic exegesis and his refusal to sanction any revolt against earthly governments.[28] While not backing away from the identification of Rome with the enemies portrayed in Revelation, this work endeavoured to assure readers that its conclusions in no way warranted rebellion. In its preface, Beverley earnestly maintained he 'could not avoid, but that the Antichristian Apostacy [of Rome] ... and its Prince, are so fathally [sic] enwrap'd in all parts of Prophecy, that they must be every where attack'd'.[29] But this incontrovertible prophetic correlation could never validate any violent action against the Catholic monarch:

> For while Holy Prophecy styles them Kings, who yet give their Kingdoms to the Beast [Rev. 17:2, 12–13; 18:3, 9], the plain Doctrinal, and preceptive part of Scripture, obliges ... to Honour those, whom It so styles Kings ... .Nor is it possible any Pretence of setting up or advancing Christs Kingdom can justifie any Rebellions, mutinous or seditious Commotions ... . And when ever that Kingdom shall Appear ... it is not as from Earth, but as from Heaven, Heavenly, Spiritual, Pure, Peaceable ... Regular, Orderly, conducted by lawful Sovereigns, even those, who till the Words of God are fulfill'd, have so given their Power.[30]

Although referring to no specific person, this is unmistakably directed to the situation in England during James's reign, expressing a belief that James, although presently under the control of the beast, would abandon that position in fulfilment of apocalyptic prophecy. Beverley would later assert that Catholic rulers would 'consider and change their Minds when God puts it into their Hearts [Rev. 17:16–17]; and therefore we ought to earnestly pray for them, whatever their Perswasions

[28] Wing gives 1684 as the date of publication for this work but within the book Beverley several times refers to his prediction of the fall of the beast in 1697, noting that this event was 10 years away. Wing's erroneous dating likely stems from a statement on the title page announcing the work was 'Printed according to a Calendar, 1684', a reference to Beverley's publication of his *Calendar* three years earlier: *SLT*, 1687, title page; Part II: 16, 25.

[29] *SLT*, 1687, sig. A3r.

[30] *SLT*, 1687, sig. A4r.

are now ... for they shall then be Instruments in his hand'.[31] However, he was also clear that, while obedience to civil authority was divinely ordained, obedience in religious matters was to God alone, because 'the rendering our Lives, our Estates, if call'd for by God, and the Edicts of Princes, cannot hurt our Consciences, but rendering our Religion to any but God and his Word, will'.[32] By this time in prison, Beverley's own circumstances showed that the distinction between civil and divine sovereignty was not so easy to navigate. The next year the path between political and religious loyalty would become even further muddied, and Beverley would speak out more forcefully on the obligations of godly English subjects.

James's accession found initial support but by 1688 the tide of opinion had turned. The king's determination to appoint Catholics to positions of political, military, and academic importance worried many, and his efforts to court political allies by offering toleration to the religiously disaffected caused further concern. The final straw came when the ecclesiastical hierarchy of the Church of England refused to publicly support James's dispensing of religious penal laws in the second Declaration of Indulgence in May 1688. The acquittal, at the end of June, of the bishops who resisted the king's policy coincided with a secret invitation to James's son-in-law, the Dutch Protestant prince William of Orange, to intervene in English affairs. By the end of 1688 William had driven James out of England, and early in 1689 William III and Mary II were made king and queen.

In the midst of these events, Beverley's *Command of God to His People to Come Out of Babylon* (1688) appeared. This tract made direct reference to events in England, and its title, alluding to Revelation 18:4, called for English subjects to reject the advances of papal 'Babylon'. Using the imagery of the whore of Revelation 17, Beverley described the current policy of toleration simply as an effort to have Catholicism surreptitiously reinstate itself in England, and he called for English subjects 'to suffer, so far as it is in our Power legally, and in our Places, to hinder this Prophetess from Seducing'.[33] With the fall of the beast only nine years away, reformed churches needed to be unyielding in their stand against Rome, and not relent 'into a Sufferance or Toleration the open, bare-fac'd, avowed Sins of Spiritual Sodom [Rev. 11:8], and its Impurities, ... lest Many Return as a Dog to the Vomit, and have Complacency in what was cast out with Detestation by a Nation and a Church'.[34] While reiterating his loyalty and the belief that James would eventually abandon his Catholic faith[35], Beverley was unambiguous in directly opposing government policy and calling for others to defy it as well. Though not apparent when it was published, this pamphlet anticipated the response to Indulgence and to the monarch himself that would develop in the summer and fall of 1688. Beverley and others perceived the results of this challenge as portending final apocalyptic accomplishment.

---

[31] *SLT,* 1687, 30.

[32] *SLT*, 1687, 28.

[33] *Command*, sig. a4r–v.

[34] *Command*, 40.

[35] *Command*, sig. a4r, 34.

The unexpected and relatively easy overthrow of the Catholic James and replacement of him by the Protestant William and Mary was seen by many as the work of divine intervention and even prophetic significance. For Beverley, whose predictions had already touted the imminent climax of Revelation's prophecies in 1697, the proximity of these events to that impending result was too auspicious to resist. The publication of a new edition of *The Command of God* in 1689 included a prefatory comment attesting 'the annex'd Discourse, I publish'd a year ago, and I cannot but look upon the present appearance of things in the World a Justification of it'.[36] Indeed, the apocalyptic refrain 'Babylon is fallen' (Rev. 14:8 and 18:2) became a popular device to celebrate the results of 1688–89.[37] Other scriptural expositors also placed the events of the Revolution in a larger eschatological context.[38] Of course, Beverley was no exception and he continued his apocalyptic output through 1690 and beyond.

In the interim stages of the Revolution there was still no certainty how the political situation of a departed king and a residing foreign prince would be resolved. In *The Late Great Revolution in This Nation* (1689), a tract clearly written before February 1689 and still referring to James as 'our King' and 'the Sovereign of this Nation',[39] Beverley reflected this monarchical ambiguity by offering a solution to the problem based on apocalyptic exegesis. He declared England 'a Land of Gods Witnesses' and its rescue from the beast a 'sudden and speedy change with so little noise, with so little, or no blood' confirmed 'God hath given ... a Sentence from heaven in this Nation, and ... exalted it above other Protestant Nations'.[40] While cautiously including the disclaimer that he would keep 'wholly within the Prophetical Sphere, touching no Civil concerns, but as naked matter of Fact for the service of Prophesie', Beverley proceeded to posit his solution for political settlement.[41] He contended that James's inability to understand the requisite stipulation of apocalyptic prophecy – that 'this Protestant Nation must have a Protestant Head' – made him unsuited to rule England and he 'should voluntarily retire from Government; till he shall see, and consider what he hath not yet duely seen'.[42] Intimating his choice for a replacement, Beverley

---

[36] Beverley, *The Voice from Heaven, Come Out of Babylon, My People* (1689), sig. A3v.

[37] See for example, *Rome's Downfal* (1689); Lewis Atterbury, *Babylons Downfall, or England's Happy Deliverance from Popery, and Slavery* (1691); Benjamin Woodroffe, *The Fall of Babylon* (1690).

[38] See for example, Drue Cressener, *The Judgments of God Upon the Roman Catholick Church* (1689); Drue Cressener, *A Demonstration of the First Principles of the Protestant Application of the Apocalypse* (1690); Benjamin Keach, *Distressed Sion Relieved* (1689); Benjamin Keach, *Antichrist Stormed* (1689); Matthew Mead, *The Vision of the Wheels Seen by the Prophet Ezekiel* (1689); John Butler, *Bellua Marina: Or the Monstrous Beast which Rose Out of the Sea* (1690); Walter Garrett, *An Essay Upon the Fourth and Fifth Chapters of the Revelation* (1690). See also Johnston, 'Revelation'.

[39] *LGR*, 8.

[40] *LGR*, 4, 6–7.

[41] *LGR*, 3.

[42] *LGR*, 8.

concluded that the nation should pray for William, 'whom God hath stirred up to be a Deliverer', who would supply the conditions in which the witnesses could finish their prophesying.[43]

The offering of the crown to William and Mary in February 1689 imposed a more forceful solution than the voluntary acquiescence by James which Beverley had suggested, though it was one he clearly supported. By the middle of 1689 he published *The Kingdom of Christ Entering its Succession* which took into account the altered political situation.[44] Dedicated to the new monarchs, crowned 'According to Prophesie', the work proclaimed Beverley 'an Ev-Angelist to this Nation' who had predicted 'the most precise Time of that Happy Revolution ... upon such undeniable Prophetic Evidence'.[45] Apocalyptic interpretation and the impending appearance of Christ's kingdom again provided the basis of Beverley's explanation for the change in rulers, an alteration not instigated by earthly revolt but instead implemented and validated by God's design. Describing the abandonment of Rome by Augustulus in AD 475 as a type for James's fleeing out of England, he found chronological symmetry in which abdication, having permitted the establishment of the beast's reign, now signalled its fall. This, in turn, supplied divine, prophetic justification for William and Mary's claim to the throne 'because Government is so necessary, that no vacuum can be allowed; The Powers therefore, that are Powers in Being, and in actual Execution of Justice, are ordain'd of God, and to be obey'd'.[46] Once more the events of the day appeared to be playing out according to apocalyptic purpose.

Through 1689 and after Beverley continued to demonstrate how correspondence with political circumstances verified his exegesis. This self-professed accuracy heightened his confidence. Beverley pronounced himself 'a Watchman to this Nation', a 'Herald of the Kingdom of Jesus Christ', a 'True Prophet', and 'an Embassador of Christ'.[47] While conceding that some might see his expositions as mere 'Apocalyptical Romance', he asked who 'can believe, that so many Prophetic Symbols, and Matters of Fact could be contriv'd so to agree; Had not He who is Supreme in Prophecy, been Supreme governour in Events also'.[48] Beverley asserted that the 'Immediate Hand' of God had intervened in 1688 to prevent England from returning to the papal fold, bringing 'a Protestant Prince ... on the very wings of Prophecy' to implement a prophetic 'Revolution'.[49] In the aftermath of that Revolution, apocalyptic prophecies were 'now big, and ready to Travel in their Completion', with the 'Affairs of Nations ... in Forming Armies, and Equipping

---

[43] *LGR*, 19.

[44] This book was published by June 1689: Edward Arber (ed.), *The Term Catalogues, 1668–1709 AD*, vol. II: 16–96 (London, 1905), 272.

[45] *KJC*, sigs. A2r, a1r.

[46] *KJC*, 43.

[47] *HR*, 1; *SLT*, 1692b, sig. A2r, Part I: 6; *FM*, sig. A1r.

[48] *PHR*, sig. b1r.

[49] *PHR*, 49; Beverley, *A Scheme of Prophecy Now to be Fulfilled* (n.p., 1691) [*Scheme*], 3; *GAV*, 10; Beverley, *The Scripture-Line of Time, from ... to ... Kingdom of Christ. Proved to be Continued* (1692) [*SLT*, 1692a], Preface (no pag.); *SLT*,1692b, Part I: 1; *HC*, broadside.

Navys ... but Subordinate to those Completions'.[50] Still, such temporal and martial concerns were important in corroborating Beverley's interpretations. In 1691 he cited William's successful campaign in Ireland, guaranteeing England's safety, and the survival of the Turks after their setback at Vienna in the early 1680s, allowing that empire to survive until the beast was brought down, as recent developments which fulfilled his prophetic expositions.[51]

Religious developments also confirmed Beverley's assertions. He adjudged the removal of the episcopal church from Scotland 'most agreeable to Prophecy' and the deprivation and replacement of English nonjuring churchmen a 'Revolution of Bishops in this Nation, as a Great Preparation for a Re-Reformation'.[52] Events outside of Britain were also prophetically significant. Commenting on the French king's revocation of the Edict of Nantes in 1685, Beverley used the description of Christ in Revelation 1:15 and 2:18 to describe 'those suffering, oppressed Protestants of France ... like Feet of Brass, now burning in a Furnace', as well as characterizing them as the 'suffering Witnesses ... now Standing on their Feet'.[53] Louis XIV took for himself the role of Antichrist and the beast in persecuting the godly 'witnesses' in France and mirroring the papal effort in attempting to achieve universal monarchy, and Beverley believed that William would act as an instrument of apocalyptic fulfilment in relieving the suffering of French Protestants.[54] Ignoring other political ends, Beverley regarded the conflict with France as a religious crusade, and proffered his opinion on William's choice of allies: 'the arms of the Protestant Refugees of France ... of Protestants in general, be more valued, and under God more Relyed [sic] upon, then mixed Confederacies, with Kingdoms and States, that yet Give their power to the Roman Beast'.[55] He eagerly anticipated military action, 'waiting at this Time, when the Kings are preparing to Go out to War for a Dawn of the Morning Star on the Suffering Witnesses ... and that Rod of Iron should begin to Break that Potters Vessel [Rev. 2:27–8]', making the 'Prophetical Assertion' that the expedition against France would end the persecution of Protestants there.[56]

Yet, in spite of all his affirmations of the English monarchy and its place in the apocalyptic vanguard, criticisms of the Revolutionary religious settlement also found a place in Beverley's writings. Exactly where the episcopal church fit in the prophetic scheme was already set out in several of his works from 1687. Using the descriptions of the churches of Asia Minor found in the early chapters of Revelation, Beverley applied the description of the church of Sardis (Rev. 3:1–6) to 'Protestant Churches, where they are protected by States and Laws' but which had 'not pursued the Principles

---

[50] Beverley, *A Memorial of the Kingdom of Our Lord Jesus Christ* (n.p., 1691) [*Memorial*], 10.

[51] *Memorial*, 3–5; *Scheme*, 3.

[52] *HC*, broadside.

[53] Beverley, *A Sermon upon Revel. 11.11* (1692), 3; *HC*, broadside.

[54] *LGR*, 11, 16, 17; *SLT*, 1692b, Part I: 8; *SLT*, 1692a, Preface , no pag.; *Memorial*, 5–7.

[55] *Memorial*, 8.

[56] Beverley, *The Universal Christian Doctrine of the Day of Judgment* (1691) [*UCD*], sig. a2v; *Scheme*, 1.

of Reformation'.[57] Sardis would be superseded by the church of Philadelphia (Rev. 3:7–13) which included those Protestants living under Catholic or Sardian-Protestant repression; the Philadelphian church would be the properly reformed Protestant church 'resting upon the consent of Christians' which would be instituted in 1697.[58] In these characterizations, Beverley was clearly distinguishing between the mandated worship of the Church of England – Sardis – and the dissenting, but more truly reformed, convictions of the Philadelphian-Protestant nonconformists. The ecclesio-prophetic designations for these positions were recurring allegorical devices in Beverley's religious commentary.

The events of the autumn of 1688 created anticipation that a reconciliation of English Protestant denominations was forthcoming. Although reminding readers at the outset of *The Late Great Revolution* of his comparisons of the established church to Sardis, in a 'slumber' and 'short of the glory intended by Christ in the Advances of his Kingdom', Beverley expressed the desire that recent results would usher in additional reform; after initial allusion to the correspondence between the persecution of Protestant dissent and the killing of the witnesses, he announced that 'the Bitterness of that Death of the Witnesses is past' because the recent direct threat from Catholicism would stir the Church of England to abandon its policies of repression.[59] In language directed at Anglican worship, Beverley hoped that 'this Revolution will be the Buoying up [of] substantial Christianity, and Protestancy, ... and that Form and Ceremony are dropping off from us, at least so far, as it hath been [a] matter of distinction, and most of all difference, and division'.[60] Beverley later looked forward to changes in religious circumstances in all three British kingdoms as further indicators of apocalyptic accomplishment.[61]

Expectation of Protestant comprehension reached its height in the late summer and fall of 1689. During these months William called for the formation of an ecclesiastical commission which would consider reforms within the Church of England, and his instructions evidenced a sympathy for the re-uniting of English Protestants in the national church.[62] In the dedication to a book from the late fall of 1689 Beverley addressed this assembly directly, calling it 'a Dawn of Fulfilling a part of the Prophecy' which would bring about the fall of the beast and the propagation of true Christianity.[63] While noting that Protestant churches protected by rulers were a solid defense against Antichrist, the tone of this tract was far from conciliatory. Making apparent his Congregational leanings, Beverley observed how the efforts of the episcopal hierarchy 'to shut the Door of those Churches, un-established by Law;

---

[57] *SS*, 47 and n. 1, 48n. 1; *SLT*, 1687, Part II: 162.

[58] *SS*, 48 n. 2, 49 n. 3.

[59] *LGR*, sigs. A3v–A4r, 5.

[60] *LGR*, 12.

[61] *KJC*, 70.

[62] For an analysis of the circumstances surrounding the summoning and meeting of the 1689 ecclesiastical commission, see Tony Claydon, *William III and the Godly Revolution* (Cambridge, 1996), 165–71.

[63] *PHR*, sig. b1r.

called by Prophecy, Philadelphian; as being only gather'd by mutual Assent' had been met in the recent past by divine retribution; this 'Recollection of Things within these last Fifty Years' not only brought to mind the fate of the Anglican church during the Civil Wars, but also intimated likely detrimental results should it continue such policies in the present.[64] Moreover, Beverley pointed out a resemblance between the episcopal structure and the government of the Catholic church, depicted as the 'feet of clay' of the fourth monarchy (Dan. 2:33–5, 40–45), and reminded his audience that some of the sufferings of the witnesses had been inflicted by the Church of England.[65]

The Revolutionary settlement did not achieve the comprehension and unity within the national church which Beverley had called for since his first move to nonconformity in the early 1680s, and he continued his critique and demands for further reform after 1689. Beverley revisited the characterization of the Anglican hierarchy as the feet of clay in another literary address from 1690, this time to the bishops of the Church of England. He advised them 'to be more watchful ... lest There should seem Any surrogation in the Reformation to the Feet of Clay; the Papacy, the Cardinalism, the Roman Hierarchy ... and so You receive the Dishonour of any part of their Fall'.[66] Beverley further distinguished between dissenting denominations and the episcopal church by labelling it the synagogue of Satan (Rev. 3:9) which had persecuted and interfered with the 'ministration of Philadelphian witnesses'; he noted how true reform had taken refuge in North America, but that the Anglican Church's 'Mountainous' power would soon be brought down 'into the Philadelphian Plain ... All Remains of that Synagogue of Sathan [sic], that casts out of the Christian Synagogue for Forms ... shall be cut off'.[67] Describing ecclesiastical courts as 'a kind of Protestant Inquisition', criticizing debates over church hierarchy and liturgy, and denying the legitimacy of the Church of England's claims to being a national church, Beverley maintained that either reform needed to occur or God would 'Punish the Outward Court-Protestancy [Rev. 11:2] of these Nations'.[68] He expected 'the whole Protestant Hierarchy of Arch-Bishops, Bishops, with all its Tumid[ity], &c. should Couch down' in 1697 with the establishment of that true Philadelphian church, 'to which the Prelaticism and Ceremonialism of the Sardian Pompous Church and They of the Synagogue shall Bow'.[69] It is apparent that the Revolution and toleration did not provide a palatable solution to all English Protestants, and some, like Beverley, still resented the subordinate status given to dissenting churches in the 1690s. Beverley continued to use apocalyptic language to describe these ecclesiastical distinctions,

---

64 *PHR*, sig. a4r.

65 *PHR*, 74.

66 Catechism, 1690, sig. A2v. See also *SLT*, 1692b, sig. A1v.

67 *GAV*, sig. a1v, 10; *FM*, 20.

68 *SLT*, 1692b, Part I: 6; Beverley, *The Pattern of the Divine Temple, Sanstuary* [sic]*, and City of the New Jerusalem* (n.p., [1690]), 8; *TYK*, 4; *Scheme*, 4.

69 *SLT*, 1692b, Part I: 6; *HC*, broadside. 'Tumid' means inflated, turgid, or bombastic: *Oxford English Dictionary Online* (http://www.oed.com).

and anticipated additional prophetic advance to rectify the religious disparity which had yet only been partially resolved.

Beverley was released from prison in the early 1690s, although again the exact date is unknown. Sometime after this, he became the pastor to a Congregational meeting in London at Cutlers' Hall in Cloak Lane on Upper Thames Street, and he was also a Sunday lecturer to Stephen Lobb's congregation in Fetter Lane.[70] In numerous writings – Beverley would publish over 20 between 1690 and 1697 – he remained steadfast in his determination that the beast would fall and the dawning of Christ's kingdom would take place in 1697. After the Revolution Beverley continued to measure the significance of events against pending apocalyptic accomplishment. Of particular importance was the death of Queen Mary in 1694. Just as the circumstances of 1688–89 had been a fulfilment of prophecy, Beverley contended that the death of the queen had to be understood in the same context.[71] He reminded readers of the failure of the Revolutionary settlement to resolve all of the issues of contention in England. Mary's important role made her death a rebuke to the nation: "When God is pleased to take away such a Person, so Eminent in the Revolution; It is, as if he would put a Disgrace, and a Dishonour upon the Revolution as to usward'.[72] The one consolation for this loss was the assurance that 'we cannot ... be far off ... from a far greater Revolution' in the coming kingdom of Christ which was only two years away.[73]

Of course the year 1697 was of supreme importance for Beverley's apocalyptic expectations.[74] In the middle of that year he published a collection of sermons concentrating on millenarian themes.[75] Printed with this was *An Apology for the Hope of the Kingdom of Christ* reiterating Beverley's chronology and re-affirming his belief in the fulfilment of his predictions. While acknowledging that no great events of apocalyptic import had yet taken place in 1697, he would not be shaken from his assurance.[76] In allusion to prolonged war with the French, Beverley anticipated the

---

[70] Walter Wilson, *The History and Antiquities of Dissenting Churches and Meeting Houses, in London, Westminster, and Southwark*, Volume II (London, 1808), 63–4; Johnstone and Robertson, *Bibliographia*, II, 424; Beverley, *The Loss of the Soul* (1694), Epistle Dedicatory, no. pag..

[71] Beverley, *A Solemn Perswasion to Most Earnest Prayer* (1695) [*SP*], Preface, no pag..

[72] *SP*, 16–17.

[73] *SP*, 21, Preface, no pag.

[74] Hillel Schwartz notes the correspondence of Beverley's predictions for the year 1697 with the start of 'public testimony' of the Philadelphian Society. The Philadelphians were founded by John Pordage and Jane Lead, and the group anticipated the imminent onset of the millennium. Beverley's ideas were even published by a German Philadelphian in 1697: Schwartz *French Prophets*, 45–50, and 50 n. 39. See *Ein Schlüssel ueber Hn. Beverleys ... Zeit-Register* (Frankfurt, 1697); *Einege Anmerckungen, ueber Herrn Thomae Beverleys ... Zeit-Register* (Frankfurt, 1697); *Herrn, Th. Beverleys ... Zeit-Register mit denen Zeichen der Zeiten, vom Anfange biss ans Ende der Welt* (Frankfurt, 1697).

[75] Beverley, *The Parable of the Ten Virgins* (1697).

[76] *Apology*, 21–3, quote at 22–3.

relief 'for the present Difficulties of Nations, to our Nation particularly, to our King, to the Councel of the Nation in Parliament: That He, whose Right it is, is now about to take to Himself his Great Power, and to Reign, and to destroy them, who have been so long destroying the earth'.[77] Unfortunately for Beverley, deliverance of the nation did not take the grand eschatological form he predicted and 1697 saw his public humiliation rather than his prophetic triumph.

Luttrell's account of Beverley's recantation of his convictions concerning 1697 was not without its epilogue. After announcing his mistake, Beverley concluded by asserting Christ's return, nonetheless, 't'was not farr off'.[78] With the failure of his expectations Beverley left his pastorship of Cutlers' Hall (his congregation is thought to have disbanded then also) and he was living in or around Colchester at the turn of the eighteenth century.[79] But, despite the passing of 1697 without apocalyptic incident, he continued to publish further assertions of the imminent manifestation of Christ's kingdom on earth.

Late in 1697 or early in 1698 Beverley wrote an account of the extraordinary political affairs of the previous year. Tellingly included on the title page was Psalm 11:2 ('For. lo, the wicked bend their bow ... that they may privily shoot at the upright in heart').[80] Beverley focused on Imperial and Russian victories against the Turks and the League of Augsburg's success against the French culminating in the Treaty of Ryswick (September 1697) as signs of God's hand in events.[81] Still not shying away from fixing dates, Beverley revised his calculations with the adjustment that 1697 must end completely and deliverance begin with the Jewish Passover in the spring of 1698. Following this, Beverley declared that if he was mistaken again, he would 'lay my Hand over my Mouth, and say with Job, I am vile; Once, yea, Twice I have spoken; But I will do so no more [Job 40:4–5]'.[82] However, Beverley's prophetic proclivities were not so easy to break.

Opening a subsequent review of significant occurrences later that year, Beverley noted that the 'great Events, I hoped this last year, have not had their Complement' and, not surprisingly considering his confident proclamations, the 'Censure of many are very severe upon me'.[83] The failure of his revised predictions in 1698 caused Beverley to undertake a more serious and convoluted alteration of his chronological computations for 1699. He put forward the theory that apocalyptic time was divided into 'indictions' or segments of 15 years, a measurement which he determined began

---

[77] *Apology*, 25.

[78] Luttrell *Brief Historical Relation*, IV, 269.

[79] Wilson *History and Antiquities*, II, 63, 64–5, 66. See also Beverley *A Sermon of Mr. Benjamin Perkins ... at Colchester, 1700* ([1701]); Arber (ed.) *Term Catalogues*, vol. III (London, 1906), 226.

[80] Beverley *A Review of What God Hath Been Pleased to Do This Year* (1698) [*Review*]. This work was published between November 1697 and February 1698: Arber (ed.), *Term Catalogues*, III, 50.

[81] *Review*, sig. a2v, 3–13, 18.

[82] *Review*, 15.

[83] Beverley, *A Most Humble Representation on a Further Review* (1698), 1.

in AD 438 at the beginning of the Jewish civil year in autumn (not at Passover as he previously contended). This, by now desperate, reasoning led to the conclusion

> we are now not in the Second Year, but so much advanced in the First Year of the Indictions ... And so we are not in the Year 1699, but 98. and so continue until the next Autumnal Equinox: so that we have to expect what God will please to do yet, ere the End of this First Year of Indicted Time of finishing, in Prophetic Count.[84]

The elapse of this deadline saw Beverley add the time of the two witnesses lying dead (Rev. 11:9), three and a half 'prophetic' days, to 1697 to come to 1700 for his new apocalyptic culmination.[85] Like any good prophet, Beverley blamed the refusal of others to recognize the significance of 1697 for causing God to postpone his promise, but he assured his readers that there would be no further delay.[86] Later Beverley would adjust the date to 1701.[87] Ever stalwart, Beverley hoped that that year inaugurated the 'Low Beginning, of singing that Song [of the thunders (Rev. 14:2–3)], vouchsafed to me through the Riches of Grace ... and that therefore it shall bring ... the Apocalyptical Expectation, I so humbly, and earnestly wait upon'.[88] Still awaiting the apocalyptic accomplishment he had staked his exegetical and ministerial reputation on, 1701 saw the last of Beverley's new prophetic interpretations. He is thought to have died in 1702.[89]

Thomas Beverley's interpretations attempted to explain the important religious and political developments of his time, demonstrating that apocalyptic prophecy remained a means to comprehend the circumstances of late seventeenth-century England. Although the frantic alterations and rationalizations of his predictions at the turn of the eighteenth century cannot help but elicit some amusement or derision from modern readers (of course the conclusion to his story is always apparent in hindsight), Beverley's thought does tell us much about belief and scriptural exegesis in the later seventeenth century. Most importantly, it reveals that apocalyptic thought had survived the change in radical fortunes after the decades of the mid-century and was readily adapted to explain the Restoration civil and ecclesiastical context. Indeed, post-1660 apocalyptic convictions were not simply leftover radical discontent, as Beverley's warnings against subversive action emphasize, and his thought emerged from very particular conditions. Moreover, with the widespread belief that divine providence had played a leading role in the heady days of 1688 and

---

[84] Beverley, *Indictions or, Accounting by Fifteens, the Great Style of Prophetic Time* (1699), 39. The use of indictions was actually instituted as a fiscal measure in the late third-century AD, and in the reign of Constantine they were made into cycles of 15 years counted from 1 September 312: N.G.L. Hammond and H.H. Scullard, *The Oxford Classical Dictionary* (2nd edn, Oxford, 1970), 544.

[85] Beverley, *The Good Hope Through Grace* (n.d.) [*GH*], sig. A3v, 38–40, 42, 53–5.

[86] *GH*, 59–60, 67–8.

[87] *Appendix*, title page, 13; Beverley, *The Grand Apocalyptical Question* (1701), 46.

[88] Beverley, *The Praise of the Glory of Grace* (1701), Epistle Dedicatory, no pag..

[89] Johnstone and Robertson, *Bibliographia*, II, 424.

1689, the deliverance of the nation from papal clutches and the replacement of the Catholic king by Protestant monarchs appeared to exemplify the resounding defeat of the enemies to the true church foretold in Revelation. However, as Beverley's commentary also shows, not all was yet resolved. Criticisms of the Revolutionary religious settlement and of the status of Protestant dissent continued, with the resolution to these problems a necessary aspect of prophetic fulfilment. Nonetheless, hope remained that events were confirming apocalyptic accomplishment, which was on its way to completion in England and ready to dawn on a wider world. In an age where scriptural explanations of the world were still predominant, the confidence that this biblical design extended to the end of the world was not so unusual, and perhaps we might sympathize with Beverley's, and others', desire to bring that apparently inevitable conclusion closer to their day.

Chapter 9

The Ghost in the Marble: Jeremy Taylor's *Liberty of Prophesying* (1647) and Its Readers

Nicholas McDowell

Intellectual and cultural historians have begun to reconsider the relationship between orthodoxy and heterodoxy as dynamic and symbiotic rather than static and oppositional. Prompted by J.G.A. Pocock's observation that 'orthodoxy generates its own scepticism, and scepticism has its own relations with orthodoxy', several of the essays in a recent collection on heterodox writing of the later seventeenth and early eighteenth centuries explore the ways in which 'a defence of orthodox belief planted the seeds of its own undoing'.[1] The self-defeating tendencies of Anglican polemic at the beginning of the eighteenth century are highlighted in Joseph M. Levine's argument that the use of historical and philological scholarship to repel deist attacks on the authenticity of Biblical texts also validated a comparative method by which the universalist claims of revealed religion could be denied. However Levine provides no examples of how Anglican Biblical scholarship was actually put to heterodox use, and so leaves himself open to the risk of simply repeating fears amongst contemporary elites about the irreligious consequences of the popular dissemination of knowledge.[2] After all, the exaltation of reason by the Cambridge Neoplatonists and 'Latitudinarian' divines was designed to combat the sectarian enthusiasm that emerged during the English revolution, but the High Church critics of the Latitudinarians repeatedly accused them of providing a nurturing soil for deist and other heterodox principles, both in their principles of natural religion and in the policy of comprehending nonconformity which they derived from those principles: 'by an *Universall Latitude*, *Comprehension*, and *Indifference* to every Sect and Party, but that of the *True Establish'd Church*, they run into the common Herd, and

[1] J.G.A. Pocock, 'Within the margins: the definition of orthodoxy', and Roger D. Lund, 'Introduction' in Roger D. Lund (ed.), *The Margins of Orthodoxy: Heterodox Writing and Cultural Response 1660–1750* (Cambridge, 1995), 33–53 (52), 1–32 (23).

[2] Joseph M. Levine, 'Deists and Anglicans: the ancient wisdom and the idea of progress', in Lund (ed.), *The Margins of Orthodoxy*, 219–39.

are *Deists*, *Socinians*, *Quakers*, *Anabaptists*, or *Independents*; *Turks* or *Jews* upon occasion, [and] take all to be equally Orthodox, as it suits best with their Interest.'[3]

In this chapter I argue that such fears and accusations did indeed have a basis in reality by recovering several instances of the radical appropriation of Anglican texts, not by deists and freethinkers but by mid-seventeenth-century figures linked to the Levellers and Quakers. I explore specifically how the writings of the Anglican divine Jeremy Taylor, who influenced the development of the Latitudinarian position, became a resource of radical Biblical criticism during the English revolution. Ironically, then, ideas associated with the evolution of Anglican modes of thought were also used to elaborate and bolster sectarian, anticlerical and sceptical positions; although importantly the radicals shared with Taylor a profound distaste for Calvinism, the dominant theological doctrine between 1640 and 1660. The role of books written by a highly learned Anglican divine in forming the anti-Scriptural beliefs of Clement Writer, an infamous radical who was accused of atheism and had no university education, provides a striking instance of how literacy created and shaped heresy in the seventeenth century, as opposed to Christopher Hill's hugely influential conception of radical ideas as autocthonous modes of folk belief that had always existed but only became visible to the literate elite (and the modern historian) with the unprecedented publishing freedoms of the 1640s.[4] This chapter thus demonstrates how heterodoxy in seventeenth-century England was produced from an interaction between elite and popular cultural configurations, and indicates how that interaction was particularly likely to occur in the urban, socially mobile world of merchants and tradesmen, who possessed the money to buy books and the literacy to understand them.[5] Finally, a seemingly unlikely relationship between Anglican rationalism and Quaker enthusiasm will shed new light on the contention that the textual and historical criticism of Scripture associated with the 'radical Enlightenment' has some of its roots in the rejection of the Bible in favour of the inner light as a rule of faith during the 1650s.[6]

Anthony Wood relates how two Oxford graduates met to engage in disputation in Folkestone, Kent on 10 March 1650. The Calvinist cleric John Reading had travelled to debate with Samuel Fisher, formerly a respected Puritan minister who

---

[3] Isabel Rivers, *Reason, Grace, and Sentiment: A Study of the Language of Religion and Ethics in England, 1660–1780. Volume 1. Whichcote to Wesley* (Cambridge, 1991), 25, 87; W.M. Spellman, *The Latitudinarians and the Church of England, 1660–1700* (Athens, GA, and London, 1993), 11–32; Henry Sacheverell, *The Character of a Low Churchman* (London, 1702), 8.

[4] See Christopher Hill, *Milton and the English Revolution* (London, 1977), 69–71; Hill, 'From Lollards to Levellers' in *Collected Essays of Christopher Hill. Volume 2: Religion and Politics in 17th Century England* (Brighton, 1986; rpt. 1988), 89–116.

[5] For the need to understand the radical culture of the English revolution in terms of an interaction between elite and popular, see Nicholas McDowell, *The English Radical Imagination: Culture, Religion, and Revolution, 1630–60* (Oxford, 2003), especially 1–21.

[6] Christopher Hill, 'Freethinking and libertinism: the legacy of the English Revolution', in Lund (ed.), *The Margins of Orthodoxy*, 54–72.

now led a General Baptist congregation in Ashford, over the question of whether 'all Christians indefinitely were equally and eternally obliged to preach the Gospel without ecclesiastical ordination, or contrary to the demands of the civil magistrate'. Fisher, Wood tells us, took 'most of his argument from Jer. Taylor's *Discourse of the Liberty of Prophesying*. After the debate was ended, our Author Reading thought himself obliged to answer several passages in the said book of Dr Taylor, which gave too great a seeming advantage to fanaticism and enthusiasm'.[7] Reading's book, *Anabaptism Routed ... With a Particular Answer to all that is alledged in favour of the Anabaptists, by Dr. Jer. Taylor, in his Book, called, The Liberty of Prophesying*, appeared in 1655.

That a leading General Baptist based his defence of illegal lay preaching on arguments taken from a text by Jeremy Taylor should give us pause for thought. Elected a Fellow of All Souls on Laud's recommendation, Taylor (1613–67) was made chaplain to Charles I in 1638 and became 'placed by the world among the highest of High Church men'.[8] He joined the king in Oxford with the outbreak of war, and from there he issued his first major publication, *Of the Sacred Order and Offices of Episcopacy Asserted* (1642). Briefly imprisoned by Parliamentary forces in 1645, on his release Taylor retired to Golden Grove, Carmarthenshire, as tutor and chaplain to the Earl of Carbery. At Golden Grove he composed many of the Anglican devotional texts for which is best known, including *The Rules and Exercises of Holy Living* (1650) and *The Golden Grove; or a Manual of Daily Prayers and Litanies* (1654). These texts develop a quietist but defiant mode of Anglican survivalism by offering the private reader a set of devotional forms by which to live in the absence of the external structures and community of the Church of England. In the preface to *The Golden Grove*, addressed to the 'Pious and Devout Believer', Taylor parodies Puritan rhetoric in the moment of encouraging Anglican survival and envisaging restoration: 'We must now take care that the young men who were born in the Captivity, may be taught how to worship to the God of Israel after the manner of their forefathers, till it shall please God that Religion shall return into the land, and dwell safely and grow prosperously' (sig. A3^{v}). Taylor seems in fact to have been imprisoned for his comments about Independency in this preface, although his friend John Evelyn records that Taylor was also conducting illegal Prayer-book services in London at this time. However he was soon released and left for the north of Ireland in 1658 to act as chaplain to Lord Conway; after the Restoration he became Bishop of Down and Connor. Taylor's writings are chiefly celebrated today for their ornate prose style, which preserved in language his keen sense of the beauty of Anglican church forms. The aesthetic appreciation of Taylor's style has, however, been at the expense of serious analysis of his thought ever since Coleridge's memorable but damaging description of his prose as 'a ghost in marble'.[9]

[7] Anthony Wood, *Athenae Oxonienses*, ed. Philip Bliss, 4 vols (Oxford, 1813–20), 3: 796. On Fisher, see also 3: 699–703.

[8] C.J. Spranks, *The Life and Writings of Jeremy Taylor* (London, 1952), 52.

[9] Ibid., 139, 290.

So what would Samuel Fisher have found in his reading of Jeremy Taylor, ex-Laudian and future bishop, to bring into disputational battle with John Reading, and what so enraged Reading that he was moved to repudiate Taylor directly in print? The text in question, ΘΕΟΛΟΓΙΑ ’ΕΚΛΕΚΤΙΚΗ. *A Discourse of the Liberty of Prophesying* (1647) is as much an intellectual response to the turmoil of civil war as Hobbes's *Leviathan* (1651), and Taylor is as concerned as Hobbes to ensure that conflict over religious difference never recurs in England. He tells us that he conceived the book in the midst of ‘this great Storm which hath dasht the Vessel of the Church to pieces’, and that he wrote ‘with as much greedinesse as if I had thought it possible with my Arguments to have perswaded the rough and hard handed Souldiers to have disbanded presently’ (pp. 2–3). Taylor set out to abolish religious conflict by defining Christian belief in terms of ethics rather than theology and by establishing the validity of toleration on the basis of the uncertainty of religious knowledge. His arguments clearly anticipate the principal ideas that came to be associated with the Latitudinarians, on whom Taylor was an acknowledged and respected influence.[10] He insists that the moral fundamentals of Christian conduct, as laid down in the Apostles' creed, are clear and in accord with natural reason, and any person who follows them lives the Christian life. However reason also tells us that there is no possibility of certainty in matters of religion beyond these fundamentals and no external authority sufficient to settle issues of speculative theology. Taylor specifically considers and rejects the claims to absolute authority of Scripture, of all methods of expounding Scripture, of tradition (including the decisions of ecclesiastical councils) and of the Pope. In the absence of certainty, all religious beliefs and practices that are not opposed to the essential articles of Christian morality or pose no threat to the security of the state should be tolerated:

> we have no other help in the midst of these distractions, and dis-unions, but all of us to be united in that common terme, which as it does constitute the Church in its being such, so it is the medium of the Communion of the Saints, and that is the creed of the Apostles, and in all other things an honest endeavour to find out what truths we can, and a charitable and mutuall permission to others that disagree from us and our opinions .... How many volumes have been writ about Angels, about immaculate conception, about originall sin, when all that is solid reason or clear Revelation, in all these three Articles, may be reasonably enough comprised in forty lines! And in these trifles and impertinencies, men are curiously busie while they negate those glorious precepts of Christianity and holy life, which are the glories of our Religion, and would enable us to live a happy eternity. (33, 44)

Taylor is emphatic not only in replacing theology with ethics as the basis of Christian doctrine but also external authority with personal reason as the rule of faith. Heresy thus becomes a matter of uncertain opinion rather than certain error:

> I am certain that a Drunkard is as contrary to God, and lives as contrary to the lawes of Christianity, as a Heretick; and I am also sure that I know what drunkennesse is, but I am

[10] Rivers, *Reason, Grace and Sentiment*, 25–6, 35–6.

> not sure that such an opinion is Heresy, neither would other men be so sure as they think if they did consider it aright, and observe the infinite deceptions, and causes of deceptions in wise men, and in most things, and in all doubtfull Questions, and that they did not mistake confidence for certainty. (pp. 38–9)

While human beings must be directed by their own reason and judgement in the absence of external sources of certain knowledge, subjective reason is of course fallible – 'even when a man thinks he hath most reason to bee confident, hee may easily bee deceived' – so no individual or group has the authority to impose their beliefs, or rather opinions, on another individual (p. 45).

Taylor was evidently reacting to Presbyterian demands for an enforced national church discipline and hoping to convince the Presbyterians, the dominant party in 1647, to allow Anglican church services to continue alongside their own: he says as much in his preface to the second edition of 1657. However as one biographer has rather condescendingly observed, 'Taylor's subjects always carried him away'; or as we might prefer to put it, Taylor followed his own arguments to their logical conclusions.[11] So he went beyond the pleas for liberty of conscience associated with the Independents in the mid-1640s and which similarly argue the necessity and virtue of uncertainty, such as Milton's *Areopagitica* (1644) and Francis Rous's *The Ancient Bounds, or Liberty of Conscience, Tenderly Stated* (1645), by explicitly stating that Catholics, given their acceptance of the Apostle's creed, should be allowed to worship freely. Taylor grants Catholics the same liberty he allows to others, freedom to hold any speculative doctrines which do not endanger either Christian morals or the state. The position on toleration to which the arguments of *The Liberty of Prophesying* brought Taylor closest in 1647 was in fact that of the Levellers. In *The Compassionate Samaritane* (1644) the future Leveller leader William Walwyn (1600–81) had addressed the Presbyterians and the Independents to argue against the imposition of religious uniformity and for universal liberty of conscience on the grounds of the 'uncertainty of knowledge in this life. No man, or sort of men, can presume of an unerring spirit ... since there remains the possibility of error, notwithstanding never so great presumptions to the contrary, one sort of men are not to compel another, since this hazard is run thereby, that he who is in error may be the constrainer of him who is in truth'.[12] Belief, for Walwyn as for Taylor, is a personal matter for each individual to derive from an ongoing process of rational examination. While Taylor had been a fellow of All Souls and Walwyn was a London merchant who had no Latin, their similarity of argument and expression is striking. For example Taylor urges men not to force others to believe through law and physical persecution – which is an impossibility in any case – but to debate the truth of their opinions through 'Argument, and Allegations of Scripture, and modesty of deportment, and meeknesse, and charity to the persons of men', so putting an end to

---

[11] *The Whole Works of The Right Rev. Jeremy Taylor*, ed. Reginald Heber, rev. Charles Page Eden, 10 vols (London, 1847–52), 5: 3; Spranks, *Jeremy Taylor*, 85.

[12] *The Writings of William Walwyn*, ed. Jack R. McMichael and Barbara Taft (Athens, Ga., 1989), 104. Cited hereafter as *WWW*.

'pertinacious disputing about things unnecessary, undeterminable, and unprofitable' (pp. 37, 44); Walwyn states that it is 'excellency in any man or woman, not to be pertinacious, or obstinate, in any opinion, but to have an open eare for reason and argument, against whatsoever he holds'.[13]

Walwyn had always insisted that a policy of religious toleration must be universal or it was nothing, and in his early writings he had daringly assumed the persona of those considered to personify blasphemy and irreligion in seventeenth-century England – the Catholic in *A New Petition of the Papists* (1641) and the Familist in *The Power of Love* (1643) – in an attempt to engage with and subvert the stereotypical depictions of their depravity used to bolster arguments against toleration. In *The Compassionate Samaritane* he was particularly concerned to argue the case of the Anabaptists against the many claims from the pulpit and in the press in the mid-1640s accusing them of irreligious beliefs and practices.[14] Taylor devotes a whole chapter of *The Liberty of Prophesying* to 'a consideration of the opinions of the Anabaptists', stating firstly the case for infant baptism, then the case against it to demonstrate his fundamental argument for toleration on the grounds of uncertainty. He applies this method of arguing *in ultramque partem* to Scriptural proofs, initially adducing the text commonly used to legitimate infant baptism, John 3.5: 'For Christ made a Law whose Sanction is with an exclusive negative to them that are not baptized [*Unlesse a man be born of water and of the Spirit, he shall not enter into the Kingdome of heaven*;]' (p. 225). Playing the Anabaptists' advocate, he points out that this text 'no more inferres a necessity of Infant's Baptism then the other words of Christ inferre a necessity to give them holy Communion, *Nisi comederitis carnem filii hominis, & biberitis sanguinem, non introibitis in regnum coelorum* ... if Anabaptist shall be a name of disgrace, why shall not some other name be invented for them that deny to communicate Infants, which shall be equally disgracefull?' (p. 232)[15] Taylor maintains such difficulties prove that there is no objective definition of heresy and that 'pretences of Scripture' are an insufficient testimony on which to base claims of theological truth.

It was presumably these arguments that Samuel Fisher used in disputation with John Reading at Folkestone, for it was this chapter that Reading answered point by point in 1655, using syllogistic, grammatical and etymological argument to prove the orthodox interpretation of the Hebrew and Greek texts. Taylor's defence of the Anabaptists certainly attracted attention: the title-page of *The Liberty of Prophesying* had described Taylor as 'Chaplaine in Ordinarie to His Majestie' and the King moved quickly to disassociate himself from Taylor's position, asking Henry Hammond to refute the chapter on Anabaptism. However Hammond's *Letter of Resolution to Six Queries of Present Use with the Church of England* (1652) is courteous and respectful, and within several months of the publication of *The Liberty of Prophesying* Taylor

[13] *Tolleration Justified, and Persecution Condemned* (London, 1645), in *WWW*, 159.

[14] *WWW*, 120–24; for further discussion, see McDowell, *The English Radical Imagination*, 24–5, 78–9.

[15] Taylor would seem to be citing John 6. 53, translated in the King James Bible as: 'Except ye eat of the flesh of the Son of man, and drink his blood, ye have no life in you.'

was one of the divines consulted by Charles over whether to extend toleration to the Independents.[16] Samuel Rutherford, Professor of Divinity at St Andrew's and Presbyterian heresiographer, was rather less emollient, naming Taylor as the joint target, with the Independent tolerationist John Goodwin, of Rutherford's sulphurous *Free Disputation against Pretended Liberty of Conscience* (1649). For Rutherford, making conscience the rule of faith above Scripture and church discipline is the first principle of scepticism and the root of libertinism. In *Anabaptism Routed* Reading explicitly locates Taylor in the context of the history of scepticism, comparing him to the Athenian philosopher Carneades, who maintained that truth is beyond human grasp, and to the Academics, who 'were wont to question the testimonie and evidence of their own senses with a *quid si falleris*? being not confident of the truth of what they saw with their *eyes*, and heard with their *ears*.' (p. 107) Taylor makes few references to his intellectual influences, but the sceptical humanist tradition did indeed play a major role in shaping William Walwyn's arguments for liberty of conscience based on the uncertainty of knowledge: Walwyn was an avid reader of Florio's rendering of Montaigne's *Essays* (1603) and the translation by Samson Lennard of Pierre Charron's *Of Wisdom* (1608). He named Montaigne and Charron as two of his favourite 'humane authors' whom he had been 'accustomed to the reading of ... these twenty years'.[17]

The danger that Rutherford and Reading identify in *The Liberty of Prophesying* goes beyond Taylor's presentation of the Anabaptists' case against infant baptism and indeed beyond his plea for toleration of Catholicism and sectarianism. They see in Taylor's rejection of the Bible as a rule of faith the origins of infidelity:

> They who deny convincing evidence in God's Word, not only erre not knowing the Scriptures, but tacitly accuse the Wisdom and Providence of God for mans salvation, of insufficiency: for how shall matters of controversie concerning faith and manners be decided without sufficient evidence? And if you think there is not sufficient evidence in Scripture to keep us from errour, and to direct us in the way of truth and salvation, in what other rule, or testimonie will you place such evidence as you would have? what in Traditions and unwritten verities? where shall we seek these, among our adversaries? nay but no man can be edified by that which is destructive; or in *Enthusiasms* and Revelations? ... nothing less than that which cannot be false can be the grounds of faith and religion: whatsoever falleth below that supreme certaintie, is but opinion at most.[18]

Taylor's original aim in demonstrating the insufficient testimony of Scripture was probably to challenge Presbyterian certitude: the Anglican tradition of rejecting Puritan Biblical fundamentalism in favour of arguments from natural reason and probability which would complement those from Scripture stretches back to Richard

---

[16] See Stranks *Jeremy Taylor*, 72–3.

[17] *Walwyns Just Defence* (London, 1649), in *WWW*, 397–9; Nigel Smith, 'The Charge of Atheism and the Language of Radical Speculation, 1640–60', in Michael Hunter and David Wootton (eds) *Atheism from the Reformation to the Enlightenment* (Oxford, 1992), 131–58 (143–57); McDowell, *The English Radical Imagination*, 74–83.

[18] John Reading, *Anabaptism Routed*, (London, 1655), 107.

Hooker. To that extent, a degree of scepticism had long 'reinforced [the Church of England's] authority and [was] part of its orthodoxy'.[19] Hooker argued that since revelation has ceased, the authority of Puritan arguments from Scripture must rest upon the 'ordinary' illumination of reason; not upon 'the fervent earnestness of their persuasion, but the soundness of those reasons whereupon the same is built, which must declare their opinion in these things to have been wrought by the holy Ghost, and not by the fraud of that evil Spirit which is even in his illusions strong'.[20] In other words, the Bible retains its infallibility as the Word of God but, in the absence of revelation, all human readers are fallible. Walwyn was accused of atheism because he had declared the Bible to be 'so plainly and directly contradictory to it self, that it makes me believe it is not the Word of God'. However he never questions the infallibility of the Bible in any of his writings; rather he agrees with Hooker and insists that all human hermeneutics are fallible, 'liable to errours, and mistakings, and are not the very Word of God, but our apprehensions drawn from the Word.' With the cessation of revelation, 'there are no true Apostles, Evangelists, Prophets, Pastors, or Teachers, endowed with power from on high, as all true ones are; by which, they are enabled to divide the word of God aright'.[21] In fact it is unsurprising that Walwyn can sound like Hooker, as Walwyn lists 'Mr Hookers *Ecclesiastical Polity*' amongst his favourite books and as early as 1641 cited Hooker in arguing for the toleration of Catholicism.[22] The Levellers would appear to have derived their sceptical arguments for liberty of conscience not only from the continental Pyrrhonism of Montaigne and Charron but from the native tradition of Anglican rationalism.

Walwyn follows Hooker, then, in challenging Puritan Biblicism by identifying a space between 'divine meaning and human reading – a space mediated by reason but therefore almost always productive of probabilities and conjectural inferences rather than certain knowledge'.[23] The distinction between their positions is that Hooker justified the existence of a clerical caste by insisting that arguments from Scripture become more probable as they are based on specialized historical and linguistic learning, while Walwyn refused to identify authoritative judgement with education and ordination, maintaining that the 'esteeme' of learning 'gets [the clergy] their Livings and preferments; and therefore she is to be kept up, or their Trade will goe downe'.[24] In *The Liberty of Prophesying*, however, Taylor explicitly questions the

---

[19] Pocock, 'Within the margins: the definitions of orthodoxy', 50.

[20] Hooker, *Of the Laws of Ecclesiastical Polity*, ed. Arthur Stephen MacGrade (Cambridge, 1989), 16–17.

[21] John Price, *Walwins Wiles* (London, 1649), in William Haller and Godfrey Davies (eds), *The Leveller Tracts* (New York, 1944), 297–8; Walwyn, *A Prediction of Mr. Edwards His Conversion* (London, 1646), in *WWW*, 232; *The Vanitie of the Present Churches* (London, 1649), in *WWW*, 327.

[22] *Walwyns Just Defence*, in *WWW*, 327; *A New Petition of the Papists* (London, 1641), in *WWW*, 59.

[23] Debora Kuller Shuger, *Habits of Thought in the English Renaissance: Religion, Politics, and the Dominant Culture* (Berkeley, Calif., 1990), 35.

[24] *The Compassionate Samaritane*, in *WWW*, 112.

very status of the Biblical texts as divine meaning, as the infallible Word of God. While he does maintain that the fundamentals of Christian doctrine as laid down in the Apostles' creed are plainly evident in Scripture, he argues on historical and textual as well as hermeneutical grounds that the Bible can provide no decisive answers concerning speculative theology.[25] It was perhaps the pressure to respond to the rise of enthusiasm in the 1640s that led Taylor to this position. The orthodox Protestant doctrine that revelation had ceased, shared by Anglicans, Presbyterians and the more conservative Independents, was the basis of the claim that only an educated and trained ministry was qualified to make an authoritative interpretation of Scripture. This claim was now furiously denied and indeed inverted by 'mechanick' preachers such as the cobbler Samuel How, who declared that 'such as are taught by the Spirit, destitute of human learning, are the learned ones who truly understand the Scriptures'.[26] Of course Taylor, like the Latitudinarians who followed him, ultimately envisaged religious difference as encompassed within an inclusive national church administered by a tithe-funded clerical caste and headed by an episcopal government. Yet if he hoped to undermine enthusiastic lay interpretation of Scripture by denying the authority of the text itself beyond the creedal essentials, he also provided radical readers with a powerful argument for the abolition of the clergy. John Reading recognized this when he accused Taylor of conveying 'ammunition' to 'known and professed enemies' of the Christian church.[27] Clement Writer was one such unlearned reader who found in the chapters on the authority of Scripture in *The Liberty of Prophesying* a scholarly basis for his radical anticlericalism.

For the Presbyterian cleric Thomas Edwards, Clement Writer (fl. 1627–58) personified the sliding scale of irreligion in England in the 1640s. First an Independent and a Brownist, then a Baptist and Arminian, Writer 'fell to be a Seeker, and is now an Anti-Scripturist, a Questionist and Sceptick, and I fear an Atheist'. Edwards devotes several pages of his voluminous heresiography *Gangraena* (1646) to a discussion of this 'arch-Heretique and fearfull Apostate'.[28] Writer might appear to be a made-to-measure invention of Edwards's polemic against the Independents and the policy of toleration which Edwards associated with them. The image of Writer fuses the stereotypes in *Gangraena* both of the Independent as sectarian extremist and of the sectarian as atheist. The opinion ascribed to Writer, that Scripture 'whether in Hebrew, Greek, or English [is] unsufficient and uncertain' is one of the first heresies listed by Edwards as gaining ground in England in the absence

[25] H.R. McAdoo emphasizes that Taylor does not reject the authority of Scripture in fundamentals; *The Spirit of Anglicanism: A Survey of Anglican Theological Method in the Seventeenth Century* (London, 1965), 70.

[26] Samuel How, *The Sufficience of the Spirits Teaching without Humane Learning* (London, 1640), 12–13.

[27] *Anabaptism Routed*, sig. A2r.

[28] *Gangraena; Or a Catalogue and Discovery of many of the Errours, heresies, Blasphemies and pernicious Practices of the Sectaries of this time* (London, 3 parts, 1646), 1: 113–16.

of a Presbyterian church discipline (1:18).[29] However Writer does not subject the Biblical texts to direct sceptical inquiry in his first, anonymous publication, *The Jus Divinum of Presbyterie* (1646), which appeared just after the accusations in *Gangraena*. He takes rather the position of Walwyn that 'no man commeth now with Divine Authority and infallible demonstration and power, to convince men' of the truth of their interpretation of Scripture, regardless of arguments 'contrived by Arts and learning'. Anything 'delivered meerly upon the credit of men' is 'uncertainly or fallibly evidenced'. The cessation of revelation thus becomes the basis of Writer's argument for the abolition of 'all distinction between Clergy and Laity' (pp. 13, 37). As with Walwyn, Writer rejects any justification of the clergy on the grounds of their learning by developing the outline of an ideological history of priestcraft: 'Objections of this Nature proceed from such as would hold captive the unlearned, under the superstitious Bond of a Romish necessity of an infallible interpreter' (p. 38). In fact he does at one point accuse priests of having 'framed all Copies and Translations' of Scripture to 'maintain their own power and standing'; however Writer himself relies on a string of Scriptural proofs to reject the *jure divino* authority of any form of church government, whether Catholic, Anglican or Presbyterian, so putting into practice his central argument that 'any man of what calling or quality, may lawfully publish or propose whatsoever he hath conceived from Scripture to the consideration of every particular mans understanding, which is each mans judge' (pp. 30, 38). Writer, as with Walwyn and Taylor, makes personal reason, or 'every particular mans understanding', the rule of faith, and similarly the uncertainty of human knowledge is for Writer the rational basis of a policy of religious toleration.

Writer was a clothier from Worcestershire who moved to London and became involved in the urban flux of radical religion in the 1640s.[30] Although a member of Thomas Lamb's General Baptist church in 1641, he seems to have followed Walwyn, with whom he was friendly and who was also originally from Worcestershire, in declining finally to attach himself to any specific sect or congregation, presumably on the grounds that he could not be certain of the truth of speculative theological doctrine. Writer was self-conscious but defiant about his lack of university education. Indeed he was unusually clear in identifying the audience he was addressing in his writings as the literate but unlearned 'middling sort', as in this retort to Richard Baxter, who had accused him of infidelity:

> I contend not to have the Reputation of learning, or being a rare and excellent Scholar ... The Reader that I expect should profit by this discourse, must neither be the careless vulgar, utterly unlearned nor any so learned as your self; for the former are scarcely capable of it, and the learned think themselves beyond it ... it is the middle sort, and plain-hearted people, who are sincere Lovers of truth, whose instruction I intend, who are neither quite above, nor quite below information, nor engaged to any party or Opinion, but

[29] For the polemical contexts of *Gangraena*, see Murray Tolmie, *The Triumph of the Saints: the Separate Churches of London, 1616–49* (Cambridge, 1977), 130–38.

[30] See R.L. Greaves and R. Zaller (eds), *A Biographical Dictionary of British Radicals in the Seventeenth Century*, 3 vols (Brighton, 1982–84).

> whose minds lye open to the evidence of Truth, by what hand soever it be made known to them.[31]

Writer's ideas about the uncertainty of knowledge and the necessity of toleration, along with his insistence that the virtuous individual must be ecumenical in the search for truth, make it clear why he would have been interested in reading *The Liberty of Prophesying* in the late 1640s. However Writer found in Taylor's text not only an eloquent expansion of the arguments that he himself had briefly sketched in *The Jus Divinum of Presbyterie*, but scholarly proofs concerning the unreliability of the Biblical texts which he could then ironically turn against his learned clerical opponents, such as Baxter and Thomas Edwards, who maintained that scholarship in the original languages provided the clergy with access to spiritual truth that was denied to the 'plain-hearted people'.

In *Fides Divina: The Ground of Faith Asserted* (1657) Writer sets out to demonstrate the insufficiency of Scripture as a rule of faith, citing 'some few modern English Protestant Authors of most eminent learning, whose Testimony herein [is] back't with such Arguments and Reasons as are evident to our own understanding and experience' (p. 2). Pride of place amongst these authors is given to '*Jer. Taylor* Dr in Divinity, and a great Scholler, [who] in his Discourse of Liberty of Prophesying pag. 61, 62, 63 shows, and by many Reasons proves that which in effect amounts to an impossibility for any man to find out a true copy or Translation, or right sense of Scripture' (p. 9). Writer refers to Section III of *The Liberty of Prophesying*, in which Taylor surveys 'considerations taken from the nature of Scripture it selfe' for the 'difficulty and uncertainty of arguments from Scripture'. Here Writer found a comprehensive series of historical, linguistic and textual arguments against the authority of the Biblical texts. Firstly he quotes Taylor on the issue of the 'many thousands of Copies that were writ by persons of severall interests and perswasions'. Taylor himself at this point offers what amounts to a brief historical analysis of the possible priestly corruptions of the text. For example he cites the claim of Justin Martyr that Jewish scribes excised phrases relating to Christ from the Psalms; as these words have only ever been restored in Justin Martyr's Bible, either one of the Fathers was at fault or all of our editions and translations of the Bible are incorrect. This is not to say that the New Testament is any more trustworthy, for some Greek copies of St Mark's Gospel have a verse 'thought by some to favour of *Manichaisme*' and so these copies were rejected by the Catholic church as inauthentic: 'Now suppose that a *Manichee* in disputation should urge this place, having found it in his Bible, if a Catholike should answer him by saying it is Apocryphall, and not found in divers Greek copies, might not the *Manichee* ask how it came in, if it was not the word of God, and if it was, how came it out?' If a verse from St. Mark's Gospel can be excised simply on the grounds that it does not agree with theological orthodoxy, 'is there not as much reason for the fierce *Lutherans* to reject the Epistle of S. *James* for favouring justification by works?' The existence of so many different versions

---

[31] Clement Writer, *An Apologetical Declaration*, (London, 2nd edn, 1658), 79–80.

of Scripture undermines the very concept of orthodox and heterodox exegesis: conventional conceptions of the Trinity are defended on the basis on 1 John 5:7 – 'For there are three that bear record in heaven, the Father, the Son, and the Holy Ghost: and these three are one' – but antitrinitarians can simply respond by 'saying the *Syrian* translation, and divers Greek copies have not that verse in them, and therefore being of doubtfull Authority, cannot conclude with certainty in a Question of Faith.'[32]

Taylor's own linguistic learning is deployed in his subsequent discussion of how in the original languages 'there are some words so neer in sound, that the Scribes might easily mistake' (p. 62). He demonstrates how a small error such as the mistranscription of a single Greek letter can change completely the meaning of a passage, and speculates how such an error proceeding from the 'negligence or ignorance of the Transcribers' might become the basis of a bitter theological dispute or the origin of a sect (p. 63). While an Anglican intellectual such as Meric Casaubon reacted to the rise of the enthusiastic interpretation of Scripture by emphasising that the authority of the Bible rested on the use of historical and philological scholarship to recover the original meaning of the texts, Taylor is emphatic that 'the knowledge of such circumstances and particular stories is irrevocably lost'.[33] The treacherous textual history of the Bible means that it can only be regarded as a human and thus fallible document; besides all the various modes of hermeneutical method are hopelessly subjective: 'Scriptures look like Pictures, wherein every man in the roome believes they look on him only, and that wheresoever he stands, or how often so ever he changes his station.' (p. 80) Taylor implicitly suggests here that to treat the Bible as a certain source of religious authority is to worship a false idol.

Writer concludes his summary of Taylor's arguments by reiterating that the 'many pregnant instances and reasons' listed by the 'learned and ingenious Doctor' prove that argument from Scripture, whether advanced by 'Councels, Fathers, Traditions ... Churches, Pope and pretenders to have the Spirit', can never be used to justify the imposition of religious uniformity (p. 14). While he makes no mention of the Apostles' creed, Writer echoes Taylor in arguing that Scripture should be treated as an ethical rather a theological guide and valued for 'such practical points as are evident to every rational mans understanding and conscience' (p. 24). Taylor's Arminian insistence on the efficacy of reason and the liberty of every man to work out his own salvation clearly appealed to Writer, who derived from his contact with General Baptists the conviction that redemption is granted to all and that damnation is the result of individual choice and action in this life. Writer fuses General Baptist soteriology with a Leveller-influenced

---

32 Taylor, *Liberty of Prophesying*, 61–2, 64; quoted by Clement Writer, *Fides Divina*, (London, 1657) 10–11. According to Thomas Edwards, when the radical Independent minister William Erbery denied the Trinity at a meeting in Marlborough, a member of the audience cited 1 John 5:7, to which Erbery replied: 'Those words were not in the Greek, but put in by some who were against the Arians'; *Gangraena*, 1:78.

33 Meric Casaubon, *Generall Learning* (1668), ed. Richard Serjeantson (Cambridge, 1999), 19-20; Taylor, *Liberty of Prophesying*, 82, quoted in Writer, *Fides Divina*, 11–12.

conception of natural rights: no external authority can be allowed to deprive 'men of that natural native Right which God hath given to every man, being born a rational Creature, to be saved by his own Faith, and therefore must have that liberty in Matter of Religion and Worship, as to be led by the result of his own understanding, and not of any other mans' (pp. 15–16).[34] Crucially, however, Writer then uses Taylor's learned demonstration of the myriad uncertainties and contradictions of Biblical scholarship as the basis of his refutation of Richard Baxter's argument in *The Unreasonableness of Infidelity* (1655) that the spiritual and temporal authority of the clergy is justified by their communication to 'the illiterate', in the sense of those without Latin and Greek, of the saving knowledge obtained from Scriptural exegesis (pp. 35–6). In other words Writer rejects the relevance of clerical scholarship to spiritual knowledge — indeed he accuses priests throughout the ages of having corrupted the Scriptural text whether 'through negligence, ignorance or design' — but at the same time he deploys learned clerical argument to prove the rational validity of this rejection (p. 2). Jeremy Taylor, Laudian chaplain, Restoration bishop and one of the most respected figures in the Anglican tradition, thus confirmed the fears of his Puritan critics by providing the intellectual resources for some of the most radically anticlerical and anti-Scriptural statements of the English revolution.[35] Indeed Taylor continued to alarm his friends and outrage his enemies by arguing against original sin in *Unum Necessarium* (1655); the Presbyterian Nathaniel Stephens pointed out in *Vindiciae Fundamenti* (1658) the similarities between Taylor's interpretation of the Fall and that advanced by the General Baptist and Putney debater, Robert Everard.[36]

We have seen how John Reading believed that Taylor's Scriptural scepticism would have the effect not of undermining enthusiasm but of encouraging claims that the Spirit within was the only true source of spiritual knowledge. Writer's use of *The Liberty of Prophesying* raises the possibility that Samuel Fisher was also influenced by Taylor's scholarly criticism of Scripture when Fisher came to declare the inner light as the only infallible rule of faith. For within months of the Restoration, Fisher, who had been converted to Quakerism in 1655, published the most strident and comprehensive rejection of the Bible as a framework for understanding man and the universe written in early modern England. Stretching to some 1,000 quarto pages, *Rusticus ad Academicos* (1660) subjects the Bible to rigorous historical and textual criticism while brilliantly satirizing the futility of the clerical application of logical, philological and rhetorical skill to Biblical exegesis.[37] Fisher's argument is grounded upon the epistemological fallacy of identifying God's Word with a material object

---

[34] On General Baptist doctrine as a reaction against the antinomian consequences of Calvinism, see Tolmie, *The Triumph of the Saints*, 73.

[35] Christopher Hill often discusses Writer but nowhere mentions that most of Writer's arguments are taken directly from Taylor; see e.g. *The World Turned Upside Down: Radical Ideas During the English Revolution* (London, 1972; repr. Harmondsworth, 1991), 261–8.

[36] William Poole in *Milton and the Idea of the Fall* (Cambridge, 2005), 55–7, shows that Stephens was right to compare Taylor and Everard on original sin.

[37] For a full account of the rhetorical strategies of *Rusticus ad Academicos*, see McDowell, *The English Radical Imagination*, 137–70.

which is subject to physical change and corruption. The seventeenth-century texts are but 'the Remote issue and Product, at the hundredth hand perhaps of God's voice in the Prophets, yea but Remote Transcripts of fallible men from the handy-work or manuscripts of the first Penmen ... the Letter is Changeable, Alterable, Flexable, Passing, Perishing, Corruptible at mans will, who may mis-transcribe'. If the text is 'yielded to be Alterable in the very *Greek* and *Hebrew* copies of it', if 'the letters, Vowels, Accents and Iotas of it are liable to be chang'd in Sound and Shape at the Wills of the Criticks', then it must be treated as an historical rather than a divine document. Yet while the Bible is 'fallible by false Interpretation and translation', the inner light of the internally resurrected Christ is 'infallible, and to be followed in what it speaks infallibly to the Conscience'.[38]

Although we know Fisher had read *The Liberty of Prophesying*, he does not cite Taylor in *Rusticus ad Academicos* and indeed makes few references to the sources of his ideas. However Richard Popkin has suggested Fisher's Biblical criticism should be placed in the context of the early European Enlightenment. When Fisher arrived in Amsterdam in 1658 as part of a conversion mission which later took him to Rome and Constantinople, he gave the job of translating two of Margaret Fell's pamphlets into Hebrew to an excommunicated Jew, whom Popkin believes was the young Benedictus Spinoza. The first Quaker missionaries in Holland had developed links with the radical spiritualist sect known as the Collegiants, whom Spinoza had joined after being expelled from the Jewish community in Amsterdam in 1656. The Hebrew translation of Fell's *A Loving Salutation to the Seed of Abraham* was published in Amsterdam in 1658 and in London in 1660; to both editions was appended a short exhortation to the Jews to convert to Quakerism, composed in Hebrew by Fisher, who had spent seven years at Oxford and was the most learned of the early Quakers. Popkin argues that the arguments advanced by Fisher and Spinoza to reject the identification of God's Word with Scripture and to argue for absolute liberty of conscience bear some comparison, and speculates on a mutual influence emerging from their acquaintance in Amsterdam in 1658. Popkin shows how the historical and textual arguments produced by Fisher concerning the ambiguity of the Mosaic authorship, the authority and origin of the Biblical canon and the development of the Hebrew and Greek languages since Biblical events were first recorded are 'strikingly novel for the time, and contain much of the material that Spinoza used in challenging the world of Jewish Bible interpreters' in the *Tractatus theologico-politicus* (1670).[39]

Popkin states that 'Fisher was moved by the Spirit, Spinoza by reason, but eventually they come to a somewhat similar vision'. However, the distinction between the inner light and reason was already becoming blurred in some Quaker circles. The

[38] Samuel Fisher, *Rusticus ad Acadmicos*, in *The Testimony of Truth Exalted*, ed. William Penn (1679), 49, 521.

[39] Richard H. Popkin, 'Spinoza and Samuel Fisher', *Philosophia* 15 (December, 1985), 219–36 (231–2); Richard H. Popkin and Michael J. Signer (eds), *Spinoza's First Publication? The Hebrew Translation of Margaret Fell's 'A Loving Salutation'*, (1987), Introduction.

Quaker missionaries in Amsterdam fell out in the early 1660s with the Collegiant sect, whose spiritualist doctrines they had recognized as similar to their own, over the rationalistic direction in which Collegiant thought was developing, partly through the influence of Spinoza. In 1661–62 William Ames, leader of the Dutch Quakers, became engaged in a dispute with Pieter Balling, leading Collegiant and close friend of Spinoza, over the nature of the inner light. This dispute resulted in Balling writing a tract, *Het Licht op den Kandelaar* (1662) in which he conceived, like the Quakers, of the inner light as superior in authority to all other sources, including Scripture; however he did so 'in terms that would permit either a rationalistic or spiritualistic interpretation', producing a concept of the natural light of reason as an infallible source of truth. Yet the learned Quaker bibliophile Benjamin Furly, who hosted figures such as John Locke, John Toland and the Third Earl of Shaftesbury at his great library in Rotterdam, immediately translated Balling's tract on the rational inner light into English as *The Light Upon the Candlestick* (1663), making no adverse comment upon its ideas. Furly's library included the writings of Samuel Fisher, as we might expect, but also of Clement Writer.[40]

Whether Fisher influenced the Collegiants or vice versa, or whether they were both influenced by Spinoza, or whether Fisher influenced Spinoza who influenced the Collegiants, remains a matter for conjecture. What becomes clear is that Fisher stands at the head of a learned strand of Quakerism which developed in part in the sectarian melting pot of mid-seventeenth-century Holland and which subjected the Christian tradition to rational and sceptical critique. Fisher's use of the *The Liberty of Prophesying* in disputation in 1650 and its central influence on Clement Writer's anticlerical Biblical criticism gives us good reason to speculate that Taylor's text played some part in shaping Fisher's learned anti-Scriptural arguments in *Rusticus ad Acadmicos*; perhaps Fisher even discussed *The Liberty of Prophesying* with Spinoza. Taylor's possible influence on Fisher coupled with the development of the concept of a rational inner light in Quaker, Collegiant and deist circles around Benjamin Furly brings us back to where we began, to the relationship between Anglicanism and deism, between orthodoxy and heterodoxy in Restoration England. There has been a growing discussion in recent years about the nature and origins of the English Enlightenment. Some scholars have seen it as a conservative and clerical movement linked to Latitudinarian rationalism; others have identified it as a radical movement and linked the development of deism and freethought to the native sectarian and anticlerical tradition of the 1640–60 period; others still have argued that the foreign influence of Spinozism in later-seventeenth century England has been underestimated.[41] This brief account of the transmission of Jeremy Taylor's

---

[40] Andrew C. Fix, *Prophecy and Reason: the Dutch Collegiants in the Early Enlightenment* (Princeton, New Jersey, 1991), 192–205 (202). On Balling's text, see Popkin, 'Spinoza's Relations with the Quakers', 27 n. 45; on Furly's library, see Hill, 'Freethinking and libertinism', 65.

[41] See e.g. and respectively J.G.A. Pocock, 'Post-Puritan England and the Problem of Enlightenment', in P. Zagorin (ed.), *Culture and Politics: From Puritanism to the Enlightenment*

Biblical criticism in the mid-seventeenth century indicates that all these theories may be correct; that Anglican, anticlerical, enthusiastic, Spinozist and deist ideas about Scripture were mixed together through complex historical and personal processes of revolution and reaction, reading and interpretation, travel and conversation.

(Berkeley, Calif., 1980), 91–112; J.A.I. Champion, '"May the last king be strangled in the bowels of the last priest": irreligion and the English Enlightenment', in Timothy Morton and Nigel Smith (eds), *Radicalism in British Literary Culture, 1650–1830* (Cambridge, 2002), 29–44; Jonathan I. Israel, *Radical Enlightenment* (Oxford, 2001; paperback edn, 2002), 599–627.

Chapter 10

Iconisms, Enthusiasm and Origen: Henry More Reads the Bible

Sarah Hutton

This essay discusses the principles of bible exegesis elaborated by the Cambridge Platonist, Henry More (1614–87), and the relationship of More's bible scholarship to the theological principles he sought to defend. Henry More is chiefly associated with the Cambridge Platonists who are best remembered nowadays as philosophers.[1] But it is their theology, more than their philosophy, which gives them identity as a group. For while there is a fair degree of variation in the philosophical positions to which they individually subscribed, they all shared a common set of theological principles, which marks them out as theological moderates. Prominent among these are their liberal theology of grace, their acceptance of the compatibility of reason and faith, their benign understanding of the divine attributes, according to which God exercises his will in conformity with his wisdom and goodness. Furthermore, their interest in philosophy was itself coloured by theological concerns, especially as an apology for religion. This is particularly true of Henry More who explicitly proclaimed his role as a philosopher to be that of religious apologist, whose aim was, 'not to Theologize in Philosophy, but to draw and *Exoterick* Fence or exteriour Fortification about Theologie'.[2] More was a prolific writer, who published many books of philosophy, but he was an equally productive writer on theological matters, notable among which are his studies of the Book of Revelation.[3] In this essay I shall

---

[1] On the Cambridge Platonists see my 'The Cambridge Platonists' in S. Nadler (ed.), *A Companion to Early Modern Philosophy* (Oxford, 2002), 308–19. On More, see S. Hutton (ed.), *Henry More (1614–87): Tercentenary Studies*, (Dordrecht, 1990).

[2] More, *A Collection of Several Philosophical Writings* (London, 1662), Preface, vi. Cited hereafter as *CSPW*.

[3] In addition to the works cited in this article, More's biblical studies included *An Exposition of the Seven Epistles to the Seven Churches* (London, 1669), A *Plain and Continued Exposition of the Several Prophecies or Divine Visions of the Prophet Daniel* (London, 1681), *An Illustration of those Two Abstruse Books in Holy Scripture, the Book of Daniel and the Revelation of S. John* (London, 1685), *Paralipomena prophetica* (London, 1685). The first volume of his *Opera omnia*, 3 vols. (London, 1675–79) contains theological writings, several of which were published in English in *Theological Works* (London, 1708) (cited hereafter as *TW*).

give an account of More's ideas on bible interpretation to show how he considered the mysteries of Christian faith were compatible with his view of Christianity as a rational religion. In particular, I shall focus on More's claim that even the most abstruse language of scripture is open to rational interpretation without sacrificing its mystery.

More's most important work of theology was his book, *An Explanation of the Grand Mystery of Godliness*, published in 1660, which he presented as being written, 'within the bounds of the confessed Truth of our Religion'.[4] This work, which tends to be ignored today, was widely read in More's lifetime, when it proved to be his most popular publication, which 'ruled the booksellers in London' between 1660 when it was published and his death in 1679.[5] Although More claimed that he wrote *An Explanation* as an act of pious gratitude for his recovery from dire illness,[6] the timing of its publication could not have been better from the point of view of establishing his theological credentials at a moment of political change and ecclesiastical retrenchment. Significantly, in this work More defends Episcopalianism at the time of the Restoration re-establishment of the Church of England. In the same work, he also distances himself from the sectarian excesses of the revolutionary period. But, equally significantly, he does not disguise his own rational, latitudinarian theology, or retract deeply held doctrines, notably his subscription to the Origenist doctrine of the pre-existence of the soul, which were viewed as heterodox by the new Anglican establishment of Charles II's reign.[7] In the context of the Restoration, More's book can be seen as a statement of a moderate position, which accepts the new ecclesiastical order, on the one hand, but argues for openness towards aspects of Christian belief and spirituality associated more with interregnum piety than with the new Anglican order. This in some measure explains why in *An Explanation of the Grand Mystery of Godliness*, More returns to the issue of the truth claims of what he regarded as the sectarian fringe, the same group of radical religionists which had formed the subject of his *Enthusiasmus Triumphatus* (1656). In that work, More had dismissed the claims to divine inspiration by a whole cluster of radical sects and their leaders, explaining their belief in their prophetic powers as mere delusion whose causes could be explained physiologically – principally attributable to an excess of melancholy humour. In *An Explanation* he accounts for their bogus prophetic claims (or 'misconceit of being inspired') in more theological terms, focusing particularly on their Christological errors. More attributes these errors to their misunderstanding of scripture, and their misconstruction of the Trinity, especially their denial of the divinity of Christ. In this book More pronounces enthusiasm as a grave danger to the Christian religion, and proposes by way of answer, a rational and historical approach to Christian doctrine, 'shewing the Reasonableness and important Usefulness of

---

[4] More, *An Explanation of the Grand Mystery of Godliness* (London, 1660), Preface, x.

[5] *The Conway Letters*, ed. Marjorie Nicolson, revised by Sarah Hutton (Oxford, 1992), 40.

[6] More, *Mystery of Godliness*, Preface, viii.

[7] See Robert Crocker, *Henry More, 1614–87. A Biography of the Cambridge Platonist* (Dordrecht, 2003).

Christian Religion in the Historical sense thereof and in reference to the very Person of Christ our saviour'.[8]

The Platonism and rational theology of the Cambridge Platonists have resulted in their being regarded as theological conservatives.[9] But, as Christopher Hill noted, men like More and Cudworth had reason to be worried lest their compliance with the republican regimes be an impediment in the 1660s.[10] This is borne out by the reaction to More's theology among Restoration Anglicans: for *An Explanation of the Grand Mystery of Godliness* did not meet with approval in the Anglican establishment. There were mutterings against More in episcopal circles (for example by Seth Ward).[11] In 1665 Francis Beaumont attacked More's book because it 'swarm'd with dangerous errours'. Among these, he complains, More's Latitudinarianism, 'Would open the door to Presbyterians, Independents Quakers, Latitudinarians' and other 'sincere and hearty enemies to our Church-government, or proud despisers of it'.[12] Although he did not mention More by name, Samuel Parker, censor to the Archbishop of Canterbury, attacked More's theology in two books published in 1666: *A Free and Impartial Censure of the Platonick Philosophy* and *An Account of the Nature and Extent of the Divine Dominion and Goodnesse*. That More was Parker's prime target is clear from the fact that he was especially critical of the Origenist doctrine of the Pre-existence of souls. As Parker's attack shows, to Restoration churchmen there was more than a whiff of heterodoxy about the principles which More upheld. And they had good reason to be concerned, for even before More engaged on setting out his theological position in *An Explanation* the appearance of a handful of Origenist texts suggested the alarming prospect that a revival of the heterodox Ante-Nicene father, Origen, was underway. In 1658 William Spencer published his edition of *Contra Celsus*, followed, in 1661, by the appearance in print of the anonymous, *A Letter of Resolution Concerning Origen*. This was followed, in 1662, by Joseph Glanvill's *Lux Orientalis*. In the same year More laid his Origenist cards on the table by including a strong defence of Origen as 'the Miracle of the Christian World',[13] in the 'Preface General' to his *A Collection of Several Philosophical Writings*.

It has long been recognized that the controversies ensuing upon the publication of *An Explanation* belong in the early history of Latitudinarianism.[14] Latterly, the doctrinal aspect of the attack on More has been brought into focus, especially his

---

[8] More, *Mystery of Godliness*, Preface, p. vi.

[9] J.G.A. Pocock, *Varieties of English Political Thought 1500–1800* (Cambridge, 1993), 310.

[10] C. Hill, *Continuity and Change in Seventeenth-Century England* (London, 1974), 265.

[11] In 1669 Edmund Elys told More that Seth Ward, Bishop of Exeter, disapproved of More's theology on this account. Cambridge, Christ's College, MS 21, letter 14. This is printed in Elys's *Letters on Several Subjects* (London, 1694).

[12] Beaumont, *Observations upon Dr More's Apologie* (London, 1665), 4, 162.

[13] *CSPW*, Preface, xxi. On More's Origenism, see D. Dockrill, 'The Fathers and the Theology of the Cambridge Platonists', *Studia Patristica*, 18 (1982), 427–39.

[14] See Marjorie Nicolson, 'Christ's College and the Latitude-Men', *Modern Philology*, 27 (1929), 35–53. Most recently see Crocker, *Henry More*.

Origenist theology.[15] In the early years of the restoration of Anglicanism, More found himself obliged, repeatedly, to defend his views, and to counter charges of doctrinal heterodoxy and of undermining ecclesiastical order. More's defence of his position against his Anglican critics is registered both in the Prefaces which he supplies to the later editions of his writings, and in his theological writings. More, in his self-defence, does not meet the charge of Origenism head on. Rather, he deflects it in conciliatory fashion by proposing that the doctrine of pre-existence of souls, while rationally plausible as a theory which explains the presence of evil in a world created by a just and loving God, is only an hypothesis. Instead, a good part of his defence of his position against his Anglican detractors takes the form of clarifications and elaborations of the principles of scriptural interpretation. For even where More's Prefaces protest his loyalty to the Church of England, while at the same time refusing to sacrifice his Origenism or his advocacy of ecclesiastical comprehension, other writings set out a series of rules for the interpretation of scripture, the application of which was to occupy him increasingly, with the publication of a whole series of works on the interpretation of prophecy. Why More should conduct so much of his self-defence in terms of exegetical theory, is not immediately apparent. Accounts of More's Latitudinarianism commonly discuss More's account of the relationship between reason and faith, but they do not connect this with his bible interpretation as such. In this essay I shall examine More's theories of biblical exegesis, and explore its connections with his defence of his position against his Anglican detractors.

Reason and apology

An Explanation of the Grand Mystery of Godliness is one of several apologetic writings in which More sets out and defends his theological position. It was followed, in 1662, by his *A Collection of Several Philosophical Writings* which not only contains an encomium of Origen, but includes two defences of a previously published work: *Defence of the Threefold Cabbala* and *An Appendix to the Defence of the Philosophick Cabbala*. These elaborate the allegorical reading of Genesis undertaken in his *Conjectura cabbalistica* (first published 1653). The republication of *Conjectura cabbalistica* along with these defensive supplements was followed in 1664 by another work clarifying More's theological views: *A Modest Enquiry into the Mystery of Iniquity*, a book that was designed to align More with the Church of England, by using the Anglican strategy of attacking Catholicism. *A Modest Enquiry* also includes an important discussion of biblical prophecy: the second part of *A Modest Enquiry*, entitled *Synopsis Prophetica*, sets out to counter the charge that scriptural

[15] On More's difficulties with Restoration Anglicanism, see David Dockrill and J.M. Lee, 'Reflections of an Episode in Cambridge Latitudinarianism. Henry More's Epistle Dedicatory to Gilbert Sheldon of his *Enchiridion Metaphysicum*', *Prudentia*, supplementary number (1994), 207–23. See also, Crocker, *Henry More*, and Hutton, 'Henry More and Anne Conway on Pre-existence and Universal Salvation', in M. Baldi (ed.), *Mind Senior to the World. Stoicismo e origenismo nella filosofia platonica del Seicento inglese* (Milan, 1996), 113–25.

prophecies are unintelligible *hocus pocus* by explaining why they are obscure, analysing their obscurity, and demonstrating 'the best way to clear and familiarize the same to us'.[16] In it More sets out four 'Rules concerning the Preference of one Prophetick Style before another'.[17] More appended to *A Modest Inquiry* a short piece entitled *The Apology of Henry More*. As the title implies, this places More's rational theology firmly within an apologetic context as a way of dealing with atheists, by recommending, 'How a man is to behave himself in this Rational and Philosophical Age for the gaining men to or the retaining them in the Christian Faith'. More's *Apology*, then, compliments *Synopsis prophetica* as guidelines for his approach to reading scripture. Taken together, this group of writings propose an elaborate system of scriptural interpretation. On the one hand, this sets clear (though broad) limits to the reach of reason in determining matters of religion, and on the other, it restricts the scope for subjectivism in the interpretation of scripture by attempting to systematize and regularize scriptural semantics, especially in the case of prophecies.

In *An Explanation of the Grand Mystery of Godliness*, More is categorical about 'the Reasonableness' of Christianity:

> I have given so solid and rational account thereof, that I am confident that no man that has the use of his Understanding shall be able ever to pretend any Reason against Christian Religion, such as it is exhibited in the Holy Writings themselves.[18]

But More's rational theology was not just aimed at rational doubters. In arguing that reason had a central place in religious matters, More sought to dispose of what he saw as the twin enemies of faith: rational atheists and irrational 'enthusiasts'. His targets were, on the one hand, the rational atheists who scoffed at the scriptures, especially the more mysterious passages as unintelligible, 'inextricable Aenigmas and Riddles'.[19] These sceptical wits he sought to win over by demonstrating that even the most abstruse passages of the bible are amenable to rational interpretation. In so doing he was also targeting their antithesis, the enthusiasts who sustained their claims to inspiration by denying reason had any place in religion. As he explains in the preface of his *Enthusiasmus triumphatus*, 'these Two unruly Guests' reinforce each other:

> For the *Atheist's* pretence to Wit and natural Reason … makes the *Enthusiast* secure that *Reason* is no guide to God: And the *Enthusiast's* boldly dictating the careless ravings of his own tumultuous *Phansy* for undeniable Principles of Divine knowledge, confirms the *Atheist* that the whole business of Religion and Notion of a God is nothing but a troublesome fit of over-curious *Melancholy*.[20]

---

[16] More, *Synopsis prophetica, A Modest Enquiry into the Mystery of Iniquity* part 2 (London and Cambridge, 1664), 211.

[17] Ibid., 259.

[18] More, *Mystery of Godliness*, Preface, ix.

[19] More, *Synopsis prophetica*, 211.

[20] More, *Enthusiasmus triumphatus*, 1–2, in *CSPW*.

Of course, by reason More meant 'right reason', or reason enlightened by true faith. It was, furthermore, affective reason, charged with emotion. More rejected what he called the Admirers of dry *Reason*'[21] as much as he did 'enthusiasts' who abandoned reason altogether. More's claim that Christianity is a rational religion did not mean scripture was reducible to a set of logical axioms, or that all the truths of scripture could be arrived by human ratiocination. For More, as for the other Cambridge Platonists, and for the Latitudinarians, the truths of scripture are not contrary to reason, even if their insights surpass the capacities of human understanding. The written word of scripture is an aid to understanding divine revelation, and the truth to be gained from it concerning the existence of God, the immortality of the soul and the existence of spirits, was more certain than philosophical truth:

> A greater Certainty, even of these things is to be drawn from the Scriptures rightly and completely understood, than from the clearest Fountains of Philosophy.[22]

Furthermore, the reasonableness of Christianity, in More's view, includes the fact that God has chosen only good men to bear witness to its truth, and the fact that its message is easily communicable.

More's *Apology* supports the rational approach of *An Explanation* by addressing the matter of the non-scriptural defence of religious belief. More's strategy is, he explains, to turn the rational weaponry of its opponents against themselves (to 'encounter those strutting Giants and Defiers of Heaven at their own weapon … I mean *Free Reason* and *Philosophy*').[23] To this end, More sets out five rules governing the use of reason in defence of religion, so as to vindicate religion 'from that vile imputation of ignorance in philosophy'. The first rule stipulates that the Christian apologist should not deny his opponent's arguments, where they are reasonable and consistent with Holy Scripture. The second rule advises him to concede rational points, but to show that they do not undermine Christianity. Rule three lays down the requirement that the 'Principles or Conclusions of Philosophy' to be used should have 'no real repugnancy with scripture', and be such as will 'most easily accordable with the Attributes of God and the *Phaenomena* of Providence'.[24] And he goes on, in Rule four, to recommend that 'the above said Philosophick Principles' should not simply be compatible with scripture (or, as he puts it, 'not really repugnant to the Divine Oracles'), but that scripture itself should actually approve of or include support for these principles, albeit in veiled form:

> … it were very desirable, that the above said Philosophick Principles which he makes choice of were not onely not really repugnant to the Divine Oracles but had some kind of countenance and approbation from them, as being either couched somewhere continuedly

[21] More, *Apocalypsis apocalypseos* (London, 1680), xvii.

[22] More, *TW*, Preface, I.

[23] More, *Apology* (London, 1664), 489.

[24] Ibid., 483–9.

under the Letter of History as a more Inward Mystical Meaning thereof, or as being glanced at in some short passages in the very Letter it self.[25]

This statement is obviously designed to permit philosophical readings of the text of scripture, and it opens the way for using non-religious sources in the interpretation of scripture. Such an accommodationist approach, however, is founded in the non-literal sense of scripture. Philosophical readings are therefore rooted in the 'more Inward, Mystical Meaning' of the scriptural text. Rule five stipulates that the rational apologist should deal with only those philosophical theories that are rational, but that this does not commit him to accepting them as true.

What was at stake was not just More's attempt to argue for the reasonableness of Christianity but his efforts to, at the same time, preserve its mystery. According to More, Christianity, as a religion, is distinguished by four qualities: obscurity, intelligibility, truth and usefulness. The obscurity of biblical language is a mark of its authenticity as the word of God, which far surpasses human capacities:

> For it is fit that Knowledge that is so far removed above humane Capacity should be received with that humble and profound Veneration which *Obscurity* and *Mysteriousness* conciliates to all Truths, but is most due to them that are the greatest and most beyond our natural Reach, as this of *Prophecy* is.[26]

More did not, however, regard obscurity as an insurmountable obstacle to intelligibility. After all, for a Platonist and erstwhile poet, obscurity of expression was hardly a difficulty. He allowed that although there are aspects of the Christian faith which cannot be reduced to rational understanding, this does not mean that they are unintelligible — as he put it in *An Account of Virtue*, 'some things are intelligible, though men know not the reason why'.[27] As a Platonist, he could take for granted that the highest truths are veiled, that spiritual things are concealed in physical form, but also that the medulla of meaning is accessible through its exterior cortex. In particular, tangible reality contains spiritual meaning: 'The Whole World is *ingens quoddam Sacramentum*, a large Sign or symbols of some spiritual Truths that nearly concern our souls'.[28] As a result, everything, in the visible world, no matter how humble or mundane, expresses some higher meaning: so we may read in the book of nature the profoundest truths of scripture. The progression from the sensible to the spiritual is suited to the understandings of men, and is part of the design of providence to enable men to work towards spiritual regeneration in which they 'ascend from sensible and Corporeal things to those things that are spiritual':[29]

> There is nothing that the Natural man is sensible of in this outward world, but the Spirit of God has made use of to prefigure and set out the condition and nature of Reward and

[25] Ibid.

[26] More, *Mystery of Iniquity*, 524.

[27] More, *An Account of Virtue* (London, 1690), 20.

[28] More, *Mystery of Godliness*, 129.

[29] More, *Discourses on Several Texts of Scripture* (London, 1692), 137.

> Spiritual things; that the Soul may receive hints to raise her self towards him that made her for to inherit Spirituality.[30]

It was, perhaps, the poet in More that lead him to pay particular attention to the written style of scripture, and, especially, to value the figurative language used. In his view, the purpose of prophetic images is partly aesthetic, to 'embellish and adorn the external Cortex of Prophecies', but also protective, to 'conceal and cover the more precious and inward' meaning.[31] Figurative language enhances understanding by appealing to the imagination. 'The schemes of speech in Prophets and Men inspired', writes More in the Preface to *An Explanation of the Mystery of Godliness*, 'are usually such as most powerfully strike the Phansie, and most strongly beat upon the Imagination, they describing things in the most sensible, palpable and particular representations that can be'.[32] At the same time prophetic utterances are not uncontrolled, but are exercises in carefully crafted rhetoric, discernible in the stylistic regularities of their writings, and therefore, More believed, amenable to critical analysis. By codifying biblical imagery, More aimed to demonstrate that prophetic utterances constituted a language that may be learned and understood like any other language – as easily as Latin or Greek. By following his guidelines, the reader 'can no more fail the right meaning of Prophecy, than he will of the rendring the true sense of a *Latin* or *Greek*, Author, keeping to the Rules of *Grammar*, and the known *Interpreters* of *Dictionaries*'.[33] More's motives were, he claimed, anti-schismatic. He aimed to put a stop to wild claims to scriptural authority, based on 'Enthusiastick Phrensie', by setting limits on the biblical exegesis, in the hope that he might, thereby 'reconcile the Sectaries to the Church of England and to shame them for separating from so Authentick a Constitution to follow the Guidance of Private Spirits'.[34]

In *A Modest Enquiry* More devotes considerable space to discussing biblical style. There are two parts to More's guide to decoding the figurative language of the prophetic bible books: the aforementioned set of 'Rules concerning the Preference of one Interpretation of the Prophetick Style before another',[35] and a lexicon of symbolic motifs, or 'iconisms', as More called them. The four rules require interpreters of prophecy to observe the 'approved Examples and Analogie' rather than the dictates of 'private phancy'; to exercise consistency by interpreting similar or identical prophetic signifiers as having the same meaning; to apply the

---

[30] More, *Mystery of Godliness*, 130.

[31] More, *Synopsis prophetica*, 213. For further discussion of More's biblical criticism, see Sarah Hutton, 'More Newton and the Language of Biblical Prophecy', in Force and Popkin (eds.), *The Books of Nature and Scripture. Recent Essays on Natural Philosophy, Theology, and Biblical Criticism in the Netherlands of Spinoza's Time and the British Isles of Newton's Time* (Dordrecht, 1994), 39–54.

[32] More, *Mystery of Godliness*, 11.

[33] More, Preface to *TW*, vii.

[34] More, *Apocalypsis apocalypseos*, Preface, iv.

[35] Ibid., 259.

criterion of the usefulness to the Church in every case; be free from prejudice or bias. To accompany these rules, More supplied a list of the most widespread rhetorical figures used by biblical prophets to 'embellish and adorn the externall Cortex of Prophecies'. Many of these are standard figures from classical rhetoric, such as metalepsis, hylasmus and synecdoche. Not all of these are familiar to readers today, for example, an example taken at random from his list of iconisms is the figure he calls 'Diorismus:

> *Diorismus*, is such a Scheme of the Prophetic style as polishes the outward letter with an appearing Sense of a very exact and determinate account of things either as to Number, Property, or specification.[36]

Such figures, claims More, are not merely ornamental, but have an epistemological function. As hc explains in the case of 'Diorismus' the use of concrete details makes a strong impression on the prophet's audience because it 'does the more strongly Strike the Phancy' and therefore 'more vigorously and palpably affect the Mind then what is more general and undetermined'.[37] More also provides a lexicon of images, which he calls 'an Alphabet of Prophetick Iconisms' or 'the chief Icastick Terms that occur in the Prophetick Style'. For example, according to this lexicon, 'Balance' signifies 'Justice'; 'Beast' stands for 'Body Politick'; both 'Horn' and 'Head' signify supreme political power. 'Desert' signifies paganism, and 'Locusts' denote 'numerous Armies of Men pillaging and destroying a Country'. 'Eye' is 'an Iconism of Knowledge' and also of 'humane Policy and Prospection'. 'Woman' too, denotes a body politic, but also, in what he calls a 'more Physical and Cabbalistical' sense, the 'domestick Eve' or bodily life and sense, 'Life, Sense, Relish of this Body'. By supplying such a list, More believed he was interpreting scripture through scripture 'attending what Scripture itself declares of them'. But it is also a rational approach, because it yields 'what Reason will unforcedly suggest or spy out concerning their Significancy and Representativeness of things'. He was confident of providing, thereby, a sure 'Method of settling and securing to our selves the true Sense of those Symbols'.[38] Although More insisted that he derived these meanings from scripture itself, the sources of his 'Alphabet of Prophetick Iconisms' were secular writings rather than bible commentators, though they did include Joseph Mede, whose synchronistic scheme for interpreting the Book of Revelation More adopts (with some modifications) in his own commentaries on the Apocalypse. More's sources include some used by Mede, such as the classical dream manuals, notably Artemodorus and the *Oneirocriticon* of Achmetes. But his range of sources goes well beyond Mede. For example the hieroglyphics of Horapollo, whence he derives his interpretation of a 'Frog' as 'an Hieroglyphick' of imperfections (though he supplements this with his own view that it is 'a fit Emblem of that *Wisedom* which is not from above').[39]

---

[36] More, *Synopsis prophetica*, 213.

[37] Ibid.

[38] More, *Synopsis*, 535 in *TW*.

[39] Ibid., 236.

By classifying and codifying recurrent images and symbols, More attempted to reconstruct a language of prophetic symbolism. And, as this scheme shows, he did not confine his exegetical method to obtaining merely historical or doctrinal readings. But it extended to philosophical truth that he believed to be encoded in scripture. By this means scripture can be interpreted allegorically, in the widest sense of the term. More continued to reassert these principles of exegesis – and, of course, put them into practice – in subsequent theological writings, especially his works on biblical prophecy. With his studies on the Jewish Kabbalah, his allegorical method of exegesis came into its own.[40] Even in his last published work, his *Opera Omnia*, More returns to these rules in the *scholia* he added to his writings. For example, in the *scholia* accompanying Book I of his *Defence of the Philosophick Cabbala*, More restates the five rules for establishing the compatibility of faith and reason, which had originally been published in his *Apology* of 1664.[41] For good measure he adds the caveat that, especially when interpreting the philosophical Kabbalah, we should be prepared to suspend judgement and submit to the authority of our superiors, even when we arrive at mathematical certainty by the application of reason.[42]

Conjectura cabbalistica

The most sustained piece of allegorical reading of scripture by More antedates his theological writings by several years. This was his *Conjectura cabbalistica*, published in 1653 and addressed to 'the Rational Spirit of free and well meaning Christians'.[43] The fact that More supplemented this with a 'Defence' and, in 1662, with a lengthy 'Appendix' justifying his method of interpretation, links it to the controversies surrounding *An Explanation of the Grand Mystery of Godliness*. And from among More's critics, there is a strong indication that it was this work that More was defending when he elaborated his views on scriptural exegesis in *A Modest Enquiry.* The young Edward Stillingfleet, future Bishop of Worcester and critic of John Locke, includes a critique of More's threefold cabbala in his *Origines Sacrae* of 1662, complaining that it has only served to cloud the meaning of scripture.

Although not a genuine kabalistical treatise, *Conjectura cabbalistica* owed its general conception to the Christian Kabbalists of the Renaissance like Reuchlin and

[40] In the 1670s More came into contact with the German kabbalist scholar, Christian Knorr von Rosenroth, ultimately co-operating with him in his project to translate the Kabbala into Latin. More contributed several pieces to the critical apparatus of Knorr's *Kabbala denudata*, 2 vols.(Sulzbach, 1677–79). On More and the kabala, see Allison P. Coudert, 'A Cambridge Platonist's Kabbalist Nightmare', *Journal of the History of Ideas*, 36 (1975), 633–52.

[41] *Opera Omnia*, vol. 3, 534–7.

[42] '*Assensum expresse suspendi ab omni re quae ullo modo videri possit dissona aut repugnans cum communio pervulgataque dogmatum Religionis nostrae intelligentia*', *Opera omnia*, vol. 3, 538.

[43] *Conjectura Cabbalistica*, p. 2, in *CSPW* (London, 1662).

Agrippa,[44] in as much as More took over the idea of a secret tradition of interpretation as 'profitable for the explaining the Literal sense as well as that more Mysterious meaning of the Text where it was intended'.[45] But the interpretative scheme adopted by More did not derive from them. *Conjectura cabbalistica* is premised on the view that 'the Mysterie of God lies not bare to false and adulterous eyes, but is hid and wrapped up in decent coverings from the sight of Vulgar and Carnal men', so that it is 'not unreasonable to conceive Moses to write *Types* and *Allegories*'.[46] The book consists of three parallel readings of the first chapter of the first book of Genesis: literal, moral and philosophical. So, for example, the work of the fourth day, the separation of day from night by the creation of 'two great lights' (Genesis 1.14–16); in the 'Literal Cabbala' More describes the placing of the sun and moon as lights in heaven, in an expanded recapitulation of the biblical text.[47] The 'Philosophick Cabbala' takes this onto a cosmological plain by introducing greater astronomical detail, by mentioning the planets, and inferring that there are many solar systems. It also proposes that the world or universe is 'a vast and immense *Aethereal* matter' or 'fluid Heaven', and interprets the two lights as being sunlight and reflected light.[48] 'The Moral Cabbala' in its turn interprets the two lights of Genesis 1.14 symbolically as, on the one hand, 'the *Sun of Righteousnesse*' or 'an hearty and sincere *Love of God and a mans neighbour*', and, on the other the inconstant light of '*Life and Knowledge*'.[49] The accompanying 'Defence' of each explains the wording and logic of the literal text of Genesis as simplified for ordinary consumption, 'words that strike the Fancy and Sense strongly' and thereby 'of easie perception to the rude people'.[50] 'The Defence of the Philosophick Cabbala' explains that the cosmological picture More gave in his account of the fourth day's work is consistent with '*Des-Cartes* his Philosophy'.[51] And 'The Defence of the Moral Cabbala' expounds verse 16 with verse 18, expanding the interpretation in the 'Moral Cabbala' by bringing in parallels from Plato and Pythagoras. Finally, in the 'Appendix' to the Philosophick Cabbala', More uses number symbolism to support his metaphysical and physical readings of the fourth day of creation (the 'Quaternary'), and answers objections to his cosmological interpretation, such as that there is no mention of the motion of the earth in the 'Judaick Cabbala'. More argues that the Mosaic account of creation contains, concealed within it, 'the Theory of the Earth's Motion'. This, he claims, is present in the inner kernel of the meaning, but has been lost to tradition. Its 'foundation', however, remains as 'a fair evidence that the Edifice once stood

[44] On Christian Kabbalism, see J. Blau, *The Christian Interpretation of the Cabala in the Renaissance* (New York, 1944) and F. Secret, *Les kabbalistes chrétiens de la Renaissance* (Paris, 1964).

[45] Ibid., 1.

[46] Ibid., 54–5.

[47] Ibid., 8.

[48] Ibid., 19.

[49] Ibid. 31.

[50] *Defence of the Threefold Cabbala*, in *CSPW*, 59, 62.

[51] Ibid., 80.

there'.[52] In the Introduction to his *Defence of the Threefold Cabbala* (published in 1662 in *A Collection of Philosophical Writings*) More explains the relationship between the letter of scripture and its inner meanings. Moses, he explains, wrote in the ordinary language of men 'accommodately to the apprehension of the meanest'. Instead of 'speaking of things according to their very Essence and real Nature', he spoke 'familiarly and condescendingly … according to the most easie and obvious conceits they themselves had of those things they saw in the world'.[53] But, Genesis contains 'under the external contexture of this narration some very singular and choice Theorems of *Natural Philosophy* and *Metaphysicks*'[54] – chief among which are a heliocentric cosmology and endorsement of the doctrine of the pre-existence of the soul. The third layer of meaning of Genesis 1.1 is 'an inward Spiritual or Mystical sense'.[55] *Conjectura cabbalistica* then, is an exercise in rational theology, which accommodates biblical literalism with a philosophical and ethical approach to scripture on the basis that the text of scripture contains multiple levels of meaning.

As an allegorical framework for reading scripture, *Conjectura cabbalistica* is obviously open to objections, not least because there are no limits on the hermeneutic possibilities to which it opens the way. To More's twentieth-century readers, his allegorical reading of the bible seems nothing if not idiosyncratic. His repeated defences of his method suggest that his ecclesiastical contemporaries were equally dissatisfied that his exegetical method accorded with received theological tradition. For all his abstruse learning, the individuality of More's approach laid him open to the objection that he was just as guilty of interpreting scripture according to 'private phancy' as the enthusiasts whom he condemned for doing just that. Not only did More's kabalistical conjectures seem to some of his Anglican contemporaries unnecessarily obscure (as Edward Stillingfleet pointed out) but his exegetical method itself smacked of heterodoxy. More's old enemy, Joseph Beaumont, never altered his views that More was theologically dubious. And he remained hostile, to the last, towards More's approach to scriptural interpretation. As late as 1690, 11 years after More's death, he railed against More's 'Psudo (*sic*)-Prophetick leaven, and *Pia Fraus*', mocking his account of prophetic imagery, and his 'strange forc't Criticisms upon the Text', adding 'when these Helps fail him, he does not stick sometimes to do manifest Violence to the Text'.[56] That More's approach was contentious in its own time is evident, as already noted from the fact that More subsequently supplemented

[52] *Appendix to the Philosophick Cabbala*, in *CSPW*, 126–7.

[53] Ibid., 50.

[54] Ibid., 51.

[55] Ibid., 55.

[56] Beaumont, *Remarks on Dr Henry More's Expositions of the Apocalypse and Daniel, and upon his Apologie Defended against his answer to them* (London, 1690), Preface, sigs. d^{v}, d(2)^{v}. Beaumont was obviously stung by More's coinage of the pseudonym, 'Streblosimus Eruentes' (normally referred to by the initials S.E.) for Beaumont in the *scholia* to his works, a name which implied Beaumont was a 'Forreigner'. Another posthumous critique of More was made by Bishop Boyle in 1680, who denounced More's quasi-kabbalistic reading of scripture in *Apocalypsis apocalypseos* as inept and ridiculous. Dublin, Marsh Library MS Z4.5.12.

Conjectura cabbalistica with a 'Defence' and a long 'Appendix to the Defence', both of which were printed with *Conjectura Cabbalistica* in More's *A Collection of Several Philosophical Writings* in 1662. And, as we have also seen, these apologetic supplements come in the context of a self-defence (in *A Modest Enquiry*) which devotes so much attention to exegetical principles. This suggests that it was not just the doctrinal content of More's beliefs that was at stake, but the method that supported it. Henry More's proposed aids to reading scripture set out in his defensive *A Modest Enquiry* entailed setting limits on the interpretations to be derived from scripture, as safeguards against enthusiasm and atheism. But his detractors in the ecclesiastical establishment could, nonetheless, argue that his rational approach itself opened the way to errors in doctrine (especially relating to the Trinity), to the rejection of revelation altogether (Deism) or to unnecessary obscurity. More was certainly no anti-Trinitarian or Deist. But he was guilty of errors of doctrine, in the eyes of his detractors, on account of his subscription to the heterodox theology of Origen. And it is on this account that his exegetical method was most suspect. And it is *Conjectura cabbalistica* which makes this apparent.

More's adoption of a multiple scheme of biblical exegesis in *Conjectura cabbalistica* has plenty of respectable precedent in Christian bible interpretation, especially the fourfold exegetical method later utilised by Christian Bible commentators (historical, allegorical, moral, anagogical). This in turn is indebted to Philo of Alexandria (*c.*20 BC–AD 40), the Jewish thinker whose authority stood high among Christian interpreters in great part because he lived in earliest Christian times.[57] The synthesis of classical philosophy and Holy Scripture achieved by Philo is based on a fourfold interpretative scheme (literal, physical, ethical and mystical). More himself acknowledges a debt to Philo whom he regarded a pre-eminent example of ancient Jewish learning, proof that the Platonists and Pythagoreans derived their teachings 'from the Divine Traditions amongst the Jews'. The general principles of More's Pythagorean/Platonic reading of the first book of Genesis are certainly indebted to Philo. But less conspicuous than Philo in More's *Conjectura* is the figure of Origen, one of the most important members of the Alexandrian school which proposed an allegorical approach to the interpretation of scripture. Origen is particularly noted both for his philosophical approach (deeply indebted to Platonism) and for his tripartite method of biblical exegesis. In his *Peri Archon* (*On First Principles*) he sets out its literal, spiritual and moral exegetical aspects, which correspond to the triple make up of man – body, soul and spirit:

> Each one must therefore pourtray the meaning of the divine writings in a threefold way upon his own soul; that is, so that the simple may be edified by what we may call the body of the scriptures (for such is the name we give to the common and literal interpretation); while those who have begun to make a little progress and are able to perceive something

[57] On Philo, see F.H. Colson and G.H. Whitaker (eds), *Philo* 10 vols (London, 1929–62); David T. Runia, *Philo of Alexandria and the Timaeus of Plato* (Leiden, 1986); H.A. Wolfson, *Philo. Foundations of Religious Philosophy in Judaism, Christianity and Islam*, 2 vols (Cambridge, MA, 1948).

more than that may be edified by the soul of scripture; and those who are perfect … may be edified by that spiritual law, which has a 'shadow of the good things to come' (Hebrews 10.1) as if by the Spirit.[58]

On this approach, Origen maintained that scripture could be understood at one level as continuous literal narrative of which the 'logical and literal meaning' can be grasped 'by the entire multitude of those believers who accept the faith quite trustfully'.[59] Nevertheless, all scripture, and not just prophecies, also has a deeper meaning, concealed within the literal exterior. The literal meaning is therefore 'a kind of outer covering and veil for spiritual meanings'.[60] Origen's allegorical approach to scripture enabled him to make sense of contradictory passages, and to explain anthropomorphisms of the Old Testament. He held that spiritual reading of this kind was particularly relevant to doctrine concerning the Father, Son and Holy Spirit. Furthermore, his method of scriptural interpretation supported some of his most controversial theological views: a subordinationist account of the Trinity, the pre-existence of souls, and universal salvation. Henry More's threefold Kabbalah matches the first three levels in Philo's scheme: literal, physical and ethical, but as a tripartite scheme it is closer to Origen's. More's Origenism, then, was not a matter of his adoption of the occasional Origenist teaching, but extended to his adoption of a rational, multi-layered reading of scripture. More is not explicit about his debt to Origen in *Conjectura cabbalistica*, making only occasional reference to Origen's views. Nor did he follow Origen in every point of doctrine (he did not, for example, agree with Origen on the matter of universal salvation), but he was, like Origen, a philosophical theologian, and a Platonising one at that. Although it is perhaps not, at first sight obvious, strong testimony to the thoroughgoing nature of More's Origenism is his approach to reading the scripture.

More's Anglican opponents had good reason to suspect that under the pretext of scriptural exegesis, More had found cover for his idiosyncratic and unorthodox theological views. For, even while he sought to reconcile philosophy and theology by demonstrating the affinities between them through an allegorical reading of scripture, so also, he continued to uphold his theological views, supporting them through his allegorical reading of scripture. Never, in any of his conciliatory restatements of his position, did More compromise or downplay his commitment to liberty of conscience. On the contrary, he continued to press the case for the national church to be comprehensive enough to accommodate all denominations barring the extremes of religious radicalism and Catholicism.[61] He insisted with increasing

58 Origen (Origines Adamantius), *On First Principles*, trans. G.W. Butterworth (London, 1936). On Origen's theology, see Henri Crouzel, *Origen*, trans. A.S. Worrall (Edinburgh: T. & T. Clark, 1989); C. Bigg, *The Christian Platonists of Alexandria*, 2nd edn (Oxford, 1913).

59 Ibid., 274, 278–9.

60 Ibid., 285.

61 See, More, *Apology*, 550.

vigour, on the relevance of millenarianism to the Christian church.[62] Although he was at pains to distinguish his millennialist views from those of the religious radicals of the interregnum by recommending his own method of exegesis as a safeguard against chiliasm and political applications of millennialism, the high profile that apocalyptical exegesis had in his theological writings meant that he always had to be on the defensive to fend off charges of guilt by association. But above all, it was his unrepentant commitment to Origenist doctrines that made his exegetical approach so potentially dangerous, as far as his Anglican critics were concerned. Although More was prepared to deflect the charges by agreeing to present the doctrine as a hypothesis rather than a dogma, he never abandoned it. [63] On the contrary, he continued to assert that, like the doctrine of the Trinity, pre-existence of souls was endorsed by scripture, especially if scripture was read according to his own rational method. And when, in later years, he encountered the genuine Jewish Kabbalah,[64] he argued, again, that a proper approach to the Kabbalah would reveal that the truths contained within it included the doctrine of the Trinity and the pre-existence of souls. He also continued to propound his theological views in more popular format, in his *Divine Dialogues* (1668), to which his allegorical approach to religious truth was particularly suited. His difficulties in getting permission to publish this book underline the fact that, despite More's indefatigable defence of Trinitarianism, he was perceived as a purveyor of unsound divinity.

The first historian of the Latitudinarian movement, Gilbert Burnet, claimed More as the forefather of the movement.[65] Henry More shares with the later Latitudinarians both a commitment to greater toleration of dissenting opinion and a rational approach to the truth of the bible. However, to locate More as a rational theologian in this way obscures the differences between him and other rational theologians of his time – particularly the Laudian legacy – and fails to account for the suspicion with which he was viewed by the established church of the Restoration. When the Origenist roots of More's rational theology are exposed, the hostility of the Anglican establishment becomes entirely explicable, and More's recent reputation as a conservative conformist becomes unsustainable. This is borne out by the fact that More's Restoration critics included the latitudinarian conformist, Edward Stillingfleet, who was later to come to prominence as a latitudinarian bishop and opponent of James II's religious policies. Soon after the Restoration Stillingfleet, like More, published his own *Rational Account of the Grounds of the Christian Faith*,

[62] Sarah Hutton, 'Henry More and the Apocalypse', *Studies in Church History*, *Subsidia* 10, (1995), 131–40.

[63] This is what he had to do in order to obtain a license for printing his *Divine Dialogues* in 1668. He did so at the insistence of Samuel Parker, the Archbishop of Canterbury's censor. See *Conway Letters*, 294.

[64] Sarah Hutton, 'More, Millenarianism and the Ma'aseh Merkavah', in J.E. Force and D.S. Katz (eds.), *Everything Connects. In Conference with Richard H. Popkin. Essays in his Honour* (Leiden, 1999), 163–82.

[65] Burnet, *A History of My Own Time*, ed. O. Airy, 2 vols (Oxford, 1897) (first published 1723), 334–5.

his *Origines sacrae* of 1664, which has already been cited above for its criticism of More's 'threefold cabbala'.[66] Like More's *An Explanation of the Grand Mystery of Godliness*, Stillingfleet's book was published at a critical time for claiming a stake in the new Anglican establishment of the Restoration. But *Origines sacrae* represents a discernibly different rational theology from More's, one that is hostile to symbolic readings of scripture of the kind More proposed. Stillingfleet's bid for acceptance by the Church hierarchy was evidently more successful than More's. For it was on the strength of this work that he was invited to write a defence of Laud, which was published as *A Rational Account of the Grounds of the Protestant Religion* (London, 1664).[67] By contrast with even a Latitudinarian like Stillingfleet, More's approach to scripture, with the theology it sustains, places him at the margins of orthodoxy in the Restoration church.

[66] *Origines sacrae: or a Rational Account of the Grounds of the Christian Faith, as told to the Truth and Divine Authority of the Scriptures, and the Matters therein Contained* (London, 1662). Edition used Oxford, 1836, 3 vols. See especially vol. 2, 108.

[67] See S. Hutton, 'Edward Stillingfleet, Henry More, and the Decline of Moses Atticus', in R. Kroll, R. Ashcraft and P. Zagorin (eds), *Philosophy, Science and Religion in England, 1640–1700*, (Cambridge, 1992), 68–84.

Chapter 11

'Directions for the Profitable Reading of the Holy Scriptures': Biblical Criticism, Clerical Learning and Lay Readers, *c.* 1650–1720*

Justin Champion

The later half of the seventeenth century saw an explosion in biblical scholarship and erudition. From the magisterial editions of the Walton polyglot to the Mill New Testament, cutting edge volumes were produced for the clerical elite and the Christian public. Alongside such pious Protestant projects were continental works of more dubious theological identity such as those of Spinoza and Richard Simon, all of which were translated for English audiences in the 1680s. This essay will examine how the seventeenth-century reader (clerical and lay) negotiated this complex and highly sophisticated set of discourses. Determining what was genuine 'Christian knowledge' and what was not, was a cultural procedure shaped in a variety of ways: in advice books on 'profitable reading', in the construction of private and ecclesiastical libraries, and in the works of bibliographical recommendation composed for clergymen scholars. The history of the book and the parallel study of reading and reception, have in recent years, become the subject of subtle and sophisticated analysis.[1] Despite the broader historiographical attention to the relationship between print and Protestantism, the number of studies devoted to exploring exactly how early modern men and women (and even children) read the Bible, and what they

* I am grateful to Nicholas Keene, Ariel Hessayon, Colin Davis, and Victor Nuovo for their comments. Audiences in London, Norwich and New Haven contributed valuable insights.

[1] See M. de Certeau, *The Practice of Everyday Life* (California, 1988) 'Reading as Poaching'. For a discussion see J. Raven, 'New reading histories, print culture and the identification of change: the case of eighteenth-century England', *Social History*, 23 (1998), 268–87; R. Chartier, *The Order of Books* (Cambridge, 1994); K. Sharpe, *Reading Revolutions: the politics of reading in early modern England* (New Haven, 2000); L. Jardine and A. Grafton, '"Studied for action": how Gabriel Harvey read his Livy', *Past & Present*, 129 (1990), 30–78: J. Raven, N. Tadmor, and H. Small (eds.), *The Practice and Representation of Reading in England* (Cambridge, 1996).

thought they were doing when they did, is relatively few.[2] Reading the Bible was the most important thing an English Protestant could do to attain salvation. But how? Where did one start? On page one and read right through? Or with the New Testament? What did one do while reading? Did one sit at a desk? In attempting to answer these questions attention will be paid to the works of powerful figures such as Thomas Barlow and Henry Dodwell who published important works on the 'de studio theologico' as well as the more popular advice books of men like Nicholas Byfield and William Lowth. The way individuals assimilated (or not) the lessons of biblical criticism will be assessed by a case study of the reading strategies of John Locke and Anthony Collins.

I

Racked with anxiety about the state of his faith and suffering from what he feared was providential illness the young Cambridge undergraduate, Isaac Archer, reflected to his diary 'I verily thinke I impaired my health by overmuch and unseasonable study'. Worried that others might overtake him in their studies, his greatest anxiety was that 'I observed that in reading God's word I could not frame by heart aright, and as I would, nor could I meditate on it, as was my duty, by reason of many idle and evill thoughts which came in, but were very unwelcome'. Despite this, Isaac had been 'diligent in reading the scriptures every day, and read them once through in a yeare for the 3 first years according to Mr Bifield's directions; yet gate I not much good for want of due meditation'. The young man assiduously noted his scriptural reading in a commonplace-book: 'I took notes out of the Bible and putt it under such heads as might suit any state and although by such industrious wayes I had a gift of prayer, I knew that except the spirit of God helped my infirmityes with groanes unutterable, Romans 8:26, I could not pray in such a manner as to please God. I found it much better to use scripture phrase, on all occasions, then to trust to parts, and pray at random'.[3] It is worth pausing to examine the language of this reflection: the phrases 'due meditation', 'diligent in reading', 'industrious wayes' combine to exemplify the sense of application and careful labour such a devout individual assumed was appropriate to encountering revelation. There are also important hints

---

[2] See I. Green, *Print and Protestantism in Early Modern England* (Oxford, 2000); S. Wabuda, 'The woman with the rock: the controversy on women and Bible reading', in S. Wabuda, C. Litzenberger, and J. Caroline (eds), *Belief and Practice in Reformation England* (Aldershot, 1998), 46–59: R. Gillespie, 'Reading the Bible in seventeenth-century Ireland', and E. Boran, 'Reading theology within the community of believers: James Ussher's "Directions"', in B. Cunningham and M. Kennedy (eds), *The Experience of Reading: Irish historical perspectives* (Dublin, 1999), 10–38, 39–59; P. Stallybrass, 'Books and scrolls: navigating the Bible' in J. Andersen and E. Sauer (eds), *Books and Readers in Early Modern England* (Philadelphia, 2002), 42–79.

[3] M. Storey (ed.), *Two East Anglian Diaries, 1641–1729* (Suffolk Record Society, 36, 1994), 60.

of the physical disposition and activities Bible reading involved. One needed to approach the book with the correct frame of mind; one read with a purpose to gather scriptural injunctions and to prepare for prayer. Importantly, for our purpose, Isaac planned his reading according to the 'directions' from 'Mr Byfield'. Earlier in his diary Isaac had described himself as 'almost continually reading the Bible or other books' desperate to catch up on his studies after an illness. Again using Byfield's book he studied 'hard to get up what I had lost in the reading of the Bible, stinting myselfe to many chapters a day'. Such intense reading, as Isaac noted, was 'not very good for my eyesight'.[4]

Isaac Archer's routines of scriptural reading may have been exceptional in their intensity, but they were not unusual amongst the Godly in seventeenth-century England. The work he had used to guide his encounters with the Holy book was Nicholas Byfield's *Directions for the private reading of the Scriptures* first published in 1618. One of the more popular works of the genre of advice books, it had reached a fourth edition by 1648.[5] Byfield's book delivered 'choice rules (that shew how to read with profit)', explained methods to enable those who could not read or write, and annexed 'pithy directions to reconcile places of scripture'. Like the shorter writing of his friend (the more distinguished) James Ussher, the work delivered advice on when and how to read both the Old and New Testaments: the bulk of the volume précised the contents of scripture and a description of the author.[6] The point was to allow an overview of each passage: 'that the reader might before he reads, mark the drift of each book and chapter, and when he hath read, might with singular ease and delight, remember what he hath read'. The 'calendar' set out which portions of the scriptures should be read in what order 'so that the whole Bible might be read over in a year. Supplementing this were 'rules for observation of profitable things in reading'. This advice was prompted by complaints from many weak Christians who affected 'their health marvellously with grief and fear, because they cannot read with more comfort and profit'. As Byfield asserted the fault in these cases was not want of 'affection to the word', so much as 'their want of direction for their reading'. Readers required a method that allowed them to identify the 'most needful places' for the development of their own Christian knowledge (and consequent growth in faith) and for the encouragement of practical piety. Reading scripture was an active business: one read with a purpose of gathering God's injunctions under 'several heads'. Following this routine even the 'simplest reader may gather great store of testimonies'. Such a gathering of 'places' would 'wonderfully fill my heart with secret refreshings, and sensible joy'. Having the fruits of reading ready to hand for re-reading would provide a means of curing anxiety and settling confusion over

[4] Storey, *Two East Anglian Diaries*, 55.

[5] See Green, *Print and Protestantism*, 147–8.

[6] See for discussion of Ussher's work, E. Boran, 'Reading theology', 39–59.

doctrinal disputes. Noting what passages raised reproof for poor conduct also meant such scriptural reading was a means for spiritual self-discipline.[7]

Byfield encouraged his readers to take a pen (or pencil) in hand when they read scripture. It was important to 'mark' the key places that 'contain evident ground of truth'. With a very practical bent, he suggested people make 'a little paper book' and draw up a small number of headings, certainly 'only so many as thou art sure thy memory will easily carry to thy reading'. When recording passages, he counselled, 'in reading, observe onely such places as stare thee in the face', and only note the reference (book chapter and verse) 'not the words, for that will tire thee in the end'. It was critical also to make an inventory of the hard and difficult passages 'which in reading I have a desire to know the meaning of': this would provide a log of details which in the company of 'preachers, or able Christians, I might have profitable questions to propound'. Byfield's advice was that this process of reading, annotation, reflection and re-reading should become a routine that was reviewed each week and each month. Incrementally over the year this 'little paper book' would build up into a significant soteriological resource: as Byfield explained, 'I am persuaded if thou fear God, thou wouldst not sell thy collections for a great price, after thou has gathered them, if it were but for the good they may do thee in the evill day, when it shall com upon thee'. John Geree ('pastor' of St Faiths', London) added to Byfield's volume further reflections and materials to improve the value of the 'private exercise' of scripture reading. Careful study of the Bible would save men and women from error. Geree was very precise in his use of the word 'study'. Simple reading was not enough, as he clarified, 'But yet to read it is not all. Legare & non intelligere, negligere etc. To read and not to understand, or not to heed, is to neglect. Such reading of scriptures is to dishonour God and them'. Special attention must be paid to the 'season of reading', so that people had both the time to read while they were affected with matters of 'special concernment'. For those who could read, but not write, then a system of marks identifying important passages was appropriate: for those who could not read then they must rely on others, if they were servants they should ensure they planted themselves in families where the 'word was duly read'.[8]

The thrust of Byfield's advice was to provide both a routine (reading every day) and a cultural practice (annotation and reflection) for the acculturation of scriptural values. The advice on reading was carefully fenced by ecclesiastical authority. The laity read scripture in order to confirm their understanding of true doctrine: that was why it was so important to deliver a clear précis and overview of the meaning and significance of each book. Reading scripture was an act of devotion. For Randall Sanderson, author of another work of advice, it was critical to read 'strictly morning, noon, night' so that 'thou shalt never want heavenly matter to take up thy thoughts'.[9] Since the first publication of the vernacular and 'Protestant' Bible there had been

---

[7] N. Byfield, *Directions for the private reading of the Scriptures* (1618, 1648 edn) 'Preface', A5–A6v [unpaginated].

[8] Byfield, *Directions,* A3; 'Second preface' passim.

[9] R. Sanderson, *An explication of the following directions* (Oxford, 1647), 2.

political anxiety and uncertainty about the dangers of an entirely undisciplined readership. Although Henrician statutes had encouraged the circulation and public access to the various authorized versions, later injunctions attempted to limit the readership of scripture to the political and social elites. Evangelical and commercial imperatives created pressures and demands which, over the course of the sixteenth century, inevitably broadened the social composition of the reading community. Much of the inter- and intra-confessional dispute between Roman Catholics and Protestants, and between Calvinists and Anglicans of the later period was fought out in the margins and typographical apparatus of the subsequent printed editions of the Bible. The addition of concordances, indexes, chapter headings, summaries, running heads, marginal cross references and philological annotation all provided means for the ecclesiastical institutions to guide and shape the reading experience.[10]

Most of the standard printed (and more importantly 'authorized') editions of the Bible were prefaced with short guides 'to the Christian reader' or the 'diligent Christian reader', which invoked the duties of careful and orthodox study. 'Considering how hard a thing it is to understand, and what errors, sects and heresies grow dayly for lack of true knowledge thereof', proclaimed the preface of a Bishops' Bible in 1599, 'we have endeavoured both by the diligent reading of the best commentaries, and also by the conference with the Godly and learned brethren' to make the meaning and understanding clear. Readers encountered the text through the mediation of a complex literary interpretation. Perhaps the most transparent method of advice was T. Grashop's diagrammatic schema 'How to take profit in reading of the holy Scriptures' which appeared in many different editions of the Bible in the Elizabethan decades. Outlining the general principles to be derived from scripture by earnest, diligent and careful reading, Grashop delivered some very practical suggestions on how to read the book. He counselled that the reader 'marke and consider' the language, idiom and context of scriptural text. If careful reading and comparative study, still left a lack of comprehension then the devout Christian ought to take opportunity to 'read interpreters, if hee be able. Conferre with such as can open the scriptures. Heare preaching, and to proove by the scriptures that which is taught'. The point of this advice was clear: there was a right way to read scripture, there were orthodox truths to be learnt, and where the reader bumped up against the limits of their own understanding they had recourse to the authoritative erudition and insight of the Church. Works like Byfield's operated against a backcloth of this type of advice which was central to the cultural purchase of the printed protestant Bible in the Stuart period. Although protestant culture encouraged the private and domestic reading of the Bible such reading was calculated to reinforce the interpretative authority of the established Church. The important distinction was between reading and interpreting the meaning of the Bible. The individual encounter with the emotive force of revelation had a powerful evangelical function; it was not conceived of as a process that empowered the individual reader to make his or her own meaning.

---

[10] B.J. McMullin, 'The Bible Trade' in *The Cambridge History of the Book in Britain. Volume IV 1557–1695* (Cambridge, 2002), 455–73.

II

Much of the confidence that Protestant churchmen displayed in their recommendations for Christian readers rested upon the conviction that revelation (even in its printed form) was inspired, inerrant and compelling. Over the course of the seventeenth century there was an accelerated corrosion of these certainties. The recovery of ancient biblical manuscripts and the application of humanist scholarly criticism to the *textus receptus* had resulted in an expansion, and flourishing, of an erudite Biblical criticism amongst Roman Catholic and Protestant communities. Debates about the merits of different codicological traditions, and the advantages of specific manuscripts, competed with discussions of canon formation, translation theory and focused disputes about (for example) the pointing systems of Hebrew vowels. This learning spawned huge folio volumes of (mainly) Latinate scholarship: lexicons, grammars, concordances, harmonies, polyglot editions were produced throughout the period. Despite much of this biblical criticism having been motivated by particular confessional interests, internal scholarly disputes, and individual hubris, the cultural consequences were complex. At one level, with such a powerful and intensive cultural investment in preserving and authenticating the integrity of the text of scripture the printed Bible became a dominant and hegemonic resource for defending the established order. From another perspective, the implications of much of the scholarly conflict suggested that, far from being certain and secure the integrity of scripture lay on fragile foundations easily shaken by robust study. By the end of the seventeenth century the reliability of revelation, as an epistemic category, and the integrity of the text of scripture, had suffered sustained, repeated, brutal and wounding assault. It was not indisputable that the word of God was inspired, inerrant or even true. Figures like Thomas Hobbes had exposed some of the elemental flaws in the supposed Mosaic authorship of the Pentateuch, as well as drawing public attention to the essentially historical process of the formation of the New Testament canon. Protestant scholars like Jean Daillé had cast doubt on the reliability of the early Church fathers' compromising the underpinning role of tradition as a foundation for scriptural integrity. Following in these footsteps, Spinoza undercut the philosophical authority of scripture by displaying the idiomatic and essentially diverse literary quality of the text. This corrosion of scriptural status was compounded by the massive (and to many compelling) textual erudition of Richard Simon, which deconstructed the textual authority of all contemporary editions, suggesting that all the world was left with were unreliable 'versions'.

By the last two decades of the seventeenth century the offensive against revelation was a matter of public knowledge. The recondite scholarly disputes that had been conducted amongst a Latinate *respublica litterorum* had spilled out into the vernacular: pamphlets, journals and sermons debated even the most sophisticated matters of philological and critical concern. One of the consequences of this controversy was that the clerical elite were profoundly aware that a public response to the threat was essential. Importantly this took two forms. There was a powerful and learned challenge to the claims of the infidels conducted in the form of scholarly rebuttals. There was also a more practical engagement. If a Hobbes or Spinoza claimed that the text of scripture was corrupt how should the Christian reader respond in their routines of scriptural reading? Clergymen designed advice to sincere readers that would allow them to absorb and refute the dangerous lessons of heterodox criticism. Delivering advice on how to read a scripture poisoned by infidel criticism was a profound antidote to the effect it might wield on the ordinary practices of diligent Christian readers. By focusing on a selection of the more significant works it will be possible to give a sense of the fundamental components of the Anglican response. One of the most powerful and effective devices for defending Anglican orthodoxy was the series of public lectures funded by Robert Boyle, inaugurated in the early 1690s. With a specific brief to challenge the threat of 'infidels' (defined as 'atheists, theists, pagans, Jews and Mahometans') the first lectures were co-ordinated to address as broad an audience as possible. Eminent figures like Richard Bentley and Samuel Clarke delivered compelling and frequently reprinted works which attached the innovative ideas of Newtonian natural philosophy to the cause of Anglican orthodoxy.[11] Although this 'scientific' dimension to the Boyle lectures has tended to dominate the historiography, substantial elements of the lectures were intended to defend the textual status of revelation. A case in point is the double series of lectures prepared by John Williams, (Chaplain to William and Mary and later Bishop of Chichester), between 1695 and 1696.[12] Deliberately calculated to rebut the arguments of Spinoza, Simon and more recently Jean Leclerc, Williams marshalled the achievements of orthodox scholarship against the challenges to the textual integrity and epistemological 'certainty' of scripture. The testimony of history and the chain of providence established the truth of revelation: as Williams stated 'here we have no reason to doubt; and where there is no reason to doubt, there is certainty'. He dismissed hostile arguments about the variable textual condition as 'not material': they were merely errors of transcription of no consequence to the true meaning of scripture.[13]

In the final lectures of his series, Williams moved to discuss the implications of these learned debates for the practical business of reading the Bible. One should 'search the scriptures' with 'humility and diligence; with impartiality and sincerity, without prejudice and prepossessions'. The intellectual disposition of the reader was the starting point for a true understanding: each reader should 'lay aside all filthyness and superfluity of naughtiness, all prejudice and interests, and receive with meekness the ingrafted word'.[14] In a subsequent lecture he described the best 'rules for interpretation' of scripture, acknowledging both the 'perspicuity and difficulties

[11] J.J. Dahm, 'Science and apologetics in the early Boyle lectures', *Church History*, 39 (1970), 172–86; M. Hunter, *Science and Society in Restoration England* (Cambridge, 1981), 183–4; M.C. Jacob, *The Newtonians and the English Revolution 1689–1720* (Cornell UP, 1976).

[12] *The possibility, expediency and necessity of divine revelation* (1695) and *The perfection of the evangelical revelation* (1696).

[13] J. Williams, *The truth of the Holy Scriptures* (1 April, 1695), 4, 6–7, 23–4.

[14] J. Williams, *Scripture the rule of faith* (3 February 1696), 3–4, 22.

of Scripture'. Most people would read the Bible in translation, but this was fine because the true sense of the original was rendered accurately 'and so again to him that understands the translation only, it is the same as if he understood the original'. Since scripture was clear in all necessary things, careful reading would enable understanding: it was, Williams insisted, almost inevitable that the sincere reader would understand these fundamental truths – 'these everyone may understand as he reads them in scripture, and which no man can read, but he must find out and understand'. The only obscurity the diligent reader would find concerned 'such points as are not in themselves necessary, and not necessary to all'. Though there were difficulties in reading the Bible 'yet they are nothing', he insisted, 'in comparison to the Plain text of it; and which no more hinders us from understanding the plan, that the spots in the sun prevent us of the light of it'. The best antidote to most obscurity was repeated daily reading: thereby 'much of the obscurity will wear off; and the phrase and style, and way of arguing will be more evident, and the matter of it makes not only the stronger impression on our minds, but be clear'd up also insensibly to us'. Routine and repeated encounter, like learning the alphabet, would create a 'kind of force to bend our minds to it'. The injunctions were straightforward: 'search, enquire and compare'.[15]

The connection between defending the certainty of revelation against the infidel and dispensing practical advice on how to read the Bible was also evident in the writings of William Lowth, prebend of Winchester and later vicar of Petersfield. In 1692 he published a successful vindication of revelation and then in 1708 a work, *Directions for the profitable reading of the Holy Scriptures*, which was frequently reprinted throughout the eighteenth century. The controversial work was a robust attack on those who undermined the sanctity of the scriptures in the name of liberty of enquiry: such people reasoned themselves into heterodoxy. Sensitive to the political dimensions of biblical hermeneutics, he was hostile to those who believed that the 'submitting to the authority of God himself to be an undue restraint upon the use of Human Reason; and the very pretending to such an authority to be one of the arts of designing priests'. Such infidels were apt to look 'upon the Bible as a book of no great value, and which the world might very well be without'. Writers like Hobbes, Spinoza, Simon all imposed on the 'unlearned reader' creating a false impression of their 'profound reading and scholarship'. The bulk of Lowth's lengthy work disputed and corrected the assertions of the 'dishonest illiterate atheists'.[16] In the less learned *Directions*, Lowth persisted in underscoring the polemic nature of his advice against the sceptics and the scorners. Untrammelled liberty of thought would lead to licentiousness in behaviour: the antidote to all this was 'industrious' reading, meditation and study. Lowth did not encourage the ordinary reading into a promiscuous reading of the Bible but aimed to identify 'what parts are fittest for them to read, and best suited to their capacities'. In answering Roman Catholic

[15] J. Williams, *Of the perspicuity of Scripture* (2 March 1696), 2, 6–7, 12, 14, 19, 30.

[16] W. Lowth, *A vindication of the divine authority of the writings of the Old and New Testament* (Oxford, 1692, 1699), ii, iv, v, 287–8.

complaints, Lowth insisted that protestant practice did not enfranchise all 'private interpretations', he said, 'as if we gave authority thereby to the meanest and most ignorant people, to judge of the sense of the abstrusest and most difficult parts of God's word'. Such liberty did indeed produce heresy and schism. To avoid such dangers he encouraged the Godly clergy 'to dedicate themselves to this employment, and bend all their studies chiefly this way, that *their lips may preserve the knowledge* of those sacred oracle; so 'tis the duty of the people *to seek the law at their mouths*'. Drawing the distinction between milk for babes and strong meat, Lowth defended the proposition that laity and clergy had different gifts of comprehension.[17]

Lowth argued that while the laity had the opportunity to read scripture because they had not made the study of scripture their business they ought to defer to the 'experts'. The protestant solution negotiated the extremes of authority and liberty: as he explained the two alternatives were 'that of locking up the scriptures, and taking the key of knowledge out of the people's hands; and the other of making every ignorant mechanick a judge of the sense and meaning of the most abstruse parts of God's word'. Everyone needed to develop 'critical skills' but there was a 'proportional industry' according to status: put simply, it was a clergyman's vocation to study scripture. For the ordinary reader exercising their judgement was essential provided that they did not follow it 'any further that they can shew that they have reason, the analogy of faith, and the phraseology of scripture on their side'. One of the most fundamental principles was to acknowledge that the Bible was 'all things to all men'; because it was written to bring 'wisdom to the simple and unlearned' the reader should not expect it to 'be writ like a regular system of philosophy'. Adapted to all capacities the best reading method was to start with the 'plainest books first'. Once well versed in these straightforward works it was possible to work up to the more complicated bits 'so they afford the greatest matter of edification to all attentive readers'. Lowth actively counselled the reader to avoid the more abstruse parts of scripture: 'the prophecies of Daniel, Ezekiel and the Revelation, which can afford but small edification to unlearned and ignorant readers'. Engaging with such portions of the Bible might be actively dangerous: misreading could be a route to impiety. The consequences of Uzzah's sin (who 'approached the ark with too much curiousity') were evident: while the injunction of 2 Timothy 3:16–17 (a ubiquitous and much debated citation) argued that all scripture was profitable, Lowth clarified 'but he does not say 'tis so to all men'.[18] This was not to advance a 'popish' defence of restricted access to scripture, but simply to recognize that different reading strategies were appropriate for different parts of the text.

Underlying Lowth's recommendations was the premise that the writers of the Old and New testaments had a harmony of purpose that combined history, prophecy and doctrine. Although the old and the new were composed at different times and circumstances 'like two faithful witnesses [they] verifie and confirm each others

[17] W. Lowth, *Directions for the profitable reading of the Holy Scriptures* (1708, 1726), iii–iv, 1–3.

[18] Lowth, *Directions*, 3–5, 6–7, 8–10.

testimony' for the coming of the messiah. One could read scripture for different purposes. The historical components had 'more of self evident truth than any history in the world'. Any obscurities could be resolved by learning and inquiry. Like many contemporaries, Lowth accentuated the role of hard work in the business of reading scripture. Some obscurity in scripture was designed to force us into inquiry, as he put it, 'to excite our industry in searching out divine truth, and make us receive it with joy, when we have discovered it'. Indeed the value of scripture truth was proportional to 'the labour we took in finding it out'. Reading with profit was hard work; it also involved the 'absolute' necessity of taking advice and counsel from clerical experts who had been placed by providence to aid the common reader. It was the greatest piece of enthusiasm for individuals to assume they had insight into scriptural difficulties without the 'help of study or human learning'. Submission and deference to the 'judgement' of those men 'who have made those studies their business and profession' was essential.[19] To benefit the ordinary reader, Lowth outlined a list of rules, starting with encouragement to read the plain books of the gospels first. While reading, one had to keep the analogy of faith in the forefront of one's mind, exercising caution in avoiding forced or contradictory interpretations. Comparing one place with another was another fundamental approach: scripture was deliberately repetitive so the reader could reconcile contradictions and familiarize oneself with the variety of scriptural idiom. Compounding deference to the interpretative agency of the contemporary church, the reader ought also to be reverential to the understanding of the primitive apostolic church. All controverted matters should be referred to the 'arbitration of the four first ages'. So, while Lowth subscribed to the protestant rhetoric of an open Bible, he also prescribed a series of complementary procedures that ensured the business of individual reading was closely circumscribed by the discipline of the established church. As he concluded, 'we ought to read the scripture with an humble, modest and teachable disposition'.[20]

The bulk of Lowth's *Directions* delivered particular recommendations concerning each individual book of scripture explaining where particular caution should be exercised. Comparative reading was sometimes appropriate to tease out the mystical from the literal reading. Many of the books of the Old Testament required 'careful perusal' to deduce the moral prescriptions from the text. As he explained the reader should 'fix his eye upon the principal design' of a book rather than 'lay hold on one single scrap or sentence'. By 'frequent reading and diligent perusal' religious instruction could be unlocked. Attention to the plain language of the gospels would lead to true faith: it was important to recall that 'Our saviour spoke with the plainness and majesty of a lawgiver, not with the niceness or subtilty of a philosopher'. When confronted with the variable accounts of the different gospels, it was important to remember that they simply related the 'same story with different circumstances'. Reading the Acts and epistles provided further witnesses to Christ's life and the providential propagation of the truth, as well as an 'authentick commentary' on

[19] Lowth, *Directions*, 27–30.

[20] Lowth, *Directions*, 30–34, 41.

the doctrinal content of the gospels. Lowth was insistent that a careful reading would provide the grounds for certain conviction in the truth of revealed religion. Those who argued that scriptural revelation was a faulty and uncertain instrument – what the deists term a 'clog to religion instead of a help' – were wrong. Such arguments misconstrued the competence of human reason which, despite being a device for understanding true doctrine, was debilitated. The 'natural blindness in things related to God' suggested that humans needed all the support in achieving religious understanding they could get. Reason was, as Lowth insisted (preserving himself from accusations of a 'popish' emphasis on mystery), the 'voice of God within us', but 'yet it is but a *still small voice,* and such as is scarce heeded, but by a listening and attentive ear'.[21] Here the shift of language from sight (associated with reading) to hearing (explanations from the Church) is significant. Lowth's short and small book was aimed at the ordinary reader, hoping to encourage good protestant reading, which simultaneously empowered the individual to examine the scriptural text, but to do so with the established interpretation at his or her elbow. This sort of reading avoided the dangerous extremes of enthusiastic rationalism and credulous ignorance.

The substance of works like Lowth's and Byfield's was that the harder one worked at excavating the true meaning of scripture the more likely one was to succeed. Fortunately in this view, the limited hermeneutic potential of the lay reader was to be perfected by the gifts of the established church. Certainly after the 1660s there was an increasing emphasis not just upon the pastoral efficiency of the established clergy, but on their learning. Much later, at turn of the century, Thomas Bray's ambitious project to ensure every parish had a library of religious tracts accessible to clergy and laity alike is one example of the emphasis on the role of learning in the public battle for edification. The idea of a learned church was a powerful cultural device for resisting the challenge of both Roman Catholicism and the fissiparous tendencies of Protestant dissent and the heterodox. Two of the most forceful proponents of clerical erudition were the Oxford figures Henry Dodwell and Thomas Barlow. Dodwell, the learned (non-juring) layman, and the successful churchman (Barlow became Bishop of Lincoln) produced between themselves two of the most influential and compelling descriptions of the duties of the cleric as scholar and teacher. Dodwell's *Two Letters of Advice* (1672), addressed to young clergymen, outlined the central duties of reading scripture, recalling that in the early days of Protestantism (under Edward VI and Elizabeth) Churchmen were obliged to read at least two chapters 'every day'. For Dodwell, correct understanding of scripture was driven by a dialogue between reading the 'original' and the historical tradition of commentators. He advised that, 'As you therefore read the scripture, it were well that after reading of any chapter you would mark the difficult places, at least in the New testament, and, when they may seem to concern any necessary matter of faith or practise … afterwards consult commentators'. The themes of careful reading and rigorous reflection were central to these directions: Dodwell suggested that after reading any commentary, the reader

[21] Lowth, *Directions*, 112, 117–20, 138–42, 148.

ought to 'recollect the sum of his discourse, by reducing them to propositions'. Reading, in this manner, produced the basic components of true belief. Having clarified such opinion the clergyman was instructed to return to the text of scripture itself again, 'and at last see how his sense agrees with the text itself'. Importantly this process was labelled 'critical learning'.[22]

For Dodwell, the Bible was a commonplace book for all other studies. Literally it was the starting point for all other enquiries. Understanding commenced by marking important passages in the margins of one's own bible. The reader made meaning from the text by comparison with parallel passages: important sections should be noted down in 'paper books prepared for that purpose'. The cultural mechanics for creating the foundations of public doctrine were bibliocentric in all senses of the word, because they focussed on the printed versions of scripture and a context of learned commentary.[23] Each clergyman, shaped by this process, became the legitimate source of theologically correct interpretation. These themes were central to Thomas Barlow's, influential and repeatedly revised, *de studio theologia* (1693, 1699) that, as befitted a former librarian of the Bodleian, displayed a profound expertise in biblical criticism.[24] The sole rule to a correct grasp of *theologia revelata* was study of the sacred scriptures which was to 'be understood by considering the text itself, and the true meaning of it'. Recommending that clergymen should own both testaments in Latin, Hebrew and Greek with full critical apparatus, Barlow identified the best editions: the octavo Greek New Testament published by Stephen Curcellus at Amsterdam in 1658 was excellent because 'it has the various lections, and parallel places, more exactly than any other I have seen; and yet the Robert Steph. edition has the various lections of 15 MSS'. Such scholarly apparatus was indispensable because it allowed the reader to collate the differences and variety of readings. Far from compromising the integrity of the sacred text, such learning enabled the critical reader to comprehend the variety of style and idiom in the originals. Consulting concordances and lexicons allowed the reader to check 'how many times the word occurs, and in what sense it is taken'. Exploring the 'circumstances' of key words (Barlow took 'faith' as an illustrative example) laid the foundation for the hermeneutic act. As Barlow explained, 'after the knowledge of words, (quae sunt rerum signa & indices) the next business will be to know the true sense of scripture signified by these words'. For this deeper stage of understanding, he emphatically insisted, 'you must consult commentators'. One did not follow these commentators blindly, but when in doubt about the meaning of a passage, the reader was encouraged to 'see what many learned men say of it; and then (by collation of them and others) judge what (or whether any) of their expositions be true'.[25] Again while the clerical reader was 'judge', they worked from materials shaped by a learned tradition. Concordances, lexicons, maps, chronologies, paraphrases, annotations were the basic components of

[22] H. Dodwell, *Two letters of advice* (1691), 27, 28, 30, 21, 232.

[23] Dodwell, *Two letters*, 232, 239.

[24] See R. Serjeantson (ed.), *Meric Casaubon. General Learning* (1999), 11–12.

[25] T. Barlow, *De studio theologiae* (Oxford, 1699) 3, 4, 5, 7–8, 9.

this encounter with scripture. Such learning was beyond the reach of most laypeople: the clergy therefore undertook critical work on behalf of their flock.

Barlow insisted that in this way regular and intense reading ensured revelation was 'imprinted on our minds'. Constant reading of the Bible 'with great application of mind' laid the foundation for true belief. Repeated encounter would acculturate the reader to the language and meaning: as Barlow explained 'various expressions will occur to our minds, and will suggest such thought to us as are to be had no other way'. Just like learning grammar as a child, the individual needed to absorb the 'phrases, and the series and order of events' by reading 'without stopping at every difficulty he meets with'. Importantly, such reading had to be active: the clerical reader 'must furnish himself with all variety of questions about religion, that he may know what to observe and enquire after'. Armed with a preset list of issues the individual then needed to display caution and care in engaging with the complex textual condition of the Bible. In order to understand any particular book, first one read it straight through a number of times 'then let him read it verse by verse and observe what the difficulties are, and try by the construction and signification of the words, and the sense of the Discourses' to make sense. After that, the instruction was, 'consult expositors'. In acknowledging that the process was 'laborious and slow' he also insisted that it was 'the most useful, and will be found at last the shortest way to true and substantial knowledge'.[26] Rooted firmly in the close examination of scriptural citation, this process of reading made a scriptural culture that created public beliefs (and thereby public authority) by the interaction between the printed text and the orthodoxy of interpretation defined by institutional hermeneutics. It was an elemental tension in Protestant scriptural politics that the printed Bible was accessible to all, yet a 'difficult' text to understand. Reading scripture was not simply a question of literacy (that is, the straightforward ability to read the work) but a hermeneutic skill. The cognitive ability to read the words on the page was not the same as being competent to understanding the divine meaning of those words. Those like Byfield, Lowth, Barlow and Dodwell, who produced works directing godly men (and infrequently women) into strategies for encountering the sacred text consistently reinforced these themes of the complexity and difficulty of a profitable reading of scripture.

The business of reading the Bible in the second half of the seventeenth century was a much more complicated activity than many historians have assumed. The physical activity of turning the pages and digesting the printed type was an experience that produced belief and conviction: it was a cognitive, epistemological and cultural act. Typically a reader from this period would encounter a very sophisticated printed Bible: using such a text required considerable practical guidance and instruction. Laid out upon the complicated typographical organisation of the page was a political hermeneutic that reflected the institutional authority of the Church of England. The individual read the text, but made meaning out of that experience, by an application of interpretative rules defined by the orthodox culture. The complexity

[26] Barlow, *De studio theologiae* 'A short method for the study of divinity', 75–9.

of this system of producing conviction was rendered even more intricate by the parallel developments of sacred erudition. As the flowering of late humanist biblical criticism became ever more central to the intellectual and confessional conflicts of the age, even the ordinary reader required instruction upon how to accommodate these findings. The critical problems produced by close scholarly analysis of the scripture also created theological implications not only for the status of revelation but by consequence raised issues about how one was to read the text. Despite these critical developments, reading scripture was still the starting point for intellectual enquiry: even the heterodox thinkers (from say Thomas Hobbes to Anthony Collins) laid the foundations of their systems of belief by rigorous dialogue with the Bible. In one very concrete sense, then, reading the Bible was at the heart of cultural change in the period. For mainstream Protestants careful reading was the means by which true faith was confirmed and propagated; for heterodox figures a similar practice of diligent and cautious reading prompted dissident beliefs. The reading strategies of one such dissident figure, John Locke, expose some of these distinctions.

III

Notoriously Locke broke controversial ground in his *Reasonableness of Christianity* (1695) by claiming that one only needed to read the gospels to achieve the fundamentals of a Christian truth. Central to this assertion was the belief that sincere reading was capable of discerning the clear meaning of revelation in the gospels alone. The remainder of the New Testament, although part of a divine mission, was not doctrinally necessary for conveying the fundamental components of the Christian faith. Whereas the gospels were designed to convey the simple and necessary proposition that Jesus was the messiah to the entire world, the *Epistles* were written on 'several occasions' for very specific audiences and circumstances. Such works required a different reading strategy: as Locke clarified, 'And he that will read them as he ought, must observe what 'tis in them is principally aimed at; find what is the argument in hand, and how managed; if he will understand them right, and profit by them'.[27] Locke's point, much expanded in the *Paraphrases*, was that understanding came by historical and contextual reading: 'The observing of this will best help us to the true meaning and mind of the Writer: For that is the Truth which is to be received and believed and not scattered sentences in Scripture-Language, accommodated to our Notions and Prejudices'. When reading the scripture one must 'look into the drift of the discourse' as opposed to culling out 'as best suits our system, here and there a period, or a verse; as if they were all distinct and independent aphorisms'. While there was only one universal fundamental truth necessary for saving belief, there were also many other 'Truths' in the Bible 'which a good Christian may be wholly ignorant of, and so not believe'. The mistake was to impose these other truths for 'fundamental articles'. The *Epistles* were composed for an audience who were 'in

[27] J. Higgins Biddle (ed.), *John Locke. The Reasonableness of Christianity* (Oxford, 1999), 164.

the Faith, and true Christians already', therefore one could not read them to learn 'Fundamental Articles and Points necessary to Salvation'. The 'occasional' truths were useful for edification but not conversion.[28] One should read different parts of scripture in different ways.

Locke expressed anxiety, both in private correspondence and his printed theological works, about the imposition of false, unnecessary and ultimately soteriologically useless interpretations on the laity by churchmen. In the *Reasonableness* Locke had shown how the gospels might be read to deliver saving belief; in the *Paraphrases* he showed how it was possible to read the *Epistles* in a constructive way. Working from autumn 1702, Locke probably sent Isaac Newton a draft of the work in May 1703, and indeed received feedback on the details of his understanding of 1 Corinthians 7:14.[29] In the preface to the printed volume, Locke addressed the issue of how any reader might understand the purpose of St Paul's letters. He admitted that 'though I had been conversant in these Epistles, as well as in other Parts of Sacred Scripture, yet I found that I understood them not'. There were a number of 'causes of obscurity' (note again that this is to be contrasted with the insistence on the clarity of meaning in the Gospels). The nature of 'epistolary writing' was a primary difficulty: as he explained, it was common that 'a well penn'd letter which is very easy and intelligible to the receiver, is very obscure to a Stranger, who hardly knows what to make of it'. The general difficulty of the Hebraic idiom of New Testament Greek was compounded by St Paul's idiosyncratic style and intellectual temper. The 'careful reader' would note many digressions ('large Parentheses'); the 'very attentive reader' would establish how 'the scatter'd parts of the discourse hang together in a coherent well-agreeing sense'; only the 'unwary, or over-hasty Reader' would be confounded by the complexity of Paul's arguments. Locke reiterated this emphasis upon attentive study, because 'if it be neglected or overlook'd will make the Reader very much mistake and misunderstand his meaning, and render the sense very perplex'd'.[30] The *Reasonableness* had suggested that the reader needed sincerity and care in order to comprehend the gospels; the *Paraphrases*, proposed a more dynamic account of the ideal 'reader'. In reading the epistles, the reader needed to forage meaning, to make connections, to work hard to contextualize statements. Unlike the gospels, the meaning of the epistles was not evident, manifest and clear: it was not enough simply to read and believe.

Locke's sensitive reaction to the stylistic and idiomatic complexities of St Paul's writings was compounded by an insight into the problems for readers prompted by the material form of the Bible. In this Locke displayed remarkable intuition about the relationship between the political implications of Biblical hermeneutics and the historical development of the printed Bible in Europe after the Reformation. As many scholars have argued, the evolution of the printed form of the protestant Bible was

---

[28] Higgins Biddle, *Reasonableness*, 165–6.

[29] E.S. De Beer (ed.), *The correspondence of John Locke*, vol. VI, no. 3287, 1–2; A.W. Wainwright (ed.), *John Locke: A Paraphrase and Notes* (Oxford, 1987), 4-5.

[30] Wainwright (ed.), *Paraphrase*, 103–4.

determined both by the potential for technological innovation and the imperative to provide a text suitable for evangelical persuasion and ecclesiastical authority. The Church of England needed a public scripture that both convinced readers to be devout believers, and in doing so, to acknowledge the authority of the established church to identify true doctrine. One of the ways in which the printed Bible had developed over the sixteenth and seventeenth centuries was the improvement of the bibliographical format to facilitate reading. Page numbers, chapter headings, marginal noted, cross references and concordances were all enhancements of the experience of reading. Put simply these aspects of the book made it easier to handle and read. As Locke pointed out, while indeed these developments facilitated reading, they did not necessarily enable understanding. It was his point that the way the printed Bible had been shaped was designed for a particular way of reading: it was one that privileged external systems of doctrine, rather than a focused engagement with the meaning of the text.

The greatest obstacle to proper reading (in Locke's view) was the division of scripture into chapters and verses, 'whereby they are so chop'd and minc'd, and as they are now Printed, stand so broken and divided'. The complaint was that 'not only the common people take the Verses usually for distinct aphorisms, but even men of more advanc'd knowledge in reading them, lose very much of the strength and force of the coherence, and the light that depends on it'. The very typographical way scripture was presented distorted the process of reading and understanding the 'Genuine sense of the Author'. The division of text disturbed the eye, such 'loose sentences … by their standing and separation, appear as so many distinct fragments'. The 'mind' of readers had become acculturated to this wrong impression from the 'cradle': most people were 'constantly accustom'd to hear them quoted as distinct sentences, without any limitation or explication of their precise Meaning from the place they stand in, and the relations they bear to what goes before, or follows'. The printed format encouraged reading 'by parcels and in scraps'. Although it has not been commonly recognized, Locke was, in fact, launching a fundamental attack upon the traditional Protestant counsel for reading the Bible. He condemned the practice of reading 'them Piecemeal, a Bit to day, and another scrap to morrow, and so on by broken intervals; especially if the pause and cessation should be made as the Chapters the Apostles Epistles are divided into do end sometimes in the middle of a Discourse, and sometimes in the middle of a sentence'. Such routine not only compromised the hermeneutic relationship between reader and text, but also underpinned a public culture of destructive citation amongst self interested parties who distorted scripture to their own ends. 'If a Bible was printed', claimed Locke, 'as it should be, and as several parts of it were writ, in continued Discourses where the argument is continued' there would be huge outcry by those who maintained their opinions 'and the system of parties by sound of words' rather than the 'true sense of scripture'. Just as Hobbes had complained about churchmen throwing 'atoms' of scripture like dust in the eyes of the laity to blind their understandings, so too did Locke remonstrate against those used scripture 'crumbled into Verses'. Men who 'snatched out a few Words … to serve a purpose' deviously appropriated sacred text 'for the Orthodoxie of his Church' rather than true belief.[31]

Distinguishing these contrary ways of reading scripture was critical for Locke. The 'sober inquisitive reader' when reading St Paul simply tried to understand 'what he meant' whereas the devious reader aimed to see in them 'what they pleased'. As he lamented, 'there are fewer that bring their opinions to the Sacred Scripture to be tried by that infallible rule, than bring the Sacred Scripture to their opinions, to bend it to them, to make it as they can a cover and Guard of them'. Because men had become familiar with the language of scripture, and internalised their own understandings of words used in society, they inevitably misconstrued the meaning of the Bible by applying anachronistic definitions. This hermeneutic distortion was not just a fault attributable to the laity but also to the learned. Even learned men of the calibre of Henry Hammond and Jean Calvin used scripture, not for 'trial, but for confirmation'. People tended to use only the expositors they agreed with or who received their brand of orthodoxy. Even those who sought help by indifferently looking 'into the notes of all commentators promiscuously', while to be commended for their admirable fairness, suffered the mischief of being distracted by a hundred competing accounts 'and so instead of that one sense of the Scripture they carried with them to their commentators, return from them with none at all'. There was, asserted Locke, a rule which would allow the reader to negotiate their way through the maze. He admitted that he had found great difficulty in understanding St Paul's epistles: 'the ordinary way of reading and studying them … left me almost every where at a loss'. The usual way of reading a chapter and then consulting the commentaries on the 'hard places … was not a right method to get into the true sense of these epistles'. Locke's proposed antidote to this fragmented experience was simple: 'to read the whole Letter through from one end to the other, all at once, to see what was the main subject and tendency of it'. Proposing a strategy that relied on reading the text, thinking about it and then re-reading it 'again and again', Locke claimed that it was possible to identify the meaning. Contrasting 'frequent perusal' with 'one or two hasty readings', Locke suggested that reading 'over, and over, and over again' would mean that by 'pains, judgement and application' coherence could be established. As he explained, having read the work 'all through at one sitting' he managed to observe the 'drift and design' of the work: subsequent reading saw an incremental increase in understanding 'till I came to have a good general view of the Apostle's main purpose'.[32]

The language used by Locke represented the business of reading as industry and effort: by labour and application (without the elevating input of priests or even faith) it was possible for the reader to understand. 'Lazy or ill disposed Readers' would fail to understand and fall into a 'superficial' account. Locke's defence of the efficacy of repeated encounter with scripture suggested that an 'attentive' disposition could achieve more than the learning of the Church and tradition. His advice was simple in summary, read carefully and compare passages: the *Paraphrases* was a practical

---

[31] Wainwright (ed.), *Paraphrase*, 105–7.

[32] Wainwright (ed.), *Paraphrase*, 109–10.

exemplar of this strategy. His ambition in reading St Paul had been to 'from his words [to] paint his very ideas and thoughts in our minds': until that was achieved 'we do not understand him'. This was not a claim to infallibility; he coyly condemned the desire to do so 'that would be to erect my self into an Apostle, a presumption of the highest nature in any one that cannot confirm what he says by miracles'. The argument defended in the *Letters* on toleration – that if I must believe for myself, I must understand for myself – was reiterated. There was no intention 'of imposing my interpretation on others': his own labour had produced 'reasons' which might carry 'light and conviction to any other Man's understanding'. Sincerely and sternly, Locke counselled that no interpretation should be followed 'beyond the evidence'. If men could each lay aside 'sloth, carelessness, prejudice, party and a reverence of men' they might find truth and salvation by earnest study of 'holy writings'.[33] Locke placed reading scripture right at the heart of the business of making Christian conviction.

IV

Locke forged his own views about the meaning of scripture in an almost compulsive relationship with the material word. His advice on methods of reading display the intellectual industry he devoted to reading, thinking, and discussing the meaning of particular passages and more complex theological problems. Despite Locke's public reassurance that he believed 'Jesus is the Messiah' many contemporaries (and subsequent historians) have doubted his orthodoxy. Clamorous accusations of 'Socinianism' against his work of the 1690s, indicted both his doctrinal treatment of Christ, and the application of 'reason' to scripture. Undoubtedly Locke knew a number of men of considerable heterodoxy and perhaps even impiety. His friendship with Benjamin Furley must have been seasoned with a frisson of danger. Connections with figures like Toland and Tindal also compromised his public reputation. However the evidence of his correspondence with clergymen like Phillip van Limborch, Jean Leclerc and Nicholas Toinard suggests that Locke found a variety of confessional approaches congenial. While it is clear that Locke did not read himself into heterodoxy, certainly he had friends who did. His relationship with Anthony Collins indicates that contact with an evidently heterodox friend was built around encounters with scripture and biblical criticism. Locke first wrote to Collins in May 1703, addressing him as a 'Philosopher and Christian'. Despite being in the 'decays and dregs' of his life, Locke enjoyed Collins' 'good company'. He also was 'exceedingly oblig'd' to the younger man for lending him various (unnamed) books. This exchange of letters persisted until the last weeks of Locke's life. Indeed Collins received his last letter posthumously.[34] It was one of the longest exchanges (some

---

[33] Wainwright (ed.), *Paraphrase*, 114–16.

[34] *Correspondence*, no. 3278, 776; no. 3648 written 23 August 1704 'to be delivered to him after my decease'; the last letter Locke sent him was no. 3640, 8 October 1704.

70 letters, only outnumbered by letters to and from Peter King) of the last months of his life.

From its initiation, the friendship between Collins and Locke was shaped by discussion of scripture and criticism. Collins regularly sought out particular editions of scripture ensuring with meticulous attention that the volume was bound to the precise instructions given by Locke. From their earliest exchanges Collins ran all sorts of errands for Locke – he carried drafts and corrections of the *Paraphrases* to printers and friends. He passed on, and received notes on, other people's books; he leant, sought out, bought and borrowed scarce and new volumes. Locke set very specific requirements about the quality of his Bibles: he sought after editions which were sturdy and useful, as he explained to Collins he wanted a 12° Bible (importantly without marginal notes) 'redy bound if you can find any one that is tolerably so for strength and use'. Gratefully, Locke acknowledged receipt, 'I thank you for the Bible you sent me. It is a good one of the kind. I wish I had another of them so bound as that you sent me and another of their ordinary binding but strong and that will open well'. This attention to the physical qualities of the binding and articulation of the page was shaped by Locke's ambitions for close study. In order to read carefully, to annotate, and to compare passages one needed a robust volume, easily opened and readily flipped backwards and forwards. By the end of his life Locke had a very clear view of the exact requirements, as he explained to Collins, 'The English one I desire may be very well bound in Calves Leather. Whereby I mean the top lines of the paper all set even of the same length, the margents all large, the pastboards strong, exceedingly well beaten, and so well sown and ordered in the back that it will lie open anywhere'. When his requests were ignored or executed incompetently Locke complained bitterly, so much so that Collins in one case prepared him for disappointment – concerning the Greek testament he had sent by a mutual friend (Peter King) Collins wrote 'I must prepare you to expect to see it not so well bound as it should be' (the binder had cut the margins too close, presumably reducing the amount of space for annotation or cross reference). Despite Collins's forewarning, Locke was incandescent with rage, offended by the running of the 'paring knife too deep into the margent, a knavish and intolerable fault in all our English bookbinders'.[35] Like others, Collins and Locke were very sensitive to the material quality of the Bibles they used because the physical book was a foundation for the extraction of intellectual truth.

In June 1704 Locke drew Collins into a greater intimacy with his own scriptural reading by inviting him to 'bestow some of your spare hours on the *Epistles to the Corinthians* and to try whether you can find them intelligible or no'. He warned, 'only permit me to tell you, you must read them with something more than an ordinary application'. Locke's intention was to encourage the younger man to prepare himself for a joint reading of his own *Paraphrases*. Collins did as instructed. He confirmed to Locke that 'I will employ all the leisure I have till I wait upon you to peruse 'em'. His reading strategy was not to entertain the discovery of any particular opinion in

[35] *Correspondence*, no. 3474, 217; no 3483, 232; no 3530, 287; no 3556, 314.

the text 'but only to endeavour to get the same ideas that the Author had when he wrote'.[36] This almost disinterested approach, allowing the text to speak for itself, was a close approximation to the sorts of advice and conduct Locke had adopted himself. As Locke explained to Peter King in late October 1704 (shortly before his death), he had originally undertaken the *Paraphrases* for his own private instruction, 'not in favour of any opinion I already had, but in search of what St Paul taught'. Recognising that his account might be novel or 'dissonant' from the commonplace interpretation, he proclaimed his 'indifferency'.[37] Whatever conclusions Locke drew from his repeated encounter with scripture, we can be certain that he had used his best judgement in refining his opinions, and also that he believed this procedure extracted divine truths from the text. Locke's approach to reading scripture was different (and evidently more intense) to that of his clerical contemporaries, he was still committed to a fundamentally 'inspired' understanding of the text. Close attentive reading was an instrument of revelation. For his young friend, Collins, such study led to very different consequences.

There is some irony in this image of Anthony Collins carefully preparing copies of the Bible for Locke's pious and sincere examinations given the reputation his own published works provoked. Collins continued his study of scripture after Locke's death. There is evidence to suggest that much of Collins's intellectual contribution was driven by his encounter with scripture. When Collins stayed with aristocratic friends like Lord Barrington it was reported that, 'as they were all men of letters, and had a taste for Scripture criticism, it is said to have been their custom after dinner, to have a Greek Testament laid on the table'. Presumably the volume was bound well enough to allow it to sit open for ease of joint reading. William Whiston reported in his memoirs that he commonly used to meet with Collins and others at the house of Lady Calverly and Sir John Hubern, for 'frequent but friendly debate about the truth of the Bible and the Christian religion'.[38] This tableau of men and women poring over the Bible, keen to make meaning is a central one to the cultural developments of the period. The Bible was in many hands, and read in different ways for different purposes. Whereas Locke read to discover the fundamental truths of the Christian religion, Collins read himself out of orthodoxy. Evidence of Collins's departure from prevailing attitudes is best illustrated in his first controversial work, *A discourse of freethinking* (1713). Traditionally this work has been regarded as part of an 'enlightened' canon that defended the rights of individual liberty of thought; in one sense a philosophical defence of the capacity and potential of human reason against the superstitious shackles of faith and religion. Considered in another way, it is possible to describe the work as a defence of a particular reading strategy. The 'right to think freely', as Collins made abundantly clear, could be reduced to a claim for the right to read without the infringements of institutional direction. Collins'

[36] *Correspondence*, no. 3565, 330; no. 3567, 322.

[37] *Correspondence*, no. 3647, 414.

[38] M. Pattison, 'Tendencies of religious thought', in H. Nettleship (ed.), *Essays* (Oxford, 1889), 70; J. O'Higgins, *Anthony Collins* (The Hague, 1970), 77.

advice was not simply an epistemological argument about the capacity of reason, but a cultural discussion, about how individuals attained opinions. Reading was a means of considering the evidence and establishing the meaning of a proposition: 'free trial, comparison and experience' were the processes by which people acquired practises and beliefs.[39]

The Bible was one of the most serious and profound sources for contemporary beliefs. It was, as Collins described it, 'a collection of tracts given us at divers times by God himself'. There was, he claimed, 'not, perhaps in the world, so miscellaneous a Book'. Because of its complexity, comprehension was a difficult business: 'to understand the matter therefore of this Book, requires the most thinking of all other Books'. One needed a range of skills and training in the 'rules of Art in Writing': languages, history, chronology, even mathematics, were prerequisites to competent reading. As Collins explained, 'Men are incapable of information either from Discourses or reading, unless they have accustom'd themselves to thinking, and by that habit are qualify'd to think of the subject whereon they hear or read a discourse'. Invoking Christ's command to 'search the scriptures', Collins insisted on the duty 'to endeavour to find out their true meaning'. Locke would have agreed, arguing that criticism was a constructive instrument for elucidating textual meaning. Collins exploited criticism to compromise the status of the book; after all 'the priests of all Christian Churches differ among themselves in each Church about copys of the same books of scripture; some reading them according to one manuscript, and others according to another'. Even if churchmen agreed on what version was authoritative, they inevitably differed endlessly 'in opinion about their sense and meaning'. There were a variety of ways of reading the Bible: the literal and the figurative, the contextual and the comparative. As he put it, 'comparing of places' discovered the 'ambiguity of words, variety of senses, alteration of circumstances, and difference of stile'. For Collins the imperative was to contradict the claims to interpretative competence advanced by the church: whereas the layman 'wants to know the truth … the Priest desires to have him of his opinion'.[40]

In the defence of freethinking, Collins had constructed an aggressive argument against the illegitimate claims of clerical hermeneutics. In his view neither human individuals nor clerical institutions could allege that they had the right to be guides for others. The later works on Christian prophecy extended these general attitudes into a focussed discussion of the difficulties of a variety of traditions of interpretation.[41] Like Locke, Collins condemned churchmen who applied their own values in distorting the supposed meaning of scriptural passages: allegorical readings of Old Testament prophecy were exposed as wiredrawn and chimerical. Indeed, in his discussion of how to understand the Pauline epistles, in *The scheme of literal prophecy* (1726), Collins deliberately invoked his friend's work in summarising:

[39] A. Collins, *A discourse of Freethinking* (1713), 5–6.

[40] Collins, *Freethinking* 10, 11–13, 14, 45, 54, 57–60, 109.

[41] See S. Snobelen, 'The argument over prophecy: an eighteenth century debate between William Whiston and Anthony Collins', *Lumen*, 15 (1996), 195–213.

'Paul ought not to be consider'd and interpreted like all other authors; from himself; from his use of words, and the connection of his discourse'.[42]

V

Writing in 1714, the controversial clergyman Samuel Clarke stated that 'the study of the scripture in the way of private judgement is not attended with any difficulty or discouragement, but on the contrary makes men orthodox'.[43] His own studies had led, notoriously, to doctrinal deviation in an account of the Trinity, and the threat of prosecution. Francis Hare, at this time, a close friend of Richard Bentley, in *The difficulties and discouragements which attend the study of the scripture in the way of private judgement* (1714) produced a satirical defence of both scriptural study and biblical criticism. The work is intriguing. French manuscript versions were circulated later in the century as heterodox texts.[44] Many contemporaries completely missed the ironic intention of the pamphlet and excoriated it as a dangerous piece of irreligion.[45] The capricious reaction (it was censured in Convocation too) to Hare's work is emblematic of the ambiguous and complex status of scriptural reading in the period. The starting point for his argument was that the business of 'thorough study' involved so many skills that it was beyond the reach of most people: it was he said, 'extremely difficult, and not to be successfully pursued, without a very great and constant application; and a previous knowledge of many other parts of useful learning'. It was absolutely necessary that a reader had a fluency in oriental, Greek and Latin languages: schoolboy learning was not enough. Parodying the argument from authority, which insisted the individual's incompetence always implied they should give way to the orthodoxy of the established church, Hare reiterated the fundamental protestant principle, 'that what ever is necessary to be believed, is plainly and clearly revealed in the scriptures; and consequently what is not plainly and clearly revealed cannot be necessary'.[46]

It was a commonplace anxiety amongst contemporaries that scriptural study ('free and impartial search into the literal sense of the scriptures') might destroy orthodoxy and produce heresy. Hare, far from condemning such enquiry, instead exposed the persecutory ambitions of those churchmen who wanted to prevent all private interpretation. Knowledge of the public doctrine ought not to qualify every

---

[42] A. Collins, *The scheme of literal prophecy* (1726), 352–3.

[43] S. Clarke, *An enquiry into the ill designs, errors etc. of Dr Clarke's (pretended) Scripture doctrine of the Trinity* (1714), 1.

[44] See A. McKenna, 'Un manuscript clandestin: Francis Hare, *Lettres sur les difficultés et découragements*' in *Les fruits de la dissention religieuse* (Université de Saint-étienne, 1998), 85–126.

[45] See for example, *Some brief remarks on a late pamphlet* (1714), supposedly written by 'A divine of the church of England'.

[46] F. Hare, *The difficulties and discouragements which attend the study of the scripture in the way of private judgement* (1714), 5, 6–8,13–14.

churchman to 'judge over the learnedest man alive'. Reiterating the protestant principle that every one had 'a right to study and judge of the scriptures for themselves', Hare drew a distinction between those clear parts of scripture which taught necessary truths, and the more obscure passages where understanding was simply a matter of opinion.[47] This is not to suggest Hare supported the 'freethinking' arguments of men like Collins: despite being associated with the new Hanoverian regime (he was a royal chaplain) he resisted the Erastian radicalism of Benjamin Hoadly's assault upon clerical power during the Bangorian Crisis in the name of ecclesiastical authority. The same routines of reading and study could produce private convictions as different as those held by John Locke, Anthony Collins and Henry Dodwell. The function of scriptural reading was protean. From one perspective, it was a shared and commonplace experience over which the Protestant state attempted to establish a measure of cultural discipline. In another context, it was a practice that unhinged private belief from public orthodoxy. In both cases there was a similar approach to the business of reading the Bible – industry, diligence, caution and application were what any reader was expected to display in order to extract plausible and true meaning. The fact that some readers confirmed their commitment to orthodoxy as a result of this activity, and others ended up on the margins of heterodoxy, is compelling evidence that the historical role of reading (rather than simply literacy) had a complicated relationship with cultural change in the period. The first evidences of 'enlightenment' can be seen then, in the intensive study of scripture, rather than the application of reason to faith.

---

[47] Hare, *Difficulties and discouragements*, 28, 33–4, 44–6.

Chapter 12

'I resolved to give an account of most of the persons mentioned in the Bible': Pierre Bayle and the Prophet David in English Biblical Culture.[1]

Alex Barber

In 1761 an anonymous pamphlet entitled *The History of the man after God's own heart* was published by R. Freeman.[2] The pamphlet complained of 'some reverend panegyrists' who had been fond of comparing the late King George II 'with a monarch in no respect resembling him'.[3] The monarch that King George was being compared to was David. The author went on to note that the primary reason for this comparison was due to the lucky coincidence that the duration of both monarchs reign had been thirty-three years. This comparison of George II with David had clearly caused the author great distress and there seemed only one way to deal with it. He would have to trouble the world with a 'new history of David'. because ostensibly he believed that David was not worthy of comparison with the recently deceased British monarch.[4]

This comparison between George II and David demonstrates the continuing cultural authority of the Bible into the mid-eighteenth century. There is little doubt that Christian polemicists had often utilized King David as an authoritative figure

---

[1] Pierre Bayle, *An Historical and Critical Dictionary*, 2nd volume, Preface, (London, 1710). I am grateful to Anthony McKenna, Justin Champion, Gianluca Mori, Nicholas Keene and Ariel Hessayon for their advice in writing this essay.

[2] John Noorthouck, *The History of the man after God's own heart,* (London, 1761).

[3] Ibid., v. Cf. William Boulton, *A sermon preached in the Baptist Meeting House, in Swift's Alley,* (London, 1760); Thomas Gibbons, *A Sermon Occasioned by the sudden Decease of his late Most Excellent and Gracious Majesty George the Second,* (London, 1760); John Palmer, *King David's death and Solomon's succession to the throne, considered and improved, in a sermon, occasioned by the Death of His late Majesty, King George the Second,* (London, 1760).

[4] Noorthouck, *History,* v.

with which to fortify monarchical authority.[5] Of course this was not simply using the Bible as a form of historical persuasion. Rather, invoking David's name was to comment upon divine providence itself. As Gerard Reedy has pointed out, in seventeenth-century England relating Scripture to a 'secular polity' involved a 'typology'.[6] In attempting to compare monarchs with David authors were thus establishing their attitudes to divine providence itself. Consequently, they were also asserting that providence had been instrumental in the nation receiving an elect leader. As the general historiographical consensus has been that such occurrences were on the decline as early as the 1680's, this typology occurring in the 1760s seems unusual.[7]

Though Cromwell had been transformed into a Davidic king – notably in the later poems of Andrew Marvell, it was with the coronation of Charles II in 1661 that the identification of England's ruler with David seems to have reached its zenith. Perhaps the most significant example was George Morley's sermon. Morley, a skilful diplomat who had been with the Royal court in exile, fully utilized this opportunity to assert the King's authority. This was no abstract oration, but a bid for political dividends. Morley was quick to suggest that those who had usurped the previous monarch were against the public good. These people were 'incensed and transported by their own passions, beyond all rules and bounds of religion, of reason, of modesty, of common honesty, nay of humanity itself'.[8] Moreover, he likened the usurpers to those who 'blew a trumpet and said; we have no part in David, neither have we any portion in the Son of Jesse'.[9]

Having attacked those who had sought to undermine the monarchy Morley set about demonstrating a positive connection between Charles II and David. At times this was not subtle: Morley simply proposed that 'our David will do as the other David tells us he did, he will rule us prudently with all his power. Psalm, 78. 71.'[10] Alongside political and cultural benefits Morley believed that God had specifically ordained David's actions. Monarchy was an establishment that was successful by succession because it was by 'divine institution'. Thus Saul and David derived their office from 'God himself'.[11] Indeed, Psalm 101 expressly contained all

[5] For the use of Davidic comparisons throughout the early modern period see Diarmaid MacCulloch, *Reformation Europe's House Divided 1490–1700,* (London, 2003).

[6] Gerard Reedy, *The Bible and Reason. Anglicans and Scripture in Late Seventeenth-Century England,* (University of Philadelphia Press; Philadelphia, 1985), 66.

[7] W. Neil, 'The Criticism and Theological Use of the Bible, 1700–1950' in S.L. Greenslade (ed.), *The Cambridge History of the Bible: Volume 3, The West From Reformation to the Present Day* (Cambridge, 1963).

[8] George Morley, *A Sermon preached at the magnificent coronation of the most high and mighty King Charles II,* (London, 1661), 14.

[9] Ibid., 14.

[10] Ibid., 29.

[11] Ibid., 20.

the advice that the new monarch needed to govern 'himself, his family, and his Kingdoms'.[12]

What is convincing in this discussion is the notion that the right of the monarchy was not only set out by providence but that evidence to support this could be found in a literal interpretation of Scripture. Thus not only was David divinely inspired but he was also a great and moral King. Undoubtedly providential theories of monarchy had longevity. John Morphew re-issued Morley's sermon in 1714 and the theory could be appropriated by both Whigs and Tories throughout the eighteenth century.[13] By 1760, however, major change had taken place. The author of *The History of the man after God's own heart* was attacking not George II as ungodly, but David. As he announced in the preface, he was convinced that the comparison with David was insulting to 'the memory of the British monarch'.[14]

To prove this he needed to write a new and complete history of David in which he would carry out a thorough investigation not only of David's life but the Bible itself. Acknowledging that he would find incontestable facts in the Old Testament, he also foresaw two problems:

I. The broken unconnected manner in which the Jewish history is transmitted down to us: which renders it impossible to give a complete narrative of any period in it.

II. The partial representation of it, as being written by themselves.[15]

The author understood that this was likely to give offence. Indeed, he was prepared for it to 'excite the indignation of many worthy persons against him, whose zeal may catch fire'.[16] While recognizing that he was discussing sacred history, the author nonetheless proceeded to argue that he should be allowed to examine the Bible with the same freedom 'which is used in reading Tacitus, Rollin or Rapin'.[17] Nor was he taking liberties with biblical writers, since 'the authority of the Lord, so continually quoted to sanctify every transaction related, constituted for the most part, nothing more than national phrases'.[18]

This pamphlet seems to illustrate a contradictory eighteenth-century attitude to Scripture: the freedom to criticize the historical truth in the Bible while recognizing its continuing religious and political authority. This does not suggest the advance of a secular attitude to scripture championed by the Deist cause of the Radical Enlightenment. However, it does illustrate the growing ambiguity of the Bible's authority caused by a century of biblical criticism. The work of Thomas Hobbes's *Leviathan* and Benedict de Spinoza *Tractatus* are well-known examples of radical

---

[12] Ibid., 30.

[13] J.C.D. Clark, *English Society 1660–1732. Religion, ideology and politics during the ancien regime,* (Cambridge, 2000), 111.

[14] Noorthouck, *History*, vi.

[15] Ibid., xi.

[16] Ibid., xiii.

[17] Ibid., xii.

[18] Ibid., xiii.

attacks on the authority of Scripture.[19] However, John Locke, Richard Bentley and John Leland also counsel against the view that Scripture was a simple choice between a historical book and divine revelation. Biblical criticism patently had many different guises and by the 1750s and 1760s the ambiguity of Scripture in this pamphlet exchange was testament to this.

Of all the authors mentioned above perhaps Pierre Bayle is the most obvious omission; both in terms of his influence on biblical criticism in England during the eighteenth century and the fact that he seems to perfectly illustrate the Scriptural ambiguity described above.[20] Bayle's influence is little understood in seventeenth and eighteenth century England because of the complexity of his work.[21] The publication and reception of his work on Comets has been virtually ignored, but it is understanding Bayle's Dictionary that has proved to be the most challenging.[22] First published in four volumes in England in 1710 and later published in two rival editions of 1734, it is a work of astonishing erudition and authority.

Bayle's representation of Scripture has divided historians as it did contemporaries. Recent studies of the Dictionary have begun to suggest that the manner in which the book was read was as important as the content of the work.[23] The Dictionary obliged the reader to consider his Bible in an intricate and thoughtful way. The article on David consists of text with marginalia containing biblical references, and footnotes displayed at the bottom of the page. Within the footnotes are further remarks that

[19] Benedictus de Spinoza, *A Treatise partly theological and partly political,* (London, 1689). In particular see Chapter IX where Spinoza uses the narration of David and Goliath in manner similar to Bayle, making that point that the bible was written by many different hands. Thomas Hobbes, *Leviathan,* (London, 1651). Hobbes uses the book of David liberally; see in particular Chapters XXXIII and XXXVII.

[20] For a recent survey of the historiography on Pierre Bayle see D. Wootton 'Pierre Bayle, libertine' in M.A. Stewart (ed.), *Studies in seventeenth century European philosophy* (Oxford, 1997).

[21] J. Dunn, 'The Claim to Freedom of Conscience: Freedom of Conscience: Freedom of Speech, Freedom of Thought, Freedom of Worship?' in Ole Grell, Jonathan Israel and Nicholas Tyacke (eds), *From Persecution To Toleration, The Glorious Revolution in England,* (Oxford, 1991), 188. For England see L.P. Courtines, *Bayle's relations with England and the English* (Columbia, 1938).

[22] Pierre Bayle, *Miscellaneous reflections, occasion'd by the comet which appear'd in December 1680 ... Written to a Doctor of the Sorbon,* 2 vols (London, 1708).

[23] J.A.I. Champion, 'Most truly ... a protestant: reading Bayle in England' in Anthony McKenna and Gianni Paganini (eds), *Pierre Bayle dans la République des lettres: philosophie religion critique* (Paris, 2004). There is ample evidence that the way in which the Dictionary was read was important in the 1720s and 1730s in England, see *The Life of Joseph Addison, Esq.; Extracted from No. III. And IV. of the General Dictionary, Historical and Critical,* (London, 1733); Pierre Des Maizeaux, *An Historical Account of the Life and Writings of the Ever-Memorable Mr. John Hales* (London, 1719); *An Historical and Critical Account of the Life and Writings of William Chillingworth* (London, 1725).

refer to cited works in marginalia.[24] Both the 1710 and 1734 versions follow this standard with a few slight variations. While consistent it was also complex. Although the entry on David only ran to some four pages, the reader was faced with nine footnotes, 24 biblical references in marginalia and a further 31 references in the footnotes directing him to other books or journals. This was some 64 references to consider if the work was to be read in its entirety completing and checking all sources.

Certainly in terms of reading the work for biblical criticism these marginalia were highly important. The reader could simply consider the main text with a Bible adjacent. He could then easily refer to the main body of the text and simply cross-reference to the Bible he was working from. The effect is dynamic, but when read the Bible consulted becomes secondary to the Dictionary since the reader is expected to start with the Dictionary and work towards the Bible. The reader can think about the fluent and simple argument in the Dictionary, but is expected to move in and out of the Bible while considering the arguments and criticisms of Bayle's work. This method is not a disguised method. It is, rather, a physical quality of reading that links the text to a physical idea of biblical criticism. In the process the Bible has effectively been demoted to a secondary text.

It is often in the footnotes that historians have sought the unorthodox, for it is here that impious ideas could be hidden. Yet this has been challenged in two ways. Firstly, it is unlikely that Bayle would have contemplated this; the censors were erudite theologians who would have easily found impiety in the Dictionary. Secondly, this is often a distortion handed down to historians by the philosophes of the High Enlightenment.[25] The footnotes were, however, highly important to Bayle's work. In the discussion that follows what will be demonstrated is that English respondents to Bayle often found the footnotes the most intriguing aspect of the Dictionary to dispute with.

In his reading of Bayle's *Pensées Diverses Sur la Comete* John Robertson has recently suggested that Bayle's notion of divine providence rested on the absolute truth of Scripture.[26] It is worth considering the reception of the David article in terms of this important idea. Indeed, this essay contends that Bayle's article did tap into the Bible's ambiguous nature throughout the eighteenth century. As Walter Rex points out, there is little doubt that the article on David is not a balanced one, magnifying 'certain selected incidents at the expense of a multitude of others'.[27] This

---

[24] H.H.M. Van Lieshout, *The Making of Pierre Bayle's Dictionaire Historique et Critique* (Amsterdam, 2001), 69.

[25] Walter Rex, *Essays on Pierre Bayle and Religious Controversy* (The Hague, 1965), 202.

[26] Pierre Bayle, *Various Thoughts on the Occasion of a Comet* (trans. Robert C. Bartlett, New York, 2000); John Robertson, 'Vico's idolatrous giants: the New Science as a refutation of Bayle', unpublished paper, IHR, 10 November 2004.

[27] Walter Rex, *Essays on Pierre Bayle and Religious Controversy* (The Hague, 1965), 235.

essay reflects the culture of reception to Bayle's thoughts, which itself reflects the precarious nature of Bayle's ideas on Scripture.

Bayle does provide the reader with an overt explanation of his attitude concerning Scripture in his *Philosophical Commentary*. On Luke 14 he declares 'I shall go upon this principle of natural reason; that all literal construction, which carries an obligation of committing iniquity, is false'.[28] As Ruth Whelan has shown, there is no doubt that Bayle's attitude to Scripture was complex and changed throughout his life.[29] However, it is this very ambiguity coupled with the complex text of the Dictionary that leads to such varied and stringent responses to Bayle. The tension in Bayle's thought on Scripture between reason and faith is nowhere more evident than in the article on David. Bayle belongs to a generation of scholars that are 'typified by an ambivalence to the biblical criticism they publicly profess to abhor'.[30] The inconsistency of Bayle's thought processes are reflected in the multiple English comments that considered him the master of the paradox.[31]

Returning to *The History of the man after God's own heart* (1761), more nuanced contemporary readings would have discerned Bayle's influence although he is only mentioned once in the text; 'I own that I subscribe to the opinion of Monsieur Bayle, who looks upon this but as another detail of the adventure at En-gedi'.[32] Thus the title alludes to the first line of Bayle's article on David, where he had commented that David was 'one of the greatest men in the world, even though we should not consider him as a Royal Prophet, who was after God's own heart'.[33] Moreover, the comment that the history of David was broken and unconnected has clear resonance to Bayle, who suggested in footnote K that Moreri had given David the wrong age when he was anointed. Bayle subsequently observed that one narrative is used to relate two different events in David's life. To him the explanation is obvious: 'I should make no difficulty to believe that it is one and the same thing, which having been reported two different ways, served for the subject of two Articles or of two chapters'.[34]

The authorship of this anonymous pamphlet has been disputed. The most prevalent attitude in England has been to attribute the book to John Noorthouck, a contributor to the *Monthly Review* and author of *A New History of London* (1773). This seems unlikely as his career seems to show no other taste for theological and political dispute.[35] Peter Annet appears a more likely candidate. A religious controversialist,

[28] Pierre Bayle, *A Philosophical Commentary* (London, 1708), 44.

[29] Ruth Whelan, *The Anatomy of Superstition: a study of the historical theory and practice of Pierre Bayle* (Oxford, 1989), Chapter 6.

[30] Ibid., 148.

[31] See for example *Reflections on man and his relation to other beings* (London, 1733), 96 'one may easily judge what design Mr. Bayle advanced so bold a paradox'.

[32] Noorthouck, *History*, 32. This comment is adjusted in the second edition of 1764 to read 'The opinion of Monsieur Bayle seems most probable concerning this adventure'.

[33] Bayle, *Dictionary*, 2nd vol., 1059.

[34] Ibid., 1062.

[35] New Oxford Dictionary of National Biography 'John Noorthouck (1732–1816)'. English Short Title Catalogue suggests that Noorthouck claims he wrote the book on

he disputed with Bishop Sherlock and wrote several other works attacking biblical figures.[36] There are similarities between them and the book on David, notably where Annet suggested that 'David found out a way to sanctify the murder of the remaining family of Saul'.[37] This theme runs throughout *The History of the man after God's own heart*. Voltaire thought the work written by Annet, as did nineteenth-century authors.[38]

The controversy surrounding the work on King David provides the historian with a picture of the cultural reception of Bayle and his work. The work of Annet in replying to the multitude of sermons binding David to George II caused a major pamphlet debate in which writers now recognized the Baylean influence that Annet had previously alluded to.[39] This uproar seems primarily to have been caused by Samuel Chandler's review of Annet's work.[40] Chandler was a dissenting minister although he is described as being much closer to the Anglican Church than many dissenters.[41] He was a prolific author and in an attack on the Catholic Church of 1735 had stated that the Holy Scriptures were 'the most ancient records of Christianity, written by the apostles and apostolical men; and because they are, even our adversaries being judges, the infallible word of God'.[42] He added that the Catholic Church had no right to 'judge … the sense of scripture'.[43]

Chandler as one of the panegyrists named by Annet took the opportunity to reply to the new history of David in 1762.[44] The review refutes completely Annet's representation of David and suggests that he has completely misrepresented the views of those who preached the original sermons. Though Chandler offers a nuanced dissection of Annet's work he does not deny him the right to interpret the Scriptures

---

David in his unpublished biography. Unfortunately I have been unable to verify this. John Noorthouck, *Noorthouck's Life. Written with his own hand*, Autograph MS 1780, Yale Osborn Shelves *c* 474.

[36] Peter Annet, *The Resurrection of Jesus demonstrated to have no proof* (London, 1744) and *The History and Character of St Paul examined* (London, 1750).

[37] Peter Annet, A *Collection of the tracts of a certain free enquirer, noted by his sufferings for his opinions* (London, 1750), 163.

[38] Ella Twynam, *Peter Annet 1693–1769,* (London, 1938), 7; Julian Hibbert, *A Dictionary of Modern Anti-Superstitionists* (London, 1826).

[39] For examples see William Cleaver, *An Inquiry into the true Character of David King of Israel* (Oxford, 1762); Thomas Patten, *King David Vindicated From A Late Misrepresentation of His Character* (London, 1762); Beilby Porteus, *The Character of David King of Israe,* (Cambridge, 1761).

[40] *The library: or, Moral and critical magazine, for the year MDCCLXII. By a Society of Gentlemen*, vol. II, 262.

[41] New Oxford Dictionary of National Biography 'Samuel Chandler (1693–1796)'.

[42] Samuel Chandler, *The notes of the church considered* (London, 1735), 3.

[43] Ibid., 5.

[44] Samuel Chandler, *A Review of the History of the man after God's own Heart* (London, 1762) [BL, 4804 bb36 has MS. Notes by John Noorthouck]. Annet's *History of the Man after God's Own Heart* is also heavily annotated [BL, 4825 aa9]. I hope to complete research on these annotations in a future article.

and to carry out an investigation into David's character.[45] Indeed, Chandler accepts that Annet has a right to consider David's reputation as long as he carried out the investigation with 'prudence and candour'.[46] He was, however, offended by Annet's depiction: he 'abuses him, calls him the most infamous names, sometimes sets him up as an object of ridicule, sometimes as an object of detestation and horror'.[47]

Chandler's review is not simply a critique of Annet's work, but a new portrayal of David's life. It is revealing for the penetration of scriptural criticism that Chandler needed to justify some of the concerns with writing a new life. He posits a twofold answer as to why the new life is difficult. Firstly, 'the history of David, in many of the transactions of his life, is very short and extremely imperfect. Facts are often times but barely mentioned, without the causes of them or circumstances attending them; in all which cases it must be difficult to pass the proper judgement on them'.[48] Secondly, Chandler notes that 'allowances should be made for the different circumstances of times and nations, their particular constitutions and forms of government'.[49] The literary consequences for Chandler were that the critic should avoid extremity when considering David; and 'I think the historian should equally refrain from much encomium and invective'.[50]

This discussion has some interesting repercussions. Rex has argued that Bayle wrote in the idiom of Calvinist understanding of David's actions in Old Testament history. Calvinists recognized David's crimes and did not try to excuse them. They also argued that David had true faith that could be detected in 'his admirable acts of repentance, in his many virtues as a ruler and in the piety of the Psalms'.[51] There is no doubt that many saw Bayle's article on David as relentless in its ability to undermine both David and the authority of Scripture. However, Chandler seems not to have taken this view. In this we can see not only the ambiguity with which people often received Bayle, but also that the way in which the Dictionary was read.

As Chandler is prepared to accept that there is a historical context to David's failings he consequently tends to not only appropriate authority to the main text of Bayle's article, but also to openly direct the reader to the footnotes. While suggesting that Annet is ignorant in the way that he contradicts the testimony of biblical historians, he allows that Bayle does not 'descend to reviling and scandal'.[52] Chandler reflects that Bayle shows David respect and 'allows him to be one of the

[45] Ibid., viii.

[46] Ibid., x.

[47] Ibid., xi.

[48] Ibid., xiii. In the collected volume of replies this section is annotated 'it is absolutely impossible to find adequate causes for some facts'.

[49] Ibid., xiii. Again this section is annotated although unfortunately too much has been cropped for an adequate translation to be offered.

[50] Ibid., xiii.

[51] Walter Rex, *Essays on Pierre Bayle and Religious Controversy* (The Hague, 1965), 207.

[52] Chandler, *Review*, xi.

greatest men that ever lived'.[53] This reflection of Bayle is taken from the main text of the work.[54] Chandler notes in a footnote that Bayle has argued 'David, King of the Jews, was one of the greatest men in the world, even though we should not consider him as a royal prophet, who was after God's own heart ... David's piety is so shining in his Psalms, and in many of his actions, that it cannot be sufficiently admired'.[55] This is an appropriation of two different sections of the main text by Chandler, suggesting that his approach to the Bible led him to often consider the main text of the Dictionary as the primary location in which to garner information.

In essence Chandler is sufficiently convinced of Bayle's sincerity that he is not prepared to question Bayle's 'real sentiments'.[56] This is motivated by his reading of Bayle ascribing piety to David. Furthermore, he recognizes that while Bayle may deride the prophet, he gives reasons for David's behaviour because he has a 'fatality, to which human nature itself is liable'.[57] Though unhappy about the effect of some of the footnotes on the position of David, there is no suggestion that he should occlude this impiety from the reader. When discussing Bayle's historical method in comparing David's actions to that of a modern day monarch, Chandler openly directs the reader to note D in the Dictionary.[58] Yet even here he is not prepared to completely attack Bayle's sincerity. If David was harsh it was justified 'by the customs of nations'.[59]

Chandler's approach to the authority of Scripture affected not only the way that he physically read Bayle but also the way in which he represented that physicality of reading to his own readers. He believed Bayle was misguided to compare the morality of the ancient world with that of the eighteenth century, but he was not ultimately impious – as shown by the main text of the Dictionary. When considering the footnotes, he found not hidden impiety but complementary comments to the main text. He also condemned Annet for appropriating Bayle, commenting that he is little more than a 'retailer ... of David's bad conduct', though he lacked 'Mr. Bayle's decency and good manners'.[60]

It is clear from the reactions to Annet's work that a number of authors in the 1760s were still sufficiently protective of the authority of scripture that they quickly sought to reply in print. It is apparent from these replies that there was a fair degree of cultural penetration for Bayle's Dictionary. Despite barely mentioning him, all of the replies to Annet recognize Bayle as one of his central sources. However, in

---

[53] Ibid., ix.

[54] Bayle, *Dictionary*, 2nd vol., 1059.

[55] Chandler, *Review*, xi, footnote *. The actual quote from Chandler is in French and refers to Pierre Bayle, *Dictionnaire Historique et Critique* (Rotterdam, 1697), 923 and 926. The quotes in English are Bayle, *Dictionary*, 2nd vol., 1059 and 1061.

[56] Chandler, *Review*, xi.

[57] Ibid., xi.

[58] Ibid, xiv.

[59] Ibid., xviii.

[60] Ibid., xxxvii, xxxvi.

these replies both the cultural authority of Bayle and the confusion surrounding his attitude to scripture can be discerned.

I

In 1755 Thomas Patten, Church of England clergyman, published a sermon. It was primarily a comment on the need of Christians to engage in theological disputes with infidels. Patten reinforced this by arguing that reason could not be a ready excuse with which to attack scripture commenting that there was a 'vanity of unbelievers'.[61] Where then did Bayle fit into this scheme? Although a sceptic, Bayle was not to be categorized with all of these infidels. Rather, he was capable of boasting that 'no question could occur, of which he was not able to defend either side with equal appearance of probability'.[62] Therefore it appears that Patten had a difficult relationship with Bayle's work. He was certainly aware that Annet was utilising Bayle and disagreed with Bayle's point of view acknowledging the 'ridiculous conceit which our author hath adopted, after Bayle'.[63] It seems Bayle was not at fault for such exploitation for Patten had satisfied himself that Bayle did not believe this point of view. Instead, Patten suggests that Annet had fallen for Bayle's tricks placed in the Dictionary. Bayle could be 'smiling to himself, while he was dressing this awkward, ill-favoured paradox; but little suspecting that so brisk a genius as our author, would ever fall so desperately in love with it'.[64] Both Beilby Porteus and William Cleaver continue this theme of attacking much of the analysis of David's life in the Dictionary and yet defending Bayle. Porteus comments that 'the most material part of his objections are borrowed from Mr Bayle; and it would have been well, if he had borrowed one thing more from him, his decency'.[65] Cleaver recognizes that Annet 'reveres and copies' Bayle, yet also argues that Bayle is eminently 'superior'.[66]

Whilst Chandler, Porteus, Cleaver and Patten's analysis of the Dictionary left room for some sincerity to be ascribed to Pierre Bayle over the David article and therefore to the whole nature of the Dictionary, Patrick Delany's work certainly did not. An Irish divine, he was on friendly terms with Swift and may have shared his Tory political inclination.[67] By the 1730s he was considered to be 'the most eminent

---

[61] Thomas Patten, *The Christian Apology. A sermon preached before the University of Oxford* (Oxford, 1755), 11.

[62] Ibid., 14.

[63] Thomas Patten, *King David Vindicated From A Late Misrepresentation of His Character* (London, 1762), 52.

[64] Ibid., 53.

[65] Beilby Porteus, *The Character of David King of Israel* (Cambridge, 1761), iii.

[66] William Cleaver, *An Inquiry into the true Character of David King of Israel* (Oxford, 1762), 12.

[67] Harold Williams (ed.), *The Correspondence of Jonathan Swift* (Oxford, 1963), vol. III, 144.

preacher we have' in Ireland and was regularly publishing work – much of it concerned with scripture. Indeed, in his comment on the state of the country in 1732 he had suggested that ill taste in the country was primarily caused by 'the strange astonishing contempt into which the Scriptures (the noblest of all writings this world was ever blessed with) have fallen for some years past'.[68] Delany explicitly argued that the use of Scripture was essential for understanding true religion. He perceived that two important and connected ideas had taken hold: men had been discouraged from studying the Scriptures, and they had lost their reverence for it.[69]

In 1740 he published his work on David. It appears to have gained some popularity – the first edition was soon followed by an Irish version of the same year. By 1745 it had been published three more times, with a fourth edition in 1759. The work ran to some three volumes and directly engaged with the controversy surrounding David's reputation. Delany was keen to emphasize that his work was not merely a hypothetical exegesis. His intention was to supply 'the light and libertine reader with matter of information and entertainment' and to avoid 'all imputation of offence and demerit with the serious, the learned, the reasonable and religious'.[70] Additionally, early in the book he surmises that this project is not merely to construct a historical project. Rather, when he considers the history of David he is also considering the 'history of the divine Providence, during the life and reign of that prince'.[71] This was significant for the Baylean project had expertly interposed in the orthodox debate concerning the prophets. Could their moral behaviour have resonance for the contemporary world? Or should their behaviour be contextualized to their period thus allowing their behaviour to be explained away?

For Delany, David's life was crucial because the world he lived in was providential. Indeed, if the reader could be induced to read his Bible correctly he would be able to witness 'the wisdom of GOD interposing, superintending, swaying and conducting them all to the purposes of his adorable Providence'.[72] In essence Delany sought to link his ideas of providence directly to the account of David in the Bible and then to the reader. If people could read the life of David in the correct way they would find a means to understand their moral duties in life; 'he will learn what degree of favour, support and success, he himself is to hope for from the divine Providence, in the upright and conscientious discharge of his duty'.[73]

---

[68] Patrick Delany, *The Present State of Learning, Religion, and infidelity in Great-Britain* (Dublin, 1732), 6. For Delany's continued interest in the bible see Patrick Delany, *Revelation Examined with Candour* (Dublin, 1732).

[69] Ibid., 9.

[70] Patrick Delany, *An Historical Account of the Life and Reign of David, King of Israel. Interspersed with Various Conjectures, Digressions and Disquisitions. In which (among other things) Mr. Bayle's Criticisms upon the conduct of that Prince are fully considered* (London, 1740) v.

[71] Delany, *David*, v.

[72] Ibid., vi.

[73] Ibid., vii.

In 1734 the Dictionary was republished under completely different terms.[74] The article on David was significantly altered. It is noteworthy that the early publishing history of the Dictionary on the continent had caused the authorities to specifically target the David article as heretical. Bayle was forced to amend much of it for republication. However, in the 1710 publication in England the original article on David was reproduced. Up until the 1730s there was little reaction it, but with the publication in 1736 of Volume IV of the Dictionary Delany demonstrates the renewed interest in Bayle's work on David.[75]

This edition was significantly less favourable to Bayle. Not only did the editors seek to add thousands more lives so that the work was more relevant to England, they also added 'reflections on such passages of Mr. Bayle, as seem to favour Scepticism and the Manichee System'.[76] Though James Marshall Osborn has commented on the technical and authorial aspect of this new edition, there has been little research on how this edition affected the reception of Bayle in England. Effectively the article on David became less complex. The reader no longer had to consider the whole work since the editors had provided an easy way to ascertain which parts of the article were likely to have been considered profane. The new editors provided the reader with 'the article as it was reformed by Mr Bayle, on some complaints against the preceding'.[77] The reader could now complete a comparison of the two articles in order to ascertain which aspects of the original had been excised. Logic suggested that that these would be the comments that contained profanity. Additionally, the editors had inserted a complete footnote in which they criticized Bayle's use of biblical translation. They retranslated the passage and give it an English context by suggesting it was a perfectly acceptable practice, as demonstrated by 'our English translators in Deut. Xxxiii. 6'.[78]

Delany worked through David's life chronologically concentrating on engaging with Bayle in two different ways. The reader is given an intricate and detailed description of the parts of David's life that Bayle has concerned himself with. This takes the form of direct criticism of Bayle's evidence and his representation of it. Here Delany largely comments on the adventure of Nabal, David's time in Gath and Ziklag, while book two contains a lengthy discussion of David's intrigues with Abner as well as a response to Bayle's comments on David's dancing and dress. What is more revealing is that Delany felt it necessary to engage with the cultural authority that Bayle had established through the Dictionary.

---

[74] A.E. Gunther, *An Introduction to the Life of the Rev. Thomas Birch D.D., F.R.S. 1705–1766* (Suffolk, 1984), 13; J.M. Osborn, 'Thomas Birch and the General Dictionary (1734–41)' *Modern Philology*, 36 (1938–39); Otto Selles, The English Translations of Bayle's *Dictionnaire* in Jens Häseler and Antony McKenna (eds), *La Vie Intellectuelle Aux Refuges Protestantes* (Paris, 2002).

[75] Bayle, *Dictionary*, vol. IV, 539.,

[75] Pierre Bayle, *A General Dictionary, Historical and Critical* (London, 1736) vol. IV.

[76] Ibid., Title page.

[77] Bayle, *Dictionary*, vol. IV, 539.

[78] Ibid., 537.

Delany is thus forced to undermine Bayle's personal reputation, though he also intimately links this reputation to that of Bayle's public identity transmitted through the Dictionary. Delany does acknowledge Bayle's erudition, agreeing that he is a man of 'allowed learning and parts'.[79] Yet it soon becomes clear that he is prepared to directly attack Bayle's learning and therefore authority via the traditional route of Bayle's reputation for scepticism. Delany argues that the reader should consider that Bayle is a 'broacher of paradoxes, an industrious dissenter from men of learning', and is keen to emphasize that Bayle should be shown little respect because so many respected men have disagreed with him.[80] But primarily he wishes to emphasize the lack of consistency in Bayle's ideas for he was 'a defender even of contrary and contradictory errors'.[81] Delany also wishes to establish that the Dictionary's erudition is for no good cause, since Bayle has been 'a known patron of all the errors that ever obtained in the world from its foundation'.[82] This is revealing as a tacit acknowledgement that when engaging with Bayle and his work the writer was faced with a conundrum. He had to engage with Bayle's public authority in order to attack his thoughts. This was no easy task and Delany sought to marginalize the situation by suggesting Bayle's reasons, 'not his authority, be weighed in this dispute'.[83]

It is difficult to establish how Delany was reading the Dictionary, though it is worth considering where he most stridently attacks Bayle. This is most evident in Chapter XX entitled 'Mr Bayle's Objections to this Part of the Sacred History considered'.[84] Here Delany objects to Bayle's method, as opposed to simply refuting a biblical interpretation of various aspects of David's life. Chapter XX is in effect a methodological commentary linked to Chapter XIX, 'David goes into Saul's Camp in the dead of the Night with one Companion. What ensued thereupon'.[85] The point can be made that in reading the work in a detailed way Delany was not prepared to reveal to the reader Bayle's literary skill of Bayle. In effect he was using his own literary method to disguise Bayle's.

Delany conceals from where he is garnering information on Bayle. Were the reader to cross reference to Bayle's Dictionary he would find it difficult to establish which part of the text Delany is referring to. Delany's initial scriptural complaint is concerned with Bayle's account of events concerning Saul and David 'in the cave, and in the camp'.[86] He observes that Bayle proposes that these events are really two different versions of 'one and the same transaction'.[87] Delany then considers Bayle's intimate reading of the Bible, suggesting that Bayle has two main reasons for this belief. Firstly, the scriptures do not comment on Saul's repeated ingratitude in

---

[79] Delany, *David*, 241.
[80] Ibid., 241.
[81] Ibid., 241.
[82] Ibid., 241.
[83] Ibid., 241.
[84] Ibid., 239.
[85] Ibid., 226.
[86] Ibid., 241.
[87] Ibid., 241.

persecuting David after the latter's benevolence. Secondly, the speeches concerning both events are textually almost the same.

Where does Delany find these comments by Bayle on the Bible? Consider the main text of the Dictionary: the final comments on David contain links to Delany's criticisms. Having commented on the holiness of David in the church, Bayle goes on to discuss the quality of that 'good book' by Abbot Choisy.[88] He criticizes the work for not placing in the margin of the year of the events and the 'places of the Bible'.[89] But when the David article is read as a whole this comment can be interpreted differently. Hitherto Bayle had been keen to point out that Choisy 'removes the difficulty better'.[90] In vacillating between criticism and praise for Choisy it seems likely that Bayle is actually highlighting the textual authority of his own work. The reader would be left in no doubt that the Dictionary possessed both biblical marginalia and precise dating in its scriptural criticism.

Bayle next inserts his own comment on authorship, commenting 'a reader is not well pleased, if he does not know whether what he reads comes from a sacred or profane author. I shall observe but few of K Moreri's faults'.[91] This is a description of the main text, and there seems little for the reader looking for unorthodoxy in the Dictionary to be concerned with. It is a simple summation of David, acknowledging that he had faults and then directing the reader to criticisms of two works both of which had been greatly admired – if not by Bayle. It is also clear that Delany has not found his criticisms of the Dictionary from the main text.

If footnote K is followed we can start to trace some of the ways in which Delany is appropriating meaning from the Dictionary. Ostensibly, the text of the footnote is an attack on Moreri. Delany, however, thought that Bayle used the attack on Moreri's Dictionary to pursue biblical criticism. Yet the structure of reading has been radically changed by Bayle with the insertion of this footnote. If one imagined an interested reader attempting to establish the veracity of Delany's claims that reader would now be faced with attempting to cross reference four books: Delany, the Bible, Bayle and Moreri.

The criticism of scripture that Delany refers to can be found within footnote K. This is bound up in an attack on Moreri. It is defined by five points, the second concerning David's persecution by Saul causing Delany most alarm.[92] In this footnote we can see the literary context of the criticism of Moreri. In a section concerning the narration of Saul's persecution of David, Bayle suggests that Moreri 'pretends that these two things so like one another happen in one year'.[93] However, Bayle does not content himself with criticising Moreri. In footnote two he reveals his own

[88] Bayle, *Dictionary*, 2nd vol., 1061.

[89] Ibid., 1061.

[90] Ibid., 1061. This comment is in footnote C and actually refers to page 1060 in the Dictionary 'Saul asked his general'.

[91] Ibid., 1062.

[92] Bayle, *Dictionary*, 2nd vol., 1062.

[93] Ibid., 1062.

thoughts on Scripture, noting 'here are other subjects of surprise'.[94] The context of this footnote is also overridden by a literary theme of narration that allows Bayle to make comparisons between the Bible and other texts.

Delany understood this connection in his close reading of the footnote and sought to separate them and undermine them separately. Nowhere does he refer to by name or intimate in his argument that he accepts the context of Bayle's criticism of Moreri.[95] Instead he first deals with Bayle's comparison of the Bible to other works, noting that 'If I saw two narratives of this nature either in Ǽlian or in Valerius Maximus I should make no difficulty to believe that it is one and the same thing'.[96] Delany found this offensive and felt that Bayle was comparing the great sacred history to 'scrap-collectors' who are 'compilers of patch-work'.[97]

In this criticism of the Dictionary it is clear that Delany is taking his arguments with which to attack Bayle from the footnotes as opposed to the main text of the article on David. Indeed, it is evident that while never admitting that he read the article in such a complex manner, Delany cross referenced through the footnotes of the Dictionary. His comment that there is not the same narrative detail in the books of Samuel as there are in 'those of Livy and or Thucydides (God forbid there should)' gives the reader a hint of the complex and intelligent nature of his reading.[98] This comment refers to a note in footnote C of the Dictionary. Here Bayle discusses whether Saul already knew David when he asked him to go against Goliath.[99] As with footnote K the reader would find little that was unorthodox. However, Bayle continued the comparison of the Bible with other books, observing that 'if such a narrative as this should be found in Thucydides, or in Livy, all the critics would unanimously conclude, that the transcribers had transposed the pages, forgot something in one place, repeated something in another, or inserted some additions to the author's work'.[100] This footnote is multifaceted – Delany clearly finds it reprehensible commenting about Bayle's method 'if this be candour, what is chicanery?'[101]

In fact Bayle ends his comment on Livy by arguing 'no such suspicions should be entertained of the Bible'.[102] The point is ambiguous, and it provokes Delany to question Bayle's sincerity. The complexity of the article means that the reader has to cross reference to be sure. Bayle concludes by remarking that 'some have been as bold as to pretend that that all the chapters, or all of the verses of the first book

---

[94] Ibid., 1062.

[95] There is little work on the influence of Moreri's Dictionary in England and none of the writers on David seem to have paid any attention to it. First published in England in 1694 and again in 1701, Jeremy Collier added a supplement to the Dictionary in 1705.

[96] Bayle, *Dictionary*, 2nd vol., 1062.

[97] Delany, *David*, 249.

[98] Ibid., 250.

[99] Bayle, *Dictionary*, 2nd vol., 1061.

[100] Ibid., 1061.

[101] Delany, *David* 250.

[102] Bayle, *Dictionary*, 2nd vol., 1061.

of Samuel are not placed as they were at first'.[103] Without informing the reader who has made this observation he goes on to argue that Abbot de Choisi's book clears up the confusion.[104] Even so, Bayle has conflicting advice about the quality of Choisi's work. That Delany has read the text in such an intricate way reflects the literary complexity of Bayle's method. The idea of the broken nature of the narration of the Bible is central to Bayle's technique. At the end of the footnote he directs the reader back to footnote K and to his comments on Richard Simon.

As with Samuel Chandler, the reader who privileged the authority of the main text would find it difficult to follow this literary thread. For Delany, however, that thread was conspicuous and needed to be pursued. Not only was he offended by the perceived denigration of David's moral authority, but in reading the footnotes in such a complex manner Delany believed that the narrative authority of Scripture was also being undermined. Were the reader to sit with Chapter XIX of Delany's work and with Bayle's article on David he would find it difficult to ascertain where in the main text Bayle has undermined David's moral authority.

There is no doubt that the Dictionary has a complex literary structure that requires and allows the text to be read in multifaceted ways. However, it is too simple to suggest that readers passively absorbed the text. Rather, their various ecclesiological and theological views meant they employed various methodologies in reading the text. Consequently, their understanding and representation of the work frequently varied. For Chandler the book was often misguided but he always thought Bayle sincere. Conversely Delany's view of the sacrality of Scripture required him to move away from the main text and analyse the footnotes. There he found offence, refusing to recognize that Bayle may have been criticising the work of other authors. For him Bayle's work on David is 'grounded upon one fundamental error; and that is, that he acted, in all his exile, merely as a private man'.[105] Driven by his belief that Scripture reveals divine providence, Delany cannot allow David to be seen as a man subject to natural reason, because he was 'elected and anointed to the Kingdom; and … the same spirit of God, which once inspired Saul with all regal virtues, was now gone over to David'.[106]

The reworking of the history of King David indicates that it was an important trope in English biblical culture persisting into the eighteenth century. This biblical figure could be represented in two ways: as a moral leader representing the ethical attributes that a man of his position should possess; or as a prophetical exemplar, anointed by God and consequently an instrument of divine providence. Bayle's engagement with the scriptural tradition contested both of these positions:

[103] Ibid., 1061.

[104] It is unclear whether Delany had read Choisi's book. The only English edition was in 1740. See Mr Labbe de Choisy, *Histoire de la Vie de David* (Amsterdam, 1692). The English version is Francois Timoleon de Choisy, *The History of the Life and Death of David* (London, 1741).

[105] Delany, *David*, 261.

[106] Ibid., 261.

the discussion in the Dictionary provoked a more complex response than simply rewriting David. Its intricate literary structure brought with it an authority that a political pamphlet could not aspire to. While there is still little agreement among historians as to Bayle's true intentions, the article on David illustrates a number of important points both about Bayle and the cultural status of the Bible and biblical commentary. Certainly biblical culture was significant to the church and public life long into the eighteenth century – even if this culture had changed significantly since the mid-seventeenth century. The sort of fundamental criticism applied to the example of David was unimaginable to Bishop Morley some 100 years previously. Despite this sophisticated and fundamental type of criticism, it remains clear that the status, meaning and significance of scriptural evidence was the starting point for cultural politics. That Bayle's article could itself be read in a number of ways is testament to the fact the early modern reader 'did not passively receive but rather actively reinterpreted their texts'.[107] Reading the Bible in the eighteenth century was not so much a question of examining a *textus receptus* as a process of making meaning for oneself.

[107] Lisa Jardine and Anthony Grafton, 'Studied for Action: How Gabriel Harvey read his Livy', *Past and Present*, no. 129 (Nov., 1990), 30.

Afterword: The Word Became Flawed

John Morrill

There are various startling images conjured up by this book. One is of Jephthah watching an army of Ammonites in headlong flight across Windsor Great Park. Another is the prospect of Robert Hooke settling down in a coffee house with Edmund Halley to discuss not comets but the dimensions of Noah's ark. A third is the 1629 purchase in Catholic Venice by the puritan Earl of Pembroke of Greek manuscripts to be gifted to the brand new Bodleian Library where they would be catalogued by Laud's assistant Augustine Lindsell. But none is more arresting than the vision of the unbending puritan Richard Rogers subjecting his flock at Withersfield in Suffolk to 103 sermons on the book of Judges. It gives the puritan doctrine of perseverance a whole new meaning – and I am referring as much to the congregation as to the preacher!

This book is about a subversive obsession: about the need of all those who, in the age of Reformation, sought to make sense of God's world by first making sense of God's Word, and how that search for understanding broke the will of those involved in the search. This was a Sisyphean labour in which Sisyphus had the right to give up and walk away.

For what the book captures perfectly is the way the Word, or at least the texts in which it was embodied, destabilises over the period. Two essays, by Rob Iliffe and Stephen Snobelen, discuss the *Johannine comma* – those disputed verses in 1 John 5:7–8 that strongly proclaim apostolic knowledge of and faith in the Trinity. This is a synedoche for the sickening realisation that the text that was the flawless Word of God, meant for mankind's instruction and as the title deeds of salvation, was itself flaky. By 1700, every single proof text of apostolic Trinitarian orthodoxy was shown to be suspect, a probable late addition. This was good news for those who, with increasing resolution, sought no longer to give improbable accounts of what they wanted to believe that the Creeds *really* meant, but to challenge the authority of the Creeds themselves. It was a pyrrhic victory, for the destabilisation of the text that St Jerome claimed to have God's *nihil obstat* on it did not lead on to an alternative ur-text of Holy Scripture, but to chronic uncertainty about the possibility of an ur-text: a Babel of voices reading discrepant texts. Hope of re-stabilising the text did not vanish overnight, as the evidence of Scott Mandelbrote's essay in this book of the febrile excitement that spread out round the scholarly world at the appearance of new manuscripts like the Codex Alexandrinus in the 1620s illustrates. But it was eroding steadily. And if the content of the canonical books became uncertain, so was certainty about what was to be treated as canonical. It was a common enough jibe of Catholic apologists, that the Bible was the Bible only through the magisterium of the Church – *sola scriptura necnon cum auctoritate ecclesiae.* But the Protestant Churches evicted the Greek apocryphal books from their Bibles. And in reading the books that remained many scholars were willing to privilege some books above others (as with Luther's intellectually threadbare belittling of the Epistle of James which so manifestly undermined his understanding of *solafideism* in the Epistle to the Romans). And they were willing to privilege non-canonical writings as pseudo-canonical. I take it this is one of the importances of Ariel Hessayon's account of the search for the books of Enoch.

Of course all this heady para-scholasticism raged far above the heads of most Christians. It would be nice to know how many even of that proportion of the population (10 per cent?) who knew substantial parts of the New Testament off by heart were aware that scholars suspected that significant gobbets of it had been added hundreds of years after they still comforted themselves that the Apostles had written it down. Stephen Snobelen shows how the Inquisitor spat the Vulgate version of 1 John 5:7 into the face of a Dutch Anabaptist ('there are three that bear record in Heaven, the Father, the Word and the Holy Ghost; and these three are one'), and how the heretic (for so he was adjudged) wiped away the spittle, saying 'I have often heard say, that Erasmus in his Annotations upon this place, proves that this text is not in the Greek or original language.' Erasmus of course felt obliged to reincorporate the disputed verse into the third edition (so that no one would have occasion to criticize him out of malice), which was to form the basis of all early modern English translations. Despite this, there was an ever-strengthening scholarly consensus that Erasmus and the Socinians were right about the text – Rob Iliffe demonstrates how Newton's painstaking research led him to this conclusion. However, the ordinary man-in-the-pulpit and therefore the ordinary person-in-the-pew was unaware of it. All available English translations down to the nineteenth century continued to translate the corrupt text, and best-selling commentaries like Matthew Henry's *Commentary* (1698) gloss it blithely enough. Even the Quaker Isaac Pennington in a 160 page exposition of the five chapters of John's first epistle published in 1656 (and trinitarianism was no load-bearing wall in his theology) took the verses at face value as part of a Johannine text.

So what this volume represents, for the most part, is the dangerous talk of professional theologians and natural philosophers who struggled to maintain that they needed to square the revelations of Himself that God had concealed in the natural world with the revelations of Himself that he had concealed in the Scriptures. It must not be taken as representative of how people, even dissenting people, read them. For that, we need to recall the Suffolk farmer William Dowsing, relaxing between bouts of iconoclasm as he carried out his official duties of cleansing the churches of East Anglia of their 'monuments of idolatry and superstition' by meticulously putting the correct biblical references into the margins of printed sermons. Or we should consider the London wood-turner Nehemiah Wallington, whose extensive notes to himself, in Paul Seaver's words 'bore [an] unremitting iteration [and yet] at times reach surprising heights of eloquence which must surely be owing to the ... constant reading of the Geneva Bible, whose cadences he made his own.' So much so that his very dreams were shaped by 'an imagination so patterned and limited by conscious concerns as to deal only in cultural clichés':

> [I] dreamed a heavenly dream: that as I was in my shop amongst my baskets I was in meditation and conference upon psalm 125: 'they that trust the Lord shall be as Mount Zion which cannot be moved'.

Or we need to turn to Oliver Cromwell, reading passage after passage looking for the parallels between God's challenge to the old Chosen People of Israel and the new Chosen People of England. His method is clear from his advice to his old Cambridge friend (and relation by marriage) Oliver St John in the autumn of 1648, as he meditated on whether it was God's Will that he, Cromwell, and the Army should be the agents of Charles I's destruction. He had let a whole series of texts mull around in his mind, waiting for a connection and a conviction to firm up. In previous weeks he had been meditating on the story of Gideon, the farmer called from the plough to winnow and to lead the armies of Israel against the host of Midian and to execute the king of the Midianites for perpetrating acts of atrocity. But in the end it was to a very different story that he turned, to Isaiah's prediction of the destruction of the corrupt leadership of the people of Israel and to the survival of a godly remnant: 'This scripture hath been of great stay with me: read it; Isaiah eighth, 10,11,14' he told St John, 'read all the chapter'. These are all radical readings of the Bible, radical encounters with the text, but the text as catalyst. A catalyst is, if I remember my school chemistry right, a substance that facilitates a chemical reaction without undergoing any change itself. Well, for Dowsing, Wallington and Cromwell, the Bible had a catalytic effect. None of them was the least concerned with Johannine commas, comparing translations of the Scriptures (though they would have strong views on the marginal glosses in different translations), and none of them would have understood Locke's denunciation of the division of scripture into chapters and verses.

This book powerfully corrects an imbalance in the existing literature, by demonstrating how scholarly treatments of Holy Writ have fallen through a gap in the standard conceptual framework between the Renaissance and the perceived modernity of Higher Criticism. But it does so at the cost of creating the gap I have just described between the hermeneutics of scholarly and of informed popular reading of the Bible. This tension is made most explicit in Justin Champion's wonderfully lucid essay, and is indeed captured in its very title: "Directions for the profitable reading of Holy Scripture": biblical criticism, clerical learning and lay readers *c.*1650–1720'. Here the guidance of Nicholas Byfield and William Lowth, or the reading practice of Isaac Archer, can be invoked to make sense of godly laymen like Dowsing or Wallington (the Bible as a catalytic converter, perhaps!), but this part of the essay fits a little uneasily with the equally probing account of Locke's deconstruction of text by (as Champion puts it) 'an almost compulsive relationship with the material word' – the physicality of the book and the mutability of the content and meaning. Alex Barber has similarly demonstrated, through a close examination of how people read

Bayle's reinterpretation of the scriptural tradition of King David, the continuing but complex influence of the Bible through the eighteenth century.

In short, this book dispels the myth that criticism of sacred texts was the preserve of radical figures – Antiscripturists and Quakers, Deists and freethinkers. In doing so, it contributes to the new meta-narrative of early modern history that demotes the importance of social experience and alienation as the driver of new thought. This book takes up the theme of Christopher Hill's *The English Bible and the Seventeenth-Century Revolution* (1993) and it opens up the discussion in all kinds of exciting ways; and not just by seeing the English Bible in a less little-Englander perspective. It shows how new hermeneutics of knowledge eroded trust in the Word at the very time that parallel hermeneutics of knowledge were increasing trust in the secrets of the Natural World. At the sharp end, the two processes interlocked in putting biblical chronology and direct divine action under intolerable pressure. Indeed, Warren Johnston's study reminds us of the continued relevance of eschatological beliefs and their importance to understanding the events of late seventeenth century England. But more generally, as the nicely nuanced essay by Sarah Hutton makes clear, it is the ingenuity with which the case for the reasonableness of Christianity – in the face of rebarbative biblical texts – was sustained through new schemes of exegesis (or, as it turns out, the refurbishment of ancient ones such as those evolved by the Jewish thinker Philo of Alexandria).

In addition to all this, the chapters in this book startle, or at least ram home, a second important and undervalued point. Amongst those who worry about the authority of scripture, denominational labels matter far less than too much historiography presumes. The protagonists of the essays published above judged one another's scholarship not by confessional tests but by other criteria. Throughout the book we find Catholics and Protestants in respectful exchange; and what might otherwise seem like exegetical oxymorons dissolve before our gaze. Sometimes the evidence is double-edged: the Spanish scholar-on-the-run, Michael Servetus, is burnt in effigy in Catholic Lyon, but burnt in person in Calvin's Geneva for his wilful misreading of scripture texts. But equally, we then find the godfather of English Socinianism, John Biddle, drawing on the 1545 Paris printing of Erasmus's edition of Irenaeus and his adoption of them as closet Unitarians; or Stephen Nye's claiming of Erasmus as an Arian Nicodemite. And, to take another example, Nicholas McDowell demonstrates the ease with which Samuel Fisher, Baptist sectary, could without a by-your-leave enlist the Laudian Jeremy Taylor as his advocate in a public disputation with the Westminster Assembly divine John Reading. This was not comfortable news to Taylor, but it created no difficulties for Fisher. Similarly, Nicholas Keene shows how biblical critics across the confessional spectrum plundered the same resources on the early Church, and used, and abused, each other's work to construct radically different visions of the authority and integrity of scripture.

I suppose I came to this volume with its original title ('The Word became flawed') expecting rather more evidence of a growing anti-clericalism. It is there, of course, in the London coffee houses and in the essays that touch on Locke. As I had expected, this book refutes the constant attempts to write the intellectual history of the seventeenth century in terms of a progressive rationalism that writes God out of the script. There is no risk here of the all too frequent mistaking of contempt for the institutions of Christianity and the High Priesthoods of Catholic, Anglican and Calvinist Dissent, being taken as evidence of atheism or religious indifference. Such arguments are confounded by the very essays in which one might most expect to find them. Hobbes's biblicism is sadly under-studied here, but there are plenty of proxies. And in fact, there is plenty of evidence in this book of how unobsessed so many radical readers were with the claims of the clergy, how ready they were to engage with sensible clerics and how ready to ignore power-crazy ones. Indeed the eclecticism that marks clerical-lay relations in this book is laid bare by these essays.

Thus the volume reminds us, as even intellectual historians need sometimes to be reminded, that ideas carry no passports and respect no frontiers. Not only are confessional divides of little relevance to those whose writings and debates are considered here, so too are chronological and geographical boundaries of little significance. Almost every chapter in this book demonstrates the ease with which anyone who thought critically about the authority of scripture thought about it in ways that showed no national or time-limited boundaries. It is an obvious enough point, but the linguistic limitations of too many anglophone scholars make too many books that we read fail to recognise this point – just look at the index of Hill's *The English Bible*.

This is a book that recovers, with impressive learning, the deep learning of those at the sharp end of holding all knowledge in creative tension. In doing so, it tells us about a neglected part of the story of how the Bible was read in the post-Reformation and pre-Enlightenment decades. It does not take us into the whole area of how visual representations of the Bible – so central to the medieval encounters with the Word made visible on every surface of every church – continued to influence how it was understood. Nicholas Cranfield's tantalising account of the Windsor panel of Jephthah and his daughter is a reminder of a much bigger story in need of telling; and he hints even more fleetingly at how important the adaptation of biblical stories (adaptations freighted with theological assumption and assertion) by librettists and composers – a process that reached its apotheosis in Handel – was in shaping that understanding. This then is a necessary volume, reminding us of much that has been forgotten, but it generates new agendas for further volumes. If the Bible is, as is so often said, the most influential text in Western culture and very specifically in post-Reformation English culture, then it is very much in need of further study. In the Royal Historical Bibliography Online, a search on 'bible' as a title-significant word for publications over the past 10 years and dealing mainly with the period 1600–1720 yields a list of seven books and 13 articles. To note that the Bible has fewer entries than for Hobbes's *Leviathan* or the writings of Gerrard Winstanley reminds us that 'present-centredness' affects what we study as well as how we study it. But that is a whole different question

Index